THE CULTIVATED FOREST

THE CULTIVATED FOREST

PEOPLE *and* WOODLANDS
in ASIAN HISTORY

EDITED BY

Ian M. Miller, Bradley Camp Davis,

Brian Lander, and John S. Lee

UNIVERSITY OF WASHINGTON PRESS

Seattle

The Cultivated Forest was made possible in part by grants from the InterAsia Initiative at Yale University, the Eastern Connecticut State University Foundation, Brown University, the Department of History at Durham University, and St. John's College of Arts and Sciences at St. John's University.

Additional support was provided by the Samuel and Althea Stroum Endowed Book Fund.

Composed in Warnock Pro, typeface designed by Robert Slimbach

UNIVERSITY OF WASHINGTON PRESS
uwapress.uw.edu

LIBRARY OF CONGRESS CATALOGING-IN-PUBLICATION DATA
Names: Miller, Ian Matthew, editor. | Davis, Bradley Camp, editor. | Lander, Brian, editor. | Lee, John S. (Researcher in Korean environmental history), editor.
Title: The cultivated forest : people and woodlands in Asian history / edited by Ian M. Miller, Bradly Camp Davis, Brian Lander, and John S. Lee.
Description: Seattle : University of Washington Press, [2022] | Includes bibliographical references and index.
Identifiers: LCCN 2022015132 (print) | LCCN 2022015133 (ebook) | ISBN 9780295751320 (hardcover) |ISBN 9780295750903 (paperback) | ISBN 9780295750910 (ebook)
Subjects: LCSH: Forests and forestry—East Asia—History. | Forests and forestry—Southeast Asia—History. | Forests and forestry—History.
Classification: LCC SD131 .C85 2022 (print) | LCC SD131 (ebook) | DDC 634.9095—dc23/eng/20220822
LC record available at https://lccn.loc.gov/2022015132
LC ebook record available at https://lccn.loc.gov/2022015133

CONTENTS

ACKNOWLEDGMENTS

This ideas in this volume began at a three-day conference, "The Wood Age in Asia: Connection and Comparison in Forest History," held at Yale University September 21–23, 2018, and organized by Kalyanakrishnan "Shivi" Sivaramakrishnan and the four editors of this volume. The conference was made possible by a generous grant from the American Council of Learned Societies Comparative Perspectives on Chinese Society and Culture, funded by the Chiang Ching-kuo Foundation; the Edward J. and Dorothy Clarke Kempf Memorial Fund; the MacMillan Center, Yale University; the Council on East Asian Studies, InterAsia Initiatives; the South Asia Studies Council. the Council on Southeast Asia Studies; and the Program in Agrarian Studies at the Yale MacMillan Center, with additional support from the Department of Anthropology, Yale University.

In addition to the chapters included here, the conference featured introductory remarks by James C. Scott, keynote speeches by Graeme Barker and Nancy Peluso, and papers by Aurelia Campbell, Sumit Guha, Kuang-chi Hung, Timothy Yang, Joshua Van Lieu, Aparajita Majumdar, and Arupjyoti Saikia. Tony Anderson, Karl Appuhn, Mitch Aso, Daniel Botsman, John Buchanan, Yuan Julian Chen, Kate de Luna, Fabian Drixler, Ben Kiernan, Faisal Husain, Joanna Linzer, Pamela McElwee, Ian J. Miller, Peter Perdue, Caterina Scaramelli, Michael Thornton, and Ling Zhang served as chairs, discussants, and round-table participants. We would like to thank them and all the other participants in the conference for their contributions to the ideas discussed in this volume.

To turn these ideas into a book, the editors would like to especially acknowledge our editor at University of Washington Press, Lorri Hagman, and two anonymous reviewers. David Fedman and Stevan Harrell provided important feedback on the introduction. Thanks also to Lynn Carlson for drawing the maps in the introduction and in chapter 3. Finally, we would like to especially acknowledge Shivi Sivaramakrishnan for his support throughout this process, without which four junior scholars would never have been able to organize this conference or this volume.

INTRODUCTION

The Cultivated Forest

IAN M. MILLER, BRADLEY CAMP DAVIS, AND JOHN S. LEE

FORESTS play a large, if sometimes overlooked role in human history. They are sites of habitation, veneration, and recreation, and above all, sources of material resources. Trees, the flagship flora of the forest biome, play an outsize role in people's lives as well. Their wood is the building material for houses and bridges, ships and carts, dikes and dams, furniture and tools. For most of history, wood was the primary fuel in most households and the main source of thermal energy for smelting metals, boiling salt, and other industrial processes. Trees also provide nuts, fruits, sap, bark, and leaves used for food, fodder, fertilizer, drugs, dyes, oils, and resins, collectively termed non-timber forest products (NTFPs). As we are increasingly aware in the age of climate change, forests also provide key ecosystem services, including carbon sequestration and soil and moisture retention, that stabilize both local ecologies and global climates. The interactions between people and trees and between human institutions and forested landscapes are neither historically nor culturally constant, but they are almost universally significant.

Many languages draw a contrast between farmland as the paradigmatic cultivated landscape and woodland as the prototypical wild one. Until relatively recently, history operated around a similar binary, assuming that farms, pastures, and cities are landscapes transformed by humans and that forests are largely what is left over, undisturbed landscapes that trend toward a natural "climax" vegetation of tall trees anywhere that sun, water, and temperature are adequate for them to grow. In this formulation, forests are a product of *natural* history, distinct from the largely agrarian environments that are products of *human* history, and forests become part of human history only when they are documented. Thus, the advent of forest history coincides with the surveys, maps, deeds, and ledgers that rendered them legible to administrators and subsequently to the historian. Perhaps the most significant watershed of forest history came with the spread of colonial and national forestry bureaus, which developed a shared set of practices and vocabularies to document—and claim—the forests.

More recently, scholars have moved away from the simplifying assumptions of colonial foresters to present the forests of Asia as *landscapes with history*. It is clear that both the composition and extent of woodlands are contingent on their pasts and not simply the products of climate, biogeochemical cycles, or topology. People describe wooded landscapes through forest surveys but also through property relations, geomancy, and complex cosmologies, and people transform wooded landscapes through fire, planting, and protective regulations, as well as with axes and saws. The documentary records of Asia encompass lineages of forest knowledge that far predate the records of European colonial empire or modern nation-states and demonstrate long-term continuities in how forests were used and understood.

The authors in this volume make use of the substantial written and oral records in Asian languages to present forests and forest users on their own terms. In chapters 1 and 2, Brian Lander and Ian M. Miller describe how forests were used and documented in early northern China and early modern southern China. Chapters 3 and 4, by John Elijah Bender and John S. Lee, trace the development of institutions to manage common-property forests in Japan and Korea. Chapters 5 and 6, by Meng Zhang and David A. Bello, describe the connection between ethnicity and different forms of forest use in the Miao frontier in China's southwestern borderlands and ritually important Manchu sites in the northern borderlands. Chapter 7, by Faizah Zakaria, depicts transitions between different colonial regimes in the Dutch East Indies and Taiwan. In Chapter 8, Larissa Pitts shows how foreign and native understandings of forests merged in the promotion of Arbor Day in China. Finally, Chapter 9, by Stevan Harrell, Amanda H. Schmidt, Brian D. Collins, R. Keala Hagmann, and Thomas M. Hinckley, uses multiple methods to study the effect of Nuosu Yi agroforestry on a regional environment in southwestern China. Collectively, this volume represents an attempt to construct a more unified framework for Asian forest history by drawing together growing bodies of historically and environmentally grounded scholarship to transcend the frameworks imposed by colonial or national histories. In addition to their individual topics, the authors engage with a broader array of scholarship on forests in East, Southeast, and South Asia.

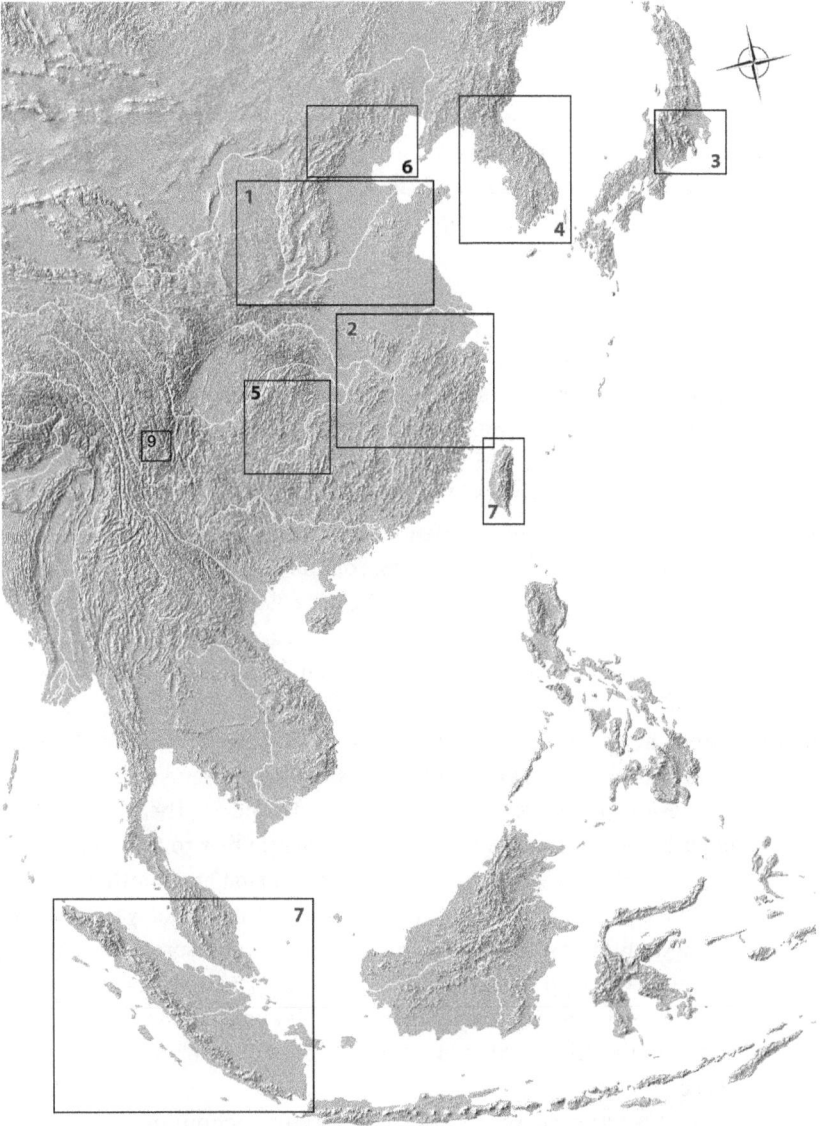

MAP I.1. East and Southeast Asia. Boxed areas correspond with the numbered chapters of this volume. Chapter 8 is not included in this map because it focuses on policy rather than any specific region. Data from Natural Earth (naturale- arthdata.com); B. Lehner, K. Verdin, A. Jarvis, "New global hydrography derived from spaceborne elevation data"; Japan Aerospace Exploration Agency, AW3D. Map by Lynn Carlson and Brian Lander.

One goal of this volume is to reconstruct alternative lineages of forest knowledge. But before we can consider these alternatives, it is important to understand the origins of the prevailing concepts used in disciplines like forestry and ecology. Throughout much of the contemporary world, forests are understood in terms first developed in Europe. The word *forest* was an administrative term first and an ecological one second; throughout Europe, it initially applied to specific jurisdictions, generally used for hunting or woodcutting, but not always particularly wooded.[1] The ambit of the term expanded as officials took greater control over wooded lands with the aim of producing more timber and fuel for the state, first in Venice in 1531, and most famously in France in 1669, under Jean-Baptiste Colbert.[2] In the late eighteenth and nineteenth centuries, German figures including Heinrich Cotta developed ideas of sustainable yield and measures of forest productivity that were widely influential in the new forestry schools and journals.[3] In the nineteenth and early twentieth centuries, colonial foresters brought French- and German-derived models of forestry to their colonies in Asia, where they designated sites *as forests*—an administrative category that allowed them to take control of woodland resources.[4] These colonial foresters were also instrumental in developing the sciences used to study forests, including the Linnean binomial terminology used to refer to plants, which was standardized in 1935.

Foresters trained in European traditions had to contend with substantial differences in colonial environments. In South and Southeast Asia, they had to adapt knowledge developed in the temperate belt to the conditions of the tropics. Early British forestry projects in Burma and southern India served as models for programs elsewhere in India, British Malaya, the independent Kingdom of Siam (which employed British advisors), and Dutch-controlled Java, which in turn provided a model for the rest of the Dutch East Indies.[5] Foresters in the American-controlled Philippines were trained in the United States, whose schools ultimately drew on the French and German models.[6]

In East and Northeast Asia, Japan became the linchpin of professional forestry in the late nineteenth and twentieth centuries. Japanese foresters trained in Germany and the United States integrated these models with domestic forestry practices and then exported and adapted these hybrids to its colonies in Hokkaido, Sakhalin, Korea, Taiwan, and Manchuria.[7] Japanese and American models were also influential in China. Although constantly contested and repeatedly revised, forestry, ecology, and botany all bear the marks of these imperial projects to standardize forest knowledge, reducing diverse ways of seeing forests to a simplified vocabulary conducive to administration and taxation. But this lineage of professional forestry was not the only model of forest knowledge available.

Long before the arrival of Europeans, people in Asia classified trees and wooded landscapes according to their own categories. In some contexts, forest oversight followed similar trajectories, namely surveying forests and recording them in voluminous land surveys, contracts, compacts, and tax records. This was especially true in the bureaucratic states of China, Korea, and Japan that are the primary focus of this volume. Aside from bureaucratic forestry, the classical Chinese pharmaceutical (*bencao*) produced by scholars across East Asia includes one of the most voluminous textual records in any language on the uses of woody plants.[8] Throughout Asia, however, most people's conceptions of trees and forests diverged from these textual corpora and were recorded only indirectly or preserved through oral traditions. Systematic classification—whether *bencao* or Linnean—depended on networks of uncredited indigenous informants.[9] But aside from the desire to encompass records in Asian languages, are there intrinsic reasons to speak of a distinctly Asian sphere of forest history? After all, trees do not respect human boundaries, be they national, cultural, or intellectual.[10]

In his classic work of historical geography, Fernand Braudel suggested that the fringes of the Mediterranean are approximately defined by the ranges of three woody plants: the date palm, the olive tree, and the grape vine.[11] While Braudel's approach has attracted both critique and revision, this focus on trees—and their dependence on the environment and on cultivation by human hands—raises interesting questions for scholars of other regions. Could we think of eastern Asia as the land of bamboo, mulberry, and tea? Can we move beyond this heuristic to define the forest history of eastern Asia as a discrete field of inquiry? In the sections that follow, we will suggest two frameworks that move Asian forest history beyond colonial and national borders—one derived from physical geography, and one from historiography—before moving on to suggest other points of historical convergence.

PHYSICAL GEOGRAPHY AND CLIMATE

The first framing device derives from the physical geography and climate of eastern Asia. Starting forty million years ago, the subduction of the Indian tectonic plate under the Eurasian plate lifted the Tibetan Plateau above the surrounding regions, forming a physical and climatic barrier that separates eastern and southern Asia—the watersheds of the Tibetan Plateau—from the rest of the continent. The Tibetan uplift also separates the weather systems of the Indian Ocean and the South and East China Seas from those of Inner Asia, creating the atmospheric conditions that produce the monsoon. To the south and east of these mountains, the seasonal monsoon dominates the climate; to their north and west, the land is too dry, and often too cold, to support extensive woodlands. We can mark the approximate ecotone where forests give way to steppes and deserts with a diagonal line stretching from northeast to southwest across China, bending west around the Himalayas and then southwest again through western India and Pakistan.

Despite its climatic separation from the rest of Eurasia, this corner of the earth contains examples of nearly the entire range of woodland biomes, from boreal forests in the far northeast, through temperate and subtropical forests in the east, to tropical rainforest and monsoon forest in the southeast, thorn forest and wooded steppe in the west, and various forms of montane forest around the Tibetan Plateau. By a second accident of climate history, the region demarcated by these mountains was also far less glaciated than most of the northern hemisphere during the last several million years. This allowed the persistence of trees extirpated from the rest of the globe, including the ginkgo, several archaic genera of conifer, and an astonishing variety of rhododendrons. The partition between the monsoon lands and the rest of Eurasia is not absolute: in the north, they fringe into the boreal forests that circle the globe; in the west, they transition into the dry steppes and deserts that cross the middle latitudes of Eurasia; in the south, many plants are widely distributed across the tropics from Africa to Oceania. Nonetheless, southern and eastern Asia feature hundreds of species of woody plants— and sometimes entire genera—not seen in forests elsewhere.

For heuristic purposes, it is useful to split our study area roughly into three large climate regions, less as an exact typology than as an exercise in explaining dynamics. The first region encompasses the temperate and subtropical regions of East Asia, from northeastern China, Japan, and Korea to Taiwan and far southern China. Here, temperature, largely determined by latitude, is the most important climatic determinant of forest composition, and precipitation is an important secondary factor. The second region encompasses the tropics of South and Southeast Asia, where precipitation is the main climatic influence and temperature gradients are far less significant except at higher elevations. Bounding and dividing these two regions is a third zone of highlands, including the Himalayas, the Tibetan Plateau, and other high mountains of northeastern India, Southeast Asia, and southwestern China. Here, elevation and rain shadow are significant climatic factors through their impacts on both temperature and precipitation.

MILLER, DAVIS, AND LEE

Temperate and Subtropical Asia

In the temperate and subtropical latitudes of eastern Asia, we can observe a continuum of vegetation varying largely by temperature but with precipitation as a significant secondary factor in the drier regions of the northwest. Starting in the north, this region borders on boreal woodlands composed mostly of larch, pine, true fir, spruce, and birch. Moving into the temperate belt that includes northern and northeastern China, most of Korea, and northern and central Japan, the boreal conifers disappear, and new species of pine share space with a greater mix of broadleaf trees including elm, lime, maple, hornbeam, and ash.[12] Still farther south, in southern China, southwestern Japan, and most of Taiwan, deciduous trees gradually give way to highly diverse broadleaf evergreen forests. The beech family—including oaks and chestnuts—predominates in many temperate and subtropical forests; their nuts have been important sources of food for millennia. Subtropical forests are also home to camphor and cassia. Distinct species of pine and cypress are also prevalent, as are several unique genera of conifer not found elsewhere in the world, including China fir and Japanese cedar. By the time we reach the far south of China and Taiwan, these subtropical trees begin to be replaced by the species of the tropics. Apart from high mountains, the natural forests of this large region have mostly been replaced with agriculture and silviculture.

Tropical Asia

Across the tropics, rainfall is generally a more important constraint on vegetation than temperature. Here it is more useful to discuss the gradients between rainforests, which are always humid, monsoon forests, which have distinct wet and dry seasons, and dry forests, which receive far less precipitation. Rainforests predominate on the islands and peninsulas—including most of the Philippines, Indonesia, and Malaysia—as well as in coastal regions or where mountains capture rainfall. Monsoon forests predominate in much of northeastern India and mainland Southeast Asia, where rainfall occurs overwhelmingly in the monsoon season. Both rainforests and monsoon forests are far more diverse than temperate or even subtropical forests, featuring an astonishing array of woody plants that almost defy classification, although colonial foresters were most interested in large timber like teak and the dipterocarp family.[13] Areas farther inland, especially in India, receive little rainfall, and drought-tolerant species predominate.

Montane Asia

Finally, an upland region stretches from the Himalayas in northern India, through the high mountains of inland Southeast Asia, into the approaches to the Tibetan Plateau in western China. Here, elevation is often the most important factor constraining vegetation through its effects on both temperature and rainfall. Direction is also significant, with southern slopes receiving more rain and sun than northern ones. Similar constraints prevail in highlands outside of the greater Tibetan uplift as well, in central Japan, northeastern Korea, and eastern Taiwan. These alpine regions often feature distinct species of pine and other conifers not seen elsewhere in the world and a wide variety of rhododendrons. Montane Asia is also the homeland of tea, which now covers large areas stretching from North India to Taiwan and Japan. At higher elevations, woody vegetation grows sparse and scraggly; at lower elevations, it fringes into the various forms of lowland forest discussed above, or just as often, into lands without substantial woody vegetation.

While suggestive of three distinct physical and climatic regions, these are very rough contours that, at best, predict the general types of woody plants that grow when and where circumstances allow. These lines themselves have moved constantly with both long-term climatic shifts and shorter-term cycles. Within these shifting zones, other factors cause substantial local variation. Woody plants can grow along rivers in regions otherwise too arid for extensive forests. This is markedly the case along the Yellow and Indus Rivers. River valleys also carve deep contours into the highlands of the Asian interior, creating steep gradients of differing vegetation. Certain soils, especially saline or podzolic ones, also place substantial limits on the varieties of trees that can grow from them. Along the deltas, salty and brackish conditions promote mangrove swamps as an important but generally localized adaptation. Granite and gneiss underlie 70 percent of the Korean Peninsula, creating slightly acidic topsoil unconducive to deep rooting. In such conditions, taller trees easily fall victim to windstorms, allowing shade-intolerant conifers, particularly pine, to thrive.[14]

Ecologists once discussed these biomes in terms of a theoretical climax vegetation. They assumed that vegetation would succeed through progressively higher forests toward a canopy whose ideal species composition was determined largely by climate, topology, and soil type.[15] This theory became unsustainable once it was clear that much of the world has never featured climax vegetation, largely due to the influence of animals, especially humans and grazing ungulates. Furthermore, the behavior of humans and other animals, the climate, and other factors affecting ecology have all changed across historic time through long-term secular patterns, stochastic events, and social and ecological intensification and collapse.[16] Rather than theorizing idealized conditions that never existed, we must therefore use climate zones as a loose framework rather than an exact typology.

HISTORIOGRAPHY

It is equally important, if not more so, to parse Asia into regions based on cultural and institutional continuities, divergent source bases, and their effects on historiography. In East Asia, the deep historical records in Chinese, Japanese, Korean, and Manchu and the legacy of strong centralized states has allowed a greater emphasis on premodern forest history than in many parts of the world. In South Asia, extensive English-language documents from the British colonial period have attracted the overwhelming preponderance of attention, permitting a high degree of nuance but overshadowing the comparatively limited attention to precolonial India. In Southeast Asia, the comparatively diverse traditions and fragmented records have meant that until recently, the greatest strength was in ethnography. Each of these regions is further subject to the imperial and nationalist historiography that has tended to obscure connections. In the following sections, we will survey these literatures before suggesting points of convergence as another framework for Asian forest history.

East Asia

The work of just two scholars has been enormously influential in suggesting an overarching framework for the environmental history of East Asia. Conrad Totman suggests that early Japanese states repeatedly devastated forests, especially in the Kansai region. He argues that it was only after the islands were unified by the Tokugawa shogunate in 1600 that regional lords developed successful regimes promoting both "negative regimen forestry" (using restrictions) and positive ones (planting for commercial production).[17] Mark Elvin argues that in China, the bureaucracy's emphasis on water-control infrastructure and warfare led to the progressive destruction of much of the original woodland and the associated "retreat of the elephants."[18] Both scholars build on substantial work by Japanese and Chinese historians, foresters, and archeologists, building in turn on early modern traditions of statecraft writing, local history, and evidentiary scholarship. Nonetheless, the frameworks offered by Totman and Elvin have been particularly influential, promoting a perception of Japan as the rare country that overcame its pre-modern tendency toward deforestation and China as a leading example of the perils of uncontrolled growth.[19] Despite these divergent conclusions, both scholars share a framework that posits deforestation—the removal of forests—as the main effect of human behavior, at least until the advent of modern forestry. While it is undeniable that humans changed the extent and composition of forests in Japan, China, and neighboring Korea, the deforestation thesis is not the last word on East Asian forest history.

Japan

In Japanese history, recent research has revealed complications in Totman's construct of 1600 as a dividing line between deforestation and positive for-estry. Long before 1600, Japan featured a number of forest users—including purveyors of forest products to the imperial household and shrines, and pro-ducers of charcoal and paper—whose activities were hidden by ledgers that identified them as agricultural producers.[20] John Elijah Bender argues in chapter 3 that Tokugawa era forestry was itself the product of many bottom-up processes of negotiation over natural resources in the Warring States period (Sengoku Jidai) that preceded it. Even after 1600, much of Japan was controlled by semi-independent lords (*daimyo*) who were at the forefront of both extractive logging and the development of new models of forest-based industry.[21] At the peripheries, the Tokugawa regime and its successor, the Meiji state (1868–1912), were active in displacing both wildlife (wolves) and non-Japanese people (Ainu).[22]

After 1868, modern Japan was a linchpin in the convergence between European and East Asian models of forests and forestry. Japanese students were sent abroad to Germany and the United States to learn forestry and botany, which they integrated with longstanding Japanese practices. As the Japanese empire expanded, imperial foresters seized control of forests in Korea, Karafuto (Sakhalin), Taiwan, and Manchuria, where they adapted their hybrid forestry models to different conditions. While promising to plant forests, they also logged extensively in the colonies to alleviate pressures on the home islands.[23] Indeed, the narrative of Japan's excep-tional forest preservation developed as part of the modern construction of nature veneration as a unique part of Japan's national identity.[24] Through-out the period, Japan's domestic preservation rested on substantial timber imports, first from its colonies, and later an informal business empire in Southeast Asia.[25]

Korea

In Korea during the Koryŏ (918–1392) and Chosŏn (1392–1910) dynasties, political decisions and cultural proclivities encouraged the growth of conifers, notably pine. By the late Koryŏ era, pine became widespread enough to achieve prominence in both literary and architectural sources.[26] The Mongol invasions of the thirteenth century further spurred the growth of pine landscapes. Mongol generals protected and harvested pine timber from southern Korea for ship construction, and Mongol horse ranches produced ecologies favorable for pine at the expense of deciduous competitors.[27] During the Chosŏn dynasty (1392–1910), pine became the centerpiece of a complex state forestry system that spanned five centuries. Chosŏn bureaucrats enacted policies that protected pine forests across the Korean Peninsula, with the timber largely reserved for warship, edifice, and coffin construction. As John S. Lee shows in chapter 4, village organizations known as pine protection *kye* developed in the latter half of the Chosŏn era to encourage the protection of forests at the local level.[28]

Korea's long legacy of state forestry also shaped its modern history in divergent ways. David Fedman argues that during the colonial era (1910–45), Japanese foresters promoted a "dualistic geographical imaginary that cast the northern uplands [of the peninsula] as a forest Eden and everything south as blighted wastelands."[29] Japanese officials and scientists critiqued the prevalence of pine on the peninsula as evidence of Chosŏn failures, even as logging companies targeted its forests for export. After liberation and division in 1945, forestry continued to be a center of domestic and international attention. The United Nations undertook reforestation projects in South Korea during the Korean War (1950–53).[30] In the 1970s, the South Korean government under Park Chung-hee launched successful reforestation policies.[31] In recent decades, South Korea has largely followed the Japanese model of importing timber from Southeast Asia to enable domestic conservation.[32] North Korea, on the other hand, experienced rampant deforestation during the 1990s, along with the collapse of the agricultural sector and widespread famine.[33]

China

Within present-day China, different regional trajectories belie Elvin's comprehensive theory of deforestation.[34] As Brian Lander argues in chapter 1, northwest China never featured extensive woodlands, and the North China

Plain was largely deforested by the Han dynasty, two thousand years ago. The very scarcity of wood resources led to early discourses promoting the protection of woodlands and probably an elaborate forestry complex near the capitals of the Qin and Han dynasties.[35] In the first millennium CE, Buddhist and Daoist groups colonized forest lands to build monasteries and developed their distinct land ethics promoting both conservation and economic exploitation.[36] North China also developed early traditions of tree planting, including mulberry and jujube on field boundaries, poplar and willow along roads and dikes, and apples, pears, and stone fruits in orchards.[37] But throughout its recorded history, North China has been dependent on timber imports. Since the eleventh century, the region's extensive reserves of mineral coal were also used to supplement its fuel supply, although they were not systematically explored until the late nineteenth century.[38]

By contrast, the hilly terrain of southern China featured relatively dense tree cover until at least the eleventh century. When demand for timber did exceed the availability of naturally seeded trees, landowners began cultivating extensive timber plantations, with a focus on China fir and horsetail pine. Other regional specializations included camphor, paper mulberry, bamboo, lacquer tree, tallow tree, stone fruits, citrus fruits, lychee, and longan.[39] As Ian M. Miller argues in chapter 2, much of this silviculture was controlled by contractual mechanisms with only a limited layer of state control. By the eighteenth century, the Yangzi River carried a flourishing traffic in forest products, including both plantation timber and logs and from naturally seeded growth in the western interior.[40] Other mechanisms—including community compacts and feng shui geomancy—developed to protect old-growth forests around graves, temples, sensitive slopes and critical watersheds.[41]

To China's northeast is a region of conifer forests that was long controlled by non-Han peoples under regional economies mixing hunting, herding and farming. As trade with central China increased in importance, peoples in this area specialized in gathering valuable forest products including ginseng, freshwater pearls and furs.[42] In the seventeenth century, one of these groups—the Manchus—conquered China, presenting a unique case of forest peoples who ruled a large agrarian region. Their Qing dynasty created a distinct set of regulations to preserve and reinforce the ecological and ethnic distinctiveness of the Manchu homeland—including its forests.[43] As many Manchus moved to cities, the Qing state worked hard to maintain their former lifeways, in part by conserving Manchuria for culturally significant hunting practices.[44] David Bello argues in chapter 6 that the borderlands between the Manchu heartland and North China witnessed conflicts between Hans and Manchus over different modes of forest use. The state of Manchurian forests shifted in the nineteenth century, as competition with Russian and Japan encouraged the late Qing governments to claim Manchuria's forests as "natural resources" rather than protecting them as cultural heritage.[45] Later Japanese foresters in the puppet Manchukuo regime promoted both afforestation and logging upon relatively similar lines to colonial Korea.[46]

Southwest China is also culturally and ecologically distinct from the predominantly Han regions of central China. Topographically, climatically, and culturally more connected to other parts of montane Asia, the region fell into the Chinese sphere of influence in the thirteenth century, when the Mongols conquered the Dali kingdom and enrolled local leaders as "native officials" (*tusi*) responsible for supplying tribute in horses, timber, and other local products. In the fifteenth and sixteenth centuries, Beijing logged the region on an unprecedented scale to feed demands for massive timbers for imperial building projects.[47] By 1730, much of the accessible old growth was gone, and the large native domains were integrated into direct rule. Subsequently, both Chinese and foreign observers traveled through the region, classifying the peoples, landscapes, and plants according to increasingly distinct and specific schemes.[48] Meanwhile, tree-planting practices and contractual management were introduced to compliment timber from the old growth.[49] Yet as Meng Zhang argues in chapter 5, even after the growth of plantation forestry in Guizhou, the Miao peoples of the region used externally imposed ethnic categories to protect their position in the timber markets.

While deforestation repeatedly emerged as a regional concern it only became a widespread problem in modern times. In the late eighteenth and nineteenth centuries, longstanding modes of governance broke down under an onslaught of migrants, including lowlanders moving into the hills in southern and central China, and Hans moving to non-Han regions of the southwest and Manchuria.[50] Between 1850 and 1950, China was repeatedly wracked by warfare that led to destruction of forests across the country.[51] Yet in between these episodes of extreme degradation, there were repeated attempts at afforestation. As Larissa Pitts demonstrates in chapter 8, in the 1920s and 30s, the Nationalist state promoted tree planting guided by both international models of Arbor Day and Chinese traditions of tomb planting.[52]

After 1950, forestry was reorganized by the Communist state along two distinct models. In the north and the borderlands, forests were often nationalized as "forest areas" (*linqu*); in southern China, individual landholdings were more often consolidated under the control of farming collectives.

"Three great cuttings" (*san da fa*) accompanied the Great Leap Forward (1958–60), Cultural Revolution (1966–76), and Reform and Opening (1980–91), with deforestation especially severe in the nationalized "forest areas."[53] Meanwhile, limited attempts at conservation focused largely on "rare and unique" animals.[54] The first significant attempts at forest conservation and reforestation date to the 1980s and were substantially expanded after serious flooding in 1998.[55] As Stevan Harrell, Amanda H. Schmidt, Brian D. Collins, R. Keala Hagmann, and Thomas M. Hinckley show in chapter 9, both local knowledge and the mass campaigns of this era leave distinct traces in the oral traditions of non-Han groups like the Nuosu Yi and in the vegetation and soil of the landscape itself.

Taiwan

Until the seventeenth century, Taiwan's indigenous people lived through agroforestry and hunting and had little contact with the Asian mainland. In the seventeenth century, however, Taiwan was sequentially colonized by the Netherlands, the Zheng family organization of pirate-traders turned state-builders, and the Qing empire. The Dutch were most interested in using Taiwan as a trading settlement to access the Chinese mainland, as well as trading with the indigenous people for deer hides and other forest products.[56] But under the Zheng family's kingdom of Dongning (1661–83), and especially with the onset of Qing control in 1683, Han settlers arrived in growing numbers, gradually clearing much of western Taiwan to produce rice and sugar cane for export to the mainland.[57] In the face of conflicts with indigenous communities, Han settlers were forbidden entry to the eastern, mountainous, half of the island. To obtain timber for warships, the Qing created an exception to this restriction—a system of "lumberjack heads" (*jungong jiangshou*) permitted to log in the eastern forests for shipbuilding timber, but who also used this position to feed the black market for camphor.[58]

The partition of Taiwan into Han and Indigenous territory continued until 1874, when in response to a Japanese raid in eastern Taiwan, the Qing opened the entire island to settlement. In 1895, with this "open the mountains and pacify the savages" (*kaishan fufan*) policy incomplete, Taiwan was transferred to Japanese control as part of the settlement of the Sino-Japanese War. Like other colonial powers, Japan initiated forest surveys, declaring all untitled land as state forest (*kanyū rinno*), regardless of its vegetation, thereby intensifying timber extraction and further classifying and resettling indigenous groups. In practice, much forested land in the west fell under Japanese corporate interests, while the former indigenous territories in the east

MILLER, DAVIS, AND LEE

were claimed by the state but only gradually opened to extraction.[59] As Faizah Zakaria argues in chapter 7, camphor extraction and surveillance of Taiwan's forest people intensified under Japanese control while also showing continuities with Qing institutions. After World War II, runaway demand for timber, rampant inflation and the continuation of the wartime production model led to chaotic conditions, until American aid aimed at modernizing the forestry sector and, in the 1980s, emphasis shifted to sustainable yield and ecological protection.[60]

South Asia

While there are no chapters on South Asia in this volume, its forest history has been highly influential on the broader field. In the context of Indian history, colonization is often seen as the key watershed of environmental change. Madhav Gadgil and Ramachandra Guha's influential work interpreted deforestation through the British colonial project, while Richard H. Grove demonstrated that colonization also brought a conservationist mindset to forestry projects in India.[61] More recent work on South Asia has critiqued this emphasis. A growing body of work on precolonial South Asia reveals substantial regional distinctions and historical developments before the arrival of European colonizers. Evidence from archeology and paleoecology suggests that the Ganges floodplains may have never been densely forested, while other regions have gone through shifts in forest cover caused by both human and climatic factors.[62] The importance of elephants to kingship and warfare led rulers throughout the subcontinent to preserve forests as reservoirs of wild elephants for capture.[63] Production of forest crops like pepper and ginger in southern India transcended the arrival of Europeans.[64] Likewise, the conceptual connection of "tribes" and indigenous, *adivasi* identities with the forest did not originate with European imperialism.[65] Research on colonial and postcolonial forestry also reveals both continuities and disjunctures from precolonial institutions.[66]

Southeast Asia

In Southeast Asia, diverse states, empires, and peoples shared a common concern with delimiting forest spaces. Whether narrated as the diffusion of Indian and Chinese influences or the hybridization of South Asian and East Asian cultural forms with local traditions, Southeast Asian political histories evince a distinction between cultivated and unsown spaces that hinges on the forest.[67] Until the nineteenth century, mainland and maritime

Southeast Asian states policed the boundary between forest and field with the language of sedentary civilization. As uplands groups kept political projects "at arm's length," agriculture tended to reflect both altitude, with settled fields below giving way to shifting swiddens above, and the limitations of lowland states to impose their rule uphill.[68] Thus the broad patterns of power in Southeast Asia fall along the tree line, and forests play a crucial role in understanding the environmental and cultural histories of the region.

Among the agrarian empires of mainland Southeast Asia, most political ecologies trafficked in dualities between governed space and unruled forest. Before 1350, the three mainland powers, Bagán in Burma, Angkor in Cambodia, and Đại Việt in Vietnam, flourished in large part through agricultural colonization. But despite expansionist ambitions, these three "charter states"—and the models they set for their successors—were limited to controlling only coasts and lowlands.[69] The rulers of Angkor venerated universal, Indic deities like Vishnu and Śiva, while Bagán—and later Burma and Siam—sponsored orthodox Theravādin teaching at monastic communities (sangha). But in the everyday spiritual world, larger religious traditions thrived alongside *nat* and *phi*, the ethereal traces of departed ancestors and other forces who guarded caves, fields, and trees.[70] The coexistence of orthodox traditions with local practices was not always harmonious. In Thailand (known as Siam until 1947), a conflict between "forest monks" (*thudong*) and sangha authorities in Bangkok with roots in the nineteenth century continued throughout the twentieth.[71]

For more modest states, O. W. Wolters's theory of the "mandala state" helps explain political ecologies that accommodated the often overlapping networks of power and control.[72] As early as the tenth century, Tai polities rested upon human connections such as trade and labor obligations, anchored by a distinction between governed space (*muang*) and the unruled forest (*pa*). After the thirteenth century, both larger Tai and Lao kingdoms, such as Ayutthaya, Chiang Mai, and Lan Xang, and smaller borderland states like Sipsong Panna (China) and Sipsong Chau Tai (Vietnam), also maintained political ecologies grounded in this environmental fissure.[73] In northern Vietnam and southwestern China, Tai modes of power became interlaced with Confucian-inflected sedentary states, a "hybrid rule" that continued well into the twentieth century.[74] This political plurality, what Thongchai Winichakuhl termed "multiple sovereignties," shaped interactions between people and trees, making timber harvesting, forest farming, and the NTFP trade a matter of layered, centripetal polities.[75]

Unlike surrounding lowland regions, the dominant model for understanding the forest history of montane Asia is not ecological but political.

Building on Willem van Schendel's conceptualization of the highlands of Asia, James C. Scott popularized the term *Zomia* to refer more specifically to the Southeast Asian part of this broader region.[76] Scott proposes that the overarching feature of the people inhabiting Zomia was that they emerged as refugees from the state building processes of the surrounding lowlands. He argues that these groups pursued multiple strategies to avoid being captured by the state, including "escape crops" that are hard to tax, shifting cultivation that is hard to survey, ethnic choices that distinguish them from state subjects, and cultural multiplicity that confounds attempts to promote unity and orthodoxy.[77] For mountain forests and the people who live in them, these commonalities cut across political, ethnic, and conceptual boundaries.

In the nineteenth and twentieth centuries, imperial and colonial ambitions extended from the coasts to the interiors, enabled by new technologies of rule, and increased demand for forest products. Many forms of extraction built on earlier forest trades, and the expansion of regional empires including the Qing and Đại Việt. Control of economically important trees like teak was often built on top of existing royal monopolies.[78] In Vietnam, upland space became a new field for imperial state building, particularly in areas once seen as foreboding to lowlands officials.[79] Yet this period also brought new colonizers—British, French, American, and Japanese—new technologies—rail lines, aerial surveys—and international demand for a newly significant suite of industrial precursors including rubber and camphor.[80] Compared to the earlier, hybrid, and overlapping political economies, these colonial empires sought to control entire commodity chains, simplifying complex ethnic, political, and cultural relations that had long interfaced at forests' edge. In chapter 7, Faizah Zakaria demonstrates that in both Japanese Taiwan and the Dutch East Indies, colonial states attempted to cut through native intermediaries in the camphor trade conducted by their Qing and Malay predecessors.

World War II, decolonization, and the Cold War recast forests across the region as sites of resistance and counterinsurgency.[81] Nonetheless, colonial forestry left legacies in the postcolonial states of the region. Resource control and resistance in postcolonial Indonesia were both rooted in structures developed under Dutch control.[82] Forest surveys from the French colonial period continue to impact the environmental goals set by both the Vietnamese state and international NGOs.[83] In Thailand, international forms of environmental knowledge continue to marginalize upland peoples including Hmong and Karen.[84] Anthropological research has challenged the sedentary logic of development policies and brought the ecological practices of forest peoples to the forefront.[85] Nonetheless, the power of bureaucrats to exploit forests and forest peoples—and their attempts to protect them under the new model of environmental NGOs—remains based in distant administrative centers, including Jakarta, Hanoi, and Beijing, as well as London, New York, and Amsterdam.

CONFLUENCES

While there are diverse local variations, we nonetheless would like to highlight three themes that run through Asian forest history. First, Asia features especially long-term written documentation of forests. This record reinforces perspectives from archeology and paleoecology; it also transcends the prevailing epistemic divides between precolonial and colonial, or premodern and modern history. Second, Asia evidenced a wide range of institutions involved in using, modifying, venerating, and regulating forests. This volume documents traditions that parallel or converge with European and American bureaucratic forestry but also traditions based on fundamentally different assumptions. Third, Asian history has numerous examples of so-called forest peoples that show the economic and ecological importance of these roles while also demonstrating how they were socially constructed.

The history of Asia demonstrates both the depth and long-term continuities of human modification of wooded environments. Asia is far from unique in this respect. However, Asia also features long-term written records that transcend multiple shifts in both political regimes and environmental trends, a depth of documentation otherwise limited to the Mediterranean and Middle East. These documents allow the addition of nuance to the results from archeology and paleoecology. In particular, written history allows researchers to understand not only how historical people interacted with forests but also what they thought about these interactions and how they changed their practices in response to changes in the forest.

This record shows that there were many significant watersheds of change in how forests were used, and how they were documented. The emergence of large agrarian empires in the late centuries BCE coincided with the first widespread threats of wood shortage in both northern China and northern India and the first significant written record of forest use. The spread of orthodox religions, including Śiva and Vishnu worship, Theravada and Mahayana Buddhism, Islam and Christianity, Confucianism, Daoism, and Shinto, each brought models of dominion that both conflicted and merged with more localized veneration of woodland gods and spirits. In the last thousand years, and especially the last four hundred, the integration of commercial markets increased demand for forest products, deepening linkages between forested regions and urban and agrarian consumers throughout Asia. This early modern integration also spurred much greater documentation of forests and forest users. Colonial forestry—including the arrival of European and North American foresters—had substantial impacts in the late nineteenth and early twentieth centuries. Colonial forestry also interacted with other models of woodland use and produced specifically Asian hybrids, whether in British India, Japanese-controlled Korea, or postcolonial Vietnam. The goals of imperial and colonial forestry variously included capturing elephants, extracting timber, suppressing insurgency, and growing a greener nation. Between and beyond these centralizing visions, forests remained sites of contestation between villagers; of commercial planting of timber and non-timber forest products; of hunting, gathering, and gleaning; and of mendicant monks and sacred trees. Indeed, while imperial, colonial, and national forestry projects have left the most extensive textual record—including many of the sources used in the chapters that follow—localized practices of burning and shifting cultivation are probably the most persistent and pervasive human interventions seen not only in Asian forests but around the world.

Finally, Asian history features numerous examples of forest peoples, ranging from the Ainu and Manchus of the northeast to the many hill peoples of Southeast Asia and the scheduled tribes of India. By viewing the histories of these groups across large time scales, it becomes increasingly clear that the distinctions between forest peoples and their neighbors practicing fixed-field agriculture have been constructed in historical time. By viewing Northeast, Southeast, and South Asia in the same frame, it is also apparent that these identities and the associated eco-social niches developed largely in response to the emergence of bureaucratic states and commercial markets. Group identities developed through patrimonial ties between the leaders of forest settlements and the rulers of agricultural ones. From Manchuria to Guizhou and Taiwan to Sumatra, people erected barriers—sometimes physical walls—between the ethnic and ecological context of the forest and the ethnic and ecological context of the farm. "Forest tribe" was not an intrinsic identity but rather a label applied to these groups by distant officials who sought to classify them and often to extract goods and labor from them. It was also an adaptation to commercial markets; as long-distance trade expanded, there was increased specialization in forest products ranging from timber to ginseng, camphor, and pepper.

This volume brings together multiple perspectives on Asian forests, ranging from early history to the near present, from Japan to Malaysia. Its chapters show that forests developed in ways that are not easily parsed into *natural history* and *human history* and that there was no single watershed of change. Furthermore, they argue that there are many distinct ways to understand forests, none of which tell the whole story. But perhaps most importantly, by exploring the deep and varied stories of the cultivated forests of Asia, these chapters show that forests have histories that need to be told.

NOTES

1   Jørgensen, "The Roots of the English Royal Forest"; Rackham, *The History of the Countryside*, 129–39, 146–51; Radkau, *Wood*, 57–70; Warde, *The Invention of Sustainability*, 60–61.

2   Venice: Appuhn, *A Forest on the Sea*; France: Matteson, *Forests in Revolutionary France*. Other examples: Radkau, *Wood*, chapters 2 and 3; Warde, *Invention of Sustainability*, 177–82, 188–92, 198–200; Wing, *Roots of Empire*; Kain and Baigent, *The Cadastral Map in the Service of the State*, 331–34.

3   Lowood, "The Calculating Forester"; Radkau, *Wood*, 172–204; Scott, *Seeing Like a State*, chapter 1; Warde, *Invention of Sustainability*, 201–27.

4   This literature is extensive. See especially: Agrawal, *Environmentality*, chapter 1; Grove, *Green Imperialism*, chapter 8 and passim; McElwee, *Forests Are Gold*, chapter 1; Peluso, *Rich Forests, Poor People*, chapters 2–3; Sivaramakrishnan, *Modern Forests*, especially chapter 4; Peluso and Vandergeest, "Genealogies," 761–812; Vandergeest and Peluso, "Empires of Forestry," 31–64.

5   Agrawal, *Environmentality*; Vandergeest and Peluso, "Empires of Forestry."

6   Bankoff, "Breaking New Ground?," 369–93.

7   Fedman, *Seeds of Control*, chapter 1 and passim; Morris-Suzuki, "The Nature of Empire," 225–42; Hung, "When the Green Archipelago Encountered Formosa."

8   Needham, Lu, and Huang, *Botany*; Métaillié, *Traditional Botany*; Federico Marcon, *The Knowledge of Nature*; Bian, *Know Your Remedies*; Menzies, *Ordering the Myriad Things*.

9   See, for example, Mueggler, *The Paper Road*.

10 James C. Scott made this observation in his introductory comments at the conference on which this volume is based.

11 Braudel, *The Mediterranean*.

12 Kolbek, Srutek, and Box, *Forest Vegetation of Northeast Asia*.

13 A more complete guide to commonly cultivated species is Jensen, *Trees Commonly Cultivated in Southeast Asia*. An online version can be found at www.fao.org/3/AC775E/AC775E00.htm.

14 In an early analysis of deforestation in Korea, Japanese forest ecologist Miyake Masahisa noted the particular vulnerability of Korean forests to

windstorms, a problem he argued was rooted in the composition of the bedrock and soils. Miyake, *Chōsen hantō no rin'ya no kōhai no gen'in.*

15 For a history of these ideas, see Worster, *Nature's Economy.*

16 See, e.g., Botkin, *Discordant Harmonies*; Gunderson and Holling, eds., *Panarchy.*

17 Totman, *The Green Archipelago;* Totman, *The Lumber Industry in Early Modern Japan.*

18 This thesis is most clearly expressed in Elvin, *The Retreat of the Elephant.*

19 For depictions of this supposed contrast in world environmental history, see for example, Richards, *The Unending Frontier,* chapter 4; Williams, *Deforesting the Earth,* 216–20; Radkau, *Nature and Power,* 112–15 and passim.

20 Amino, *Rethinking Japanese History*; Aoki, "The Role of Villagers in Domain and State Forestry Management," 255–75.

21 Roberts, *Mercantilism in a Japanese Domain.*

22 Walker, *The Conquest of Ainu Lands*; Walker, *The Lost Wolves of Japan.*

23 Fedman, *Seeds of Control*; Morris-Suzuki, "The Nature of Empire"; Hung, "When the Green Archipelago Encountered Formosa."

24 Fedman, *Seeds of Control.* On nature in the Japanese national identity more generally, see Thomas, *Reconfiguring Modernity.*

25 Dauvergne, *Shadows in the Forest*; Clancey, "Seeing the Timber for the Forest"; Fedman, *Seeds of Control.*

26 For analysis of the tree composition of Korean historical buildings, see Pak and I, "Uri nara kŏnch'uk e sayong toen mokchae sujong ŭi pyŏnch'ŏn," 9–27.

27 Lee, "Postwar Pines," 319–32.

28 Lautensach observed red pine-dominant forests emerging across similarly deforested landscapes in late colonial Korea. Lautensach, *Korea,* 136.

29 Fedman, *Seeds of Control,* 50.

30 Brady, "Sowing War, Reaping Peace," 351–63.

31 Bae, Joo, and Kim, "Forest Transition in South Korea," 228–33.

32 Fedman, *Seeds of Control,* 235–36.

33 Yu, "The Rise and Demise of Industrial Agriculture in North Korea," 75–110.

34 Nicholas K. Menzies made this point even before Elvin's major work came out; see Menzies, *Forest and Land Management in Imperial China.*

35 Miller, "Forestry and the Politics of Sustainability in Early China"; Sanft, "Environment and Law in Early Imperial China"; Schafer, "Hunting Parks and Animal Enclosures in Ancient China."

36 Gernet, *Buddhism in Chinese Society,* 116–29 and chapter 3; Marks, *China,* 138–41; Schafer, "The Conservation of Nature," 279–308; Elverskog, *The Buddha's Footprint.* Note that Marks has been updated with a new edition, titled *China: An Environmental History* (2017). References here and throughout are to the 2012 edition.

37 On East Asian traditions of fruit tree cultivation, especially grafting, see Métailié, *Traditional Botany,* 482–533.

38   Several scholars have argued for the growing use of coal in the eleventh century, especially in the Central Plains. See Hartwell, "Markets, Technology, and the Structure of Enterprise"; Golas, *Science and Civilisation in China 5.13 Mining*, 186–96. On the exploration of coal reserves in the nineteenth and twentieth centuries, see Wu, *Empires of Coal*.

39   Miller, *Fir and Empire*; McDermott, *The Making of a New Rural Order in South China*, chapter 6; Menzies, *Forest and Land Management*, chapter 6; Needham, Lu, and Huang, *Botany*, 355–427.

40   Zhang, *Timber and Forestry in Qing China*.

41   Menzies, *Forest and Land Management*, chapter 4–5; Coggins, "When the Land Is Excellent."

42   Kim, *Ginseng and Borderland*.

43   Bello, *Across Forest, Steppe, and Mountain*; Schlesinger, *A World Trimmed with Fur*.

44   There is a large and growing field of study on the Manchus, often called the "New Qing History." In addition to Bello and Schlesinger, see especially Crossley, *A Translucent Mirror*; Elliott, *The Manchu Way*; Rawski, *The Last Emperors*.

45   Chi, "Chinese Resource Modernity."

46   Caffrey, "Transforming the Forests of a Counterfeit Nation."

47   Campbell, *What the Emperor Built*; Miller, *Fir and Empire*, chapter 7; Menzies, *Forest and Land Management*, chapter 7.

48   There is an extensive literature on this topic, including: Anderson and Whitmore, *China's Encounters on the South and Southwest*; Herman, *Amid the Clouds and Mist*; Sutton, "Ethnicity and the Miao Frontier in the Eighteenth Century"; Weinstein, *Empire and Identity in Guizhou*; Hostetler, *Qing Colonial Enterprise*; Giersch, *Asian Borderlands*.

49   Zhang, *Timber and Forestry in Qing China*; Meng Zhang, "Financing Market-Oriented Reforestation"; Zhang Yingqiang, *Mucai zhi liudong*.

50   There is extensive scholarship on the degradation of the late eighteenth and nineteenth centuries: Marks, *Tigers, Rice, Silk, and Silt*; Averill, "The Shed People and the Opening of the Yangzi Highlands"; Osborne, "The Local Politics of Land Reclamation"; Osborne, "Highlands and Lowlands"; Vermeer, "The Mountain Frontier in Late Imperial China"; Vermeer, "Population and Ecology"; Ch'en, "Nonreclamation Deforestation in Taiwan," Ts'ui-jung Liu, "Han Migration." A useful summary is provided in Marks, *China*, chapter 5. This text is updated. For the interpretation of this period as a breakdown in formerly functional systems, see Bello, *Across Forest, Steppe, and Mountain*, chapter 5; Miller, *Fir and Empire*, conclusion.

51   Caffrey, "Transforming the Forests"; Muscolino, *The Ecology of War in China*.

52   In addition to chapter 8 in this volume, see also Songster, "Cultivating the Nation in Fujian's Forests."

53 These three cuttings are covered in some detail in Smil, *The Bad Earth*, 15–25. See also Shapiro, *Mao's War against Nature*, 80–86; Marks, *China*, 276–87. As Smil points out, the PRC continues to substantially manipulate forest cover statistics to promote a picture of continuous reforestation that is belied by the specifics

54 Coggins, *The Tiger and the Pangolin*; Songster, *Panda Nation*.

55 Smil, *The Bad Earth*; Shapiro, *Mao's War against Nature*, 80–86; Economy, *The River Runs Black*, 64–68; Richardson, *Forests and Forestry in China*; Démurger, Hou, and Yang, "Forest Management Policies" 17–41; Marks, *China*, 288; Yeh, "The Politics of Conservation."

56 Koo, "Deer Hunting and Preserving the Commons"; Andrade, "Pirates, Pelts, and Promises."

57 Shepherd, *Statecraft and Political Economy*; Ch'en, "Non-reclamation Deforestation"; Liu, "Environmental Change."

58 Ch'en, "'Jungong jiangshou' yu Qingling shiqi Taiwan de famu wenti."

59 Kuang-chi Hung, "Green Archipelago Encountered Formosa"; Hung, "Zhanhou chuqi zhi Taiwan guoyoulin jingying wenti, 64–66.

60 Hung, "Zhanhou chuqi zhi Taiwan guoyoulin jingying wenti"; Zheng Chinlong, "Ershi shiji Taiwan de shequ linye zuzhi," 1–5.

61 Gadgil and Guha, *This Fissured Land*; Grove, *Green Imperialism*.

62 Morrison, "Conceiving Ecology and Stopping the Clock."

63 Trautmann, *Elephants and Kings*.

64 Morrison, "Pepper in the Hills"; Morrison and Lycett, "Constructing Nature"; Prange, "'Measuring by the Bushel.'" On the role of South-Southeast Asia trade networks in the early VOC (Vereenigde Oostindische Compagnie), see Dijk, "The VOC's Trade in Indian Textiles with Burma."

65 Sivasundaram, "Trading Knowledge"; Parpia, "The Imperial Mughal Hunt"; Singh, "Forests, Pastoralists and Agrarian Society in Mughal India"; Guha, *Environment and Ethnicity in India*.

66 A relatively recent survey of this extensive scholarship is provided in Sivaramakrishnan, "Forests and the Environmental History of Modern India."

67 Coedès, *The Indianized States of Southeast Asia*. For a critical response, see Mus, *India Seen from the East*.

68 Scott, *The Art of Not Being Governed*. As the robust discussion that followed Scott's work attests, state avoidance might also mask forms of state engagement that pass modestly below the political radar.

69 Lieberman, *Strange Parallels*, 23.

70 Lieberman, *Strange Parallels*, 231.

71 Tiyavanich, *Forest Recollections*.

72 Wolters, *History, Culture*, 27–41, 126–54.

73 *Sipsong*, meaning "twelve" in Tai, indicated the plurality of *muang* polities, each led by a *chao* or "lord." On the *muang*, see Davis, *Imperial Bandits*, 5; Hanks and Hanks, *Tribes of the North Thailand Frontier*, 31–32.

74 On the endurance of Tai Lüe power holders after Qing reforms, see Giersch, *Asian Borderlands*. For Tai modalities in imperial and French colonial Vietnam, see Davis, "Black Flag Rumors and the Black River Basin."

75 Winichakuhl, *Siam Mapped*, 84–88; Tambiah, "The Galactic Polity," 69–97.

76 Schendel, "Geographies of Knowing." See also Michaud, "Editorial"; Davis, "Review of *The Art of Not Being Governed*."

77 Scott, *The Art of Not Being Governed*.

78 Bryant, "Burma and the Politics of Teak," 143–61; Peluso, *Rich Forests, Poor People*, chapter 2.

79 On imperial Vietnam, see Davis, "The Production of Peoples"; Baldanza, "Books without Borders."

80 Peluso, *Rich Forests, Poor People*, chapters 3–4; McElwee, *Forests Are Gold*, chapter 1; Bankoff, "Almost an Embarrassment of Riches"; Bryant, "Burma and the Politics of Teak."

81 Peluso and Vandergeest, "Political Ecologies of War and Forests."

82 Peluso, *Rich Forests, Poor People*.

83 McElwee, *Forests are Gold*.

84 Forsyth and Walker, *Forest Guardians, Forest Destroyers*.

85 The path-breaking example: Conklin, "The Relation of Hanunóo Culture to the Plant World," reprinted in Conklin, *Fine Description*, 196–260.

THE CULTIVATED FOREST

CHAPTER ONE

DEFORESTATION IN EARLY CHINA

How People Adapted to Wood Scarcity

BRIAN LANDER

U NTIL quite recently, most of the energy and materials that people in China used came from plants. Plants were the ultimate source of all food, woody plants were the main fuel for cooking and heating, and wood was used to make buildings and tools.[1] For the first few millennia of their existence, sedentary agricultural communities were small enough that there was usually plenty of wood available. But as populations grew and farmland replaced woodlands, people increasingly found it difficult to find all the wood they needed. They adapted in various ways, including by regulating forest exploitation, growing trees as crops, importing timber, and by developing technologies to use less wood. Evidence for the use, and scarcity, of wood in China during the Zhou-Han period (ca. 1045 BCE–200 CE) shows that the lowlands of the Yellow River valley, especially the North China plain, were the first regions in East Asia to confront a scarcity of timber, a situation to which people and states adapted in various ways.

Even though wood was essential, it was such a mundane topic that early Chinese writers rarely addressed it directly, and we have surprisingly little evidence on it. But references to wood are scattered through the ancient texts, and we can combine these with evidence from pollen and charcoal that have been preserved underground to understand changes in woodlands and people's use of them. The forests that remain in the region, all of which grow on slopes too steep to cultivate, also provide an important indication of what trees were available to early people. Of course, there is also a considerable body of information on trees planted for their fruits, nuts, and other uses, but here we will focus on trees used for their wood.[2]

Homo sapiens have inhabited East Asia for tens of thousands of years, but it was only with the growth of farming societies that populations began to outstrip the wood supply. Agricultural populations congregated in low-lying arable valleys and plains, and they tended to gather wood near their settlements or in places from which they could easily transport it, so their impact on forests was highly localized. Even as the spread of farming replaced the natural ecosystems of flat areas with grain fields, hilly or waterlogged areas that could not be used to grow crops were used for cutting timber, pasturing livestock, and foraging for food, firewood, and medicines. Most of the forests in the mountains of the Yellow and Yangzi River valleys have been cut and regrown many times over the millennia, though of course, the least accessible areas were cut less often.

The transition from a landscape in which humans were just one of many animals to one in which they were the dominant ecological force happened very gradually. Stone Age farmers frequently abandoned worn-out fields and cleared new settlements elsewhere, a practice that is sustainable as long as populations remain low, though it replaces old-growth forests with a mosaic of forest succession types. As human populations increased, the amount of time between clearances would have declined, and people would have been forced to farm lower-quality land that would previously have been left alone. The replacement of the region's forests with farmland was not a wave of deforestation but a gradual process in which the length of time any given tree grew before being cut down diminished. Certain areas and sites that had excellent conditions for establishing a farming village would have been repeatedly occupied and cleared over the millennia. The fruit and nut trees that people planted remained part of the forest that grew back. Incidentally, the creation of sacred tree groves that were off-limits to axes began with the spread of Buddhism in the first millennium CE. People in early China did plant trees on important sites, but unlike people in many other parts of the world, they did not worship them.[3]

THE TREES IN THE HEARTLAND OF CHINESE CIVILIZATION

The northern hemisphere's broadleaf and coniferous forests arose around the pole over sixty million years ago, a time when the climate was warm and Eurasia was connected to North America.[4] As the world cooled, these forests moved south and spread across both continents. Over the past fifteen million years, the earth continued to cool, and rain-blocking mountains rose that made the centers of both continents too dry for forests, which were gradually replaced with grasslands and deserts while the forests remained on the east and west of each continent. Over the past two million years, the climate has fluctuated dramatically, and glaciers have repeatedly plowed over Europe and North America. Because plants could freely migrate over a vast area stretching from Malaysia to Siberia and the latter region was too dry for ice sheets to form, East Asia's flora was spared the extinctions of the other two regions and has the most diverse flora of all northern temperate forests. Anyone acquainted with the plants of North America or Europe will find much that is familiar in North China's forests.

It is difficult to guess what the vegetation of North China's lowlands would look like without human modification (something ecologists call "potential natural vegetation") or to reconstruct how prehistoric people affected it. No forests remain in the lowlands, and little research has been done on the fossil pollen of the North China plain itself. The region's average annual temperature is roughly 14°C (57°F), and its annual precipitation ranges from 600 mm around Xi'an in the west to just under 1,000 mm on the coast of Jiangsu. This suggests that the west of the region would have been dominated by shrubby grasslands, with woodlands in wetter areas, and that as one traveled eastward, the amount of tree cover would have gradually increased, becoming dense forest in the southeast of the plain north of the Yangzi River. Most of the region's vegetation would have reflected its local hydrology, with more trees in lower, wetter areas and more herbaceous and shrubby vegetation in drier areas. To the north and west, the vegetation gradually faded to steppe and desert, while the surrounding mountainous regions received more rain and were mostly forested.[5]

The most common timber trees in lowland North China over recent centuries have been fast-growing ones like paulownia, pines, and poplars, the latter of which have become by far the most common trees.[6] Other widely planted native trees include ornamental cypresses, pagoda tree, and willows, as well as indigenously domesticated fruits and nuts like mulberries, cherries, peaches, apricots, pears, chestnuts, and jujubes.[7] All these trees would have been present in North China's forests, but many other species that grow slowly or have no obvious use have been eliminated. Oaks were among the most common trees across much of North China, and the broader beech family predominated in the forests of the Yangzi valley.[8] People gradually replaced oaks with trees that grew faster but whose wood is often softer and weaker.[9] The rugged Qinling Mountains are still covered in biodiverse forests and surely resemble the forests that once grew in the lowlands. These forests included a wide variety of broadleaf trees as well as conifers such as hemlocks, firs, spruces, yews, plum yews, and numerous species of pines and cypresses.[10] Larch, fir, and spruce are still common in the high mountains.

Although their natural habitats are now restricted to remote mountains in China, many East Asian trees are widely planted as ornamentals across the temperate world.

Although we have a general understanding of the species involved, it is still difficult to imagine what the forests of China looked like thousands of years ago. There are no natural lowland environments remaining anywhere in East Asia, and mountainous areas with wild forests have climates and soils that are very different from those of the lowlands. Even the mountain forests have been logged continually over the past millennia, so there are no old-growth forests. Also, animals can play important ecological roles, but many of China's animals have been extirpated from much of their former ranges or driven to extinction.[11] We can expect that future paleoecological research will uncover that some trees endemic to lowland North China are now extinct.

WOOD USAGE IN EARLY CHINA

Historian Joachim Radkau estimated that nine-tenths of wood used in pre-modern Germany was burned as fuel, and I would not be surprised if the same were true in ancient China.[12] Wood used for building and tools can last for decades, while people tend to cook every day. The need for fuel would have kept a strain on the forests surrounding all populated areas. It should be emphasized that even overexploited forests with few large trees can still produce a lot of firewood, so obtaining wood to burn is a completely different affair from obtaining good timber, which requires that trees be left for decades to grow. "Cutting trees," a poem from *The Book of Odes* (Shijing; ca. 900–600 BCE), is usually assumed to be a lumberman's work song, and it gives the impression that logging was one form of labor service that people had to provide to their lords.[13] In later centuries, firewood must have been one of the most important of the products of the mountains, marshes, and forests that are frequently referred to in ancient texts. When one imagines a densely populated farming area with little wooded land, it becomes easy to understand the importance with which early thinkers viewed regulating wood.

The *Huainanzi*, written in the second century BCE, lists the abuses associated with each of the five phases (or elements), which notably included wood. It summarizes the problems created by burning too much wood:

> Frying, boiling, roasting, grilling, the quest to blend, equalize,
> and harmonize [flavors], trying to capture every permutation of
> sweet and sour in the manner of Jing and Wu; burning down

forests in order to hunt, stoking kilns with entire logs, blowing through tuyeres and puffing with bellows in order to melt bronze and iron that extravagantly flow to harden in the mold, not considering an entire day sufficient to the task. The mountains are denuded of towering trees; the forests are stripped of cudrania and catalpa trees; tree trunks are baked to make charcoal; grass is burned to make ash, [so that] open fields and grasslands are white and bare and do not yield [vegetation] in season. Above, the heavens are obscured [by smoke]; below, the fruits of the earth are extinguished.[14]

In other words, people burn wood for cooking, hunting, smelting metal, and making charcoal, and this wastes wood, chars the ground, and causes air pollution. The expression "burning the forest to hunt" later became an expression used to indicate any self-defeating activity, but the critical tone of this passage suggests that the phrase is being used literally, which is not surprising, because there was a long tradition of hunting with fire.[15] The mention of charcoal in this passage is significant. Charcoal is much lighter to transport than firewood and is preferred for indoor burning because it produces less smoke. But producing it requires considerable work and wastes a lot of wood, so it would be produced only when there were large numbers of people who lacked fuel and were willing to pay the cost of producing and transporting it from forests to their towns. It may also have been preferred for smelting. Like many mundane things, charcoal is rarely mentioned in early texts, and we have no idea how common it was.[16]

While most wood was burned, it was also used in a variety of other ways. While the walls of buildings could be built of timber, earth, or bricks, wood was the material of choice for roofs in almost all Chinese architecture, which were covered with thatch or wood-fired ceramic tiles. Wood was also used to build a wide variety of things, such as tools, boats, bridges, and fences. Artisans knew which types of wood should be used to make each type of thing, selecting for attributes like hardness, flexibility, durability, and appearance. As commerce and industry expanded over the first millennium BCE, artisans used more and more wood to fire pottery, smelt metal, and evaporate salt.[17] Metal production required such enormous quantities of wood that "the limiting resource in pre-modern iron productions is *wood*, not ore."[18] For this reason, metal production and salt production were often carried out in remote forested areas. The second century BCE *Discourses on Salt and Iron* (Yantie lun) notes that "the places where salt is crystallised and iron smelted are in most cases in mountains and on rivers near to iron and charcoal."[19] The government produced considerable amounts of iron at that time. An estimated ten to fifty thousand convict laborers worked in state foundries, and empire-wide annual iron production may have been around five million kilograms.[20] This would have burned a lot of wood. Moreover, these iron foundries produced massive numbers of metal implements and for the first time gave common people access to iron axes that made it easier to cut down trees.

The increasing wealth and power of political elites beginning in the Warring States period led to an increase in monumental architecture.[21] This must have required larger timbers than had been needed before, some of which probably had to be sought in distant forests. The First Emperor had timber brought hundreds of miles from the Yangzi valley to build his enormous palaces, which suggests that accessible larger trees of the Yellow River valley had already been logged.[22] As discussed below, forests in the western Yellow River valley were cut because their trees could be floated downstream to the valley's population centers. All these uses of wood had their impacts on forests and woodlands.

EARLY EVIDENCE FOR DEFORESTATION

At least seven thousand years ago, communities in the Yellow River valley were already damaging the vegetation around their communities enough that when it rained, the soils eroded into waterways in quantities that are still visible to scientists.[23] Over the past few millennia, the amount of sediment in the Yellow River has increased as more and more people have cleared vegetation for farming.[24] Our earliest written evidence of overcutting and overgrazing dates to the Warring States period (481–221 BCE), and the most famous is this passage from Mencius:

> The trees on Ox Mountain were once beautiful, but because it is near a big city, they were all chopped down with axes. Can this be considered beautiful? The vegetation does get respite over the days and nights and is watered by the rain and dew, so it is not that no new shoots grow, but then cattle and sheep come and graze on them. That is why the mountain is so bald. People see its baldness and assume it never had trees on it, but is that the nature of the mountain?[25]

Given the archaeological evidence that people had been transforming vegetation in the region for millennia by this point, Mencius's awareness of overcutting and overgrazing is not surprising. But it is remarkable that he considered these topics obvious enough to serve as metaphors for the destruction of people's innate goodness. Although our evidence from earlier periods is too sparse to say anything conclusive, it seems to be in the second half of the first millennium BCE that populations in substantial areas of the North China plain began to outstrip the ability of the region to produce adequate wood supplies.

Some of the most useful textual evidence on how people perceived forests comes from comparisons of the material wealth of different regions, several of which reveal that the North China plain was lacking in timber. Both *Strategies of the Warring States* (Zhanguo ce) and *Mozi* include a passage in which Mozi attempts to convince the ruler of the southern state of Chu (also called Jing) not to attack Song by arguing that Song was too poor to be worth the expense of invading:

> Jing has Yunmeng, filled with buffalo, rhinoceros, buffalo, elaphures, and deer, and the Yangzi and the Han are full of fish, tortoises, giant turtles and alligators—enough to feed the empire. Song, on the other hand, is known as a land that even lacks pheasants, rabbits, and foxes. So this is like exchanging meat and millet for dregs and lees. Jing has tall pines and beautiful catalpa, *piannan* and *yüzhang* trees while Song has no timber.[26]

Song lay in the heart of the North China plain, which was the most densely populated area in East Asia at this time (it is the cluster of dots to the right of the center of figure 1.1). Writing in the second century BCE, Sima Qian likewise names Zou, Lu, Song, Liang, and eastern Chu, all in the North China plain, as places that lacked timber.[27] A similar point is made in *Discourses on Salt and Iron* (first century BCE), which enumerates various regions with plentiful timber and then contrasts them with the North China plain, which was so lacking in timber that people had to reuse coffins to bury their dead.[28] The North China plain was an enormous expanse of flat arable land that had no hills or mountains, so most of its land was farmed. In contrast, the two densely populated areas of the west—Sichuan's Chengdu plain and Shaanxi's Guanzhong basin—were surrounded by forested mountains and thus did not lack for timber. The people of the mountainous and sparsely populated south had no lack of timber at this time.

The passages just cited can be supplemented with the earliest extant empire-wide population records, which date to 2 CE. They reveal very clearly

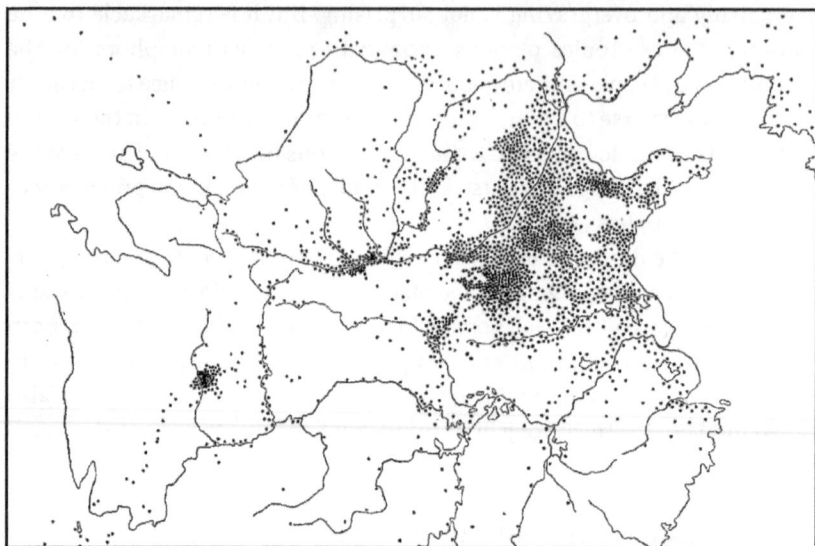

FIGURE 1.1. The population of the Han dynasty in 2 CE as recorded in *Han History*. Image from Hans Bielenstein, "The Census in China during the Period 2–742 AD," plate 2, cropped and redrawn to reflect the Han era coastline as depicted in Tan Qixiang, *Zhongguo lishi dituji*, 2:14.

that the North China lowlands were the main centers of human population in East Asia (see figure 1.1). Although the Han did not have the capacity to count every person, it did control most of the major agricultural centers, so this is probably a fairly good record of human population in the Yellow and Yangzi valleys. South of the Yangzi valley, the Han controlled only the fertile river valleys and the transportation corridors between them. The populations of remote mountainous regions were too sparse to repay the cost of administering them. The total population of the empire was about sixty million. The picture of population density revealed in the census corresponds well with the passages cited above. By the third century BCE, the North China plain was so heavily populated that many people were lacking in both protein and timber, which pushed them to develop new ways of producing and consuming resources.

As commerce expanded over this period, the invisible hand of the market reached farther into the forest. Commodities that could make a merchant rich in the second century BCE included timber, firewood, bamboo, metals, and tree commodities like fruits and lacquer.[29] This reveals that businesses were involved in timber extraction and in producing metal in forested regions. The ability of urban elites to pay large sums for good timber made it profitable for loggers to head farther into the forests.

As this second-century BCE passage reveals, one way they did this was by floating wood downstream:

> *Piannan* and *yuzhang* are the most famous kinds of wood in the world. They grow in the deep mountains and the slopes of river valleys. When they stand upright, they are more distinguished than all the trees on big mountains. When they are chopped down, they can be used by people for ten thousand generations. The logs float down the streams of mountain rivers and come out in remote country. Going along the course of rivers, eventually the logs reach the area of the imperial capital. The work of axes allows them to display their patterns and colors: perfectly solid, straight grained, densely fine, tall and straight. Insects and wood-worms cannot penetrate them, rain and dampness cannot harm them. . . . Of this wood, the best is the possession of the emperor and the princes, while wood of lesser quality is bestowed on lords and ministers.[30]

This passage uses rare timber as a metaphor for talented people. Readers surely knew that prized timber was scarce enough that loggers went into remote areas to find it. It is not the only early record of people floating wood downstream. A passage in *Huainanzi* describes an official who made his subjects cut trees in the winter and float them down the river in the spring to sell. Although income from this region tripled, the ruler told the official that the people worked hard the rest of the year and should be allowed to relax in winter.[31] The fourth-century CE *Records of the States South of Mt. Hua* (Huayang guo zhi) records that when officials from the state of Qin had built the Dujiangyan irrigation works in Sichuan more than six centuries earlier, they made sure that waterways were still available to float catalpa, cypresses, and bamboo from the mountains down to Chengdu.[32] This was the beginning of a long tradition, whereby rulers sought out ever more remote sources of old-growth timber, that culminated in the eighteenth century, when the Qing dynasty could no longer find large timbers anywhere in its enormous empire.[33]

The practice of floating wood downstream, which was common in medieval and modern Europe, had many consequences for people living along those rivers and for forests.[34] First, forests from which timber or firewood could be easily floated to population centers were easily cut, leaving less convenient waterways as the next best option. Loggers often modified waterways to facilitate wood movement by straightening them, building special spillways or even damming waterways to ensure adequate water for a single burst of wood flotation. In many places, there was only enough water in specific seasons, which made it a seasonal activity, as suggested by the *Huainanzi* passage above. Logs could disrupt fishing and damage shores, weirs, and bridges, so it led to conflict and required negotiation with those who used the rivers for other things.

The fact that people in the early Han were floating wood downstream is clear evidence that there was scarcity in population centers. This leads to the question of when people began to actively protect forests and to grow wood for their own use.

STATE CONTROL AND MANAGEMENT OF FORESTS

As human populations grew and woodlands diminished, people sought new ways to get wood. Control of land and human labor was the key to political power in preindustrial times, so states, non-state elites, and common people often struggled over land ownership and land use. This was especially true of arable land, but by the second half of the first millennium BCE, states extended their control over previously communal land and then instituted rules about how it should be used.[35]

We can dimly see this occurring in our sources. In the early Zhou period, much of the best arable land was held by aristocratic lineages whose estates would have included some woodlands and wetlands and had people appointed to manage them.[36] The forest wardens referred to in texts of this period were probably more like gamekeepers of princely estates than officials of public lands.[37] Much of the rest of the forested land seems to have been held in common or to have not been owned by anyone and was thus available for common people to collect firewood, forage, hunt, and cut timber. As the various states fought increasingly long and expensive wars over the course of the first millennium BCE, they strove to find new sources of income.[38] The minister of war of the southern state of Chu "recorded the ground and fields, measured the forests in the mountains, added up the wetlands and marshes, distinguished hills from tombs, noted barren and saline ground, calculated border wetlands, graded reservoirs and weirs, grazed livestock in marshy places, divided fertile land into grids, and adjusted the levies based on the income of each area."[39] In other words, he surveyed all the land, not only the arable, to ensure that the state could extract as much as possible. This happened in other states as well.[40]

There was surely plenty of resistance to these power grabs, but our only record of it comes from conservative Confucians, many of whom were members of the declining lower aristocracy, who resented the increasing power of centralized states. For example, one scholar attacked the Duke of Lu for being "greedy for the profit from the mountains, forests, grasslands and marshes, competing with the people in gaining the wealth from the fields, fisheries, firewood and edible plants."[41] Mencius likewise criticized the Duke of Qi for barring commoners from foraging in his imperial parks, noting that he should not be surprised that the people resented him for abolishing their traditional access to forest resources.[42] It is worth considering the possibility that farming communities had systems of sustainable wood use that were eroded by increasing state control. As governments took over their forests, people would be more likely to take as much from them as they could than to manage them carefully. The need for state management may have been partly created by these dynamics.

By the third century BCE, the states had achieved direct control over many forests. *Offices of Zhou* (Zhou guan; Zhou li) describes officers of mountains, forests, rivers, and wetlands who were in charge of regulating all hunting and fishing and providing animals and fish for sacrifices.[43] *The Annals of Master Lü* (Lüshi chunqiu, third century BCE) states that in the spring, "the foresters enter the mountains and make a tour of inspection to see that the trees have not been felled or trimmed."[44] Likewise, Xunzi explains that "the duties of the master of forests and game are to prepare rules for burning, to care for the resources of the mountain forests, the lakes, and the marshes, such as the grasses and the trees, the fish and the turtles, and the hundred other edibles, opening and closing them according to the season so the state will have enough to satisfy its needs, and raw materials and resources will not be depleted."[45]

Many of the Warring States philosophers commented on the need for the protection of forests, which shows both that the overexploitation of resources was a widespread problem and that people were aware that state regulation was necessary for sustainable management.[46] Most of these thinkers came from the North China plain. The earlier opposition to state control was replaced in this period by advocacy for effective state regulation of woodlands.

The ideas in Warring States philosophical texts on preserving resources were eventually written into law. Qin's *Statutes on Agriculture* were excavated from a tomb in 1975 and include this passage:

> In the second month of spring one should not venture to cut
> timber or mountain forests or block or dike water courses.
> Except in the months of summer one should not venture to burn

weeds to make ashes, to collect [indigo], young animals, eggs or fledglings. One should not . . . poison fish or tortoises or arrange pitfalls and nets. By the seventh month [these prohibitions] are lifted. Only when someone has unfortunately died and one fells [wood for] the inner and outer coffins, is this not done according to the seasons.[47]

We have no way of evaluating how successfully Qin enforced these laws, but we can presume that they had some effect in areas where state control was strong. This statute continued to be issued by the subsequent Han dynasty, and various other texts from the same period advocated seasonal prohibitions on the cutting of trees.[48]

Our best evidence of government interest in logging are maps discovered at Fangmatan, Gansu, in the 1980s and dated to the third century BCE. They represent maps made by Qin officials to survey timber. Appropriately enough, these were discovered at a modern logging station in a mountainous and forested region south of Tianshui, Gansu. This area, cited as a source of good timber in several early texts, has been logged on and off for well over two thousand years. Like the rest of the Qinling, the area is mountainous and densely forested, useful for forestry but not for agriculture. From that area, logs could be floated down the Wei River to the capital region. This made it considerably more practical for logging than areas of the central Qinling Mountains that were closer to the capital but very difficult to extract logs from.[49] There is no evidence that state officials produced these maps, but administrators commonly used maps in the period, and the tomb is assumed to have belonged to an official.[50] These maps could have been made for Qin offices that logged this region to provide timber for state use, but it is also possible that Qin used these maps to manage and tax private logging operations.

The six maps from Fangmatan form a group; one map is a larger-scale depiction of two adjacent watersheds, and the others are smaller scale "close-ups" of different areas (figure 1.2 is one of the latter). The maps are structured around the network of waterways they depict, and this also provides a general idea of the layout of the mountains. The maps include the names of towns and villages, streams and gullies, and mountain passes. They also note stands of trees and distances to reach them and in one case a road or path. There are several mentions of pine, one of paulownia (*tong*), and a reference to a place called "poplar gorge," but several other wood-related words are either unknown or ambiguous. It is unclear if one key term means "poles/ tree trunks" or "cut down," making it impossible for us to tell if it indicates

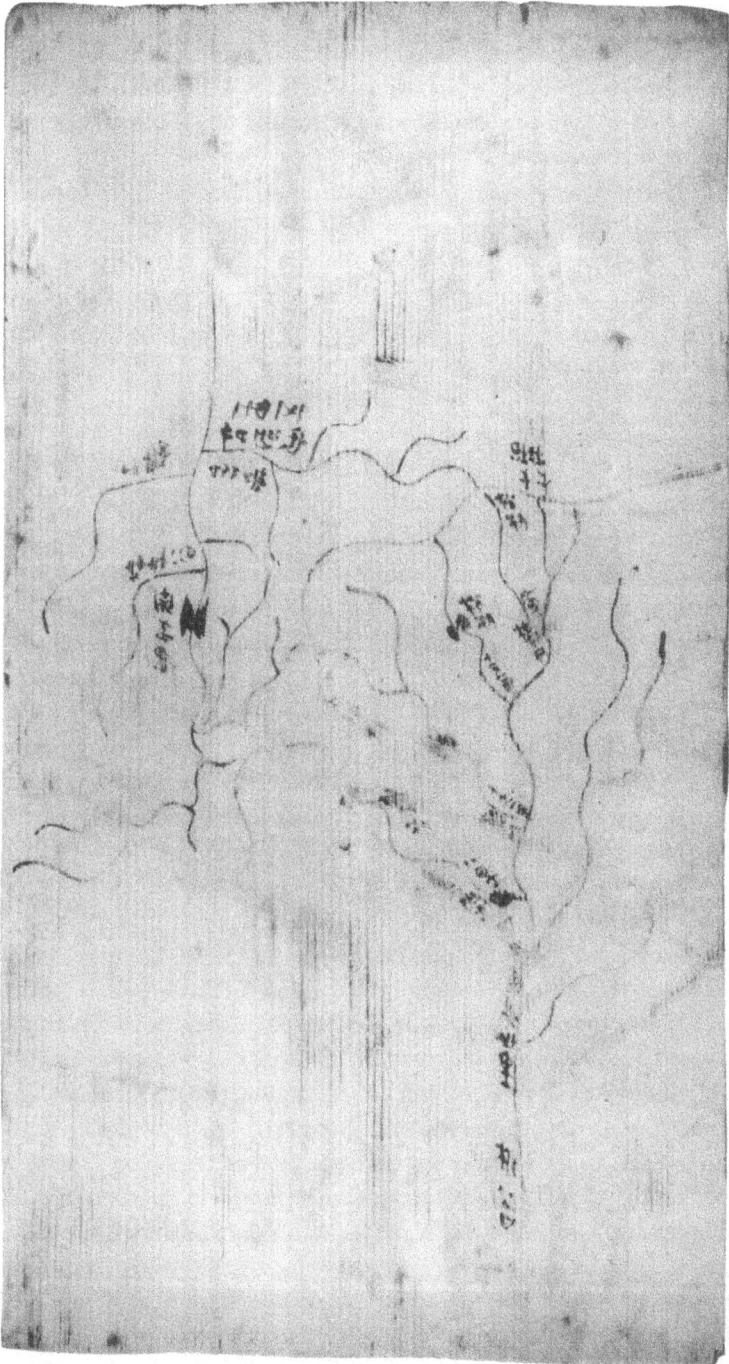

FIGURE 1.2. A map on pine wood excavated from a third-century BCE tomb at Fangmatan, Gansu. The lines depict waterways. Image from Chen, Sun, and Yan, *Qin jiandu heji*, 349. Courtesy of Chen Wei and Wuhan University Press.

timber resources or a lack of trees. In either case, these maps suggest a systematic large-scale logging operation. Given the size of the Qin state and the extent of its many projects, it must have needed a lot of timber, so there is nothing surprising about these maps. Maps were used at various scales of the administration, from the central government to local administrators, for a variety of purposes, including the exploitation of resources.[51] We can be sure that the Fangmatan maps are a random discovery of a type of document that were quite common at the time, and we can hope that more such documents will come to light and tell us more about how the state managed forests and wetlands.

THE ORIGINS OF SILVICULTURE

Managing woodlands was the first step in dealing with wood scarcity, but by the time there were tens of millions of people in North China's lowlands, they needed more intensive strategies for procuring wood.[52] The North China plain had no hills or mountains that could be reserved for timber, so farmers began to grow their own timber as crops, a practice that can be considered the beginning of silviculture in China. We know from archaeological evidence that farmers were cultivating peaches and apricots four thousand years ago.[53] *The Book of Odes* includes those two fruits as well as cherries, pears, and jujubes. Since arboriculture was already part of the agricultural system, people would have no trouble growing timber trees, but they did not need to plant them if they had access to other wood. So the real issue is to determine when they needed to actively work to grow trees because they had no access to wild woodlands.

Westerners visiting the North China plain during the late nineteenth and early twentieth centuries noted that although there were no remnants of natural forest, some villages grew enough paulownia and poplar in small timber plots that they were able to export it.[54] This had become possible both through their skill in growing trees and by the use of good arable land for the intensive cultivation of trees, something that would have been unthinkable in ancient times when there were still forests to exploit. People must have begun to plant trees for timber in overpopulated parts of the North China plain no later than the Warring States period, which ended in 221 BCE.[55]

The Book of Odes mentions people growing trees in their yards.[56] The earliest evidence for people planting timber trees comes from Ode 50, which is traditionally considered to commemorate the founding of a new settlement. It reads, "They built the mansion at Chu, planting about it hazel and chestnut trees, paulownia, catalpa and lacquer trees which, when cut down, might afford materials for zithers."[57] It is difficult to separate the planting of trees in a new town with the symbolism that was often associated with the planting of trees in this period, when people also planted trees as boundary markers and on tombs and altars.[58] People also planted trees for their own coffins, which was convenient for their descendants and probably also had symbolic value.[59] The *Offices of Zhou* also gives the impression of landscapes in which planted trees were common. It discusses several officials whose duties included dealing with the planting and management of trees, making clear that people were generally concerned about the symbolic and practical function of trees in various contexts.[60]

The earliest evidence for larger numbers of trees planted for timber seems to come from the "Categories of Land" *diyuan* text, which was written around 250–100 BCE and is now found in the *Guanzi* anthology. The fifth section of the text contains rhyming lists of which plants can be grown in specific types of soils.[61] For example, "The five *su* soils are fully suitable for paulownia and oak trees and there is no place where their trunks do not grow tall. Numerous other trees, including elms and willow, wild mulberry, and mulberry, cudrania and serrated oak, pagoda tree and poplar grow in profusion, quickly reach maturity, and have limbs that are straight and long."[62] It is possible that these trees were being planted for entirely ornamental purposes, but the desire for tall and straight trees makes clear that these authors were interested in producing good timber.

Centuries later, *Essential Arts to Nourish the People* (Qimin yaoshu) reveals that timber was planted as a cash crop on large aristocratic estates and discusses methods for growing various trees.[63] It was written during the fifth century CE in the North China plain and makes clear that silviculture was well established by then. It also discusses other practices typical of intensive land use, such as keeping pigs in pens and raising fish in ponds. All these reveal that the people of the plain had adapted to the lack of freely accessible natural resources by developing more labor-intensive methods of producing food and materials.[64]

CONCLUSION

The dense populations in the lowlands of the Yellow River valley gradually replaced woodlands with farmland, and people found themselves lacking in wood. While people in more mountainous regions could manage forests on slopes too steep for farming, those in the lowlands had little option but to buy wood from elsewhere or to devote precious farmland to growing trees. People in early North China developed many methods to deal with wood scarcity, such as finding ways to use wood more efficiently, managing woodlands, and planting trees. As the population of East Asia subsequently grew, other regions experienced similar problems and were able to draw on these methods.[65] In fact, it was often people from the Yellow River valley who brought these methods themselves, since migration out of North China was one driver of population growth in other regions. Moreover, many of the texts cited in this chapter became the classical corpus studied by educated people across East Asia. For example, most educated people in early modern East Asia knew Mencius's story of the deforestation of Ox Mountain, and many of them memorized it. The process described in this chapter is thus connected to the subsequent history of woodland exploitation across East Asia, because people were often familiar with many of the classical passages described above.

NOTES

1   Most daily-use implements in early twentieth-century rural China were made of wood and bamboo; Hommel, *China at Work*.

2   On China's remaining forests, see Wang, *The Forests of China*; on fruit and nut trees, see Spenger, *Fruit from the Sands*; and Lander, *The King's Harvest*, chapter 2.

3   Hara, "Kodai Chūgoku ni okeru jumoku e no ninshiki no hensen." A classic study of tree worship is found in chapters 9 and 10 of Frazer's *The Magic Art and the Evolution of Kings*.

4   At that time, these forests already had broadleaf genera like alder, birch, maple, oak, poplar, and walnut and deciduous conifers like dawn redwood (*Metasequoia*), ginkgo, and larches (*Larix* and *Pseudolarix*), all still found in China. Willis and McElwain, *The Evolution of Plants*, 225–64, 315; Manchester et al., "Eastern Asian Endemic Seed Plant Genera and Their Paleogeographic History."

5   On the climate and ecology of the west of this region, see Lander, "Birds and Beasts Were Many."

6   These are *Paulownia tomentosa*, presumably *Pinus tabulaeformis*, and poplars including *Populus tomentosa* and *P. simonii*. Lowdermilk and Li, "Forestry in Denuded China," 129, 137–39.

7   The most common cypresses are Oriental arborvitae, weeping cypress, and Chinese juniper.

8   Wang, *The Forests of China*. The main oaks of the north are *Quercus acrodonta*, *Q. acutissima*, *Q. aliena*, *Q. baronii*, *Q. dentata*, *Q. dolicholepis*, *Q. mongolica*, *Q. serrata*, and *Q. variabilis*. Ring-cupped oaks are considered

either a subgenus of oak or a separate genus (*Cyclobalanopsis*). Other genera of the beech family common in China are chestnuts, chinquapins, and stone oaks.

9   Menzies, *Forestry*, 615–16.

10   Woody broadleaf plants of North China's forests include sweetgum, holly, birch, alder, hornbeam, hazel, catalpa, katsura, dogwood, persimmon, redbud, honey locust, hackberry, chestnut, beech, walnut, hickory, wingnut, linden, paper mulberry, ash, crab apple, rowan, cork tree, willow, buckeye, goldenrain tree, tree of heaven, snowbells, zelkova, and elm. See glossary for scientific and Chinese names. For distribution maps of woody plants in China, see Fang, Wang, and Tang, *Atlas of Woody Plants*.

11   Lander and Brunson, "Wild Mammals of Ancient North China."

12   Radkau, *Wood*, 19.

13   The *Odes* were composed between roughly 900 and 600 BCE. "Cutting trees" (Fa mu) is Ode 165. Odes 300, "The Closed Temple" (Bi gong), and 305 "Warriors of Yin" (Yin wu) also mention logging. Waley and Allen, *The Book of Songs*.

14   He, *Huainanzi jishi*, 8.595–96; Major et al., *Huainanzi*, 281–82.

15   Fiskesjö, "Rising from Blood-Stained Fields."

16   An early Han mathematical text refers to someone collecting charcoal to deliver to a government post; Dauben, "*Suan Shu*," 146.

17   It has been estimated that the slag excavated at Tonglüshan, one of the largest known Bronze Age copper mines, required three thousand cubic meters of timber to produce. Dazhi shi tonglüshan gu tongkuang yizhi baohu guanli weiyuanhui, *Tonglüshan gu tongkuang yizhi kaogu faxian yu yanjiu*, xi.

18   Wagner, *Iron and Steel in Ancient China*, 258; Radkau, *Wood*, 92–112.

19   Wang, *Yantielun jiaozhu*, 5.68; Gale, *Discourses on Salt and Iron*, 33.

20   Barbieri-Low, *Artisans in Early Imperial China*, 236.

21   Hung, "The Art and Architecture of the Warring States Period."

22   Qian, *Shi ji*, 6.256; Nienhauser, *The Grand Scribe's Records*, 149.

23   Rosen, "The Impact of Environmental Change"; Zhuang and Kidder, "Archaeology of the Anthropocene"; Kidder and Zhuang, "Anthropocene Archaeology of the Yellow River"; Rosen et al., "The Anthropocene and the Landscape of Confucius."

24   Xu, "Naturally and Anthropogenically Accelerated Sedimentation"; Mostern, *The Yellow River*.

25   The Mencius quote is my translation; see Lau, *Mencius*, 6A.250–51.

26   Crump, *Chan-kuo ts'e*, 563; Liu Xiang, *Zhanguo ce*, 279; Also found in Johnston, *The Mozi*, 50.727.

27   Qian, *Shi ji* 129.3266; Qian, *Records of the Grand Historian*, 444.

28   Wang, *Yantie lun jiaozhu*, 3.42; Gale, *Discourses on Salt and Iron*, 20.

29   Qian, *Shi ji*, 129.3253–84; Qian, *Records of the Grand Historian*, 448–54.

30 Wang, *Xinyu jiaozhu*; Ku, *A Chinese Mirror for Magistrates*, 101–4.

31 He, *Huainanzi jishi*, 18.1270; Major et al., *Huainanzi*, 18.733.

32 *Huayang guo zhi*, 3.30.

33 Miller, *Fir and Empire*, chapter 7.

34 Radkau, *Wood*, 112–18.

35 Lander, *The King's Harvest*.

36 See the Lai *pan*, Nangong Liu *ding* (JC2805), Tong *gui* (JC4271), Mian *gui* (JC4240), and Mian *fu* (JC4626) in Li, *Bureaucracy and the State in Early China*, 206–11.

37 Durrant, Li, and Schaberg, *Zuo Tradition*, 34–35 (Yin 5), 1584–85 (Zhao 20).

38 Hsu, *Ancient China in Transition*.

39 Durrant, Li, and Schaberg, *Zuo Tradition*, 1154–55 (Xiang 25); Yang, *Chun qiu Zuo zhuan zhu*, 1106–08; Sun, *Zhouli zhengyi*, 300–1.

40 Miller, "Forestry and the Politics of Sustainability."

41 Wang, *Xin yu jiaozhu*, 8.124; Ku, *A Chinese Mirror for Magistrates*, 110; Yang, *Chun qiu Zuo zhuan zhu*, 1417 (Zhao 20).

42 Lau, *Mencius*, 1B.28–31.

43 These officials are called *shan yu, lin heng, chuan heng*, and *ze yu*; Miller, "Forestry and the Politics of Sustainability," 606–7; Biot, *Le Tcheou-li*, 105–6; Sun, *Zhouli zhengyi*, 1198–209. See also Swann, *Food and Money in Ancient China*, 121. Although it claims to depict earlier times, the *Offices of Zhou* was probably composed in its current form sometime around the third century BCE.

44 Knoblock and Riegel, *The Annals of Lü Buwei*, 6.155; see also page 653.

45 Knoblock, *Xunzi*, 1:9.106.

46 Sanft, "Environment and Law"; Miller, "Forestry and the Politics of Sustainability."

47 Hulsewé, *Remnants of Ch'in Law*, 22 (document no, 2.3–6); Yates, "Some Notes on Ch'in Law," 248.

48 Barbieri-Low and Yates, *Law, State, and Society*, 712; Rickett, *Guanzi*, 2:124–25, 208, 221.

49 Yan, "Tianshui Fangmatan muban ditu xintan"; Chen, Sun, and Yan, *Qin jiandu heji (si)*; Hsu, "The Qin Maps." For a succinct review of how different scholars have dated these texts, see Wang and Li, "Fangmatan Qin ditu linye jiaotong shiliao yanjiu," 5. The *Han shu* states that the mountainous Tao and upper Wei River valleys had large tracts of forests, so people built their homes with wood, in contrast to rammed earth and bricks in regions further east. Shi Nianhai notes that the region was also a major logging area in the Song Dynasty; Shi Nianhai, *Huangtu Gaoyuan lishi dili yanjiu*, 125, 149–50; Wang Xianqian, *Han shu buzhu*, 28.2824; Wang, *Yantielun jiaozhu*, 3.41.

50 Hsing, "Lun Mawangdui Han mu 'Zhujun tu' ying zhengming wei 'Jiandao fengyu tu'"; Harper and Kalinowski, *Books of Fate and Popular Culture*, 21.

51 Rickett, *Guanzi*, 1:387–91; Jia, *Zhouli zhushu*, 597. On Qin, see Lander, *The King's Harvest*.

52 Miller, "Forestry and the Politics of Sustainability"; Sanft, "Environment and Law."

53 Spengler, *Fruit from the Sands.*

54 Lowdermilk and Li, "Forestry in Denuded China," 137–39; Menzies, *Forestry,* 667.

55 There are differences of opinion on when silviculture began in China; see Lander, "The Retreat of the Forests."

56 Most notably Ode 76, "Jiang Zhongzi."

57 It is unclear if *yi tong* refers to one tree or two, but I simply translate it "paulownia." Translation based on Legge, *The She King,* 81.

58 Cook, "Ritual, Politics and the Issue of *feng,*" 217–20; Miller, "Forestry and the Politics of Sustainability," 604; Jia, *Zhouli zhushu,* 335, 819.

59 Jia, *Zhouli zhushu,* 480.

60 The phrase *shu yi* has often been considered to refer to the planting of trees, but that is not certain, since *shu* used as a verb simply means to plant. Jia, *Zhouli zhushu,* 344, 368.

61 Needham, Lu, and Huang. *Botany*; Hara, *Kodai Chūgoku no kaihatsu to kankyō.*

62 Rickett, *Guanzi,* 269.

63 Shih, *A Preliminary Study*; Menzies, *Forestry,* 611.

64 For a description of how this dynamic transformed pig husbandry, see Lander, Schneider, and Brunson, "A History of Pigs in China."

65 See Miller, *Fir and Empire* and chapter 2 in this volume.

CHAPTER TWO

FORESTRY BY CONTRACT

Knowledge, Ownership, and the Written Record in South China

IAN M. MILLER

Forests in China have been subject to intensive human use since the dawn of written records, with forms of forest management varying widely by region. Southern China, wetter than the north and with highly varied topography, featured different tree species and developed different forms of silviculture. For centuries, the region was oriented toward using the wooded mountains to supply high demand for fuel and timber in the river valleys and in the north. Nonetheless, even this wood-rich region eventually came under the threat of shortages. Starting around 1000 CE, fears of wood scarcity—like those that gripped North China over a millennium earlier—came to the south.[1] These prompted an epochal shift in how people conceptualized forests, how they managed forests, and the extent and composition of the forests themselves. At the conceptual level, forests moved from the domain of shared natural abundance to the domain of exclusive and potentially valuable property. At the institutional level, people shifted from claiming *forest products* by applying labor—cutting wood, gathering fruit—to claiming *forest plots* by owning the land underneath. They began to claim ownership of woodland in the mountains, much as they had long claimed ownership of farmland in the valleys. At the environmental level, diverse, self-seeding, mixed broadleaf forests gave way to anthropogenic plantations of conifers, bamboo, and other commercially valuable species.[2]

The silvicultural revolution was predicated on a documentary revolution—the advent of texts attesting the new ways that people managed forests. In particular, the shift of claims from forest products to forest plots necessitated new ways of documenting ownership. The traditional way of making a claim to timber was to mark a symbol on the trunk, either while it was standing or after it was cut. This technique was widespread throughout Chinese history, including both the mark of "imperial timber" (*huangmu*) and private owners' signs. It is also seen in other regions and contexts, such as the "king's broad arrow" used to mark North American white pines claimed for the British Navy.[3] But to extend a claim from a single tree to an entire plot necessitated a different form of documentation, marking the boundaries of the land and noting ownership of everything within those borders. While this could be done in situ with stones, ditches, or other markers, it was increasingly done with two forms of written document: land registers (or "cadasters"), which were generally held by the state as a central documentation of tax responsibilities; and deeds, which were held by the owner as proof of title. Forest owners also developed other contractual documents to apportion specific rights within forest plots, including rental, shareholding, and logging agreements. These two source bases—cadasters developed to meet the needs of governments and deeds and contracts developed to meet the needs of landowners—now serve as the principal sources for the forest history of southern China.

In the past several decades, the discoveries of thousands of forest deeds and contracts have further revolutionized this field. Concentrated in several discrete locations in present-day Anhui, Jiangxi, Zhejiang, and Fujian, these documents describe forms of forest management that prevailed across the broad but largely contiguous mountainous region at the borders of these four provinces.[4] The earliest regional corpora of forest contracts in terms of both content and date of discovery is from Huizhou.[5] The Huizhou contracts show the development of forest management from 1200 onward, including the emergence of sophisticated shareholding mechanisms.[6] A second regional collection uncovered in western Zhejiang largely concerns the nineteenth and early twentieth centuries, showing how local management changed across the transition from the imperial period to the Republic of China.[7] Finally, tens of thousands of documents from northwestern Fujian have only begun to receive consideration in either Chinese- or English-language writing.[8] Collectively, these regional collections of deeds and contracts cover multiple locations within the highlands of southeastern China and document over seven hundred years of change.

In addition to contractual documents, there are two other major genres of text with extensive records of forest management: agricultural manuals and cadastral records. Each of these corpora provides a different perspective on the silvicultural revolution, but none shows as much variation or change as the contractual materials. Written by and for local officials concerned with promoting best practices, the coverage of silviculture in agricultural manuals attests tree planting from an early date but is otherwise relatively superficial. Silvicultural knowledge did develop over time, with manuals from the seventeenth, eighteenth, and nineteenth centuries showing more attention to varieties of both trees and soils than was paid in earlier texts. Nonetheless, the fundamental planting techniques they document did not change significantly between the late twelfth and early twentieth centuries.

The cadastral documentation paints a somewhat different picture, dominated by two episodes of rapidly shifting forest oversight bookending a longer period of far more gradual change.[9] Between 1149 and 1391, forests were reported in tax books for the first time. This initial wave of forest registration was highly significant to the silvicultural revolution.[10] It was followed by a comparatively slow rate of change over the next five centuries as forest oversight spread to new regions but also underwent a high degree of attrition. Between 1914 and 1945, there was another wave of rapid change as the Republic of China once again attempted to centralize tax records. The changes under the Republic were both significant and astonishingly similar to simultaneous shifts in forest oversight elsewhere in the world. Nonetheless, throughout this long period between the mid-twelfth and mid-twentieth centuries, the documentation of forests in official cadasters was superficial and largely related to tax payment. Between the major shifts in state oversight before 1391 and after 1914, changes in the cadastral regime were relatively minor and therefore did not lead to significant change in forestry practice.[11]

By contrast to both the minimal change in documented silvicultural techniques and the highly episodic shifts in cadastral record keeping, changes in the contractual forest record were both continuous and significant. The changes to forest contracts over this long period did not reflect fundamentally new forms of forest cultivation, forest use, or even forest ownership. Instead, novel clauses were added to clarify the subdivision of forest resources within a given plot. In effect, contractual forestry reproduced many of the types of usage rights formerly governed by custom but now demarcated them within the boundaries of each plot. Instead of the state making a blanket and largely unenforced claim to all wild land, individual landowners now pressed specific claims to bounded parcels of forest. Under the pressures of population growth, an expanding money supply, and increased demand for forest products, these claims were increasingly delineated in writing to provide proof in case of dispute. In short, the first wave of the silvicultural revolution was largely cadastral: the demarcation of territorial boundaries. Its second wave was basically contractual: the specification of cash values and fixed durations for the use of these demarcated plots. Deeds and contracts were far from exclusive to the forestry sector; indeed, forestry documents were adapted from contractual forms first used in farming, and similar contracts proliferated widely across Chinese society. Nonetheless, the specific conditions of forestry—its long time horizons, high degree of uncertainty, and difficulties with oversight—were particularly complex.

SILVICULTURE AS AGRICULTURE

The basic techniques for planting trees were well known long before South China's silvicultural revolution. China's first significant text on estate management, Jia Sixie's sixth-century *Essential Arts to Nourish the People* (Qimin yaoshu), is also the first to clearly describe techniques for cultivating trees, principally the tree species of the north. A section on orchards and hedges gives instructions on growing fruit trees, including jujubes, peaches, apples, plums, and apricots.[12] In keeping with the importance of sericulture in China, it also gives instructions on cultivating mulberry trees, whose leaves were fed to silkworms.[13] Jia also details coppicing methods for elms and poplars, the most important source of fuel and small poles.[14] Other sections explain techniques for planting willows, pagoda trees, catalpa, and bamboo.[15]

By the ninth century, estate silviculture grew increasingly widespread, including in the south, and featured a stratum of expert tree planters. The Tang essayist Liu Zongyuan (773–819) left a biography of "tree-planter Guo the hunchback."[16] *The Book of Tree Planting* (Zhongshu shu) is also attributed to "Guo the hunchback," although some scholars suggest this may have been the product of the twelfth or thirteenth centuries. This book represents a somewhat new genre, organized according to the planting calendar and by the different types of cultivated plants. In addition to its novel organization, *The Book of Tree Planting* is notable for its highly detailed instructions documenting an entire year of garden and orchard cultivation. It also contains instructions on planting southern China's two major timber trees, including extensive details on planting pine from seeds, and far more minimal notes on planting fir from cuttings.[17] Even if *The Book of Tree Planting* was not written until later, other documents from the tenth and eleventh centuries confirm that similar techniques were in wide use. The poet and essayist Su Shi (1037–1101) records a similar method of planting pines, while eleventh-century temples in Hangzhou and Jiangxi boasted extensive plantings of fir trees.[18] But unlike fruit, fuel, and mulberry trees, conifers like pine and fir were largely planted for ornamental purposes on temple and noble estates, not for timber production.

In the twelfth century, silviculture went through a revolution, expanding beyond its previous emphasis on fruit, mulberry, and fuel trees to produce large volumes of timber for commercial markets. While this shift rested on some changes in tree planting techniques, the basic methods for planting pine and fir had been known since the ninth or tenth centuries at the latest. Instead, the breakthrough in timber cultivation responded principally to commercial opportunities. Growth in demand for wood, met with an inadequate growth in supply, almost certainly meant rising prices. Entrepreneurs responded by finding more wood to market; when there was not enough to log from natural growth, they turned to planting trees.

The first clear indication of large-scale investments in tree planting comes from the miscellaneous writings of a minor scholar named Ye Mengde (1077–1148). Ye begins by describing his plans to grow timber to repair his house:

> If every year I planted one-thousand pines, three hundred poles each of tung and fir, and bamboo wherever there was a free crack, after five years there would be five thousand pines, and one-thousand five hundred poles each of tung and fir. After thirty years, as my house became worn out, I could cut them to rebuild it. I would have more than enough bamboo for my needs by only taking those damaged by wind and frost or that invaded the roadway. This year I have accumulated several thousand poles of bamboo in the forest, and there are pines and firs of up to three feet [*chi*, approximately one meter] [in circumference] all over the place.[19]

Despite Ye's conceit that this timber was to repair his house, it is obvious that he in fact created a substantial commercial investment, with thousands of poles of timber. This is further confirmed by Ye's conclusion, where he remarks that despite his advanced age, he planned to continue planting trees to leave as a legacy to his heirs.[20] While Ye was the first to leave a record of commercial timber plantings on this scale, he was far from the only one. Later that century, Yuan Cai (ca. 1140–90) wrote his famous *Precepts for Social Life* (Yuanshi shifan, 1163), a manual instructing the heads of gentry families on how to run their affairs. Like his predecessor, Yuan is most cognizant of the value of timber as a long-term investment. He writes, "It is really not a difficult thing to plant mulberry, fruit, bamboo and timber trees in the spring, and after ten or twenty years, enjoy the profits." He even suggests that families plant ten thousand fir trees when daughters were born to sell for their dowries when they reached marrying age.[21] By the late thirteenth century, *Essentials of Agriculture and Sericulture* (Nongsang jiyao, 1273) further disseminated information on tree planting. But in keeping with general developments in the genre, most of these instructions were reprinted from earlier texts, some of them centuries old, rather than reflecting new methods.[22]

Later manuals continued to document much the same silvicultural techniques throughout the rest of the millennium. In 1639, Xu Guangqi's *Complete Book of Agricultural Administration* (Nongzheng quanshu) was presented posthumously to the Ming court.[23] This massive work of scholarship represented the culmination of centuries of agrarian expertise, presented specifically for official use. Xu, a polymathic talent who collaborated with Jesuits and who sometimes known by his baptismal name, Paul, collected information from dozens of earlier texts, including many of those cited above, and added his own notes. While shorter than the sections on agriculture or sericulture, *Agricultural Administration* contains the longest section on silviculture of any premodern Chinese text. Xu provides notes, some of them original, on how to cultivate dozens of different trees, but this information was clearly a small fraction of the knowledge accumulated by South China's thousands of independent tree farmers.[24]

Agricultural Administration was not the last word on tree planting. In the eighteenth and nineteenth centuries, there were regional attempts to promote tree crops as alternatives to agriculture in mountain areas, as in *Hunan Provincial Precedents* (Hunan shengli, ca. 1800).[25] Nineteenth-century reformers including Bao Shichen built on these efforts. In *Four Arts to Nourish the People* (Qimin sishu, ca. 1840), Bao suggests that in the mountains, trees make more suitable crops than grain. Some new information surfaces in Bao's notes. He considers red and white soils suitable for tea on shady slopes and for bamboo on sunny slopes, while those far from water are better planted with tung, pine, fir, or tallow trees; black and yellow soils are suitable for pine and fir on the shady side and lacquer tree on the sunny side. He notes that "while the profits are somewhat delayed, they can be estimated at a ten-fold income."[26] This adds some additional detail to the notes provided by earlier authors. Nonetheless, like Xu Guangqi, Bao Shichen was probably recording the existing practices of tree farmers rather than suggesting fundamentally new techniques. Numerous planting techniques and fundamentals of botanical knowledge are documented in these manuals, but their central purpose was to disseminate a basic recognition of different forms of agriculture, sericulture, and silviculture among officials circulating throughout a wide empire. New techniques may have enabled the silvicultural revolution, but they were not the principal locus of change.

CADASTRAL FORESTS

The second potential source of change in forestry practice comes from the land surveys that registered forests for tax payment and could also serve as documentation of land title. As noted above, an enforceable claim to own the entire plot of timber was necessary for planters to be confident of recouping their upfront investment in planting trees rather than just logging them. In fact, there is evidence that forest surveys were significant to securing land title and thereby encouraging their owners to make these investments, especially after key land surveys in 1149, 1315, and 1391, which nudged forward the budding revolution in tree planting.

Like silviculture, land surveys have a very deep documented history in China. Forests were at least nominally included in some of the earliest known surveys in southern China, conducted by Chu in the Huainan region in 548 BCE, which encouraged nascent understandings of land ownership.[27] Nonetheless, the Chu surveys seem to have been something of a false start. For the next several centuries, land oversight focused on farms, and forest oversight focused on labor. Woodlands were largely treated as part of the open-access commons called "mountains and marshes" (shanze).[28] There were significant shifts in this policy starting in the fifth century CE, when Yang Xi (d. 468) proposed:

> Formerly the mountains and marshes were cleared by burning to
> grow bamboo, timber, and miscellaneous fruits into dense
> groves . . . ranked officials of the first and second grade should
> now be permitted to occupy three qing of forest [shan, about
> forty acres]; fourth grade [officials], two and a half qing [thirty-
> three acres]. . . . ninth grade [officials] and commoners, one qing
> [thirteen acres]. All [forests] are to have fixed measurements
> recorded in the registers.[29]

Yang's logic is clear: because labor went into clearing natural landscapes and planting them with "bamboo, timber and miscellaneous fruits," forests should be treated like other landed properties—measured and recorded in the registers. In practice, estates developed forest plantations on the premise of secure property rights secured by these surveys. Anecdotes from this era describe both monks and aristocrats cultivating orchards, tea plantations, and fuel coppices.[30] Nonetheless, delimited forest properties remained of limited extent, and there were occasional crackdowns on magnates who monopolized more than their allotted share of the wilds.[31] The seventh-century *Tang Code with Commentaries* (Tanglü shuyi) still marked the "mountains and wilds" (*shanye*) as common-access land, with labor the only legitimate way to claim forest products.[32]

This tension between growing private claims to forests and an official ban on "occupying" wooded commons remained in effect until the twelfth century, when there was a clear trend toward both the state's and private landowners' enclosing forests as delimited properties on a wider basis. Forest enclosure started with an abortive attempt to establish state forest oversight in the first three decades of the century, and a more successful movement to include forests in the general-purpose land surveys of 1149. The 1149 surveys were effective in documenting forest boundaries in much of Jiangnan, northwestern Zhejiang, and parts of Fujian. These were followed up by a reorganization of land into six standard categories, including forests (*shan*, literally "mountain") in 1315, that were further reduced to four categories in the 1380s and 90s. Subsequently, forest registration in official cadasters spread across much of southeastern China.[33] This provided a small but useful tax base for the state and an important centralized record of title in places where the records were well maintained. The cadastral surveys of the twelfth and fourteenth centuries were therefore a key impetus enabling landowners to claim bounded forests and to spread forest plantations beyond the bounds of noble estates and temple complexes, confident that they would have proof of ownership. But after 1391, there was relatively little change in cadastral forest records; further tax reforms largely changed accounting practices rather than land surveys. Instead, cadastral recordkeeping went through a slow process of attrition. Occasionally—as in 1581—this trend was reversed by more active land surveys. But more often the loss of cadastral records was hastened by neglect and warfare.

If the 1149 surveys represent one bookend on this period of cadastral forest records, the other end is marked by the forest laws of the Republic of China after 1911. One of the first acts of the Beiyang government, in the 1914 *Forest Law* (Senlin fa) and accompanying 1915 *Detailed Regulations for Implementation of the Forest Law* (Senlin fa shexing xize), was to require all owners to register their forest deeds in a new set of government cadasters. All other properties would be considered "ownerless" and claimed as state forests. These trends toward centralization of records and nationalization of resources were continued under the Nanjing government's *Temporary*

Regulations for National and Public Forests (Guanyoulin gongyoulin zanxing guize) in 1931 and the 1945 *Forest Law* (Senlin fa).[34] These policies were markedly similar to the transformation of forest ownership rights in Japanese colonial Taiwan after 1895 and Korea after 1910.[35] As in Taiwan and Korea, the new laws led to a massive spike in forest disputes, as claimants rushed to present even the oldest and vaguest records as evidence of ownership. But Republican era governments—Beiyang, Nanjing, and regional—lacked the capacity to conduct land surveys. Instead, the main effect of their policies was to centralize forest registration by compiling evidence from deeds and other forms of contract, some over four hundred years old by that time.[36] In other words, while land registration could be a major force promoting private forest ownership, between 1391 and 1914, there was little change in the cadastral regime, except through its extension to new territories. Instead, deeds and contracts were the main documents supporting changes in the claims made to forest resources.

CONTRACTUAL FORESTRY

With state interventions confined to collecting taxes and supporting land title, private forest owners were left to innovate most of the mechanisms specific to forest management. Private records noting forest boundaries are extant as early as the first century CE and become substantially more common in the ninth through eleventh centuries, but they overwhelmingly apply to the forests around graves and give boundaries but not acreage.[37] Then, starting in the twelfth century, forest owners began to modify the formats of the deeds and contracts used to buy, sell, and rent agrarian land to fit the specific needs of forest management. This is attested directly in a handful of deeds preserved from Huizhou from the 1200s and indirectly in other records from the period. By the 1400s, new contractual mechanisms became increasingly elaborate. Owners divided forests into shares to divide the ownership rights to forests without the need to subdivide parcels or enumerate individual trees. They created partnerships (*huo*) to compensate tree planters with shares in the future timber harvest in exchange for their labor. Active markets for forest shares allowed stakeholders to cash out before the trees they planted matured enough to cut. Shareholders also developed contractual mechanisms to specify responsibilities for fighting fires and reporting theft, both of which were significant hazards on plantations of timber that took upward of twenty-five years to reach marketable size. Many contracts from this period specified methods for planting trees, generally including an initial term when seedlings or cuttings were interplanted with dry crops like wheat and hemp, an inspection after three to five years to confirm that the young trees had matured properly, and logging upon the agreement of all major stakeholders, generally after twenty-five to thirty years or more.[38] These planting techniques were not new, largely representing an elaboration and standardization of methods documented in the twelfth-century household manuals and probably known since the ninth century. Instead, it was the contractual and financial mechanisms that represented the areas of greatest development.

To demonstrate the complex forms of management developed in the fifteenth and sixteenth century, it is worth quoting at length from an unusually complete forest deed. In 1520, a Huizhou tree planter named Tan Jing sold his stake in a forest plot to one of his uncles. The deed of sale demonstrates some of the complexities involved. It reads in full:

> Tan Jing previously contributed to the collective purchase of Hu Yuanqing's cadastral registration and the associated forest plot in *bao* number five in the area called "east spring." Together with uncles [Tan] Yongxian and Tan Yongfang, [Tan Jing] also bought an unspecified number of sections [on this plot] that were planted with fir by Tan Gong and his cousin Hongjing. [Tan Jing] also collaborated with Tan Qi to plant another section with fir, and worked with a group to plant another forest section with seedlings. Today he is selling the above forest plot and the other items held under his name, including all shares of fir seedlings that he planted or purchased. These several items are included with this deed and sold to be placed under his uncle Yongxian's name. This will consolidate [ownership] for easier management. The parties met face to face and agreed on a current value of 1.7 taels of silver.[39]

This deed establishes four significant features of the forest and its management. First, it records the source of land title; Tan Jing and several unspecified relatives bought the plot from Hu Yuanqing. This information, including the plot location in both administrative and local terminology and the tax registration, was enough to support the Tans' ownership against rival claims. Second, the deed records the arrangements for planting the plot with fir seedlings. It was divided into sections, each of which was planted by a group of Tans, who thereby acquired stakes in the timber. Third, it notes the shareholding arrangements, which included both ownership shares in the underlying plot (*zhufen*) and labor shares based on planting trees (*lifen*), each of which could be bought and sold.[40] Both types of shares carried a stake in the timber harvest, but only ownership shares retained a stake in the land after it was logged. In this case, Tan Jing's uncle Yongxian had clearly acquired the majority of both types of shares, which would have given him the principal voice in deciding when to log the plot. Finally, the deed specifies a price for Tan Jing's various shares as agreed on by the two parties. It does not state how they arrived at this valuation, but it presumably combined some notion of fair value for Tan's labor and capital investments, with a rough assessment of the future value of the timber.

Few individual contracts are as complete as Tan Jing's deed of sale. The overwhelming majority of land deeds give only an abbreviated specification of land title, shareholding arrangements, and a price. Most tenancy or partnership contracts simply specify the name of the plot and the number of shares allotted to the laborers. There are a handful of other, more comprehensive forms of documentation. When lineage corporations held forests, they often produced centralized registers and regulations.[41] As shareholding grew more fragmented over time, other shareholder groups also produced similar forms of records. Villages also created community compacts to elaborate the rights and restrictions on harvesting trees, on private and especially on common-use land. But for the most part, the contractual record is both sparse and scattered. This suggests that expertise—contractual and silvicultural—was widespread in tree-planting communities.

The Tan deed represented something of a midpoint in the development of contractual forestry in Huizhou. On the one hand, it shows substantial elaboration of shareholding and planting practices. On the other hand, the Tans who were involved as owners, planters, and managers of this forest still overlapped. By the late sixteenth and seventeenth centuries, this type of arrangement within the family appears to have declined in favor of increasing separation between three main strata of forest stakeholders. People like Tan Jing's uncle Yongxian gradually became absentee landlords, perhaps more accurately described as absentee investors, a group that owned shares of many forests but participated only indirectly in managing their properties. The people who planted trees soon became a permanent underclass, filled mostly by bondservants and landless tenants, bound the forests they worked, but with little hope of acquiring large or long-term stakes in the timber harvest. Finally, logging was increasingly performed by migrant laborers working on short-term contracts.

While starting later than contractual records in Huizhou, the evidence from northwestern Fujian suggests that its forest economy developed along largely related lines. A contract from Yongtai County from 1786 reports on the complexities that developed in a set of forest plots over the previous two centuries. In the late 1500s, Zhang Chaotong, Zeng Xue, and Cai Tiansheng bought several plots of taxpaying forest (*shuishan*). "At that time, they did not establish boundaries to divide it, [instead] the three surnames agreed to a contract establishing four shares, with the Zeng and Cai collectively holding two shares and the Zhang family holding two shares." Further complications developed over the years. Starting in the 1740s, Zhang Ruizhong, an heir to some part of the two Zhang shares, gave his shares to Zhang Yuzhao as collateral on a loan. Ruizhong asked two uncles and a younger brother to help him put up the silver needed to redeem his share, agreeing to a four-way split; his brother Ruizhi took one share, his uncles split one share, and Ruizhong kept two. By 1786, each of these "small shares" were further subdivided through either inheritance or partible sales, and two additional families, the Lins and the Chens, owned shares in the Zhang portion of the forest. A contract was drawn up to clarify these complex shareholding arrangements and to specify that any profits from selling timber, or rights to dig graves, raise buildings, or cultivate the land, were "evenly divided according to the shares."[42]

As in Huizhou, some owner-operators in northwestern Fujian planted their own trees and even rented additional land to raise the value of their investment. But research on more than three thousand deeds and contracts from this region reveals that most forest owners rented their plots to cultivators rather than participating actively in the management.[43] By the late nineteenth century, some of these forest landlords, such as the Zhangs of Yuezhou, had even developed printed forms to facilitate rental agreements on their substantial forests (note that ____ indicates a blank left in the original form):

> Forest rental contract: ____ ancestor of Yuezhou bequeathed this
> taxpaying forest, located in the 29th township of this county.
> Within it, there is one plot at ____ location, with the local
> name ____. Today it is agreed with ____ to pay ____, [the money]
> exchanged in full along with the contract. Within the boundaries
> ____ can do ____ in accordance with the contract. If their activities impinge on others, they are not allowed to use this contract
> as pretense to forcibly ____ and are not permitted to transfer
> it to others of their own accord. Each year, they contract to
> submit ____ rent, which [branches of the] Zhang family take turns
> receiving. Today, desiring evidence [of the transaction], this
> contract in one page is enclosed to retain as proof.
>   Specific terms are enumerated below. [44]

In extant printed contracts, the specific term *enumerated below* includes buildings, graves, planting trees, growing mushrooms, making charcoal, kilning, and cutting wood to make tools. Duration varied, with planting contracts lasting until the trees were cleared and mushroom-farming contracts until the logs used to grow the mushrooms became rotten; contracts for buildings and graves covering long periods of time, and most others, renewed annually. According to the Zhang family regulations, printed contracts *only* were to be taken as legitimate, and "handwritten contracts on blank paper" were to be reported to the authorities as forgeries.[45] The Zhang contracts show some clear differences from those used in sixteenth and seventeenth century Huizhou; in particular, shareholding appears to have been limited to the owners of underlying land rights, with tenants paying cash rents rather than shares in the timber harvest. This may have reflected both regional differences and changes in the market over time, as the introduction of more silver to the market made it easier to express capital-labor relationships in cash.

Documents from western Zhejiang demonstrate another line of differences in the functioning of forest contracts. One key difference was between regions with well-maintained cadasters and those where private contracts were among the only evidence of forest ownership. As noted above, Huizhou had an especially strong cadastral record, and deeds tended to note the location of forest plots in the official record books. This was also true in Yongtai, although the practice of noting "taxpaying forests" in some contracts suggests the existence of a complimentary category of "non-taxpaying forests." Yet nontaxpaying forests did not lack documentation entirely. In a comparative study of two jurisdictions in Zhejiang, Du Zhengzhen contrasts a region with a strong cadastral record rivaling Huizhou—Yanzhou Prefecture—with another with an almost total absence of cadastral forest records—Longquan County. In fact, sixteenth-century Yanzhou had the highest proportion of officially reported forest acreage of any prefecture surveyed, while Longquan's near absence of cadastral records was probably quite typical of large swaths farther south and west.[46] In other words, Yanzhou and Longquan represent the two ends of the documentary spectrum in southern China. It was not just state practice that maintained this difference in records; it was also documentary culture. In Huizhou, residents kept their own cadasters during an interregnum in the 1350s and 60s.[47] Likewise, in the wake of the Taiping armies' destroying the land registers in 1860–61, Yanzhou residents created their own township-level cadasters. In this documentary culture, cadastral records were necessary to prove forest ownership, so locals created them when the state was unable to do so.[48]

By contrast, Longquan was granted a blanket tax exemption for forests during the late 1300s and had very few forests on the official books for the next six hundred years. Instead, locals relied almost exclusively on privately circulating deeds and contracts as proof of ownership. From the perspective of the early twentieth century, when they were required to register their ownership with the Republican state, this was a serious issue, making it especially hard to establish forest ownership. Nonetheless, Longquan, like Yanzhou, regularly produced timber and other products for export markets. Its residents were seemingly able to do this without a central registry of title as backup. The disputes that emerged over forest ownership in the 1910s and 1920s often centered on precisely those properties whose ownership was the least clear; claimants used the *Forest Law* of 1914 as an excuse to try to shore up highly dubious claims using decades- or centuries-old records. Despite the absence of government accounts of boundaries and ownership, Longquan's forest markets were seemingly able to operate on contract alone for centuries, albeit at some loss of clarity and uniformity.[49] This contrast with the documentary cultures of Huizhou, Yanzhou, and Yongtai suggests that forest documentation does not map easily onto forest use or composition. Areas with widely ranging documentary cultures could have very similar forms of forest economy and forest ecology. Indeed, all four of these jurisdictions were within the same broad mountainous regions where four southeastern provinces come together. Likewise, the use of similar forms of document could suppress substantial differences in forest ecology between different parts of this region or significant changes in the extent and composition of forests over time.

CONCLUSION

In the last thousand years, southern China underwent an epochal change as people developed new ways of thinking about and managing the wooded landscape and transformed the extent and composition of forests themselves. This revolutionary change was predicated on techniques that gave people control of the entire lifecycles of the woody plants they cultivated, from planting to thinning to logging. For people to invest labor in intensive silviculture, they also needed to be reasonably confident that they would recoup the profits of cutting these trees after several decades of growth. To promote this confidence, the state developed surveys and records of forest ownership, while individual planters used land deeds and tenancy and logging contracts as evidence of their claims. Together, contract and cadaster transformed the ownership of forest resources from claims to the timber felled by one's own hand to more blanket assertions to control all the trees standing on a given plot. All these conditions—silvicultural techniques, centralized land registration, and individual proof of ownership—were present in southern China by the mid- to late twelfth century. Collectively, they were the keys to the revolutionary changes in China's forests. But after the initial transitions toward private ownership and more intensive cultivation, these three aspects of forestry did not play equal roles in the further shifts that ensued. After the thirteenth century, there was little further change in either the silvicultural techniques documented in agricultural manuals or the cadastral records kept by the state, at least not until the early twentieth century. Instead, the greatest shifts in forestry are seen in the deeds and contracts used to document transactions between small groups of owners, workers, and managers.

In the past several decades, tens of thousands of seemingly banal forest deeds and tenancy, logging, and shareholding contracts have been discovered in the mountains of southeastern China. While research on these materials is still in its infancy, they demonstrate a degree of vibrant commercial activity that enabled the cultivation of trees in the mountains to feed demand for timber, fuel, and other forest products in the cities. These documents also give insight into the small changes in contractual terms used to manage a complex economy little touched by the state. Parties to these contracts used them to distribute risks and profits among shareholders, to manage the different potential uses of a single forest plot, including timber, tea, charcoal, mushrooms, and graves, and to provide proof of ownership. They show a substantial range of strategies that differed by plot and by jurisdiction, and that changed over time. However, what these contracts show in common is the increased fragmentation of forest rights as ownership claims were subdivided into shares and usage rights were parceled out according to increasingly specific terms and given cash values and fixed durations.

Seen from the long-term perspective, usage rights that had formerly been managed according to unwritten custom reemerged in written contracts; claims that had formerly been secured by labor were now purchased with cash, and forests that had previously been common or open-access land were now held as exclusive properties. Seen from the global perspective, similar renegotiations of usage rights—under different institutions with different forms of documentation—can be seen in other early modern contexts, including Japan and Korea, as well as in farther-flung regions such as France and Germany.[50] Even within southern China, there were substantial differences in how rights were apportioned—including both shareholding and multiple forms of tenancy—and how rights were documented—including both contract and cadaster. In that respect, the differences in documentary regime depended more on legal and political culture than on changes in the forests themselves.

With such a large yet fragmented corpus of records, we are susceptible to the hazard of missing the forest for the trees—and indeed, of missing the trees for the paper trail. Is it possible to zoom out from these records of individual transactions to say something not only about the legal, cultural, or managerial trends in forestry but about environmental change as well? Here, I suspect, we have reached the limitations of the records, which have neither the scope nor the focus to say much more about the environment. As noted above, jurisdictions scattered through a broad region with relatively similar forests produced very different documentary records. Likewise, the records of a single region may easily suppress substantial ecological change about which their authors were little concerned. Nonetheless, these contracts place forests at the center of some of the most important trends of this era: the changes wrought by commercialization, state-building, large-scale migration, and political upheaval. While the detailed contours of these changes demand further research, the fragmentation and commodification of forests were tied to the prevailing trends of period: population growth and market penetration. They show how some of the oldest claims made by humans—to control the fruits that they gathered—were reinterpreted, contested, subdivided, and recorded. In turn, these finely delineated claims to own land and its flora anticipate some of the further shifts toward enclosure, partition, and commodification of forests and their products seen in the last hundred years.

NOTES

1   On wood scarcity in North China, see Lander's chapter in this volume.

2   For more detail, see Miller, *Fir and Empire*.

3   Albion, *Forests and Sea Power*, chapter 6.

4   Another collection from the Qingshui River valley in eastern Guizhou is considered by Meng Zhang in chapter 5 of this volume and not addressed in detail here. In addition, see Zhang Yingqiang, "The Qingshuijiang Documents."

5   Huizhou is now divided between Anhui and Jiangxi but was historically a single prefecture in Song Jiangnan, the Ming Southern Metropolitan Region, and Qing Anhui.

6   A useful review of the extensive Chinese-language literature on this diffuse documentation is provided in Kang Jian, "Ming Qing Huizhou shanlin jingji yanjiu huigu." On the discovery of the Huizhou "archive," see McDermott, *The Making of a New Rural Order in South China*, 16–38.

7   These documents are introduced in Du and Wu, "Longquan sifa dang'an de zhuyao tedian yu shiliao jiazhi."

8   See Zheng Zhenman, "Ming Qing shiqi de linye jingji yu shanqu shehui."

9   Note that most of the original cadasters have been lost. For information on their content, scholars rely principally on summary records in gazetteers and institutional compendia, as well as a handful of extant examples.

10 Miller, *Fir and Empire*, chapter 2 and throughout.

11 The one exception, covered in detail in Miller, *Fir and Empire*, chapter 3, is the reform of the labor service, which I argue pushed foresters into the commercial and contractual labor market.

12 Jia Sixie, *Qimin yaoshu*, 5. Note that in this chapter, dates for digital editions indicate the publication dates of the print editions on which they are based. For digital sources, I have preferentially given chapter numbers and subsection titles rather than page numbers in reprint editions, as this allows readers to find the source text more easily across editions.

13 Jia Sixie, *Qimin yaoshu*, 5.45, "Growing Mulberry and Chinese Mulberry" [Zong sang zhe].

14 Jia Sixie, *Qimin yaoshu*, 5.46, "Growing Elm and Poplar" [Hong yu baiyang].

15 Jia, *Qimin yaoshu* , 5.47–5.51.

16 Liu Zongyuan, *Zhongshu Guo tuotuo zhuan*, 0592.

17 Guo Tuotuo, *Zhongshu shu*, 1–3. In this chapter, *fir* refers principally to "China fir," *Cunninghamia lanceolata*.

18 Su Shi, *Dongpo zaji*, quoted in Chen Rong, *Zhongguo senlin shiliao*, 34–35; "Products" [*wuchan*] in Zhang Ji'an, *Jiaqing Yuhang xianzhi*, quoting the *Xianchun Lin'an zhi*; "Ten-thousand *shan* temple" [*wanshan si*], in Zhu Xi, *Hui'an xiansheng Zhu wengong wenji* 2.

19 Ye Mengde, *Bizhao lühua*, 2.

20 Ye Mengde, *Bihan lühua*, 2. This and all other quotes are my translations.

21 "Timely planting of mulberry and timber" [*sangmu yinshi zhongzhi*], and "Advance planning" [*zaolü*], in Yuan Cai, *Yuanshi shifan*, 2–3.

22 *Nongsang jiyao* 6.

23 Xu Guangqi, ed., *Nongzheng quanshu*.

24 *Nongzheng quanshu*, 38.7a. Translated in McDermott, *The Making of a New Rural Order in South China*, 384.

25 "Encouraging the people to plant miscellaneous grains on empty mountain land in this county" [*xian you yushantu quan min zaizong zaliang*]; Wu Dashan et al., *Hunan shengli*, 7.5a-21b. Despite the name, this also encouraged the planting of tree crops.

26 "Suitability of soils" [*rentu*], in Bao Shichen, *Qimin si shu*, vol. 1a.

27 Von Glahn, *The Economic History of China*, 54; Weld, "Chu Law in Action," 76–97.

28 Du, "Ming Qing yiqian dongnan shanlin de dingjie yu quequan," 118; Miller, *Fir and Empire*, 23–24.

29 "Biography of Yang Xi" [Yang Xi zhuan], *Song shu*, quoted in Du, "Ming Qing yiqian dongnan shanlin de dingjie yu quequan," 118.

30 Examples of estate forests are referenced in Lewis, *China's Cosmopolitan Empire*, 25–26, 126; Elvin, *The Pattern of the Chinese Past*, 80–82. On Buddhist temple forests, see Gernet, *Buddhism in Chinese Society*, 116–29; Walsh, *Sacred Economies*, chapters 4 and 5; Marks, *China*, 138–41; Menzies, *Forest and Land Management in Imperial China*, chapter 4; Schafer, "The Conservation of Nature," 282–84, 288. Note that Marks has been updated with a new edition, titled *China: An Environmental History* (2017). References here and throughout are to the 2012 edition.

31 Du, "Ming Qing yiqian dongnan shanlin de dingjie yu quequan," 118; Elvin, "Three Thousand Years of Unsustainable Growth," 25.

32 Miller, *Fir and Empire*, 25–27.

33 Miller, *Fir and Empire*, chapter 2.

34 Du, "Wan Qing Minguo shanlin suoyou quan de huode yu zhengming," 78–80. There are two interesting shifts in terminology in the 1910s that demand further study. First, the prevailing term for "forest" changed from *shan* or *shanlin* (literally "mountain" or "mountain grove"), which had been in use since late antiquity, to *senlin* (literally "dense grove"), which was derived from the modern Japanese usage of the same characters (*shinrin*) to translate Western terms for *forest*. Second, there is a partial shift from the use of "state-owned" (*guanyou*) to "nationally owned" (*guoyou*) that reflects the growing conceptual importance of the nation.

35 Fedman, *Seeds of Control*, 86–98; Hung, "When the Green Archipelago Encountered Formosa."

36 Du, "Wan Qing Minguo shanlin suoyou quan de huode yu zhengming," 90–91.

37 Du, "Ming Qing yiqian dongnan shanlin de dingjie yu quequan," 119–20.

38 Chen Keyun, ""Cong 'Lishi shanlin zhichan bu' kan Ming Qing Huizhou shanlin jingying," 73–84; McDermott, *The Making of a New Rural Order in South China*, chapter 6; Miller, *Fir and Empire*, chapter 4.

39 Zhang, *Zhongguo lidai qiyue huibian kaoyi*, 809, no. 653.

40 Chen Kuyen, "Ming Qing Huizhou shanlin jingying zhong de 'lifen' wenti." See also McDermott, *The Making of a New Rural Order in South China*, chapter 6.

41 See, for example, McDermott, *The Making of a New Rural Order in South China*, chapters 4–6; Chen, "Cong 'Lishi shanlin bu.'"

42 Quoted in Zheng, "Ming Qing shiqi de linye jingji yu shanqu shehui," 151–52.

43 Zheng, "Ming Qing shiqi de linye jingji yu shanqu shehui," 152.

44 Quoted in Zheng, "Ming Qing shiqi de linye jingji yu shanqu shehui," 152–53.

45 Zheng, "Ming Qing shiqi de linye jingji yu shanqu shehui," 153.

46 Miller, *Fir and Empire,* 47.

47 Miller, *Fir and Empire,* 54, map 2.2.

48 Du, "Wan Qing Minguo shanlin suoyou quan de huode yu zhengming," 86.

49 Du, "Wan Qing Minguo shanlin suoyou quan de huode yu zhengming," 80–86.

50 See chapters 3–4 in this volume and Matteson, *Forests in Revolutionary France*; Warde, *Ecology, Economy, and State Formation.*

CHAPTER THREE

FIGHTING OVER NATURE

Resource Disputes in Central Japan during an Age of Instability,
1475–1635

JOHN ELIJAH BENDER

I n the mid-fifteenth century, the Japanese archipelago descended into an era of prolonged turmoil. Social order, conflict resolution, and institutions of governance foundered, resulting in widespread violence and instability. Over one hundred and fifty years of civil war raged. Conflict was endemic, afflicting all aspects of daily life for those who lived through the era. And then, in the late sixteenth century, several decades of rapid, sweeping sociopolitical changes ended generations of bloodshed. When swords were sheathed and arrows lowered, a new order emerged.[1] Consistent upheaval gave way to stability, and violent conflict was replaced by bureaucracy. This new order proved remarkably durable, lasting without serious challenge for over two and a half centuries.

While elite samurai waged wars for territorial supremacy, the stakes were more prosaic for the vast majority of the island's inhabitants during the Warring States (ca. 1450–1600), or late medieval, age. As little means for smooth dispute resolution existed, struggles over local resources necessary to sustain daily life became life-and-death affairs. Although studies have traditionally focused on arable land, forests, too, were violently contested spaces. Their importance was every bit as high as that of the most productive paddy land. While the cadastral survey has commanded much attention in studies of daimyo domain-building and sixteenth-century "unification," forested lands were also heavily managed environments and were no less important than their arable counterparts in premodern societies.[2] In late medieval Japan, the difference between forest and arable land was clear discursively, administratively, and economically. But ecologically, forests were part of a web of local resources critical to the functioning of the whole. As such, building reliable, nonviolent mechanisms for dispute resolution in local forests was a necessary part of reestablishing order. Because forests were a key site of conflict, examining how those conflicts were resolved provides a glimpse of underlying processes that made the transition from widespread disorder to widespread peace possible in late medieval Japan.

Tracing a high-stakes but very localized conflict in this way allows us to see the component pieces of Japan's early modern transformation. In Kai Province (modern Yamanashi Prefecture), we can see two seemingly opposed trends coalesce: de facto local control and increasingly effective central (domain-level) authority.[3] The Takeda, a warrior lineage that came to dominate the region, built their domain and became regional magnates by functioning as local guarantor and dispute mediator. Their interest in maintaining order while tapping into local productivity actually dovetailed with the desires of local communities to assert their claims to resources; in other words, conflict resolution proceeded from the ground up as institutionalization of local practice. These roles had to be worked out against a backdrop of endemic instability. Any dispute resolution mechanisms were only as effective as they could be applied. For that reason, it took several generations and much trial and error for this reciprocal relationship between local and regional lord to develop.

Resolution of these kinds of disputes created a conceptual and legal framework that guided control of local forests and other resources for the next few centuries. The conditions of "common usage rights" (*iriai* or *iriyama*) and related terminology were fleshed out at this time. Definitions of different types of forest were laid down. As arrangements between Takeda officials and local residents became more explicit, they became the genesis of woodland management institutions. These relationships grew ever more bureaucratized and commercialized as time went on, but important foundations that began here endured—namely the high degree of control residents claimed over local resources.

For Kai, where agriculture was limited, both subsistence and commercial use of forests loomed comparatively larger than in other regions. However, research on the early modern *satoyama* indicates that even in heavily agricultural areas, forest resources were essential.[4] Farming always depended on a reserve of forest products. Conversely, defining *forest* as a distinct place and source of specific resources was in reference to those things outside of it.

KURECHI

Kawaguchi   Myabayashi/Mt. Otare   Shimo
                                        no mizu

Lake   Myohoji and
        Jozaiji temples   Omuro
        Kobayashi Owari   Sengen
        Estate   Shrine
                           SHINKURA
UPPER YOSHIDA

                           LOWER
                           YOSHIDA

        Funatsu Checkpoint

                    Fuji Sengen Shrine
                    (Kitaguchi Hongu)

                Edo   Kobayashi Izumi
              (Tokyo)   Estate

Mt. Fuji

                                        2.5
                                    Kilometers

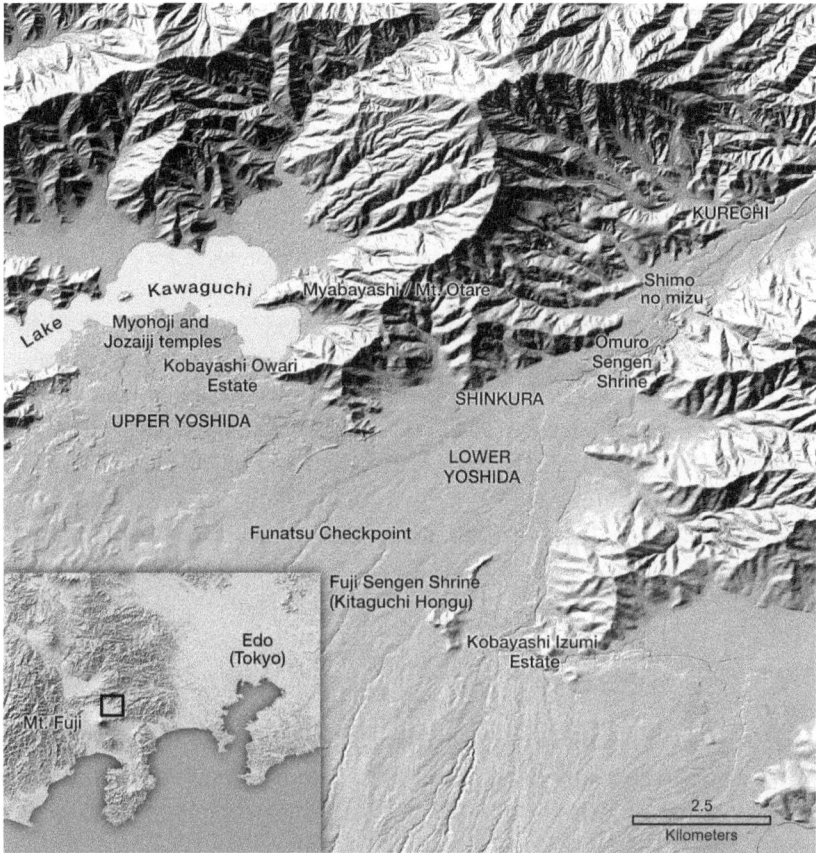

MAP 3.1. Yoshida and surrounding regions, noting places named in the text. Data from Natural Earth (naturalearthdata.com); B. Lehner, K. Verdin, A. Jarvis, "New global hydrography derived from spaceborne elevation data"; Japan Aerospace Exploration Agency, AW3D. Map by Lynn Carlson and Brian Lander.

Examination of a series of resource disputes in a community on the northern foothills of Mt. Fuji shows how these new procedures were forged and solidified. It reveals how contests over local environment reconfigured a variety of sociopolitical relationships at multiple scales. Yoshida, today Fujiyoshida City, was a dynamic crossroads of travelers and trade in the medieval age (see map 3.1). The religious sites around Mt. Fuji attracted pilgrims of all sorts, even during the tumultuous era of civil war. Several dozen temples and shrines in the area relied on pilgrimage as a major source of revenue.

These institutions also sponsored markets, their other major source of income. Yoshida was located along one of the few routes through Kai Province, making it a major entrepot for travelers and trade in and out of the region (see map 3.1). Because of its high elevation and mountainous terrain, farmers here could not grow enough food for the area to be completely self-sufficient. Instead, residents relied on a combination of locally grown crops, almost exclusively in dry fields, and imported rice and fish. Residents therefore depended on their own local resources and on access to imported goods for their survival and prosperity.

Yoshida was a geopolitical crossroads in the civil war era. It sat at the intersection of three territories belonging to competing regional warlords. Each of these magnates vied for influence in Yoshida, primarily by incorporating local warrior houses as retainers and tapping into the local economy by offering residents tax exemptions in exchange for confirmation of various usage rights. But none of these arrangements were clearly established in the sixteenth century. The fluid political situation meant a great deal of uncertainty for local residents. Essentially, they could not rely upon external forces to endorse and protect their claims until there was a demonstrated willingness and ability to do so. There was no reliable way of knowing whether a local landlord, temple, or distant daimyo could actually provide assistance if some entity encroached upon local claims. Further complicating matters was the fact that communities consistently found themselves at odds with other local actors competing for the same limited local resources. This kind of small-scale conflict was far more widespread, and potentially disruptive, than clashes between samurai armies emblematic of the era.

As a site of travel and exchange, Yoshida qualifies as an "urban space" in Amino Yoshihiko's analysis, despite its small size and provincial location.[5] This had a number of implications for the socioeconomic hierarchy that developed in Yoshida. At all levels, residents depended on a combination of commerce and local products, and competition for limited resources was substantial. The local elite in Yoshida consisted of the clergy staffing various shrines and temples, heads of artisan guilds who operated in the area, and military retainers of the Takeda with landed estates. If pilgrims did not patronize religious sites or if trade was disrupted and markets declined, religious leaders faced serious economic hardship. Likewise, the major artisan groups in and around Yoshida were primarily porters and lumberjacks, both of whom relied on interregional commerce for their livelihoods.[6] Local warriors, too, derived their income from a combination of limited agriculture supplemented with commercial exchange.

Almost all lower-status individuals in Yoshida were connected in some way to religious institutions or to artisan guilds and their associated operations. They made their living by growing what food they could, usually wheat or potatoes, using local forests for a variety of raw materials and supplementing these activities with income in trades. Despite socioeconomic divides in late medieval Yoshida, all residents were dependent on the same combination of local resources and interregional trade for their livelihoods.[7] Mutual dependency did not always ensure social harmony. Conflicts could and did occur along a variety of fault lines within Yoshida, but was most frequent between ordinary residents and wealthy local warriors, who tended to own significant amounts of land. Far fewer villagers were attached to the households and estate operations of local warriors compared to the numbers associated with shrines, temples, and guilds. Local warriors also became subordinate to more elite, distant warrior houses over the course of the sixteenth century. This meant that of the elite in Yoshida, it was local warriors who were the most likely to have interests that did not coincide with the community at large. The Kobayashi lineage in Yoshida demonstrates this point. For most of the sixteenth century, the wealth of this warrior house derived from tolls collected at the major highway checkpoint (*sekisho*) in Yoshida and the sale of marketable timber.[8] This created a structural tension between Kobayashi and the rest of the community. Collection of tolls benefited only Kobayashi and their retainers. Additionally, the Kobayashi house often wished to exploit the same forests for timbers that other residents depended upon for daily necessities.

It is clear that the forests of late medieval Yoshida were thoroughly anthropogenic. In what remains the most extensive study of premodern Japanese woodlands in English, Conrad Totman argues that human activity disrupted a climax ecology that only recovered much later as the result of regenerative forestry.[9] Episodes of particularly intense timber exploitation came in the seventh to ninth and sixteenth to eighteenth centuries. It was only through rigorous state regulation and the commercialization of tree plantations beginning in the seventeenth century that Japan avoided becoming "an eroded moonscape."[10] For all its many merits, our ecological and historical understanding has evolved significantly since the genre-defining *The Green Archipelago* was written. There was no premodern climax ecology to disrupt. Particularly in a mountainous area such as Yoshida, woodlands had always been managed environments, exploited for all kinds of resources—a cultivated forest, in short. Certainly, the late sixteenth century disputes examined here indicate a complete integration of forest use into the daily lives of all residents in Yoshida. Moreover, focusing on elite regulation as the driving force behind changes in forest management practices from circa 600–1850 tells only half the story at best. State regulation was far less formative than it might appear from this perspective. This chapter identifies continuities in local practices that not only persisted from the late medieval into the early modern era but in fact shaped regulations that were installed at that time. Even as increasingly interventionist domanial policies restricted forest use in early modern Japan, local usage practices remained largely unaltered, if more clearly delineated. There is little to suggest that population pressure strained forest resources per se. Rather, consumerism increased competition for commercially viable forest products and shaped the kinds of forests that elites wished to maintain.[11]

Premodern Yoshida shows us a cultivated forest, and one with a comparatively impressive textual tradition as well. Surviving historical records from Sengoku Japan are notoriously sparse. Much of what has survived is terse, incomplete, or both. The prevalence, then, of forest disputes in the limited number of local sources speaks to their centrality. The next sections examine the ways that these disputes transformed local society and played important roles in the evolution from late medieval chaos to early modern stability.

OVERCOMING DISORDER, ESTABLISHING PROCEDURE

Everyone in late medieval Japan had force at their disposal. Daimyo armies were the largest military assemblages of the era, but they were one of many. Religious institutions, local samurai, and even local communities had the ability to resort to coercive force when necessary. Medieval Yoshida was no exception. The village militia (*wakashū*) frequently acted as the defender of local claims to resources.[12] In the civil war era, it was incumbent on locals themselves to protect their interests and resolve conflicts. Violence was common when disputes arose, and the mechanism used to deal with those disputes was the village militia.

Yoshida's militia, like that of other late medieval communities, was not an insignificant force. In 1475, after a year of severe flooding that exacerbated an ongoing famine, the residents of Yoshida killed a local warrior landlord named Kawaguchi and eliminated his lineage. Later accounts indicate that the conflict likely arose over water use. By killing Kawaguchi, Yoshida villagers removed a disruptive competitor for a crucial local resource, which at the time was especially scarce.[13] Whatever the proximate cause, this dispute demonstrates the violent nature of conflict resolution at the time and shows that Yoshida villagers had the muscle to eliminate a warrior landlord. There is no evidence of a process or judicial mechanisms in place. Two parties to a dispute contested directly, and one of them was forcibly eliminated.

Contentious and often violent resource disputes appear to have been widespread in late medieval Japan. Fights over forests predominate in local records from late medieval Yoshida. This indicates the crucial role of forest resources—residents literally fought to the death to secure and maintain access the resources forests provided. Under such circumstances, any entity that could help solidify resource claims and fend off challengers could represent a valuable ally to local villages. In Yoshida's case, evidence for convergence between the interest of the village and those of regional elites with the means to act as guarantor of local resource claims does not appear until the 1530s. Disputes over a roughly thirty-year period from 1533 to 1557 show an emerging procedure and a nascent discourse of ownership, authority, and rights. Nonetheless, violence still figured prominently in dispute resolution, only becoming nonviolent and procedural decades later.

In the late 1520s, Yoshida experienced a multiyear string of calamities that included famine, a surge of refugees, and commodity shortages.[14] Extreme weather in 1533 then led to a water dispute between Yoshida villagers and a local warrior landlord named Watanabe Shōzaemon (dates unknown).[15] Although fair weather prevailed around the New Year, late spring turned out to be exceptionally dry. Water levels at Lake Kawaguchi ran low.[16] In the midst of this drought, a fire broke out on the sixteenth of the third month and consumed a large portion of Yoshida. According to a local monk chronicler, "Everything but Jōgyōji was burned."[17] It was a devastating conflagration. As residents salvaged what they could from burned-out structures, the rain returned. From the fifth to the eighth months, Yoshida was inundated, drought quickly turning into flood. The deluge drowned crops, causing a poor harvest and further hardship.

Sources are frustratingly mute on cause, but it is not hard to imagine how the recent drought, fire, and sudden return of heavy rains could disrupt water supplies and lead to conflict. One can almost feel the desperation of Yoshida villagers in 1533 who destroyed newly constructed sluices on Watanabe's estate. Most likely, the new infrastructure had the potential to divert a greater share of water to Watanabe than villagers deemed acceptable.[18] Timber used in sluice construction may also have been at issue. Though not mentioned in this instance, later examples show Yoshida villagers moving quickly to deny local warriors access to forests claimed by the village. Whether the sticking point was water or lumber (or both), the ensuring dispute between Watanabe and Yoshida shows that the former had encroached on resources claimed by the village. Their response was swift and unequivocal: destroy the offending structures.

Unlike the violence of 1475, which saw Kawaguchi murdered in his own residence, at this time, county-level elites were employed to help resolve the matter. Oyamada Nobuari (1488–1541), Watanabe's superior who resided some twenty miles east, intervened. After hearing testimony from "many people," the Oyamada lord backed Yoshida's claims over those of his own retainer.[19] Villagers' destruction of the sluices was justified and their resort to property damage thus legitimated. The decision implied that Watanabe had unjustly tampered with local precedent was duly punished. Note that the punishment, destruction of Watanabe's sluices, was initiated by locals and came first. Only after that did villagers successfully validate their actions via the authority of the county lord Oyamada. Yoshida used an external elite to prevent encroachment of a local rival.

This case and its resolution are significant both because it entailed direct action and procedure and because the local community was ultimately legitimated by a superior operating at a different geopolitical scale. Although none were killed, this dispute still resulted in violence. That trend continued for some time, advancing toward proceduralization in fits and starts. For various reasons, respecting local precedent proved to be the most effect means of resolving conflict and maintaining stability from the perspective of the new military elite. Over time, this precedent became more firmly entrenched, and it was relied on as the basis of dispute resolution for several centuries.

Over the next few decades, two developments emerged that had a lasting impact. The first was the creation of regularized procedure for resolving disputes. These functioned as lawsuits in which the regional magnate was mediator. Second, locals began making appeals for conflict resolution directly to the daimyo. That helped to solidify a convergence of interest between the very elite (Takeda) and very local (Yoshida), while at the same time curtailing the influence of local and county-level elites, those like the aforementioned Kawaguchi and Watanabe. Direct appeals to the regional authority resulted in continuation of the trend toward giving preference to the claims advanced by local communities.

For over ten years in the mid-sixteenth century, Yoshida Village and a local warrior house named Kobayashi disputed various forest and water rights. These disputes drew in the Oyamada, Kobayashi's lord, as well as the Takeda, Oyamada's superior. Decisions rendered over the course of these disputes initiated a transition toward de facto ownership for residents. Rather than claims to resources being linked to office, status, or investiture from a superior, occupancy came to determine control.[20]

The Kobayashi lineage existed in Yoshida since at least the late fifteenth century and achieved prominence there by the early sixteenth. They provided major funding for several riparian projects, led the local militia in a successful invasion defense on at least one occasion, and controlled a checkpoint that oversaw traffic in and out of Yoshida.[21] Their local influence earned them recognition as *yorioya*, unofficial patron or guardian of Yoshida.[22] By the 1550s, there were two branches of the Kobayashi, each occupying strategically important and economically lucrative areas of Yoshida.[23] The line headed by one Kobayashi Owari no kami (d. 1584?) held an estate on the southern shore of Lake Kawaguchi, upstream of Yoshida and thus influential over the village's water supply. A second Kobayashi line headed by one Izumi no kami (d. 1580) held the Funatsu checkpoint mentioned above (see map 3.1).

The first significant clash between Yoshida and Kobayashi was over water distribution and forest access, initiated by construction of a new Kobayashi residence. In 1556, Kobayashi Owari no kami decided to build a new estate and dug wells and built fields for the new complex.[24] He had expressed his plans to do so to his lord, Oyamada Nobuari (1540–65) but ran into stiff resistance from Yoshida villagers.[25] Unnamed villagers objected to the digging of new wells and felling of trees but were "repeatedly mistreated" by Kobayashi when construction began. Villagers disapproved of Kobayashi's use of a local forest called Miyabayashi for timber (see map 3.1). Later documents reveal that this forest had been used as a source of raw materials by Yoshida since the late 1400s and that it was considered collective property exclusive to the village.[26] In response, the Yoshida "group of twenty" gathered and confronted Kobayashi's followers as they worked.[27] The encounter does not appear to have turned violent, but it ended in standoff, halting construction. The Yoshida group and Kobayashi's retainers then traveled to the Oyamada estate on the other side of the mountains northeast of Yoshida. It was here that the two sides pleaded their cases to the young Nobuari, a youth of only sixteen years at the time. The inexperienced leader found himself in a difficult position. Kobayashi Owari was several decades his senior, not to mention one of his most influential retainers. On the other hand, Nobuari could ill afford hostilities erupting within his territory, lest his lord Takeda Shingen (1521–73) be forced to intervene militarily. After several days, Nobuari failed to render a decision.[28]

Kobayashi's envoys eventually returned home, but the Yoshida "group of twenty" pressed on to Kōfu, some thirty miles farther north. There they presented their case directly to the daimyo Shingen and justified their claims based on logic or "reasonableness" (*dōri*).[29] Shingen determined that Kobayashi Owari no kami should not build a new estate; he must abandon the project and dismantle whatever had already been completed.[30] To dissuade future overzealousness by Kobayashi, Shingen took the further step of stripping him of his position of *yorioya*.[31] In other words, the regional magnate officially recognized that Kobayashi had no elevated status within Yoshida. Instead, Shingen ordered his county deputy, Oyamada Nobuari, to oversee Yoshida directly. Villagers were apparently pleased with this resolution, although in the short term, it led to further conflict.

Yoshida appears to have been emboldened by Shingen's intervention on their behalf, and he pressed their advantage against Kobayashi. Later in 1556, the Yoshida Village council (*hyaku-yo nin*) deliberated and sent another appeal to Oyamada Nobuari.[32] Once again citing "repeated mistreatment," they leveled charges against the other prominent Kobayashi in Yoshida, Izumi no kami.[33] Later events strongly suggest that the underlying source of friction at this time between Yoshida and Izumi no kami was again disputed forest access at Miyabayashi. This same issue had Yoshida and Kobayashi Owari at loggerheads only moths before. In this case, Kobayashi Izumi responded to the village's claims by sending a retainer of his own to Nobuari. The retainer offered apologies on his behalf for the rancor with Yoshida but advocated for his lord's perquisites at Miyabayashi. Discussions must have been intense, for Izumi's proxy made the twenty-mile journey to and from Oyamada's estate three times in a single day.[34] Once again, the Oyamada lord could not render a decision. His hesitance might be explained by inexperience, or perhaps the young Nobuari was savvy enough to realize he was caught between a rock and hard place. Intervention here meant alienating either his retainer or the village, and he wisely opted to leave the decision to his superior.

Kobayashi Izumi then adopted the tactic used previously by Yoshida and appealed directly to Shingen. He dispatched another retainer to Shingen's seat at Kōfu. It took until the following year (1557) for Yoshida and Kobayashi Izumi to be informed of the Takeda lord's decision. Shingen decided that Kobayashi Izumi could remain at his estate; however, like his relative, he too would no longer be recognized as *yorioya* in Yoshida.[35] In this way, the Yoshida Village council had successfully lobbied the regional elite to remove both Kobayashis from positions of local influence.

The Kobayashi lineage challenged these decisions without delay, but they were upheld in no uncertain terms. Kobayashi Izumi sent an envoy to Nobuari in the second month of 1557, objecting to his diminished local status.[36] It was to no avail. Nobuari's officials merely reiterated that

Kobayashi did not have the authority to unilaterally appropriate local resources for his own ends. His relative Owari no kami was again expressly forbade from building a new estate. This was a tacit acknowledgment by Oyamada that the territory and resources of Yoshida Village belonged to the community collectively, and it was the village council, not wealthy local warrior landlords of the area, that was the primary representative of that community. This was a very significant step, although it did not immediately result in smooth conflict resolution over local resources.

In the tenth month of 1557, Yoshida villagers cut timber from Miyabayashi for construction of riparian works along the Katsura River (see map 3.1).[37] They had just recently blocked both Kobayashis from using Miyabayashi and clearly felt it belonged to them. Despite that, the Kobayashi Izumi lineage attempted to lay claim to this forest in 1557. One of Izumi no kami's sons led a group of followers out to Miyabayashi as Yoshida woodcutters labored there and ambushed them. They confiscated the villagers' tools and had the workers "severely beaten."[38] Yoshida's response was unambiguous. The village militia marched out to Kobayashi Izumi's estate, surrounded the residence, and demanded return of the tools. Kobayashi and his followers found themselves under house arrest unless they returned Yoshida's property. It was a standoff, so Oyamada Noburai was once again brought in to adjudicate. Villagers allowed Kobayashi to dispatch a messenger to Nobuari, who was actually away on campaign in a neighboring province at the time. The messenger returned with news that Nobuari did not believe that any wrong had been committed. He thereby acknowledge that the villagers' demands that their tools be returned were reasonable and that their use of force was justified. Kobayashi refused to accept this. He sent a second messenger, this time directly to Shingen in Kōfu. But the Takeda lord upheld judgment in favor of the village, dispatched an official to Yoshida to enforce compliance, and the matter was resolved without further strife. Shingen's decision "restored the relationship" between Yoshida and Kobayashi; in other words, it prevented further violence over this issue.[39]

Contemporaneous sources do not report how exactly the relationship between Yoshida and Kobayashi was restored. But later documents reveal the terms of the 1557 settlement to have been the following. Miyabayashi did indeed belong to the village but was to be reserved for essentials only, such as Yoshida's 1557 riparian project.[40] Kobayashi was explicitly barred from using Miyabayashi, and instead, the Oyamada were granted permission to harvest a limited number of timbers for construction each year from that forest. In other words, the Kobayashi got none of what they requested. The

Oyamada gained limited usage rights to the area, and Yoshida essentially got to keep using Miyabayashi as they had been for several generations by this point.

The Yoshida versus Kobayashi midcentury dispute shows an in-between point along a spectrum from direct confrontation, which tended towards violence, to a kind of half-procedural, half-direct means of dispute resolution. In this case, both stages of the dispute began with a confrontation. Parties on both sides moved swiftly to back up claims, and both sides had ready military force available. Both sides also appealed to county- and regional-level superiors to advance their local interests. Two local claimants leveraged outside elites in order to establish what amounted to ownership of a place. Yoshida had seen only two decades before that county-level lords (Oyamada) *could* act as guarantor of their local claims, even against the lord's own followers. The 1556–57 dispute demonstrated that that was the case at an even larger, regional level as well. The Takeda thus became a powerful patron for Yoshida. But it took some time, several decades in fact, for this arrangement to be worked out. It became established only once its effectiveness could be *demonstrated*. New mechanisms of dispute resolution were conceived, contested, and executed all at the same time. In the chaotic Warring States environment, it is not hard to see why progress toward formal procedure inched forward unevenly and protractedly. But by the seventeenth century, Warring States settlements appear to have become entrenched as the basis for resource use rights.

FORMALIZATION OF PROCEDURE AND LOCAL OWNERSHIP

An early seventeenth century forest dispute in Yoshida shows how late medieval resource disputes became the foundation of rights and conflict resolution well into the early modern era. In 1635, Yoshida contested competing claims to Mt. Otare from the nearby villages of Kurechi and Onuma (see map 3.1).[41] This dispute was fully procedural, resulting in no direct confrontation or violence. The dispute began when Kurechi and Onuma endeavored to use Mt. Otare for slash-and-burn fields.[42] This Mt. Otare was in fact Miyabayashi, still an important resource cache for Yoshida after many generations.[43] As such, Yoshida vigorously opposed encroachment on their territory. But instead of sending out the militia, they filed suit. The village council submitted a petition to the local magistrate (*bugyō*) under Akimoto Yasutomo (1580–1642), a Tokugawa retainer entrusted with what had previously been Oyamada territory and that included Yoshida.[44] In their petition, Yoshida argued in no uncertain terms that the forest belonged

to them. The other villages' claims to this area were completely unjusti-
fied. Yoshida leaders based these claims on three primary factors. Fore-
most was that the forest had been designated as Yoshida's source for
miscellaneous raw materials (*karishiki*), and as such, they had paid a portion
of these materials as tax since the early 1600s.[45] Furthermore, other villages
had been denied usage and development rights to Mt. Otare forest in the
past. And finally, the area had been designated as under Yoshida's responsibility for previous road and river construction projects.

Yoshida officials began their appeal by citing tax obligations as a proxy
for ownership. According to the Yoshida suit, the village had paid a materials tax on Mt. Otare for some thirty-two years.[46] This entailed collection of
undergrowth and other plant materials to be used as fodder, fertilizer, and
raw materials for goods including thatch and rope. Yoshida paid this tax on
Mt. Otare because it was where the village gathered these materials for their
own use. The fact that Yoshida residents were the ones using this place and
paying taxes from it meant it belonged to them. Yoshida explicitly denied
that Kurechi or Onuma had any justifiable claim to Mt. Otare. The logic at
work here is straightforward but significant: Yoshida paid taxes on Mt. Otare
because they were the ones that used it, and therefore, it belonged to them.

The next points in the suit proceeded in a rough reverse chronology, tracing the genesis of the village's claim to Mt. Otare through the early seventeenth century and back into the sixteenth. It begins by noting that in the
1590s, Shinkura Village was denied rights to develop a parcel of land between
Mt. Otare and an area called Shimo no mizu, along the banks of the Katsura (see map 3.1).[47] Yoshida had prevented this by appealing to the magistrate at Funatsu, who endorsed Yoshida's claim to this parcel of land, asserting
that it was considered part of Mt. Otare. As evidence of that decision, the
1635 appeal points to the fact that Yoshida paid a tax (*kuji*) on materials collected here.[48] The next point describes the assignment of construction duty
in the 1620s, which further supports their assertion that the contested area
belonged to them. In 1620, there was a large-scale dredging of the Katsura
River, and part of the project involved building a road that ran parallel to
the river along Mt. Otare. Yoshida was tasked with building a section of this
road upstream (southwest) from Shimo no mizu as part of their construction duty (*fushin-yaku*).[49] Their assignment of this section of the road indicated that it was within "their" territory.

Yoshida's appeal then jumps further back in time to demonstrate the long
history of effective ownership of Mt. Otare. Cited here are decisions from
some of the very same sixteenth century disputes examined above. First,
Yoshida asserts that in the late fifteenth or early sixteenth century, Lower

Yoshida, adjacent to Shimo no mizu, had developed new dry fields and used materials from Mt. Otare.[50] The appeal continues that "for four generations [of Oyamada lords] . . . and afterward," Yoshida had cut lumber and undergrowth at Mt. Otare.[51] The assertion here is quite clear: Mt. Otare belongs to Yoshida and it has for the past century. The four generations of Oyamada lords described here span nearly the entire 1500s. In other words, the mid-sixteenth century settlements to the Yoshida/Kobayashi disputes had established Yoshida's claim to Mt. Otare and were its continued basis here.

In this way, Yoshida justified generations of usage rights to this forest and asserted effective ownership of this place. Kurechi and Onuma's claims were rejected outright. There was no experience of use that would legitimate their rights to use this forest. Yoshida alone had enjoyed access to Mt. Otare's resources for over a century, as demonstrated via dispute resolutions and tax obligations. That meant that in the 1630s, Yoshida had ample evidence for customary practice and official decree showing that they effectively "owned" Mt. Otare. It was a convincing case—exclusive use affirmed over generations.

Responses to Yoshida's 1635 appeal have not survived, but we know from subsequent documents that Yoshida's position prevailed. Mt. Otare is explicitly named as belonging to Yoshida in documents from the eighteenth (1759) and nineteenth (1806) centuries, which specify that the village is to pay a materials tax on resources collected from the forest.[52] These documents describe Mt. Otare as Yoshida's source of timber for riparian construction projects, and specifically as land to be left uncultivated to provide the village with miscellaneous forest products.[53] Yoshida's effective ownership of the forest was maintained according to the same logic as the 1635 appeal, which in turn was justified by late medieval precedent. That precedent, as we have seen, was established through a combination of violence and negotiation over several generations. Dispute resolutions achieved as early as the first decade of the sixteenth century thus continued to serve as the basis of property claims into the nineteenth century. Local settlements regarding resource use endured as founding principles of local administration from the era of Sengoku daimyo well into the early modern era. These practices were solidified in Kai around midcentury, and the instances in the 1530s and 1550s in Yoshida show a transitional moment when the new terms of use, rights, and ownership were contested. As the 1635 example shows, subsequent lords endorsed these decisions with little or no modification. For them, respecting local precedent had long been established as the most expedient way to maintain stability, a key mandate imposed upon local administrators by domain and Tokugawa officials.[54] They became standard practice and accepted common law.

There was no shortage of conflict in late medieval Japan. Yet examination of a place such as Yoshida shows the centrality of local resource disputes to local residents even within the larger context of territorial wars prosecuted by elites. Ways developed to resolve those disputes without violence were painfully birthed over the course of the sixteenth century. Their effect was small in scale but crucial. No lasting peace could be achieved without local stability. Once conflict resolution over the most contentious issue of resources could be achieved without violence at the local level, it opened up space for broader stability, first at the domainal level and ultimately across the archipelago. Peace was thus reestablished from the ground up, and in many parts of Japan, that ground was forested.

CONCLUSION

Resource disputes in Yoshida went from violent clashes to legal disputes and played a key role in ending Sengoku era warfare. It was not only a procedural evolution but a discursive one. The logic behind dispute resolution became more complex. The general evolution can be characterized as a shift from a dispute as a battle, what Fujiki called "battle disputes" (*kassen sōron*) and exemplified by events such as the 1475 attack on Kawaguchi, to a complimentary relationship within the sociopolitical hierarchy.[55] Consider the following points from the above examples. The 1475 instance was unmistakably violent, amounting to naked force. Kawaguchi ran afoul of Yoshida villagers and was killed. Later, when Yoshida confronted Watanabe in 1533, the village ultimately "won" a decision from Oyamada Nobuari. Yoshida's extended disputes with Kobayashi in the 1550s then reveals several new concepts at work. Village envoys presented the logic or "reasonableness" of their claims, and the lord Shingen deemed their position to be "correct" (*tadashii*).[56] They condemned both Kobayashi Owari no kami and Izumi no kami on the basis of crimes (*hibun*) that they had perpetrated against the village. This was not just naked force but a discourse of logic and ownership. Analyzing the same period, Nishikawa Kōhei describes this fundamental shift in the discourse of ownership as a transition from "service logic" to "location logic."[57] The former renders access in exchange for service obligations to some elite entity, while in the latter, access is based upon proximity and daily use. Nishikawa's point is that "location logic" came to prevail in late medieval Japan. Elites tapped into local resources by recognizing (and defending) the legitimacy of local claims, in exchange for a portion of yield. Yoshida gives us evidence of how that process actually unfolded.

When the regional warlord Shingen rendered the verdict in 1557, it was not understood as a victory for Yoshida, although they did achieve their goals vis-à-vis Kobayashi. This settlement resulted in a "restoration" (*naosu*) of the relationship between the Kobayashi Izumi lineage and Yoshida villagers.[58] In other words, there was now a clear idea of how the relationship between these two entities *should* function. Furthermore, it established a mutually beneficial relationship between small-time Yoshida and the daimyo. The village got help resolving a local problem, and the Takeda quashed a potentially disruptive conflict. This was one of the first instances of common interest between the very top (Takeda) and the very local (Yoshida) in late medieval Kai. That trend grew stronger over the next several decades, and by the turn of the seventeenth century, it was entrenched.

As the dispute between Yoshida and two nearby villages in 1635 demonstrated, sixteenth-century precedent was convincing. The village reasserted its exclusive claim to the forest at Mt. Otare by submitting a formal appeal to the territorial lord. No record survives of a competing claim to this forest from that point onward, and its association with Yoshida is explicitly reiterated as late as 1806. Further investigation will be needed to determine just how lasting these sixteenth-century precedents really were and how widespread the trends examined in Yoshida were.[59] This study presents direct examples as late as the early nineteenth century, but influences may extend beyond that point in time. Examination of communal agricultural property suggests that some joint landholding practices whose genesis can be traced to the late sixteenth century persisted even into the 1970s.[60] Even if practices applied to forests, waterways, and other local resources were not quite so long-lived as that, it is clear that they played a key role in shaping early modern stability.

Yoshida's late medieval resource disputes add nuance to the broader history of common resources. What appears to be a fairly straightforward story of a fragmented, weak medieval state giving way to a more institutionalized, central early modern one with greater coercive force in sixteenth to seventeenth century Japan fits uneasily in prescribed boxes. Common local use of Yoshida's forests generally fits the schematic "predictors of success" for an enduring common pool resource laid out in Elinor Ostrom's classic *Governing the Commons*.[61] But a few points about the nature of *iriai* in late medieval Yoshida complicate the picture. The first is that Ostrom's three-tier division of operational, institutional, and constitutional mechanisms for resource use were all being contested and enacted simultaneously during the widespread conflict of late medieval Japan. The example of Yoshida indicates an indirect institutionalization that relies on customary practice and precedent, which never achieved constitutional formalization despite enduring for over two centuries. Furthermore, throughout premodern Japan, and particularly in the early modern era (1600–1868), there was significant slippage between prescribed behavior and actual practice. This was by design, and for local villages, it allowed for a high degree of flexibility and autonomy.[62] In late medieval Yoshida, the need for collective *defense* created a strong impetus for maintenance of common resources.

The importance of collective property and the prevalence of violence in premodern Japan is unquestioned. But we still lack a clear picture of the relationship between the two. Common property in late medieval Japan can be considered the "primarily explanatory variable" for the existence of self-governance at the village level.[63] Furthermore, examples from Yoshida show that defense played the major role in shaping collective resource claims since these were initially secured via force with the village militia.[64] External elites did not create space for local management, a component Ostrom's study identified as crucial, but were rather leveraged as muscle to enforce customary practice and enshrine local precedent.

In that sense, local environmental management in Yoshida evolved in the opposite direction of what happened to villagers in revolutionary France. The village of Charquemont in eastern France experienced state encroachment on traditional forest-use rights in the late eighteenth century, which led to increased discontent and violence.[65] In Yoshida, villagers coopted the authority of regional elites to strengthen local resource claims, entrench them, and ultimately prevent violence.[66]

Villages gained a mechanism for enforcing their claims but were largely left to administer collective property themselves. Elites gained a mechanism for tapping into the local economy and thereby reduced the potential for local upheaval. Local landlords such as Kobayashi appear to have been the most persistent obstacle to rural tranquility, not unlike what occurred in the heavily agricultural *kantō* around the same time.[67] Regional magnates, in this case the Takeda, became guarantors of local resource use rights. They upheld Yoshida's claims primarily against small-time rivals that included local warrior landlords and neighboring villages. In early modern Germany, a similar convergence of interests occurred between local villages and the regional elite. The duke's capacity to serve as dispute mediator and to enforce local regulations in sixteenth-century Leonberg underlay local elites' acceptance of state authority after 1550.[68] That same basic arrangement was primarily responsible for the long-term durability of the Edo period socioeconomic order. Fighting over nature transformed late medieval chaos into early modern order.

NOTES

1   The "Great Peace" of the Tokugawa Period (1600–1868) stretched for some two hundred and sixty eight years. I refer to the "Tokugawa," "early modern," or "Edo Period" to describe the sociopolitical system in place during these centuries which maintained the Great Peace.

2   John Hall's pioneering research is representative of this kind of scholarship in English. See especially Hall, *Government and Local Power in Japan*; and Hall, Nagahara, and Yamamura, *Japan before Tokugawa*.

3   Warring States domains (*ryōgoku*) functioned as largely independent states headed by a regional warlord called daimyo. These domains and their administrative structures survived in only slightly modified form through the Tokugawa period.

4   *Satoyama* refers to rural settlements that used a combination of arable land, forest, pasture, waterways, and other ecologies in concert to support local livelihoods. These often featured some form of common property and a high degree of local autonomy. Although the term itself dates from the mid-eighteenth century, this style of rural environmental use is many centuries older. For an overview of *satoyama* studies, see Arioka Toshiyuki, *Satoyama*; and Shidei Tsunahide, *Shinrin wa mori ya hayashi dewa nai: watakushi no shinrinron*.

5   Amino contrasts premodern urban spaces with rural settlements, which were largely insulated and self-sufficient. His major point is that although there were only a handful of cities in premodern Japan, there were many "urban spaces." Amino, *Rethinking Japanese History*, 74.

6   One indication of the importance of transportation trades in Yoshida is the repeated levies for post horses (*tenma*) by the Takeda beginning in the 1520s.

7   Access to water and forest stand out in local conflicts in Yoshida as particularly contentious. Residents relied on forests for everything from food, fertilizer, animal fodder, fuel, and building materials to miscellaneous raw materials for items of daily use. Arable land was a relatively limited but important resource, as was pasture. Some late medieval disputes occurred over roads, which Kristina Troost suggests should be considered resources in the medieval period, along with fishing, trade, and shipping rights. Troost, "Common Property and Community Formation," 22.

8   For details on the local warrior lineages in Yoshida, see Osano, "Takeda ryōgoku no dogōsō to chiiki shakai"; Nishikawa, *Chūsei kōki no kaihatsu— kankyō to chiiki shakai*.

9   Totman, *The Green Archipelago*.

10   Totman, *The Green Archipelago*, 1.

11 Tighter controls of forests and the promotion of regenerative forestry by the state (daimyo domains) were primarily focused on sustaining supplies of marketable timber. These first emerge in the late seventeenth century, as urban consumerism drove the centralization and commercialization of timber markets. For an example of commodification as being the driving force behind both increased forest regulation and ecological problems, see chapter 3 of Luke S. Robert's study of the Tosa domain, *Mercantilism in a Japanese Domain*.

12 Militias varied in form as did other aspects of village organization across the archipelago. Most *wakashū* comprised the fighting-aged men of a community and carried out various guard, policing, and defense duties for the village.

13 Fujiyoshida-shi shihensan-shitsu, *Myōhōji-ki*, 4.

14 Fujiyoshida-shi shihensan-shitsu, *Myōhōji-ki*, 25–26.

15 Fujiyoshida-shi shihensan-shitsu, *Myōhōji-ki*, 28.

16 Fujiyoshida-shi shihensan-shitsu, *Myōhōji-ki*, 27.

17 Fujiyoshida-shi shihensan-shitsu, *Myōhōji-ki*, 27.

18 Fujiyoshida-shi shihensan-shitsu, *Myōhōji-ki*, 28.

19 Fujiyoshida-shi shihensan-shitsu, *Myōhōji-ki*, 28.

20 Nishikawa Kōhei focuses on this shift in "Sengoku-ki Kai no kuni ni okeru zaimoku no chōsetsu to yamazukuri."

21 Osano, "Takeda ryōgoku no dogōsō," 332. The invasion occurred in 1516 and was led by forces from neighboring Suruga Province under the Imagawa daimyo house. *Myōhōji-ki*, 16.

22 Fujiyoshida-shi shihensan-shitsu, *Myōhōji-ki*, 44–45. Osano speculates that the Kobayashi leveraged their sponsorship of riparian improvements to achieve recognition as *yorioya* in Yoshida. See Osano, "Takeda ryōgoku no dogōsō," 329.

23 For the divergence of two Kobayashi lines, see Shibatsuji, *Takeda-shi kashindan jinmei jiten*, 320–21.

24 Fujiyoshida-shi shihensan-shitsu, *Myōhōji-ki*, 44.

25 This Nobuari was the third of three Oyamada family heads with the name Nobuari. Shibatsuji, *Takeda-shi kashindan*, 231.

26 Fujiyoshida-shi kyōiku iinkai, *Fujiyoshida-shi shi shiryō-hen dai sankan*, 556–57.

27 Fujiyoshida-shi shihensan-shitsu, *Myōhōji-ki*, 44. The "group of twenty" was most likely a cohort of village militia leadership and younger members of the village council who served as messengers and envoys for the council itself. See Nishikawa, *Chūsei kōki no kaihatsu*, 102–3; and Fujiki, *Sengoku so sahō*, 18, 24, 33.

28 Fujiyoshida-shi shihensan-shitsu, *Myōhōji-ki*, 44.

29 For an analysis of the discourse of reasonableness and its use in disputes, see Eason, "The Culture of Disputes in Early Modern Japan, 1550–1700."

30 Fujiyoshida-shi shihensan-shitsu, *Myōhōji-ki*, 44–45.

31   Fujiyoshida-shi shihensan-shitsu, *Myōhōji-ki*, 44.

32   Fujiyoshida-shi shihensan-shitsu, *Myōhōji-ki*, 45. For analysis of the term *hyaku-yo nin*, see Nishikawa, *Chūsei kōki no kaihatsu*, 102.

33   Fujiyoshida-shi shihensan-shitsu, *Myōhōji-ki*, 45.

34   Fujiyoshida-shi shihensan-shitsu, *Myōhōji-ki*, 45.

35   Fujiyoshida-shi shihensan-shitsu, *Myōhōji-ki*, 45.

36   Fujiyoshida-shi shihensan-shitsu, *Myōhōji-ki*, 45.

37   Fujiyoshida-shi shihensan-shitsu, *Myōhōji-ki*, 45.

38   Fujiyoshida-shi shihensan-shitsu, *Myōhōji-ki*, 45.

39   Fujiyoshida-shi shihensan-shitsu, *Myōhōji-ki*, 46.

40   Nishikawa, *Chūsei kōki no kaihatsu*, 104–5.

41   Fujiyoshida-shi kyōiku iinkai, *Fujiyoshida-shi shiryō-hen dai sankan*, 556.

42   Fujiyoshida-shi kyōiku iinkai, *Fujiyoshida-shi shiryō-hen dai sankan*, 556.

43   Nishikawa demonstrates the link between Miyabayashi and its early modern name Mt. Otare in *Chūsei kōki no kaihatsu*, 103–4, 107.

44   Akimoto Yasutomo's official in Yoshida is unnamed. Interestingly, the Akimoto seat was located at Funatsu, the checkpoint that had once been held by Kobayashi Izumi no kami. See Nishikawa, *Chūsei kōki no kaihatsu*, 106.

45   Fujiyoshida-shi kyōiku iinkai, *Fujiyoshida-shi shiryō-hen dai sankan*, 556.

46   Fujiyoshida-shi kyōiku iinkai, *Fujiyoshida-shi shiryō-hen dai sankan*, 556.

47   Fujiyoshida-shi kyōiku iinkai, *Fujiyoshida-shi shiryō-hen dai sankan*, 556. In this document, time frames are not expressed in eras or years but rather by who was the county warrior landlord at the time. For instance, it references Oyamada, Kobayashi, and subsequent warrior lords who held sway in the area after the Tokugawa supplanted the Takeda in Kai Province.

48   Fujiyoshida-shi kyōiku iinkai, *Fujiyoshida-shi shiryō-hen dai sankan*, 556.

49   Fujiyoshida-shi kyōiku iinkai, *Fujiyoshida-shi shiryō-hen dai sankan*, 556. Construction duty was a type of corvée labor that formed part of villagers' tax obligations in the late medieval and early modern eras.

50   Fujiyoshida-shi kyōiku iinkai, *Fujiyoshida-shi shiryō-hen dai sankan*, 556. The dating is imprecise because it references the lifetime of a local warrior landlord (Kobayashi Dōkō, d. 1535) rather than a specific year. For information on generations of the Kobayashi lineage, see Shibatsuji, *Takeda-shi kashindan*, 316–20.

51   Fujiyoshida-shi kyōiku iinkai, *Fujiyoshida-shi shiryō-hen dai sankan*, 556–57.

52   Fujiyoshida-shi kyōiku iinkai, *Fujiyoshida-shi shi shiryō sōsho 4, mura meisaichō*, 21, 24. Nishikawa Kōhei discusses these documents in detail in *Chūsei kōki no kaihatsu*, 103–4.

53   This is the underlying logic of *satoyama*—local forests are to be kept and managed as a cache of necessary resources for the community.

54   On the importance of maintaining local stability above other concerns in the early modern era, see Roberts, *Performing the Great Peace*, especially chapter 4.

55 Fujiki argues that the most prevalent type of conflict in the Warring States era was violent clashes over local resources and that communities understood these confrontations to be part and parcel of late medieval warfare. See Fujiki, *Sengoku no sahō*, 14.

56 Fujiyoshida-shi shihensan-shitsu, *Myōhōji-ki*, 47.

57 Nishikawa, "Sengoku-ki Kai no kuni ni okeru zaimoku," 13.

58 Fujiyoshida-shi shihensan-shitsu, *Myōhōji-ki*, 47.

59 Research from other areas and eras of Japanese history suggest that they were both widespread and long lasting. See the works of Sano, Fujiki, Nishikawa, Vesey, and Tonomura cited in this study, as well as Garrett, "Bad Neighbors and Monastic Influence," 377–402.

60 Brown, *Cultivating Commons*, 2.

61 Ostrom, *Governing the Commons*, 88.

62 Relatively high local autonomy has long been recognized as a key characteristic of the Tokugawa order. For analysis of workings and functions in maintaining stability, see Roberts, *Performing the Great Peace*; and Brown, *Central Authority and Local Autonomy*.

63 Troost, "Common Property and Community Formation," 23.

64 Others have pointed to the role of estates (*shōen*) and tutelary shrine associations (*chinjū, miyaza*) in the formation of common property. While these predate the late medieval era, all such associations took on defensive functions during the Warring States era, and new associations were formed for the purpose of collective defense. My point here is not to deny the existence of these earlier structures but to emphasize that in the late medieval period, their most essential function was military. For lingering *shōen* connections in Kai Province, see Nishikawa, *Chūsei kōki no kaihatsu*, 236. For the role of tutelary shrines, see Hitomi, *Community and Commerce in Late Medieval Japan*, 9–14.

65 Matteson, *Forests in Revolutionary France*, 3.

66 Alexander Vesey provides examples of how a village near Edo leveraged elites in the same way to protect their resource claims vis-à-vis a large temple complex that was the major landowner of the area in the early modern era. See Vesey, "Temples, Timber, and Negotiations," 70–71.

67 Michael Birt argues for a strong local impetus to push samurai landlords out of late sixteenth-century agricultural villages in order to obtain more favorable tax assessments. See Birt, "Samurai in Passage," 369–99.

68 Warde, *Ecology, Economy and State Formation in Early Modern Germany*, 24.

CHAPTER FOUR

THE SYLVAN LOCAL

The Pine Protection Kye *in Late Chosŏn Korea, 1700–1900*

JOHN S. LEE

S PANNING over five hundred years, the pine administration (*songjŏng*) system of Korea's Chosŏn dynasty (1392–1910) was the longest continuous state forestry regime in world history.[1] Established in the early fifteenth century, the pine administration system consisted of hundreds of pine forests across the Korean Peninsula reserved for "state use" (*kugyong*), largely for edifice, warship, and coffin construction. It was a system envisioned by bureaucrats and sustained through a network of magistrates, military officers, and wardens. The protection of a single, easily identifiable conifer instilled predictability and perpetuated the key role that pines played in Chosŏn society and culture. As a result of government policy, *Pinus densiflora, Pinus thunbergii*, and related *Pinus* trees became the dominant sylvan species across much of the Korean Peninsula.[2]

Yet a question remains. How did a preindustrial, agrarian polity maintain a complex forestry system for half a millennium, and how did state and society make the necessary adjustments to protect pine forests for generation after generation? An answer can be found at the local level with the rise of a particular organization in late Chosŏn Korea from the late seventeenth through the mid-nineteenth centuries—the pine protection *kye* (*kŭmsonggye, songgye*).[3] The *kye* was a type of mutual-aid organization that proliferated in the latter half of the Chosŏn era and could be found across the Korean Peninsula in both urban and rural areas. *Kye* functions ranged from granary and forest management to supporting funerary rituals and collecting taxes. They were usually composed of most adult men within a village, but leadership and organization were often further subdivided along

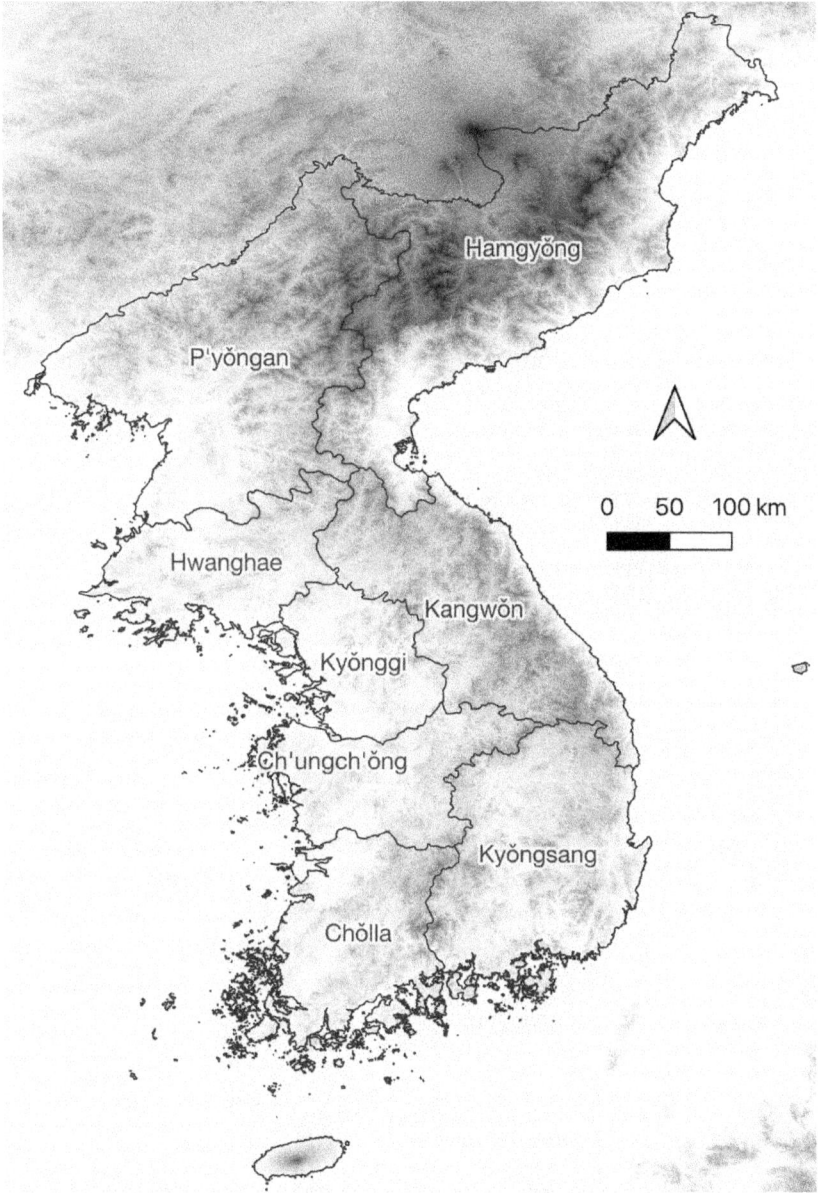

MAP 4.1. Provinces of Chosŏn Korea. Data from Japan Aerospace Exploration Agency, AW3D; DIVA-GIS (diva-gis.org); Rikugun Sanbōkyoku, *Chōsen zenzu*. Map by Ian M. Miller and John S. Lee.

status lines. In general, members of the *kye* made initial financial contributions for common goals. To avoid recurring contributions, most *kye* engaged in profit-seeking activities to earn extra income, such as by renting fields or selling wood. Depending on the activities and financial health of the *kye*, members might also be asked to make supplementary labor or monetary contributions as necessary.[4]

Pine protection *kye* were a form of *kye* that spread throughout Chosŏn Korea in the eighteenth and nineteenth centuries. Their social composition and functions varied, but they shared a common dedication: the regulated usage of local pine forests. In some areas, such as along the western coast and in the island zones, the Chosŏn state ordered villagers to form pine protection *kye* to meet government objectives such as timber protection and wood procurement. In other areas, especially along the upper Naktong River basin in southeastern Korea, local elites utilized the pine protection *kye* to protect their own social and economic interests. In these cases where local elites dominated the *kye* rosters, they used by-laws to protect assets such as gravesite groves and limit commoner access to nearby woodland. On the other hand, there were other pine protection *kye* whose membership were more inclusive and whose operations reflected more egalitarian, collective actions.

The pine protection *kye* of southern Korea emerged as a local strategy for protecting critical sylvan resources in an era of administrative expansion, rising economic competition, and significant environmental change, notably the protection and spread of pine forests. Three particular figurations of pine protection *kye* can be identified: as part of the state forestry system; as mechanisms for local elite dominance; and as local forms of common resource management.[5] Pine protection *kye* provide a critical lens into the link between rural organization and environmental change in Korean history and additionally invite comparison with the emergence of localized or community forestry in early modern and modern Asia.

BACKGROUND: STATE, SOCIETY, AND FORESTS IN THE LATE CHOSŎN ERA

The key organs of the Chosŏn state were threefold: a hereditary monarch; a central bureaucracy staffed by an ascriptive elite, the *yangban*; and lower-level administrators that included hereditary clerks and military officers. *Yangban*, meaning the "two orders" of the civil and military bureaucracy, included state examination passers, upper bureaucrats, and their kin and descendants, as well as country families who engaged in Confucian practices and education and could claim some sort of *yangban* descent. From the seventeenth century onward, certain *yangban* lineages would dominate important positions in central politics while the majority of their status-group compatriots lived in the provinces. There, through powerful organizations and state-sanctioned privileges such as exemption from military service, they would dominate local social and economic life through the end of the dynasty.[6]

Amid the layers of *yangban* dominance, however, numerous changes were unfolding across the Chosŏn economy and environment. After the devastating Japanese invasions of the 1590s, known in Korea as the Imjin War (1592–98), the Chosŏn government underwent a long period of recovery and reform. While *yangban* elite dominated the upper echelons of the bureaucracy, administrative expansion entailed the mobilization of other institutional elements, including the military and clerks. Government projects such as construction and forestry required the recruitment of the local population to serve as corvée. The latter half of the Chosŏn dynasty was also an era of economic and cultural efflorescence. The capital, Hansŏng (present-day Seoul), grew beyond a mere administrative center into the beating heart of the Chosŏn economy. Commercialization and tax reforms brought new opportunities—and demands—to the Chosŏn countryside.[7]

Forests were central to administrative and commercial expansion in the late Chosŏn era. From the seventeenth century onward, the Chosŏn government expanded the pine administration system to ensure supplies for shipbuilding and edifice construction. The original iteration of the state forestry system included 291 protected forests in 1448. By 1808, the number of state forests had expanded to 678 sites.[8] The majority of state forests were located along western and southern coasts. In the seventeenth and eighteenth centuries, the Chosŏn government expanded state forests into the island zones of the southwest, the mountains of Kangwŏn Province, and the hills of the upper Naktong River basin. In accordance with the expansion of state forestry, the government extended the capacities of military garrisons and clerks. The procedures of forest administration varied based on location and context, but the system shared a common principle: the primacy of the pine atop the sylvan hierarchy.

However, the Chosŏn state lacked the wherewithal to manage its fiscal system, let alone forestry, through government agents alone. Preindustrial states required brokers and middlemen to perform the vast capacities of governance. In late Chosŏn Korea, for duties ranging from forest protection to tax collection and funerary expenses, village *kye* filled a key gap. Administrative changes further transformed local society in the late Chosŏn era.

Kye in southern Korea that had been restricted to lineage and basic village functions in the fifteenth and sixteenth centuries diversified into new sectors and functions. New taxation systems instituted in the seventeenth century required village-level cooperation to gather necessary resources and share burdens. Some *kye* that were originally designed to raise moral standards and to cultivate Confucian practice became more akin to fiscal contracts by which village inhabitants used pooled income to finance local schools, infrastructure, irrigation, and the needy. A shared piece of land, such as a forest, was a common way to produce the necessary income.[9]

Thus, pine protection *kye* cannot be seen as strictly serving the interests of the state. Koreans in the late Chosŏn era of all status groups needed wood for daily use. Moreover, an increasingly commercialized economy provided ample profits for villagers willing to organize the tasks of forest management. Even so, these pine protection *kye* all had something in common: an organized dedication to protecting a tree that had become synonymous with state usage. Their nomenclature reflected the successful dissemination of a particular discourse dedicated to "pine administration." Even in the workaday crevices of Chosŏn village life, pine was king.

A BRANCH OF STATE FORESTRY: THE STATE AND PINE PROTECTION *KYE*

In the late seventeenth and early eighteenth centuries, the Chosŏn government attempted to use pine protection *kye* as cogs in the broader expansion of state forestry. In 1710, the government urged residents along the coasts of Ch'ungchŏng Province to form pine protection *kye* for the sake of managing state forests. Government sources lament diminishing timber supplies for shipbuilding and edifice construction. Accordingly, all villagers within thirty *li* (approximately 110 kilometers) from the coast were to form pine protection *kye*, appoint wardens, and report any violations to the local magistrate.[10]

However, top-down efforts to mobilize pine protection *kye* were largely unsuccessful. Most villages along the Ch'ungchŏng coast did not follow prescriptions from above to form their own pine protection *kye*, and the government continued to rely on soldiers, clerks, and inspectors to maintain and surveil state forests. There were some exceptions. On Anmyŏn island on the far western tip of the T'aean peninsula, local pine protection *kye* continued to provide timber management services for the state until the end of the dynasty.[11]

The synergy between the state and the pine protection *kye* was more pronounced when the initiative came from below. For instance, in 1860, 121 villages in Hadong district in southeastern Korea chartered a pine protection *kye*. Their charter starts with the following quote from a 1788 iteration of the government regulations: "In the governance of the state, there is nothing more important than the protection of pines."[12] Whether the villagers actually believed this is doubtful, but the pine association document evidences a local counterpart to state forestry that emerged during the eighteenth and nineteenth centuries.

The Hadong pine protection *kye* is a fitting example of local society operating within the state forestry framework. According to the Handong *kye* charter, the villagers decided to create the *kye* to address the deteriorating condition of the state forests and private woodlands in the area. At the time of the charter's composition, the Chosŏn government maintained ten state forests in the area.[13] According to the association charter, each village in Hadong district was to appoint two wardens to patrol the local pine forest. The wardens maintained the state forest boundaries, putting up restriction postings (*kŭmp'yo*) and checking for any violations, notably evidence of slash-and-burn agriculture and illegal logging. The wardens would then submit periodic reports regarding the condition of local forests to the magistrate's office.[14]

To further ensure compliance, villagers also agreed to utilize the five-household system (*o'ga chakt'ong*), an idea derived from Chinese legalist thought that ostensibly organized villages into five-household units that maintained collective responsibilities for the payment of taxes and adherence to laws. The system was encouraged by officials throughout the Chosŏn era but with little effect. Only in the eighteenth century was there any effective local implementation of the five-household order, largely due to the further systemization of villages as administrative units.[15] In the case of the Hadong pine protection *kye*, villagers worked together to selectively log mature pine timber, which they then sold to the military or government-licensed merchants to help pay off taxes or other communal obligations. If any villagers were caught violating forestry ordinances, associated households could be punished as well.[16]

Why did the villagers of Hadong agree to work closely with the state? The Hadong pine protection *kye* may have been an exceptional case of a large, particularly well-organized set of villages living in close proximity to multiple state forests. Accordingly, cooperation with the state allowed villagers to maintain some autonomy and ensured access to forest resources.

A similar symbiotic relationship can be found in a *kye* founded in 1819 in the hamlet of Onjŏng, Yŏnp'ung County, near present-day Koesan in Ch'ungch'ŏng Province. There, villagers formed a pine protection *kye* in response to rampant deforestation in their vicinity. Their *kye* rules, titled the Onjŏng Pine Protection Regulations (Onjŏngdong kŭmsong chŏlmok) specifically outlined measures to punish and fine illegal logging.[17] The Onjŏng *kye* relied on a close relationship with local government authorities. The members cite government regulations as a basis for forming their pine protection *kye*, and perpetrators from "outside the villages" were reported to local authorities for further punishment. In turn, one sees a glimpse of how *kye* formation allowed members to internally discipline violations. Outsiders, on the other hand, were put at the mercy of state authorities.

The vast majority of pine protection *kye* in late Chosŏn Korea, however, did not demonstrate a comparable level of state-local synergy. Numerous *kye* charters cite government forestry regulations and hail the importance of pine, but their actual practices reflected local desires to maintain exclusive usufruct rights. While pine protection *kye* made some efforts to protect government forests, such efforts were secondary to the far more important task of maintaining primary access for specific groups. For many local *yangban* in particular, the purpose of the *kye* was to keep the state out, not in.

MECHANISMS OF DOMINANCE: LOCAL ELITES AND PINE PROTECTION *KYE*

The first recorded pine protection *kye* can be traced to a community compact (*hyangyak*) from the hamlet of Kŭman near Naju in southern Chŏlla Province.[18] In 1681, a magistrate named Yi Hŭiryong (1639–97) oversaw the formation of a *kye* among the village elites, and the charter included provisions for the protection of local forests. Local *yangban* in the hamlet, notably members of the Naju Chŏng lineage, later used the *kye* system to expand forest restrictions and to accordingly secure gravesite groves. New regulations set by the Chŏng clan in 1715 and 1718 restricted general access to pine forests around Kŭman.[19] The Chŏng clan allowed villagers to gather a limited amount of mulch and undergrowth in the spring for fertilizer. Mature timber was harvested in the autumn, in carefully prescribed amounts, for wider usage and sale, with the proceeds communally managed by the *kye*.[20]

The Kŭman village elites used a bifurcated system of stratification that restricted non-elite land-use practices while also instilling nominal cooperation. The Chŏng lineages and allied families occupied an exclusive "upper *kye*" (*sanggye*) and wrote most of the *kye* rules. Non-elites were organized into their own "lower *kye*" (*hagye*) that could consult with the upper branch members. The lower *kye* appointed its own steward (*kamgo*) to guard the local pine forest and maintain logging restrictions. According to historians such as Na Sŏnha, the upper-lower stratification of Kŭman's *kye* was designed to preserve elite interests. Elites maintained their status and local autonomy while ensuring village-wide cooperation to promote agricultural productivity and protect key assets such as timber.[21] Non-elites received *yangban* guarantees of forest regulation and, most importantly, protection from government wardens and military officials.

The initial 1681 regulations largely focus on punitive measures, a pattern also seen in other pine protection *kye*. Logging violations were subject to fines paid in rice, with fines escalating based on number of trees logged. The *kye* even restricted collections of dead or wilted pines to five per household. Households going through hard times could purchase wood from upper *kye* members. In 1715, local elites issued even stricter amendments. Illegal loggers received beatings with a club, with the punishments extending to those who illegally cut pine branches. Masters were also held accountable for their slaves and servants. If a slave was caught more than three times violating pine protection regulations, his or her household head had to pay a fine in the form of a bottle of alcohol and five side dishes. The slave was also clubbed twenty times.[22]

The formation of the Kŭman's forest regulations has to be further situated in the broader social and political context of southern Korea in the early eighteenth century. Tensions between centrally appointed magistrates and local *yangban* were an ongoing drama throughout the Chosŏn era. By 1700, numerous local elites were losing that battle; in effect, they were losing influence over administrative affairs.[23] Local *yangban* devised strategies for dealing with their increasing alienation from political power. These "localist strategies," historian Martina Deuchler argues, entailed the consolidation of kinship groups and bolstering their social and economic role in their communities.[24] Local elites sponsored private academies, upheld key family rituals such as the ancestral cult, and organized mutual funds to support their kin. As the Chosŏn administrative state expanded its tax collection and resource management capacities from the mid-seventeenth century onward, resentful locals further entrenched themselves in community affairs and jealously safeguarded their autonomy.

The Kŭman pine protection *kye* exemplified the preservationist impulses of the local *yangban* in southern Korea during the late seventeenth and early eighteenth centuries. The *kye* allowed elites to protect their assets and autonomy while achieving greater prominence in their villages via control over a key resource. The Chŏng family used the *kye* figuration to enlist village-wide cooperation in protecting key assets, notably their gravesite groves. Simultaneously, Kŭman's elites made an explicit pact with the state: in exchange for carrying out the state forestry regimen, the government sanctioned the Kŭman *kye*'s autonomy over the implementation of forest management.

Local elites also formed *kye*-type organizations to protect critical resources, notably forests, from external forces: their neighbors, vagrants, and the state. In 1756, a magistrate near Andong in southeastern Korea ordered the felling of a number of pine trees located in the private grove of the Ŭisong Kim lineage. The magistrate had been angry at the Kim family for supporting a rival political faction. The government then took the felled timber as a tax levy. In response, the Kim lineage formed a pine protection charter. Two men from the family were to be appointed "tree protection officers" who patrolled the pine grove and tended to its affairs. The incident demonstrates that the government had the authority to appropriate pine timber as it saw fit. However, such arbitrary actions could also engender local resistance and spur organizational formation.[25]

Andong is part of the upper Naktong River basin constituting the northern portion of Kyŏngsang Province. This region was a center of Confucian scholarship and a den of proud local elites during the Chosŏn era. The region sprouted Korea's most renowned neo-Confucian scholar, T'oegye Yi Hwang (1501–70), numerous illustrious lineages, and the most influential Confucian academies and scholarly circles outside of Seoul. In turn, the region was marked by robust local organizations, including a plethora of *kye* of various types. Pine protection *kye* emerged in upper Naktong basin during the late Chosŏn era as local residents faced new anxieties: rising competition over forest resources and an increasingly intrusive state.

Pine protection *kye* in the upper Naktong basin shared certain characteristics that reflected the region's localized figuration and powerful local elite. Pine protection *kye* in the region tended to be centered around lineage organizations. A notable example is the Pine *Kye* Resolution (Songgye Wanŭi) from Sŏnsan County in present-day Kumi in northern Kyŏngsang Province. Kumi is famous for the being the hometown of Pak Chŏnghŭi (Park Chung-hee, 1917–79), former president of South Korea. In the Chosŏn era, the area was part of a prosperous agricultural and riverine transport zone.

The Pine *Kye* Resolution was composed in either 1802 or 1862 by 178 men from Sŏnsan County dedicated to managing local pine forests. As typical in communities throughout early nineteenth-century Korea, the *kye* bifurcated into "upper" and "lower" branches. The upper branch was composed of seventy men from the most prominent families in the area. The lower branch was a far more diverse group of lower *yangban* and commoner origin.[26]

The authors of the resolution bemoan the overemphasis on timber production that defined their era. The Sŏnsan pine protection *kye* begins its charter with a quote from Mencius: "If axes and bills enter the hills and forests only at the proper time, the wood will be more than can be used." The authors go on to note:

> Surely, are [Mencius'] words not about the affairs of our day? If trees inevitably become timber after having matured, and only after they become timber can they have uses, then in life there is no concern for their soil; in death, no regrets for about their growth. Moreover, wherever people live, there are forests. The forests provide shade; the pines and spindles block sunlight. How can we only speak of using trees for timber?[27]

Shade (*ŭmnye*) is a geomantic term referring to passive *ŭm* (Chinese: *yin*) energies that balance active *yang* forces. The Sŏnsan *kye* leaders, in a sense, were decrying the materialistic exploitation of sylvan landscapes. Thus, trade-offs between economic and geomantic concerns—at times complementary, in others conflicting—were yet another source of anxiety for local elites throughout the late Chosŏn era. Local elites in other communities regularly used geomantic discourses to control land-use practices across their communities.[28] Just as early Chosŏn bureaucrats sought to corral the sylvan dependencies of the very people they governed, local elites feared the myopia of their social inferiors, particularly their lack of consideration for painstakingly managed ecologies and geomantic fortunes.

In terms of the regulatory procedures, the Sŏnsan pine protection *kye* did not greatly differ from its late Chosŏn counterparts. The *kye* banned any unregulated felling of pines in the hills that surrounded the county's villages. Dead pines were regulated on a case-by-case basis, most likely to maintain fire and erosion controls. On hillsides prone to wildfires, the *kye* installed comprehensive protections on all trees including "miscellaneous trees" (*chammok*) other than pine. Punishments were accorded according to highest, middle, and lowest degrees. Twelve out of the fifteen Sŏnsan *kye* regulations deal specifically with types of bans and their respective punishments. A later addendum to the Sŏnsan *kye* regulations actually mentions very little about pines but instead lists several new rules related to the maintenance of social propriety and the management of *kye* funds.[29]

In other parts of Korea, a combination of population growth and economic conflict further drove the formation of pine protection *kye*. In the eighteenth and nineteenth centuries, Seoul and the broader capital region in Kyŏnggi Province experienced an influx of new residents attracted by new commercial opportunities and economic growth. A notable example of economic and demographic shifts spurring *kye* formation can be found in Kajwa near present-day Pyŏngt'aek, about sixty-five kilometers southwest of Seoul. Kajwa was part of a larger area comprising Yangsŏng Prefecture and Sogoni district in southern Kyŏnggi Province that experienced significant demographic and economic expansion in the latter half of the eighteenth century. In the eighteenth century, the southern Kyŏnggi region grew more integrated into a flourishing economy emanating from Seoul. Villages such as Kajwa became part of a network of markets and hubs connecting the capital and the southern provinces.[30] Estimates include a 20 percent population increase in Yangsŏng between 1757 and 1789 and a 63 percent rise in Sogoni in the same time span.[31]

Demographic and economic growth, in turn, spurred greater competition over forest resources. The residents of Kajwa formed a series of pine protection *kye* that were chartered in an 1838 document, the "Pine Protection *Kye* Roster" (Kŭmsonggye chwamok).[32] In justifying the formation of the *kye*, the leaders cite ecological devastation wrecked by avaricious commoners:

> The customs change day by day, and the people do not know the
> bans [on pine logging]. They even pull out everything to the
> roots and load them onto oxen and horses for transport, bridles
> and reins one after another on the road. Consequently, forests
> that were once green are now red. Forests that were once dense
> are now denuded. The gravesites and tombs of the noble
> households are also degraded, and they wail that the tiger and
> dragon are collapsing.[33] If the court's pine restrictions fall apart,
> then where indeed would there be orders coming from above and
> reform happening from below?[34]

In its organization and purposes, the Kajwa pine protection *kye* was similar to *yangban*-led *kye* in other parts of Korea. The *kye* was separated along upper and lower branches, and according to stated custom, the members maintained the upkeep of gravesite groves and the surrounding forest. In practice, the upper branch dominated the *kye*. The roster lists forty-five members in the upper branch, largely from the noble Chŏnju Yi and Susŏng

Choe clans, and only six people are listed as representing the lower branches. The upper branch accordingly used the pine protection *kye* to protect their primary interests, namely gravesite groves and fuelwood production. The pine protection *kye*, nominally a form of cooperative resource management, was a powerful tool for the reproduction of a stratified social order.

COMMON-POOL RESOURCES: VILLAGE SOCIETY AND PINE PROTECTION *KYE*

Did all pine protection *kye* neatly align with the designs of *yangban* and the state? Pine protection *kye* largely circumscribed government and elite interests within the structures of a highly stratified, bureaucratic society. *Kye* were certainly collective in their function and figuration, but their outcomes usually reinforced status and economic divisions. Nevertheless, it is important to note that the collective nature of forest conservation could unite different elements of a Chosŏn locale around a common goal. Pae Suho and Yi Myŏngsŏk, in their comprehensive study of Korean pine protection *kye*, conclude that numerous Korean pine protection *kye* exhibited principles consistent with Elinor Ostrom's conceptions of effective commons management.[35] Pine protection *kye* preserved local forests as common-pool resources over multiple generations. Appropriators devised, applied, and monitored their own rules to control their usage. Most importantly, numerous *kye* survived for long periods of time amidst shifting environmental and political contexts.

The longest-enduring *kye* in Korea featured more egalitarian structures that distributed decision-making and outcomes across status groups. For instance, the *kye* regulations of a village called Hoeryong in Tamyang County in Chŏlla Province, dated to 1816, ensured that all illegal loggers, "even those of *yangban* background," would be reported to government officials.[36] *Kye* organization and strong collective practices continue in Hoeryong to the present day.[37] The Hoeryong residents initially established their *kye* regulations in response to a famine that struck the area in 1814 and 1815. As agricultural production collapsed, vagrants wandered the area looking for food, and the nearby forests became depleted of useful timber and fuelwood. The villagers of Hoeryong responded to the crisis with organizational vigor. People of "high and low" status banded together to establish regulations on issues ranging from tax collection and fiscal management to forest protection and social propriety. Forest usage, in particular, was regulated to secure communal village income in the form of fuelwood and timber sales.[38] The income, in turn, would be used to support expenses such as funerals, education, and tax payments.

The Hoeryong *kye* was distinctive in that it did not involve a separate pine protection organization. Rather, forest usage was regulated as part of the village's general communal obligations, others of which included famine and epidemic relief, corvée labor duty, and preparation for key ceremonies and rituals. Perhaps due to its traumatic origins in a time of famine, the Hoeryong village *kye* was distinctive in its egalitarian spirit. The regulations open *kye* membership to all village residents and prescribe equal punishments for violators from all status groups.

A similarly long-enduring, egalitarian figuration can be found in the village of Kurim in Yŏngam County in Chŏlla Province. In 1768, a group of Kurim villagers formed a pine protection *kye* that was entrusted with the management of the local pine forests.[39] *Kye* members patrolled the forests, replanted trees, and even doled out punishments to unpermitted loggers. Villagers who logged pines without permission from the *kye* could be denied access to collective resources such as fuelwood and the village well. They could also be cut off from *kye* funds for funerals and economic relief.[40] In turn, the Kurim pine protection *kye* periodically logged mature pines and sold them, with the proceeds going to the collective *kye* funds.[41] The Kurim *kye* continues to operate to the present day. Its contemporary undertakings have expanded beyond the protection of trees to supporting local schools and the management of a fish farm. Even so, the Kurim *kye* retains its collective structures, including the persistence of collective-choice arrangements, the monitoring of appropriator behavior, and the use of graduated sanctions for violations.

Similar levels of longevity and collectivity can be found among pine protection *kye* from Kŭmsan and Kyeryong in Ch'ungch'ŏng Province. In both cases, the *kye* expanded in the late Chosŏn era amid rising competition over forest resources. Like their counterparts in Kurim and Hoeryong, the Kŭmsan and Kyeryong *kye* had wide membership from across status groups with commoners in leadership positions. In Kŭmsan, members maintained a respectful relationship with the Chosŏn state, cooperating with government officials to report and punish trespassers. The Kŭmsan *kye* continued to maintain themselves in accord with the policies of the Japanese colonial state (1910–45) and the Republic of Korea in the twentieth century.[42] In Kyeryong, the *kye* maintained a complex hierarchy of forest officers who shared a variety of surveillance, planting, and administrative duties.[43] These *kye* survive to the present day thanks to a litany of reasons: proximity to valuable forest land, positive relations with government institutions, and effective common-pool arrangements.

CONCLUSION

Pine protection *kye* directed by the state, for the most part, died with the Chosŏn dynasty. Gravesite groves and communal forests fascinated Japanese ethnographers, but ultimately, Korean woodland claims required documentary evidence demanded by the new colonial state. Japanese forest officials developed a new framework for woodland ownership that reclassified forests into four ownership categories—imperial, national, public, and private. Private ownership of woodland required registration backed by proof of ownership in the form a "land register, land area calculation, and sketch map."[44] According to historian David Fedman, *yangban* were quite successful in registering private claims thanks to their "easy access to historical documentation verifying ownership claims and deep enough pockets to cover the cost of surveying."[45] With private ownership ascertained by the new colonial state, many *yangban*-led pine protection *kye* lost their necessity.

Commoners and other small-scale agriculturalists, on the other hand, faced woodland dispossession. Confusion regarding the necessity of surveys and a lack of historical documentation produced meager numbers of smallholder claimants. The result was a "land-tenure framework designed to permit a bare minimum level of access to Korean farmers and afford a maximum degree of control" to colonial foresters.[46] Ironically, Japanese forestry officials also had held the pine protection *kye* in high regard, seeing in them a conservationist tradition similar to Japan's own *iriai*, the collective arrangements through which Japanese villages had also maintained forests.[47]

Overall, pine protection *kye* can be seen through a tripartite lens: as branches of a long and complex state forestry system, as tools of local elite dominance in an early modern society, and as effective forms of commons management that endure to the present day. The pine protection *kye* can also be compared to other forms of communal forest management that lasted throughout the preindustrial era. Political economist Elinor Ostrom's theories of effective common-pool resource management focused on woodland institutions from Swiss and Japanese history.[48] The endurance of the respective institutions exemplified the efficacy of communal forest ownership and accordant modes of monitoring, conflict resolution, and decision-making. However, Ostrom notes that while these "cases clearly demonstrate the feasibility of robust, self-governing institutions . . .

the origins of these systems are lost in time."[49] In the case of the Korean pine protection *kye*, their origins and modus operandi can be understood through the existent historical record. An expanding state forestry system and local socioeconomic competition spurred the formation of pine protection *kye* in the late Chosŏn era. A centuries-long political emphasis on pine circumscribed group nomenclature and functional emphases. Relationships with the state and among intervillage groups were decisive in shaping the fate of local society and woodland usage in the last three centuries of Korean history.

NOTES

1   By *forestry*, I refer to institutionalized practice of managing, protecting, and planting forests. *State forestry* thus entails the institutionalization of forest usage through laws and edicts and the accordant management of the forests through bureaucratic functions and personnel.

2   For an examination of the Chosŏn state forestry system in English, see Lee, "Postwar Pines."

3   All romanization of Korean in this chapter follows McCune-Reischauer conventions.

4   The majority of the English-language scholarship regarding the Korean *kye* has focused on their role in modern South Korea and their usage by the Korean diaspora. For representative works, see Campbell "Kyes and Mujins," 55–68; and Kennedy, "The Korean *Kye*," 197–222. For an English-language summary of colonial era *kye* and their functions, see Stephens, "Agriculture and Development in an Age of Empire," 202–6. For a comprehensive Korean-language study of *kye*, see Kim, *Han'guk sahoe chojiksa yŏn'gu*. The most comprehensive Korean-language study of Korean pine protection *kye* can be found in Pae and Yi, *Sallim kongyu chawŏn kwalli rosŏ kŭmsonggye yŏn'gu*.

5   Pak Chongcha'e categorizes pine protection *kye* based on whether they were led by the state, local elites, or villagers. Pak Chongch'ae, "Chosŏn hugi kŭmsonggye ŭi yuhyŏng."

6   For comprehensive analysis of the Chosŏn elite, see Deuchler, *Under the Ancestors' Eyes*.

7   For a summary of the late Chosŏn economic and social context, see Palais, *Confucian Statecraft and Korean Institutions*, 18–21, 92–113.

8   For a full description of the expansion of state forestry in late Chosŏn Korea, see Lee, "Postwar Pines," 319–32.

9   For an example, see Deuchler, *Under the Ancestors' Eyes*, 351. For a fuller explanation of brokers and their role in Chosŏn administration, see Lee, "The Rise of the Brokered State," 81–108.

10   *Pibyŏnsa tŭngrok, sukchong*, 36.11.13 (1710). All entries from Chosŏn court records are cited in reign year-month-day format.

11   *Anmyŏndo minho kŭp wŏnyŏk kŏhaeng chŏlmok.*

12   *Songgye chŏlmok*, 2b, 1860, Kyu 2329. Further analysis of this document can be found in Pak, "Chosŏn hugi kŭmsonggye ŭi yuhyŏng," 192–93; Pae and Yi, *Sallim kongyu chawŏn kwalli rosŏ kŭmsonggye yŏn'gu*, 96–103.

13   *Man'gi yoram*, 5:12b, 1808, Kyu 1151.

14   *Songgye chŏlmok.*

15   For further context regarding the five-household system in Chosŏn Korea, see Deuchler, *Under the Ancestors' Eyes*, 261–62; Chŏng, *Chosŏn sidae hyangch'on sahoesa*, 267–71.

16   *Songgye chŏlmok.*

17   Pae and Yi, *Sallim kongyu chawŏn kwalli rosŏ kŭmsonggye yŏn'gu*, 137.

18   Pak Chongch'ae, "Chosŏn hugi tonggye ŭi unyŏng kwa hyangch'on chojik," 165–98.

19   Na, "16–17 segi Naju sajok ŭi chonjae yangsang kwa hyanggwŏn ŭi ch'ui," 107.

20   Pae and Yi, *Sallim kongyu chawŏn kwalli rosŏ kŭmsonggye yŏn'gu*, 356.

21   Na, "16–17 segi Naju sajok ŭi chonjae yangsang kwa hyanggwŏn ŭi ch'ui," 104–7.

22   Pae and Yi, *Sallim kongyu chawŏn kwalli rosŏ kŭmsonggye yŏn'gu*, 360.

23   Deuchler, *Under the Ancestor's Eyes*, 256–65.

24   Deuchler, *Under the Ancestor's Eyes*, 266.

25   Deuchler, 371; Mun et al., *Chosŏn yangban ŭi saenghwal segye*, 403–7.

26   Pae and Yi, *Sallim kongyu chawŏn kwalli rosŏ kŭmsonggye yŏn'gu*, 117.

27   *Songgye wanŭi*, 2b-3a, n.d., Ko 5129–30.

28   Choe Wŏnsŏk, "Chosŏn hugi yŏngnam chibang sajok ch'on ŭi p'ungsu tamnon," 265–74. For connections between geomancy and forest protection in China, see Coggins, "When the Land Is Excellent," 97–126.

29   *Songgye wanŭi*, 5a-5b.

30   Han, "Chosŏn hugi kajwa tong kŭmsonggye ŭi unyŏng kwa kinŭng," 153–54.

31   Han, "Chosŏn hugi kajwa tong kŭmsonggye ŭi unyŏng kwa kinŭng," 150–52.

32   *Kŭmsonggye chwamok.*

33   *Tiger and dragon (yongho)* is a geomantic term for auspicious areas around a gravesite or home.

34   *Kŭmsonggye chwamok*, 2b-3a.

35   Pae and Yi, *Sallim kongyu chawŏn kwalli rosŏ kŭmsonggye yŏn'gu* 6, 9; Ostrom, *Governing the Commons*, 58–61, 88–102.

36   Pae and Yi, *Sallim kongyu chawŏn kwalli rosŏ kŭmsonggye yŏn'gu*, 110.

37   Pae and Yi, *Sallim kongyu chawŏn kwalli rosŏ kŭmsonggye yŏn'gu*, 114–15.

38   Pae and Yi, *Sallim kongyu chawŏn kwalli rosŏ kŭmsonggye yŏn'gu*, 114.

39   "Kurim taedonggye [The Kurim village *kye*]," in *Kurim taedonggye chi*, 55.

40   Kim, "18–19 segi sŏnamhae tosŏ yŏnan chiyŏk songgye ŭi chojik kwa kinŭng," 23.

41   Kim, "18–19 segi sŏnamhae tosŏ yŏnan chiyŏk songgye ŭi chojik kwa kinŭng," 24.

42   Kang Sŏngbok, *Kŭmsan ŭi songgye,* 65-66.

43   Kang Sŏngbok, "Sallim munhwa ŭi chinsu, Kuksabong songgye wa tongje," 118–21.

44   Fedman, *Seeds of Control,* 80.

45   Fedman, *Seeds of Control,* 82.

46   Fedman, *Seeds of Control,* 97.

47   Fedman, *Seeds of Control,* 77.

48   Ostrom, *Governing the Commons,* 61–69.

49   Ostrom, *Governing the Commons,* 103.

CHAPTER FIVE

FRONTIER TIMBER IN SOUTHWEST CHINA

Market, Empire, and Identity

MENG ZHANG

S OUTHWEST China was gradually incorporated into the central empire over the early modern period after centuries as an ethnically diverse area peripheral to direct imperial administration. The so-called Miao frontier was a broad area encompassing parts of today's Hunan, Guizhou, and Guangxi provinces and is so named after the various indigenous groups that were collectively labeled by imperial agents as the Miao people. Accompanying the forces of administrative and military expansions of the imperial state was the economic incorporation of this frontier into a nascent and expansive national market system. During the eighteenth century, the development of a timber industry in the Miao territories was greatly facilitated by migration, market integration, and improved water transportation. Timber produced in the Miao frontier became increasingly important in satisfying the demand for construction materials in the middle and lower reaches of the Yangzi River. The timber market in Jinping County at the upper end of the Yuan River in southeastern Guizhou (see map 5.1) rose to be a regional hub where timber merchants from afar conducted business with the Miao sellers through the mediation of bilingual local brokerages.

The timber market in Jinping was the newest segment of an interregional timber trade system along the Yangzi River and its tributaries that was sending five million logs annually to the eastern coast by the mid-eighteenth century.[1] Not surprisingly, many of the business practices that had become entrenched in the eastern metropole spread to this frontier market along the steps of itinerant merchants. Most notably, these included the use of a peculiar algorithmic system for timber measurement and pricing, the

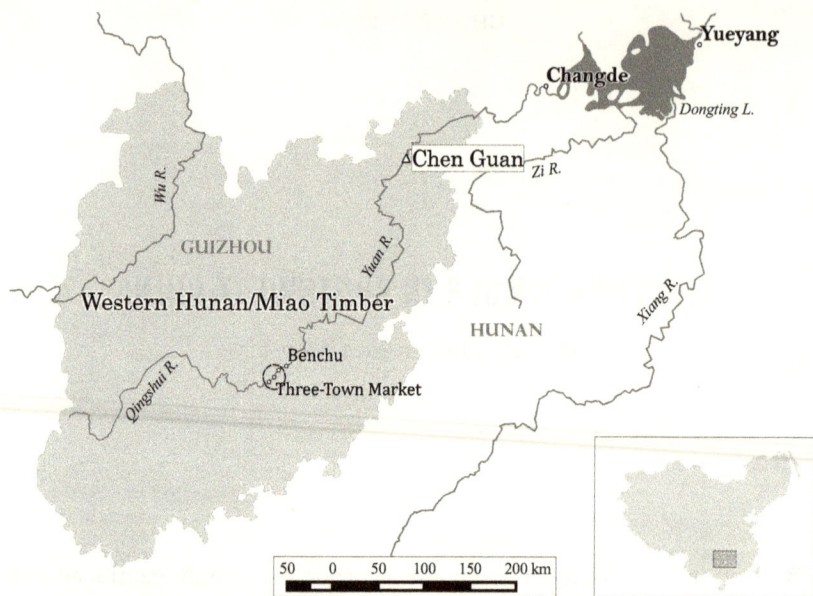

MAP 5.1. Timber markets and trade routes in the Miao frontier. Map by Meng Zhang.

organization of merchants into groups based on native-place origins and the functioning of brokerages as intermediaries for long-distance exchanges.[2] The empire-wide institution of licensed brokerage (*yahang*), in particular, had become the primary conduit for the indirect market regulation by the largely laissez-faire state. By the time the Jinping market began to flourish in the second half of the eighteenth century, the Qing state had completed its overhaul of the national licensed brokerage system in the spirit of ensuring market access and fair trade and eliminating excessive interference and exactions by local officials.[3] In the frontier setting, however, this overall consideration of promoting fair transactions according to market principles had to be reconciled with other priorities of ensuring stability and interethnic harmony. The presence of extra-economic considerations was similar to David Bello's study of the northern imperial tombs and hunting grounds in chapter 6 of this volume, although the exact nature and implications of such considerations differed. As later discussions will show, timber brokerages on the Miao frontier had similar business operations as their counterparts in the metropole but faced different administrative environments.

Repercussions of the state's frontier policies helped shape the practices of timber trade in Jinping. The imperial officials' concerns about ethnic tensions and social instability committed them to maintaining a monopoly system at the Han-Miao ethnic border even after the initial economic rationale withered away. In practice, however, merchants—Han and Miao alike—strategically took advantage of the state's frontier discourse, ethnic labels, and administrative priorities to their own advantages. The changes that the Qing empire brought to this ethnic and ecological frontier were actively negotiated on the ground between the state's various local representatives and merchant groups whose competing economic interests were often be expressed through and helped define their ethnic identities. The Miao frontier that emerged from such intricate negotiations turns out to be very different than the one imagined by the empire's ethnographic projects.[4]

FRONTIER TIMBER AND THE EXPANSION OF EMPIRE

The incorporation of the southwestern frontier into the interregional timber trade system was part of a larger political and social process that accompanied the expansion of the Ming-Qing empire. Such expansionist endeavors culminated in the Qing emperor Yongzheng's decision in the early eighteenth century to abolish native chieftainships and extend direct bureaucratic administration by state-appointed officials, which ignited extensive Miao revolts that took the Qing state more than a decade to suppress.[5] This and other large-scale military operations in the region carried out by the Ming-Qing state over the centuries required considerable investment in building infrastructure and collecting local intelligence. Roads and rivers that were initially built, repaired, or dredged to facilitate military operations later facilitated the more mundane movement of people and commodities. Regular administrative units were made out of previous native chieftain territories, and the term *Miao frontier* (*Miaojiang*) came increasingly to refer administratively to specific counties and districts rather than to an ambiguous, boundless, untamed land. Gazetteers about the local environment and transportation routes were first produced by government offices and later also released by commercial publishers, providing guides to travelers.[6] The local non-Han groups, often collectively labeled "Miao" in both official and popular discourse, were further categorized with adjectives ("Flower Miao," "Cave Miao," and so forth) or by indications of their varying degrees of acculturaltion ("raw Miao" versus "cooked Miao") in ethnographic works that sought to make legible classifications out of diverse local customs.[7] Such infrastructural, administrative, and epistemological constructions of the "Miao" people and the "Miao frontier" laid the ground for enormous economic and environmental transformations.

The focus of this study, the Yuan River basin in eastern Guizhou and western Hunan, was a subregion of the larger "Miao frontier" and became an important source of timber. Factors that increased the ability of Han merchants to access this timber included improved transportation conditions, better knowledge of the landscape, and more familiar administrative structures. To varying degrees, these were all by-products of state expansion. An area of richly forested hills inhabited by diverse Miao groups, it began to supply large amounts of timber for both state and civilian use in the eighteenth century. The establishment of sub-prefecture civil offices in the newly pacified areas brought administrative practices that the Han Chinese merchants were well versed in and familiar authorities whom they knew how to interact with—although that by no means guaranteed they could always get what they wanted, as later sections will show.

Another event significant to the development of the timber industry in this region was the mobilization of local laborers to dredge the Qingshui River (the upper stretch of the Yuan River) during the 1730s military campaign.[8] Originally carried out to facilitate the movement of military forces and supplies, the dredging opened the export route for timber and non-timber forest resources along the river valley to the Yangzi River through Dongting Lake (see map 5.1). Since then, timber produced from the Yuan River basin, known as "timber from the Miao territories" (*Miao mu*) or "timber from western Hunan" (*xi-Hu mu*), became increasingly important in satisfying both the state's procurement of imperial timber as well as market demands from the prosperous lower Yangzi River region. Based on the taxation data from a customs station on the Yuan River, the monetary value of timber exported from the Yuan River basin grew from about three hundred thousand silver taels in 1730 to eight hundred thousand taels by 1800. With a rough estimation, this probably represented about 15 to 30 percent of the overall Yangzi River timber trade by 1800.[9]

Timber export from the Yuan River basin was a combination of logs cut from primary and secondary forests and those from cultivated plantations. The attraction of the Miao frontier to imperial agents and merchants alike lay in its abundance of large timber from natural forests. The annual quota of timber tribute demanded by the central state included more than a thousand large-sized logs that had to be cut from old-growth forests, which brought the procuring officials and their merchant delegates from the responsible provinces to the frontier Miao markets in search of the required varieties.[10] The more accessible forests along the river valley gradually disappeared. But deforestation was not the whole story. Similar to the case of the Nuosu community in southwestern Sichuan as discussed in chapter 9, local agroforestry practices were important counter forces to unsustainable extractions in the Miao frontier. As in many other areas of southern China, where and when the right conditions existed, market-oriented tree cultivation prospered in the Yuan River basin. Similar silvicultural and contractual practices as seen in eastern provinces came to spread widely among the Miao communities. Most popular was the intercropping of China fir for timber and tung oil trees or other perennials for non-timber products.[11] An eighteenth-century local gazetteer stated:

> Previously, the Miao people did not make profit from pine and fir. The trees in the mountains were left to grow on their own, even their names were not known. Nowadays pine and fir are being widely planted, the lands look lush and prosperous. The area is close to river transportation. Every year, timber is cut down and rafted to flow down the river to be sold in Hongjiang, Changde, and other places. People's livelihood improves increasingly.[12]

Some officials also actively promoted the planting of timber and fruit trees among the Miao.[13] By the turn of the nineteenth century, tree planting had spread to what were considered less acculturated communities, such as the "Black Miao."[14] Moreover, as seen in some other places in southern China, the challenge of long-term investment posed by the nature of tree growth was solved by the flexibility of shareholding. Landowners, tenant planters, and interested investors claimed their rights to the end profits through divisible and tradable shares. Such contractual practices can be seen in the large number of Chinese-language documents preserved in the Miao communities, which I have analyzed elsewhere.[15]

Whether from natural forests or managed plantations, timber logs of all sizes and varieties from the upper tributaries of the Yuan River gathered at the first market at Jinping before making their way into the interregional arteries. With the expansion of timber trade, Han merchants from eastern provinces became a powerful group in the frontier market. It became a concern of the state to regulate the behavior of the timber seekers in order to prevent potential social disturbances caused by their exploitation of the Miao. As early as 1732, Guizhou surveillance commissioner Fang Xian remarked on the influx of Han merchants deep into the mountains and the occasional conflicts that resulted when they pressured the locals into accepting lower-than-market prices.[16] Fang proposed to ban the access of Han merchants and to preserve the forests for imperial acquisitions only. He also suggested that direct contact between procurement officials and the Miao sellers should be severed and the procurement of imperial timber be conducted exclusively through the local Guizhou officials who were more familiar with the delicate situations in this frontier area. Fang's policies, if implemented, could have amounted to the enclosure of a broad area of imperial forests with the rights of access monopolized by the local government in Guizhou, potentially leading to a more interventionist form of state forestry in which officials dealt directly with the forest communities without merchant intermediaries.

However, Fang's proposals were never acted on.[17] In fact, Fang's segregation position was a minority view during his time. Instead, the emperor and a group of assimilationist Guizhou officials were contemplating the long-term feasibility of acculturating the Miao and assimilating them fully into the economic as well as cultural realm of China proper. The following decades saw Han settlers and merchants move steadily into the area. In 1747, Hunan governor Yang Xifu took several measures to rectify malpractices in the official purchases of imperial timber, including forced sales in the Miao areas. Yang did not go so far as Fang Xian's proposal of full segregation but emphasized fair trading and official supervision. Yang's original memorial and his regulations were erected as stelae in front of his office building in the provincial capital of Hunan. Now, two and a half centuries later, among the local manuscripts recently discovered in the Miao area, hundreds of miles from the provincial capital, we find handwritten copies of those stelae preserved by the local Miao dealers with exactly the same content as Yang's original memorial that is now preserved at the National Palace Museum in Taipei.[18] Apparently, the Miao timber sellers were well aware of these policies and ready to invoke them to protect their interests.

THE THREE-TOWN BROKERAGE SYSTEM

The Jinping timber market was located at three adjacent towns, hence I refer to it as the "three-town market" in this study.[19] During the Qing military campaign in the 1730s, these three towns were granted the exclusive right to take turns on a yearly basis to open timber brokerages and facilitate the transactions between Miao sellers from the mountains and Han buyers from afar.[20] The town in turn was said to be "under the duty of managing the river" (*dangjiang*) that year.[21] Local tales usually attribute the introduction of the rotating monopoly system to Zhang Guangsi, who was the governor of Guizhou at the time and an important figure in the pacification of the area. I have not found direct evidence, such as memorials by Zhang or stelae records from that era, that could support this claim. However, the notion that the rotating monopoly system was a precedent set by Zhang during the Yongzheng emperor's reign was mentioned repeatedly by the representatives of the three towns as well as local magistrates in adjudicating later court disputes over the right to "manage the river," which referred to the privilege to open timber brokerages.[22]

The three towns' exclusive right to open timber brokerages was a deviation from the empire-wide licensed brokerage system. By sticking to the "managing the river" nomenclature and avoiding self-reference as "licensed brokerages" (*yahang*), the Miao brokers of the three towns were permitted to operate freely as *legal unlicensed* brokerages and were never required to go through the normal procedure to obtain a license and pay annual fees to extend their legal status. Moreover, because timber was not a taxed commodity in this prefecture, the three-town brokerages did not bear the official responsibility of collecting commercial taxes from the trade as licensed brokerages often did.

The three-town monopoly was initially established for its practicality. In the years immediately after the military conquest, the area around the three towns was on the edge of any effective control that the state could exert in the newly incorporated Miao territory. In the eyes of many Qing officials, the Miao people of the three towns, who were bilingual in both the Chinese and the Miao languages, were ready mediators of trade. The newly incorporated territories further to the west should be kept as a prohibited region from the disturbances of the Han merchants so as to forestall ethnic conflicts. A placard issued by the Guizhou governor in 1801, for example, stated that the residents of the three towns were initially of the same origin as the "Black Miao" who brought timber from upriver mountains, and should continue working as brokerages to gain a better understanding of the customs of the "Black Miao."[23] In the following century and a half, concerns about ethnic tensions and social stability committed the state to the three-town monopoly system at this location despite recurrent challenges from downriver Han-Chinese towns and the fact that its status as a border region became increasingly dubious as the gradual acculturation of the local people rendered less relevant the initial rationale of mitigating cultural and linguistic barriers at this particular location.

Brokers, sellers, and buyers constituted to be the main actors in the three-town market. Timber brokers in the three towns, although without official licenses (for reasons detailed below), were no different from the licensed brokerages in the non-frontier provinces in terms of their actual business operations. The primary task of the brokers was to match sellers and buyers, which might take a long time when the purchase list of the buyer included a variety of products. They also provided lodging, assessed the quantity and quality of timber, helped arrange storage and transportation, negotiated the price, managed the account books for both sides, and sometimes extended short-term credit to sellers in need. In exchange for these services, they extracted a 4 to 5 percent commission fee from the transaction price.[24]

Timber sellers were often called "guests from the mountains" (*shanke*). Big sellers often started by trading the timber harvested from their own family holdings and then extended their businesses into upstream mountainous areas, sometimes with working capital obtained from the three-town timber brokerages.[25] By the early nineteenth century, some Miao families came to control extensive mountain lands. The stories of their rise to fortune invariably featured some kind of speculative investment at the right market timing.[26] These local powers formed alliances, intermarried, and occasionally engaged in disputes when their interests came into conflict.[27] The rise and fall of the great mountain-owning families became popular folk legends. For example, a popular tale was the story of how three big surnames sued one another into decline. Copies of legal documents from the 1830s, which seemed to be the factual basis of the dramatized oral tradition, revealed that the disputes first began as ordinary civil matters of alleged timber thefts and property infringements and finally escalated into mutual accusations of colluding with local rebellious groups—a most serious accusation indeed.[28] Regardless of the actual substance of such contentions, both the legal documents and the dramatized popular stories attest to the widespread familiarity with the imperial administrative apparatus among the Miao communities by the nineteenth century as well as active local agency in strategically deploying the judicial system toward various personal objectives.

Timber buyers in the three-town market were called "guests from the rivers" (*shuike*). These were itinerant Han merchants who usually formed loose associations based on their native-place origins. The most prominent merchant groups were referred to as the "three large groups and five assisting groups" (*sanbang wuxiang*). It is by no means surprising that the dominant "three large groups" in this Miao market were the same as the leading groups in the national market: the eastern merchant groups of Huizhou, Linqing, and Jiangxi. They pioneered the export of timber from this area for mass consumption in the early seventeenth century and sometimes worked concurrently as the delegates of the state to procure tribute timber for imperial uses. The "five assisting groups" were merchants from nearby prefectures in Hunan and Guizhou, who started as local agents or employees of the three large groups and later became independent timber traders.[29] Entering the nineteenth century, some merchants from the Middle Yangzi provinces also came to purchase timber in the three-town market. These were sometimes referred to as the "eighteen small groups."[30]

Sellers, buyers, and timber brokers of the three towns negotiated among themselves to set up boundaries of each group's market reach. A boundary tablet erected in 1797 was engraved with an agreement between the timber brokerages and the "three large groups," stating that beyond that point was the moorage area for the sellers to stock their timber, and the buyers should not trespass. Although it was framed as a clarification of the docking areas for sellers and buyers, this agreement was primarily a protection of the timber brokerages' business; the buyers could not bypass the brokers to purchase directly from the sellers, and the sellers could not float their rafts past the three towns to sell in the markets farther down the river.[31] The context of this agreement was the incessant challenge to the three towns' monopoly from nearby towns. In this long-lasting fight, upriver buyers and downriver sellers came to form alliances with one party or another in pursuit of their own interests.

"STRUGGLE FOR THE RIVER"

The fight over the right to "manage the river" became an enduring theme almost as soon as the institution was established. Benchu, a Han-dominated town just a few miles downriver (but under the jurisdiction of a different prefecture), was the most insistent competitor seeking to overthrow the monopoly of the three towns. The residents of Benchu repeatedly applied to the authorities for official licenses (*yatie*) to open brokerages. The conflict between Benchu and the three towns escalated into a series of violent conflicts and lawsuits from 1798 to 1806. The details were preserved in official memorials, private copies of legal documents from the court cases, and an account in the local gazetteer. The events also became the basis of a popular local ballad called the "The Tale of the Struggle for the River" (Zhengjiang ji).[32]

The first major conflict erupted in 1801. A leading merchant from Huizhou—one of the "three large groups" of buyers—requested to purchase land in the three towns to build a meeting hall for his native-place association. The request was rejected by the three towns' brokerages. Wu Shiren, a native of Benchu, took advantage of this rift and invited the buyers of the "three large groups" to trade in Benchu instead. Wu even talked some prominent buyers into accusing the three-town brokers with the charge of "manipulating the market, obstructing free trade, and impeding tax revenues" at a number of domestic customs stations along the Yangzi River that depended on taxing timber to fulfill their revenue quotas.[33] The case quickly drew high-profile attention from the central Boards of Revenue and Works, which held direct jurisdiction over these domestic customs, and from several provincial governors of the middle and lower Yangzi region. Inquiries from these administrations pressured the Guizhou governor to attend to the matter immediately.[34] Despite this, the three-town privilege was left intact at the conclusion of the investigation. The case did not turn out favorably for Wu Shiren either, since he ended up being exiled, not least because he violently blocked the water route through the three towns.

A few years later, in 1805 and 1806, a group of furious Benchu shopkeepers resorted to more extreme means. They blocked the water route again and even set five timber rafts on fire, causing a total stoppage of the market. Forty-some big rafts and hundreds of merchants were stuck.[35] Representatives of "three large groups and five assisting groups," as well as the leading Miao sellers, all sided with the three towns to condemn Benchu and submitted petitions to authorities.[36] Merchants of the "three large groups" delegated with the task of procuring imperial timber tribute claimed that tribute mission could be in jeopardy if their rafts continued to be blocked. Under such indignation, the rotating monopoly of the three towns was once again confirmed by the joint judgment of the provincial administrative and judicial commissioners of Guizhou.[37]

Despite their misconduct, Wu Shiren and other advocates of Benchu were correct that the state's preservation of the three towns' monopoly seemed to contradict the general principle of guaranteeing free market access when dealing with charges of market manipulation and illegal brokerage. According to the established licensed brokerage system, newly opened markets, such as the timber market around Jinping, should be issued a quota of brokerage licenses by the provincial government. Any individual—be it a resident of the three towns or Benchu—who met a set of criteria could apply to obtain a license by paying a certain amount of annual fee. Licensed brokers were in principle protected by law enforcement against illegal brokers who did not pay for the official license and thus operated at lower costs. Illegal brokers who charged commission fees for the trade they mediated were often accused of "privately exacting illegal taxation" (*sichou yashui*) when licensed brokers brought a suit against them in a court of law.[38]

Therefore, the accusation against the three towns, brought by Wu Shiren and others, that these timber brokerages did not have official brokerage licenses and were illegally collecting levies on commerce by forcing the sellers and the buyers to trade through them, was a legitimate and serious charge. After all, the request of Wu and his sympathizers was only for the application of the empire-wide licensed brokerage system in this relatively new market. For this reason, they soon won the attention and even support of market regulating agencies on all levels.[39]

Indeed, the accusation against the three towns was not without ground. The timber brokerages in the three towns were not incorporated into the regular licensed brokerage system until 1889. The three towns' privilege in opening timber brokerages was rooted in the favorable policies toward the Miao people issued by the first generation of frontier officials. As mentioned above, it was a deliberate official choice to refer to the three-town system by the "managing the river" nomenclature and to avoid any references as "licensed brokerages." The three-town brokers were permitted to operate legally as private brokerages and were never required to obtain a license. Because timber was not taxed at this location, the three-town brokerages did not act as tax intermediaries, a usual responsibility of licensed brokerages in other places. In refutation of the accusation of "illegal collection of commercial tax," the three towns emphasized that they were not performing the tax collecting functions of licensed brokerages at all, and their commission fees were not illegal levies on commerce but only compensation for the services that they provided at an amount agreed upon by all parties.[40]

The overriding consideration behind the officials' repeated rejection of Benchu's petition to normalize the Jinping market was the destabilizing political consequence of introducing competition from the Han community of Benchu into the timber brokerage business, a livelihood that had been promised exclusively to the Miao people of the three towns. The disputes between the three towns and Benchu happened in the middle of a Miao revolt from 1795 to 1806. Indeed, the Miao loss of economic resources to Han settlers was the chief cause of their revolt. The slogan of the rebels was to expel Han migrants and reclaim the land that they took from the Miao (often as collateral for unpaid loans). Advocates of Han migration and Miao assimilation learned the hard way that extensive acculturation of Miao individuals to the Chinese language and administrative norms did not necessarily carry with it a sense of loyalty to Qing rule.[41] Although the Miao litigants involved in the three-town/Benchu dispute were not part of the revolt, Guizhou officials nonetheless considered pacifying Miao resentment and protecting their economic interests as the first priority in preventing the unrest from spreading.

The following remarks by the provincial and prefectural officials of Guizhou are a representative example of the rhetoric regarding the situation:

> When guest merchants lodged in the three towns, it was customary to pay a 4 percent fee to cover the house rent, water labor, security, raft tying, and other miscellaneous services, so that the *impoverished Miao people* [qiong Miao] in the three towns could have a means of living. . . . The town of Benchu was a Han community under the jurisdiction of the Tianzhu County of Zhenyuan Prefecture, and little timber was produced there; it went without saying that Benchu had nothing to do with Maoping [one of the three towns] and other areas in the Miao frontier. How dare the rogues of Benchu constantly attempt to seize the profit?
>
> [The current arrangement] had been working for over a hundred years; the merchants and Miao people lived in peace with it. If we make even the slightest change, I fear not only that the Miao people in the three towns would lose their means of living, but that other Han towns down the river might also all follow the example of Benchu and set up brokerages and levy fees, then there would be no stop to lawsuits, and timber merchants would suffer endlessly. More importantly, *it might upset the stability of the Miao frontier.*[42]

Apparently, interethnic fissions and frontier instability were at the center of official concerns. The residents of the three towns used and expanded on this official rhetoric when portraying themselves in petitions. They appealed to officials that "we *impoverished Miao people* [qiong Miao] set up the brokerage business and depend on it for a living," and if Benchu's violent blockage of the river was not stopped, then "not only will we suffer, but all the Miao area along the river would be badly impacted as their timber could not find buyers. In a word, as long as those treacherous people are not eradicated, timber merchants will not come, and we poor Miao can have no reliance for life."[43] The upriver Miao sellers, in support of the petition of the three towns, lamented their own loss over so many cut trees that could not be sold. They referred to the competitors from Benchu as the "treacherous Han" (*Hanjian*), while emphasizing their common Miao identity with the three-town brokers, who "spoke the Miao language and understand the dialects of

Huizhou and Jiangxi" and "always gave fair prices and stuck to the proper silver standard."[44]

In fact, however, by the 1800s, cultural and language barriers were no longer as overwhelming as they had been in the 1730s. Acculturation was in process. As discussed above, Miao people in the upstream valleys had adopted Chinese-language contracts and increasingly turned to the local administration for dispute resolution. Many of the large land-owning families had produced degree holders by taking advantage of the favorable Miao quotas in the civil service examinations.[45] This is not to say that the Miao had become fully assimilated but that their emphasis on the common Miao customs and languages in their appeals to Qing officials reflected less about actual communicational difficulties with Han merchants than their strategic use of the state's ethnic policies to fend off Han competition.

BREAKDOWN OF THE THREE-TOWN MONOPOLY

While the three-town-monopoly stayed intact for the first half of the nineteenth century, by mid-century, the Qing state was forced to shift priorities under unprecedented foreign and domestic challenges. Amid several large-scale rebellions (including a major Miao revolt) that almost toppled the Qing and in the face of increasing pressure from Western powers, the Qing state had to improvise new ways to raise revenues to pay for its modernization reforms. The frontier distinctions of the Miao timber market were discarded as its timber came to be taxed just like in the metropole. As was happening in other parts of the empire, local militias were founded under the cosponsorship of the state and rural gentries, and the transit Lijin taxes on timber were collected at increasing numbers of tax stations established along the rivers to support military expenses.[46] Timber brokerages in the three towns were required to increase their commission fees, and the increased revenue was claimed by the prefectural government to pay for its policing expenses.

The final breakdown of the rotating monopoly of the three towns only came in 1889, when Guizhou province, under pressure to generate more tax revenues, eventually issued brokerage licenses to Benchu and two adjacent towns, which were thereafter referred to as the "outer three towns" (*wai sanjiang*). After some back and forth, the old three towns of Jinping finally responded by applying for the official licenses as well and came to be called the "inner three towns" (*nei sanjiang*).[47] The initial permission to open brokerages was obtained by a couple of big surnames in each town, which became an inheritable right that was passed on to their offspring.[48] Yet the official brokerages of the inner and outer towns did not immediately enter into free market competition; rather, they divided up the customer base. The right to purchase timber through the brokerages of the inner three towns, which had firsthand access to better timber supply, became a privilege of the "three large groups and five assisting groups," while other merchant groups had to trade through the outer three towns. This last attempt by the inner three towns and the traditionally dominant merchant groups to hold onto any tenuous exclusivity was short-lived in the face of new players; by the end of the nineteenth century, compradors of Japanese companies came to eclipse the power of the "three large groups and five assisting groups." Equipped with much more capital, they purchased more than 80 percent of the timber produced in the Yuan River basin.[49] Indeed, the penetration of foreign capital into the timber trade was prevalent by this point throughout the nation. The nominal division of the inner and outer three towns was eventually abandoned in 1916, by which time "the three large groups and five assisting groups" existed in name only.[50] The business of brokering timber trade was no longer an exclusive privilege but a prevalent local livelihood. In the 1910s, the total number of timber brokerages in these three towns reached more than eighty among a population of around three thousand households.[51]

CONCLUSION

The evolution of timber-market management in this frontier area reflected the shifts in the Qing state's priorities. The eighteenth-century state was willing (and could afford) to tailor economic policies to its frontier concerns. In regular timber markets, the Qing state usually upheld the principle of equal and fair market entrance—although the application of the principle to specific cases could be subject to the interpretation of individual magistrates. Brokerage licensing fees, though not onerous, were not negotiable. In the Miao frontier, by contrast, not only were license fees waived, concerns about ethnic tensions and social stability committed the state to a monopoly system at the perceived Han-Miao border even after the initial concern about cultural and linguistic barriers to trade withered away. The examination on the timber trade in this region reveals a more multifaceted picture of the Miao frontier than the simplistic understanding that economically unsophisticated natives were deprived of their land and other resources by encroaching outsiders. Episodes of fighting over the rights to open timber brokerages demonstrate that the state's ethnic policies and administrative priorities were all strategically utilized by the involved economic agents, including the Miao locals, to achieve their respective interests.

While the eighteenth- and early-nineteenth-century state was concerned mostly with the pacification of frontier society, from the mid-nineteenth century onward, successive national challenges forced the late Qing state to extract whatever revenue that could be generated from local commerce. In both the metropole and the frontier, previous priorities broke down under new pressures. In this context, ensuring a livelihood for a minority popula-tion against Han competition came second to the urgency of paying for the modernization of the military and strategic industries. Not only was it no longer tenable to mark off an exclusive niche in the frontier market for the Miao, but the entire trading system along the Yangzi River (and for that matter, China's domestic market in general) became increasingly porous to foreign players. The three Miao towns lost their monopoly, and the tradition-ally powerful merchant groups lost their market dominance to newly rising parties that were backed by more abundant foreign capital. Notwithstanding such ruptures, these changes in the late nineteenth and early twentieth century could be viewed in a broader light as continuities of earlier trends to make frontier forests more legible, accessible, and responsive to market forces that were driven by demands from elsewhere and less entangled with the local particularities of indigenous rule, identity, and livelihood. In this regard, the transformations in the Miao frontier can be compared with similar pro-cesses in the camphor forests of colonial Taiwan and the Dutch East Indies, as delineated in chapter 7. This was the end of the frontier exception. The transformation of the three-town market at the turn of the twentieth century was a microcosm of the changes in the national timber market, where foreign capital and foreign timber came to the center of the stage.

NOTES

1   For details of this estimation, see Zhang, *Timber and Forestry in Qing China*, chapter 2.

2   For the ingenious *longquan ma* system of timber measurement and pricing, see Zhang, *Timber and Forestry in Qing China*, 72–79; Lu Yin, "Wo ye laitan Longquan ma"; Tang Bingnan, "Hankou ce mucai zhi fa."

3   These measures included quinquennial audit of licensed brokerages, prohibition of monopolization and illicit charges, centralization of the authority to issue brokerage licenses, and fixation of the number of brokerage licenses in long-established markets. For details of these reforms and how they affected the timber trade, see Zhang, *Timber and Forestry in Qing China*, chapter 4.

4   For how the Qing state used ethnography to pursue its imperial ambitions, see Hostetler, *Qing Colonial Enterprise*.

5   There is a vibrant literature on the late imperial incorporation of southwestern borderlands and the local histories of choices and resistance. For some exemplary studies, see Herman, *Amid the Clouds and Mist*; Giersch, *Asian Borderlands*; Atwill, *The Chinese Sultanate*; Shin, *The Making of the Chinese State*.

6   For the spread of knowledge about travel routes and local conditions through commercial publishing during the Ming-Qing period, see Chen Xuewen, *Ming Qing shiqi shangye shu*.

7   See Diamond, "Defining the Miao"; Deal and Hostetler, *The Art of Ethnography*; Hostetler, *Qing Colonial Enterprise*. In this study, I use the term *Miao* in accordance with its Qing usage, which referred to broader groups than its contemporary meaning of one of the fifty-six officially recognized "nationalities" (*minzu*). For example, today's Dong nationality was grouped under the Miao during the Qing.

8   Liang Cong, *Qingshui Jiang xiayou cunzhai shehui*, 212–17; Zhang Yingqiang, *Mucai zhi liudong*, 28–35.

9   This estimation is based on the revenue data from Chen Guan, the customs station at Chenzhou in western Hunan. For details of the data and my estimation methods, see Zhang, *Timber and Forestry in Qing China*, 68–72.

10 For a systematic study of the Qing tribute timber system, see Zhang, *Timber and Forestry in Qing China*, chapter 1.

11 For the development of commercial tree cultivation in the Miao frontier, see Zhang, "Financing Market-Oriented Reforestation"; Zhang Yingqiang, *Mucai zhi liudong*. For earlier developments of such practices in eastern provinces, see McDermott, *The Making of a New Rural Order in South China*; Miller, *Fir and Empire*.

12 *Qianlong Qingjiang zhi*, 1:79.

13 *Qiannan shilue*, 9: 9b–10a.

14 *Qiannan shilue*, 13: 11b.

15 See Zhang, *Timber and Forestry in Qing China*, chapter 3.

16 GZD, 000840.

17 *Qingdai Gongzhong dang zouzhe ji Junji Chu dang zhejian ziliao ku* (hereafter GZD), 402002884.

18 *Jinping xianzhi*, 1538–41.

19 The three towns are Maoping, Wangzhai, and Guazhi in Jinping County, today part of the Qiandongnan Miao and Dong Autonomous Prefecture.

20 *Dongzu shehui lishi diaocha*, 36; Wu Zhenyu, *Qian yu, juan xia*, "Liping mu."

21 *Guangxu Liping fu zhi*, 3a: 32b; Liang Cong, *Qingshui Jiang xiayou cunzhai shehui*, 216–17.

22 See, for example, a petition sent by representatives of Wangzhai in 1817 in *Jinping xianzhi*, 1536–37.

23 *Jinping xianzhi*, 1523–24.

24 *Dongzu shehui lishi diaocha*, 32.

25 *Dongzu shehui lishi diaocha*, 28–29. For stories of the rise and fall of the Yaos in local oral tradition of the Miao, see Cheng Zeshi, *Qingshui Jiang wenshu zhi fayi chutan*, 159–66. For the brokerages' practice of extending trade credit to sellers in the Qingshui valley, see Cheng Zeshi, *Qingshui Jiang wenshu zhi fayi chutan*, 174. The practice was widespread in timber markets elsewhere, for example, see Chen Ruizhi, "Hangzhou mucai ye de neimu," 111–12.

26 *Dongzu shehui lishi diaocha*, 29–30.

27 Intermarriages between the Yaos and the Jiangs were evident from the Yaos' genealogy compiled during the Daoguang era (1821–1850); see Cheng Zeshi, *Qingshui Jiang wenshu zhi fayi chutan*, 171.

28 For a detailed analysis of the folklore and the legal documents on several related lawsuits, see Cheng Zeshi, *Qingshui Jiang wenshu zhi fayi chutan*, 166–73.

29 There are different opinions on the exact places of origin of the five *xiang*. A legal document from 1827 identified the five *xiang* as merchants from Changde, Deshan, Hefo, Hongjiang, and Tuokou of Hunan Province, all of which were timber markets along the Yuan River. Another opinion views the five *xiang* as from several districts of the Tianzhu County, which was adjacent to Jinping. See *Jinping xianzhi*, 1537; *Dongzu shehui lishi diaocha*, 30; Zhang Yingqiang, "Cong Guazhi 'Yishi Yongzun' shike."

30 Zhang Yingqiang, "Cong Guazhi 'Yishi Yongzun' shike."

31 For the full text and a detailed analysis, see Zhang Yingqiang, "Cong Guazhi 'Yishi Yongzun' shike."

32 "The Tale of the Struggle for the River" is recorded in *Dongzu shehui lishi diaocha*, 36–37.

33 They especially appealed to the Longjiang Customs Station in Nanjing. For more details on the customs duties on timber, see Zhang, *Timber and Forestry in Qing China*, chapter 2.

34 See the judgment of the Guizhou governor in 1801, the joint report of the prefects of Guiyang, Anshun, and Liping in 1806, and the joint announcement of the Guizhou administrative commissioner and commissioner of justice in 1806 in *Dongzu shehui lishi diaocha*, 38–39, 42–43. See also *Guangxu Liping fu zhi*, 3a: 33a.

35 The details of this outbreak and the causes that led to it are summarized in a memorial of Guizhou governor Fuqing on Jiaqing 12 (1807).7.28, the First Historical Archives of China, 04–01–08–0119–004.

36 For the full text of these petitions, see *Dongzu shehui lishi diaocha*, 39–42.

37 For the full text of the judgment, see *Dongzu shehui lishi diaocha*, 42–43.

38 For example, the stele records in Suzhou show that the local officials have always upheld this principle. For judgment on disputes over the "market

manipulation" of some timber brokerages, see *Ming Qing Suzhou gongshang ye beike ji*, no. 74 and 76.

39 *Dongzu shehui lishi diaocha*, 39.

40 *Guangxu Liping fu zhi, juan* 3a, 32a, and 35.

41 Sutton, "Ethnicity and the Miao Frontier."

42 *Dongzu shehui lishi diaocha*, 38–39, 42–43. Emphasis added.

43 *Dongzu shehui lishi diaocha*, 39–40.

44 *Dongzu shehui lishi diaocha*, 41–42.

45 *Jinping xianzhi*, 1511–13, 1517.

46 Zhang Yingqiang, *Mucai zhi liudong*, 85–90.

47 *Guangxu Liping fu zhi*, 3a: 34–37.

48 Jiang Dexue, *Guizhou jindai jingji shi ziliao xuanji*, 339. [In the bibliography, it should be "Jiang Dexue" with no comma.] [Changed]

49 These compradors were mostly from Hubei and had close associations with native banks based in Hankou. *Dongzu shehui lishi diaocha*, 31–32.

50 *Dongzu shehui lishi diaocha*, 44–45.

51 There were eighty-four timber brokerages in 1909, among which thirty-three in Wangzhai, thirty in Maoping, and twenty-one in Guazhi; see *Jinping xianzhi*, 521. Population information is from the 1914 survey; see *Dongzu shehui lishi diaocha*, 2.

CHAPTER SIX

SPLINTERED HABITATS

*The Fragmentation of Ecotone Northern China's
Imperial Woodland Complexes*

DAVID A. BELLO

C HINA'S ecotone woodlands contained spaces integral to some of the most important ritual sites—hunting preserves and royal tombs—of China's last dynasty, the Qing (1644–1912). Timber resources were certainly at issue, but possession of dead wood was not the only split between ruling elites and their subjects. Keeping woodlands alive as habitats was also a critical point of contention for the dynasty's Manchu rulers.

An emerging literature on the economic exploitation of China's woodlands persuasively demonstrates the human historical contingency that marks these ecosystems.[1] In productive contrast, however, more environmentally oriented approaches offer an under-acknowledged collateral branch "lineage of forest knowledge" that emphasizes human dependency on nature rather than human exploitation of it. There is no question that the human impact on woodlands in China has been—and continues to be—immense, but influences have been mutual, as woodlands have deeply conditioned people, especially in preindustrial periods.

In all time periods, ecological processes have been the prerequisite for human sustenance. Economics has systematically recognized this vital support only recently as "ecosystem services." When simply conceived of as "the multiple benefits provided by ecosystems to humans," the concept appears as "an inherently anthropocentric construct" in so far as its services are evaluated purely in their utility to humans.[2] This construct is only strengthened by the common impression that ecosystem services—when acknowledged—are free. However, the alarming slowdown of photosynthesis caused by sunshine-blocking industrial smog in northern Hebei province exemplifies the costs hidden within ostensibly free ecosystem services like sunlight and air exploited for primary needs like cultivation.[3]

Ecosystem services do not just deliver what specialists term provisioning services (like food or fresh water), regulating services (like climate cycles), and supporting services (like soil formation). They may also provide cultural services that can be recreational, aesthetic, or spiritual.[4] Like many ecosystems, woodlands include all four, but it is usually not possible to maximize these services simultaneously. Historically, humans have generally chosen to enhance food production as much as possible at the expense of all other considerations, and this is certainly true of the imperial Chinese state.

By the Qing, provisioning services throughout much of northern China were under serious pressure from both human activities and ecological conditions. The part of the region that falls within what has been called China's "farming-pastoral ecotone" constitutes a transitional gradient through different types of forest and grassland vegetation, with accompanying emergent variants in climate, soil quality, overall biodiversity and—most critically—precipitation.[5] Consequently, the northern China ecotone, including parts of southern and eastern Inner Mongolia and western and northern Manchuria, is agriculturally fragile in comparison with wetter climates to the south of it.

This fragility is largely a product of precipitation instability. The region's average annual rainfall is currently about 350–400 mm, reaching as high as 500 mm to 600 mm in peak years and dropping to lows of 100 mm to 250 mm in drought years.[6] These conditions fluctuate along the edges of minimal water requirements for the ecotone's traditional crops, including sorghum, barley and millet, which optimally need about 450–650 mm per year. They were nevertheless grown as staples where the average annual rainfall in present-day Hebei province (called Zhili during the Qing) is 300–450 mm. Some studies have found the northern China ecotone even drier during the northern hemisphere's last major cooling interval—known as the Little Ice Age (ca. 1400–ca. 1900)—that covered nearly the whole Qing period. This suggests that the ecotone overall experienced lower than average precipitation during the Qing and was about 1°C colder than at present.[7] When examined on a centennial scale, however, the ecotone was probably significantly warmer and wetter during the eighteenth century than in either the seventeen or nineteenth centuries, which allowed for agricultural expansion in some locales.

Historical climatology has yet to reach consensus on China's Little Ice Age regional conditions, which, nevertheless, are among the world's best documented through tens of thousands of entries for the eighteenth century alone. Recent studies based on these records, however, generally confirm a cooler, drier region than had existed during the preceding Medieval Warm Period (ca. 1000–ca. 1300), with correspondingly fragile conditions for agriculture.[8]

This climate, especially in terms of precipitation, could affect ecotone forests. One recent extended study found that sparse ecotone rainfall inhibited the growth structure of one key regional tree, the Japanese white birch: "Precipitation is no longer suitable for large-scale forest growth. The forests all appear on the shady slopes of low mountains and tall sand dunes. Under substantial external environmental disturbance, the patches become smaller and the height of birch trees decreases." Another study observed that a lack of water is the main inhibitor of forest growth in steppe areas of the southeastern part of the ecotone.[9]

This certainly does not mean that only stunted forests existed in northern China's forest-steppe ecotone. Along the ecotone's eastern and southern fringes, steppe steadily transitioned into large tracts of various birch, pine, linden, larch, maple, and oak species. Nevertheless, habitats for both plants and animals were patchy and easily disrupted. This is in contrast to southern China climes, which enjoyed more favorable conditions. Precipitation up to triple that of northern China created more congenial habitats for commercial silviculture of fast-growth species like the China fir.

The relationship people cultivated with trees in northern China was, consequently, different from that nurtured in southern China. There were, of course, quite fundamental similarities in the use of wood for fuel and building materials, but other forms of economic and cultural interaction were distinct. Some aspects of these relations, like those between China fir and south China silviculturalists, were formed from relatively stark ecological differences. Others arose from more complex interplays of nature and culture.

Like its dynastic predecessors, the Qing maintained important ritual spaces where provisioning services were restricted or entirely prohibited. The dynasty's founders were not ethnic Chinese (Han) but Manchurian forest peoples most accustomed to a combination of herding, foraging, and agriculture. The main imperial hunting ground of Mu-lan (Ma: Muran) was accordingly maintained in large measure as an enormous preserve for the managed pursuit of game for ritual or military training purposes.

More traditional imperial Chinese cultural services were delivered by the dynasty's two main royal interment sites (Qing Dongling and Qing Xiling). These woodland ecosystems not only provided habitat for the foraging of flora and fauna in Mu-lan but were also held to concentrate cosmic energy (qi) vital for the ancestral maintenance of dynastic generational continuity. Trees could certainly be culled, especially in Mu-lan, whose vast tracts of woods supplied major state projects, mainly tomb and temple construction. Yet even these extractions, which perhaps did contribute to the reserve's nineteenth-century decline, were intended mainly for the preservation of Inner Asian traditions.

Pressure for provisioning from these cultural woodlands, especially in the form of trespassing Han farmers and lumberjacks, rose steadily to unsustainable levels by the nineteenth century. As the following sections on the hunting grounds and tombs will show, however, Inner Asian elites and their Han subjects were often in conflict more over the degree of woodland exploitation than whether or not any exploitation should occur. This difference was nevertheless environmentally explicit; the elite ideal of limited consumption was pursued—however imperfectly—for the preservation of Inner Asian cultural identity. Han pursuits were motivated by more material subsistence concerns. As Qing subjects eking out a living on the farming-pastoral ecotone, Han people's legacy generally appears as a provisional appreciation of woodlands. Conflict over woodland ecosystem services often appears as a diametrical opposition between one group living out its regional woodland heritage and another simply trying to survive in the region's woodlands. This conflict occurred within the context of a long-term trend of deforestation, which had become acute throughout north China proper.

Mu-lan and the dynastic tombs—as imperial woodland complexes originally assembled for elite cultural purposes—came under increasing subsistence pressure from subjects hungry for farmland and fuel around the Zhili ecotone. Although trees appear to lie at the root of these contradictions, woodlands were never just sites of timber conflicts. Instead, they were habitats networked through climate and soil conditions that sustained wildlife and particular ways of human life. These networks could not be reduced to lumber, nor could they be casually severed by administrative fiat or crude plunder without unraveling their many environmental interdependencies that sustained conditioned forms of nature and culture—whatever human assumptions may have been.

A WOODLAND ECOSYSTEM UNDER ENVIRONMENTAL PRESSURE

Something of the complexity that informed environmental relations in the Zhili ecotone during this period may be conveyed by a 1751 report in Manchu from Zhangjiakou, located just south of the Great Wall about 194 km northwest of Beijing on the southern edge of the empire's steppe borderland. Zhangjiakou was "under pressure, fuel difficult to obtain, coal for purchase scarce." Resident dynastic subjects, mainly Han peasants, had to depend for fuel "on grass and wood cut, taken and purchased" in herding areas of the dynasty's pastoral Mongol subjects north of the Great Wall. For several years, residents had had "to go gradually farther out to cut fuel from the wooded and grassy mountains, which made it very expensive and caused "great distress . . . for Han commoner households."[10]

Fortuitously, a coal deposit was discovered close to Zhangjiakou just over the Great Wall, and there was a proposal that the coal be shared between Han and Mongol locals. However, borderland interethnic dynamics, a product of the Qing empire's unification of Inner Asia and China proper, complicated the proposed solution of opening coal pits on the northern, mainly pastoral side of the Great Wall to supply the more urban-agrarian south. The report argued that "the Mongol way of life is to gather dung and cut grass and wood for burning and does not rely on coal." Its author feared that if mines were opened, Mongols "who had never been able to dig" coal would "have to recruit Han commoners to dig for them." This would require a competitive, quarrelsome cohabitation that would "greatly harm the locality."[11] The coal was therefore left in its pastoral ground.

In this case, the Qing central authorities thought their pastoral Mongol subjects ignorant of coal and solely dependent on dung, grass, and wood for fuel. This made disruptive interaction with Han Chinese, who alone were considered experienced in working coal, inevitable. Resource extraction under multiethnic borderland conditions was certainly difficult to manage once initiated. In 1735, Inner Mongolian forests in the Muna range were being stripped of tens of thousands of trees by around ten thousand Han trespassers. By the 1880s, Jilin, the Manchurian homeland of the Qing rulers and therefore off limits to Han, was itself losing pines in comparable quantities as poachers cut into its foraging preserves.[12]

As the problems controlling and apportioning woodland across Inner Mongolia and Manchuria reveal, the Qing faced a set of pressures that were both cultural and ecological (i.e., environmental). The empire's environmental diversity complicated dynastic management of ecosystems like woodlands, whose scarcity could push people beyond the confines of their local cultures and ecologies into more conflicted spaces.[13] The problem, from a Manchu-Mongol perspective, was that agrarian Han were more dependent on trees as fuel than were pastoral Inner Asians, who could rely on livestock manure. Moreover, dung and even grass—if not coal—were more readily renewable resources than wood.

Northern China's woodlands had gone into general decline before the Qing, which helps to explain the motivations of Zhangjiakou's Han population. Official and private attempts to encourage silviculture, and even reforestation, were occasionally made. Huang Liuhong (1633–ca. 1710), as a district magistrate in both Shandong and Zhili, offered a variety of financial incentives, penalties, and exhortations for cultivation of elm, willow ash, and pine "to provide shade in summertime and fuel in winter."[14] Han farmers, according to a late Ming source, however, offered a dismaying list of silviculture disincentives: saplings were expensive and scarce; guards were required to stop poachers and grazers; trees were vulnerable to arbitrary state confiscation. Trees also used up scarce water reserves.[15]

The Qing record suggests a limited implementation of state reforestation, which appears only sporadically, mainly restricted to a single spate over about twenty years from the mid-1730s. Even at this time, it is likely that no large-scale reforestation was ever carried out, despite forty-nine provincial proposals and claims of saplings planted in the millions. Instructively, after this spasm, most memorials to the throne advocating regional reforestation were largely restricted to imperial hunting grounds and imperial tombs.[16]

Likely the most regular form of state promotion of green space outside these elite ritual zones was realized in periodic attempts to enforce regulations governing the exploitation of reeds and plantation of willows to maintain water conservancy infrastructure. Reeds were harvested wild from state wetlands, primarily for construction materials. In contrast, willow stands were supposed to be regularly planted to reinforce dikes and, as such, may have constituted the most common and extensive implementation of state silviculture. As one 1801 memorial makes clear, however, willow cultivation required proper oversight best delivered by troops assigned to river conservancies rather than through reliance on comparatively amateur, ephemeral, and sometimes corrupt local civilian initiatives. Such operations could involve tens of thousands of saplings and strictly prohibited illicit agrarian conversion of ground cover in flood control terrain.[17] However, along the ecotone itself, which lacked major waterways and hydrological infrastructure, even small-scale operations were probably fairly uncommon.

Northern China woodland conditions seem to have further declined into the nineteenth century. One Western observer recorded in the 1870s that "from Hankou to Beijing, all mountains and hills are destitute of trees and shrubs. . . . If it were not for the [water storing capacity of the soil formation called] loess, Northern China would be a desert."[18] This surely overstates the situation, but it does echo general impressions of both contemporaries and historians of a nineteenth-century transition from scarcity to crisis. In some north and northwestern China areas, conditions can be roughly measured by decline of biodiversity and habit. Southern Shaanxi, for example, experienced a drop in tiger attacks after the Jiaqing reign (1796–1820). In other places, however, the record is ambiguous. In 1741, a Suiyuan garrison successfully requested an allocation of twenty muskets to protect livestock that were "being constantly ravaged by tigers." This might indicate that tigers in this comparatively urbanized area of the Inner Mongolian ecotone were being pushed into pastures by habitat contraction. There are other signs, however, that game remained plentiful north of the Great Wall but almost nonexistent south of it; one 1749 report asserted that China proper garrisons could carry out hunting exercises only in neighboring Inner Mongolia.[19] Such distinctions indicate gradients within the ecotone itself, arising from more intensive agriculture south of the wall and largely, and less disturbing, pastoral practices to its north.

Trans-ecotone habitat contraction became more explicit by the early decades of the nineteenth century, likely accelerated by a change in temperature. The annual imperial hunt at the Mu-lan preserve, for example, was terminated in 1820 after years of futile attempts to arrest game declines. One groundbreaking study has found significant correlation between Little Ice Age climate fluctuations and the rise and decline of Mu-lan. It argues that a comparatively warmer eighteenth century promoted the agrarian expansion that emerged in some ecotone locales. Development was subsequently undermined by a colder nineteenth century, which actually began circa 1788. Less hospitable climate created the sort of resource shortages that drove preserve poaching that became so pronounced at this time. Although not the only driver of Mu-lan change, climate clearly interacted synergistically with other social and natural conditions.[20] Thus, the ecotone, certainly exceptional in many ecological and cultural terms, was not a pristine zone hermetically sealed from the environmental historical processes that connected China proper to Inner Asia.

THE MU-LAN HUNTING GROUNDS: CLASSICAL AND COMPARATIVE CONTEXTS

The Qing did not begin the tradition of imperial Chinese hunting rituals, which stretch back into antiquity. Some of the earliest records already show that these rituals, which excluded most people from large woodland areas full of much-needed natural resources, caused tensions between rulers who used these woodland ecosystem services for mainly cultural purposes and their subjects who used them for largely provisional purposes. One of the most famous exchanges on these tensions occurred between the Confucian philosopher Mencius and King Xuan of Qi:

> King Xuan of Qi asked, "It is said that King Wen's royal park was seventy *li* square. Is that so?"
> Mencius replied, "It is reported so in the histories."
> "As big as that!"
> "Even so, the people found it small."
> "My park is only forty *li* square, and yet the people consider it too big. Why is this?"
> Mencius said, "True. King Wen's park was seventy *li* square, but it was open to woodcutters as well as catchers of pheasants and hares. As he shared it with the people, is it any wonder they found it small? When I first came to the borders of your state. . . . I was told that there was a park forty *li* square on the outskirts of the capital, where the killing of a deer was treated as an offence comparable to killing a man. This turns the park into a trap forty *li* square in the midst of the state. Is it any wonder that the people consider it too big?"[21]

This is a classical summary dialogue of imperial China's social conflict over woodland ecosystem services, which is more concerned with what sort of human access will be permitted than with how the ecosystem itself can be preserved. This priority seems to have driven the sort of destabilizing extractions of trees inflicted by Qing authorities themselves in Mu-lan during the second half of the eighteenth century, as discussed in more detail in the next section.

Fragmentary records of dynastic parks into the Tang period (618–907) tend to emphasize their primary cultural service role as suppliers of sacrificial meats for ancestral temples and as grounds for ceremonies that included such sacrifices. The Supreme Forest parks of both the Qin (221–206 BCE) and the Han (202 BCE–220 CE) contained large tracts of forests and fields filled with animals and vegetation of various sorts. They also contained built structures and retained a large staff of foresters acting as both procurers and guards. The example of these parks, as well as their classical predecessor, King Wen's royal park (the Numinous Enclosure, or Lingyou), resonated down the centuries, reaching the works of no less a Qing author than the Qianlong emperor (r. 1736–96), who considered his own chief preserve of Mu-lan as commensurate with them.[22]

With the onset of Inner Asian conquest dynasties, hunting spaces and cultures reached unprecedented development for practical—even existential—purposes. The emperor Liao Taizong (r. 927–47), second ruler of the Inner Asian conquest dynasty, the Liao (907–1125), spoke for Inner Asian elites in general when he stated that "our hunting is not merely the pursuit of enjoyment, but a means of practicing warfare!"[23] The Mongol Yuan engaged in the chase on a much greater scale than its predecessors. The empire's summer capital in Mongolia, Shangdu, "was, by all accounts, used mainly as a game reserve and hunting park by the imperial family once the imperial city of Dadu/Khanbaligh (Beijing) had been completed." However, preserves were also maintained in the vicinity of Beijing and elsewhere.[24] The Yuan's Inner Asian successors, the Manchu Qing, certainly inherited these traditions but had a much more extended opportunity to put them into unprecedented practice on a much more systematic level, with much more ethnically complicated results.

THE HUNT FOR INNER ASIAN IDENTITY AT MU-LAN

Mu-lan, as part of the imperial summer capital complex of Chengde, or the Mountain Retreat to Escape the Heat (Bishu Shanzhuang) in Rehe beyond the Great Wall, was the most important Qing hunting ground. For 140 years, from 1681 to 1821, the Mu-lan forest-steppe ecosystem delivered a range of services, but its main function was cultural.[25] Trees were integral to the design of the complex. Many of the retreat's built spaces were landscaped around a featured tree species. Chinese pines, however, probably predominated before and after construction and "may be considered the backbone" species of the complex. As such, pines may have comprised about 50 percent of parkland and garden coverage, with thousands being transplanted during the retreat's existence.[26]

In 1782, the Qianlong emperor explained at length the intent of the Qing royal house's establishment of the complex during the reign of his grandfather, the Kangxi emperor (r. 1654–1722). His explanation reveals not only the import of the multigenerational cultural ecosystem services Mu-lan provided but also the dependency of those services on forest-steppe ecological diversity:

> My Imperial Grandfather built the Mountain Retreat as a means
> of commemorating feats of arms and of pacifying the frontier
> peoples . . . My Imperial Father [the Yongzheng emperor

(r.1722–35)] ... personally advised that ... "my male descendants should follow the example of my Imperial Grandfather and conduct military training at Mu-lan, so as not to forget our family precepts" ... Since the Han and Tang, what dynasty has gone without imperial lodges and country parks? Suchlike was no more than a waste of the people's wealth and self-indulgence. In extreme cases, these led to the fall of the dynasty; an unworthy example to be on guard against.

The Mountain Retreat of today is situated outside the [Great Wall] passes, where it is actually intended to give weight to the practice of war, not to the veneration of literati culture ... The high mountains and steep cliffs, the state of water and forest, the roaming of stork and deer, the enjoyment of hawk and fish; when to these are added the buildings for reflection on the precipices and pavilions beside the brooks and the fragrant grasses and ancient trees, things have a natural attraction that makes one forget worldly cares.

Compared to the imperial lodges and country parks of the Han and Tang, the Mountain Retreat is surpassing in every respect. Yet, to become besotted with such a place, forgetting all else, would be for me to have reprehensibly contrived a snare from what I have done with ... the Mountain Retreat.[27]

In the view of these Qing emperors, the primary service delivered by the Chengde complex in general, and Mu-lan in particular, is a proper Inner Asian milieu for military training of elite mounted troops. The Qianlong emperor's main concern regarding the legitimation and sustainability of these services reveals a distinction between Han and Inner Asian traditions in terms of the propriety of cultural services on offer in imperial hunting parks. As construed here by the emperor, Han imperial culture's more recreational use of forest-steppe areas was illegitimate to the point of dynastic collapse. Purely recreational services would demilitarize—and implicitly Sinify—Inner Asian environmental relationships constructed out of hunting, or as I have elsewhere termed this process of environmental identity formation beyond mere subsistence, "venery."[28]

Earlier in his reign, the emperor had confronted this issue at least once. In 1741, one of his Han Chinese censors, Cong Dong (1687–?) memorialized that he "feared the [emperor's] retinue considers hunting amusement. Capital officials, being so very distant from the emperor's presence, steadily fall into idle complacency. . . . Battue hunting [should] be temporarily suspended." The emperor's decree in response offered an Inner Asian lesson for the edification of an official who occupied one of the most distinctively Han jobs—including a remit to admonish the emperor—in the imperial bureaucracy. The emperor lectured that in antiquity, various seasonal hunts in spring, summer, fall, and winter were all conducted with military matters in mind: "Our dynasty's military preparedness far exceeds that of previous dynasties. . . . If the hunt is abandoned in peacetime and ignored, then Manchu troops will become practiced in leisured, playful ease, and steadily lose their skill at mounted archery."[29]

The Chengde complex was also the site of elaborate diplomatic and other ritualized cultural activities not necessarily connected to hunting and Manchu military identity. However, the high Qing emperors of the Kangxi, Yongzheng, and Qianlong reigns all stressed that the complex's primary role was to use its forest-steppe resources for the reproduction of this identity as part of the core of their dynastic enterprise. As subsequent events demonstrated, Mu-lan could not fulfill this role without woodlands, because they formed the basic habitat for the wild animals Manchus needed to chase in order to become full-fledged Inner Asian soldiers.

State problems with the maintenance of the Mu-lan habitat are quite visible with the onset of the nineteenth century, but it is possible to discern much earlier deforestation pressures on its forest-steppe ecosystem. In a gloss of his 1749 poem, "Passing through the Ongni'ud [Mongol] Tribes," the Qianlong emperor noted that his neighboring Mongol vassals dispatched patrols to stop "those who enter the hunting enclosures to cut down trees and poach beasts."[30]

Such incursions, which probably did not extract more than a few thousand trunks, seem relatively minor compared to the massive legal state timbering operations in Mu-lan hunting enclosures for large-scale construction projects. In 1767, for example, 34,279 trunks were cut from twenty-two hunting enclosures. A year later, 120,615 trees were cut down in four enclosures. In 1771, a further 75,285 trees were cut from several enclosures. Figures from subsequent years into the 1780s were commensurate in scale.[31] One 1771 report concerning the final construction stages of Chengde's iconic Potala Temple (Putuozongcheng Miao) can represent the requirements of a large individual construction project, which in this case required the transport of over fourteen thousand trunks that would have to be hauled by 450 carts.[32] For comparison, one 1812 timber poaching case involving eight men particularly upset the Jiaqing emperor (r. 1796–1820) because they had brazenly employed twenty-three carts to haul out their illicit wood.[33] If a comparable load capacity is assumed, the poachers would have been transporting about seven hundred trunks. This is not to dismiss poaching, which leaves behind few statistics, as entirely irrelevant to Mu-lan deforestation. However, official extraction, both licit and otherwise, seems to have had far greater resources at its disposal and more extended opportunities to fell trees at greater orders of magnitude.

The immediate effects of these large-scale extractions of trees, many of which appear to be pine or maple species, is hard to judge. It is, however, probably no coincidence that the succeeding Jiaqing reign saw serious declines in wildlife that officials attributed to both poaching and diminished forest cover. Within the first decade of the nineteenth century, the emperor was complaining almost annually about hunting conditions in Mu-lan, which he generally linked to reduced forest cover. In 1802, for example, he recalled that when he had hunted previously, a record was made" each time and "the number of wild beasts encircled was quite numerous." Although there had been no imperial hunt for a decade, when the emperor "went to call for deer this time, there were very few. This appears to be the result of an everyday practice of just letting intruders poach wild beasts and cut down trees."[34] Another case from 1804 affords a more extended evaluation by the emperor and, so, merits closer examination.

A memorial by Khalkha prince consort Lhawang Dorji (1754–1816), who had already been sent on a number of inspections of hunting ground enclosures in Mu-lan, stated that four had no deer and that an additional forty enclosures had "extremely few." There were also the remains of an apparent timbering operation that left behind stumps, burned trunks, and a crisscross of transport cart ruts amid storage huts. He concluded that these operations, which had included game poaching, were the main cause of a drop in the deer population."[35]

The emperor, in the tradition of his forefathers, stressed in his response that "the hunting enclosures are important areas of military training where it is natural that there should be stringent inspections to prevent acts of tree and deer poaching." Significantly, he also acknowledged that "for many years there have been major projects that require cutting of state timber," but he refused to take full responsibility for the results. Instead, he charged that his local officials, in "overseeing such matters have handled things poorly," an apparent reference to only the most recent legal extraction operations in 1799. They had "allowed bandits casual entrance to set up their own stores and huts to cover up illicit tree-felling. Lumber, to be carried beyond the boundaries for profit but not yet transported, remains piled on the roadside in uncountable quantities." The emperor alluded to the classical text *Mencius* in summing up the situation: "Truly, this is 'setting the mountains and valleys alight and burning them, so that the birds and beasts flee into hiding.'"[36]

From the damage done to Mu-lan's ecosystem, measurable in declining catches that dogged many of the Jiaqing emperor's hunting expeditions, he concluded that the perpetrators must have colluded with local officials. He interpreted this collusion as a crisis of state security:

> This is why there is now actually no difference between the
> state's battue enclosures where the autumn hunt has been
> conducted for more than a century and the lumber yards of
> Shengjing and Jilin [in Manchuria]. Yet, the rituals for the labor
> and study of war have been conducted under such deficiency for
> a string of years; how can they amount to anything appropriate?
> There must be stringent punishment for this.[37]

Two years later, in 1806, however, the Jiaqing emperor was dispatching minions back into Mu-lan enclosures to search for more trees that could be cut for imperial tomb projects.[38] By 1810, the emperor was repeating many of the complaints he had made in such detail six years earlier in 1804. Game was scarce, and there were traces of horses and carts amid much-reduced woods. The emperor lamented:

> When I followed my Deceased Father, the Qianlong emperor to
> call deer, the many encirclements were all in areas of tall trees,
> lush grass and the animals were most numerous . . . [But now]
> the battue grounds personnel . . . allow nearby Han commoners
> and Mongols to fell timber without authorization and poach
> animals. . . . [Mu-lan] lies above the passes and was presented by
> Mongols as battue grounds in the seventeenth century to provide
> for the chase. . . . It is not the same as a normal park and so
> should naturally be restricted to prohibit pasturing and fuel
> gathering.[39]

By the first decade of the nineteenth century—ten years prior to the Jiaqing emperor's termination of the imperial hunt at Mu-lan—the complex's woodland ecosystem services had visibly declined. The ostensible reason—especially favored by Qing rulers—has generally been considered poaching of various resources by multiethnic official and private interests. However, large extractions of vast tracts of woodland, concentrated in the second half of the eighteenth century (with two high points being 1768–69 and

1786–88), suggest that a contributing cause of this decline was the authorized extraction of hundreds of thousands of trees, along with an unknown amount of illicit timbering. The immediate problem for the dynasty, however, was not the ensuing shortage of wood but the woodland wildlife habitat, on which Qing military identity depended for its proper formation.

In this respect, Mu-lan deforestation's ultimate imperial measure might be gauged by the number of crack cavalry not trained. Woodland ecosystem wildlife was the prerequisite for the training of elite Inner Asian horsemen. Hunting-as-military-training was not merely a matter of having men kill animals. It required uncultivated tracts of forests, grasslands, and water. Such tracts—undeveloped "wilderness" (*huang*) in agrarian perspective—would have been almost totally converted to the cultivation of China proper farmers as tax-paying peasants. When properly managed within restrictions that often appear as "cultural," these wildernesses reappear as reproductive habitat, first, for wild animals, who would then nonverbally transmit forest knowledge to Qing bannermen lineages. In the extraordinary perspective of this foraging, boreal dynasty, living woodland ecosystems became organic to imperial identity in unprecedented ways not just cultural but existential—ways intimately environmental. Under such tutelage, indigenous knowledge acquires a new, interspecies significance.

By the late eighteenth century, serious contradictions between cultural and provision woodland services, as well as some contradictions internal to cultural services, were seriously disturbing the Mu-lan ecosystem. In a further contradiction, its ensuing decline was a multiethnic accomplishment of Mongol and Han poaching and authorized imperial extraction. Dynamics in the Qing imperial tomb complexes were different. Although Chengde certainly experienced Han agrarian pressures, these were complicated by the presence of neighboring Mongols, who for the most part were pastoral and thus more interested in selling timber to Han buyers while hunting for their own sustenance. Competition for woodland ecosystem services in the imperial tomb complexes of Qing Dongling and Qing Xiling seems to have been much more polarized between Inner Asian ritual and Han agricultural practices.

THE QING IMPERIAL TOMBS: CLASSICAL CONTEXT

Woodland interment sites had constituted spaces of social distinction from at least the late Warring States period (ca. third century BCE). This was ostensibly the time at which a major ritual text of Chinese antiquity, *The*

Record of Rites (Liji), in its discourse on "The Royal Order" (Wangzhi), ruled, "Commoners are interred without coffin ropes or steles . . . without a tumulus or trees." Some funerary practices were more egalitarian than these elite prescriptions. All, for example, "from the Son of Heaven on down" were charged to mourn parents for three years without engagement in other affairs.[40] Nevertheless, prominent impositions on the landscape, especially as tall mounds that mimicked mountains (*ling*) and lines of trees that recalled forests, were, along with accompanying ritual architecture, the primary expressions of elite interment held to have stretched back into the paradigmatic Zhou dynasty (ca. 1046–256 BCE) of classical antiquity.

Ideally, royal domains in general were to be marked off by trees. Another authoritative treatise on rulership from the late Warring States period, *The Classic of Rites* (Zhouli), affirms that a ruler should "establish his kingdom" at the geographical center and "lay out his 1,000 *li* royal demesne by raising a palisade of trees [*fengshu*]" to demarcate the borders of his authority.[41] By the succeeding imperial period, *fengshu* had become a synecdoche for the lavish practices of royal interment. Both *The Record of Rites* and *The Classic of Rites* aver the primacy of the majestic visibility of the royal tomb complex. It is critical for these spectacular royal spaces to be readily marked as such by their target audience, whose identity as royal subjects is partly formed precisely by their inculcated ability to recognize the markers of a dynastic space and act accordingly—mainly by keeping out.

Mausoleum landscape had not always been of central dynastic importance. At times, emphasis was placed on ways not recognizing these spaces for very material reasons. An extended rationale of this obscuring viewpoint was provided by the Wei dynasty (220–65) emperor Wendi's 223 decree regarding his own funeral arrangements. The emperor observed that the exemplary sage rulers of antiquity were buried so as not to disturb the woodland or farmland environs of their tombs. He thus concluded that his own tomb did not need to conform to *fengshu*; there would be

> no mausoleum structures, guard barracks or spirit road [of statues]. This burial will be a hidden one so that those who wish to find it cannot. . . . I want to ensure that successor dynasties will not know its location, so that it will grant them no fuel, conceal no gold, silver, copper or iron . . . From antiquity to today, there has never been a defunct state whose tombs have likewise not been dug up [for plunder]. Since the rituals have fallen into confusion, there has not been a single tomb of the rulers of the Han Dynasty that has not been dug up [for

plunder] ... such calamity comes from the lavish burial style of *fengshu*.[42]

Concealed royal interment persisted among the Wei's immediate dynastic successors, but the lavish funerary landscape practices of *fengshu* eventually reasserted themselves, undergoing another alteration during the centuries of Inner Asian conquest that preceded the Ming. By late imperial times, however, *fengshu* royal interment had not only been reestablished but had also achieved an unprecedented imposition of a landscape.[43] As Wendi of Wei foresaw, however, these complexes also attracted unwanted attention from imperial subjects who saw very different panoramas as they looked over Qing mausoleums under conditions of mounting woodland scarcity.

Environmental interdependency between culture and ecology—more specifically, between people and trees—is of particular interest here. The ecological realities on which royal interment literally rested were constituted by material limits imposed on individual or group spatial appropriations. These realities also mandated specific adaptations as long as these people invested ecological spaces with ecosystem service values, whether these values were aesthetic or existential. Indeed, the distinction between these two values becomes rather blurry once the analytical approach moves away from an extreme position of social construction to accommodate the interests and effects of nonhuman ecology in which cultural systems are inextricably embedded.

ENTOMBED WOODLANDS

Qing royal interment was deeply informed by previous dynastic practice, particularly the *fengshu* innovations of its immediate predecessor the Ming. During the Ming, interment complexes were transformed into sprawling "natural parks" full of "100,000 pines" and "1,000 deer."[44] By the Qing, the Qianlong emperor could assert that in repairing flood damage at Fuling, the mausoleum of the dynastic founder Nurhaci that lay beyond the Great Wall in Shengjing (Mukden), "*fengshui* was of the utmost relevance." The built space of imperial mausoleums was determined by these principles, of literally "wind and water," that were themselves constructed by nature as well as culture.[45]

Built space was nevertheless a comparatively small-scale problem in interment complex management. The extent main Qing mausoleum complex, Dongling (Eastern Tombs) absorbed over 2,500 km² of well-watered, forested hills of Zunhua Prefecture (125 km northeast of Beijing). Only about 48 km²

　　　　　　　　　　　BELLO

of this expanse, however, was built space, where five emperors, four empresses, and five concubines were entombed between 1663 and 1908.[46] Dongling was the largest Chinese imperial mausoleum complex ever assembled. Its commensurately lavish resources were thus attractive both to Qing rulers concerned with legitimation and domination and to their subjects concerned with production and consumption. While these motives were not inevitably incompatible, they proved difficult to keep at equilibrium under dynamic environmental conditions.

Dynastic authorities had initially disturbed the area's socioeconomic equilibrium by the decision to locate Dongling in an underdeveloped area. The influx of groundskeepers and military personnel, whose main task was to keep nearby commoners from plundering both the tombs and their encircling woodlands, flooded a rural backwater with thousands of people. The military garrison for the built space zone alone numbered 1,200 Manchu cavalry, with an additional 3,100 Han infantry patrolling the much more extensive wilderness zone beyond from a number of encampments. Costs for maintaining these large garrisons were accordingly immense. In 1899, seventy-one thousand silver taels was spent on troop provisions alone. Some of these effects may also be seen in some tree poaching cases between 1849 and 1866, mainly perpetrated by first offenders desperate for firewood. The pattern of these cases suggests to one authority signs of the economic stress created by the complex's enormous demands on local resources.[47]

There were other costs borne not necessarily by the state but by its resident subjects. The mausoleum complex's typical frontier mix of military and civilian residence complicated local administration. The ensuing horde of newcomers increased pressure on local resources, which were not very developed in agrarian terms. Many original residents lost their land and were burdened with additional corvee duties.[48]

Qing-style decoupling of woodlands from fields also required detailed administrative distinctions, many unique to the area's conversion into the main Qing royal interment site. Spatial complications emerged as ongoing attempts to regulate the ritually intricate interment site within a series of—mainly—concentric zones. Hierarchical spatial divisions were definitive of all such sites subject to *fengshu* regimes. Built and natural woodland spaces were divided into a "anterior enclosure" (*qianquan*) and "posterior dragon" (*houlong*), respectively. In basic feng shui terminology, dragons were undulating elevated stretches infused with abundant qi and, as such, constituted a requisite part of the interment site. These spaces were further distinguished by the anterior enclosure's trees landscaped in ranks (*yishu*) and those of the posterior dragon, a "sea of trees" (*haishu*) that were left to flourish naturally. Such abundance understandably drew incursions, which required further zoning of the posterior dragon woodland space. These zones increased in access restrictions the closer one moved toward the sacrosanct central built spaces of the mausoleums, whose immediate environs were surrounded by a rectangular feng shui enclosing wall (*fengshui weiqiang*). Eventually, three of these concentric zones were laid out along color coded painted wooden perimeter posts and rocks. The innermost zone of maximum restriction was delineated by red posts, themselves surrounded by an outer ring of unpainted "white posts" and, finally, an outermost ring of green posts.[49] In addition to these zones behind the mausoleum, there was also a much more extensive *guanshan* zone, which basically encircled the green zone and was constituted of lesser hills opposite the anterior enclosure in the foreground where surplus qi (*yuqi*) from the main site was believed to concentrate. This area was not brought under fully articulated regulation until the 1820s.[50]

Restrictions generally concerned the extent to which residents new and old could access resources, particularly timber. Initially, the red zone was completely off limits. The green and white zones were less restrictive, although highly disruptive activities like soil excavation, quarrying, and working charcoal kilns were not allowed anywhere. These regulations—laid down sometime between the 1663 establishment of Dongling and 1774—were not altered until 1804, when limited excavation and silviculture was permitted in the white zone. Penalties for other violations were also reduced outside the red zone. This relaxation appears as the first formal indication of spatial concessions made by dynastic authorities to their subjects' pressing material needs.[51]

Reports on the actual enforcement of these regulations, however, indicate a greater degree of flexibility extended to cultivators as early as 1741, when one official deliberation decided to let commoners "forage and cultivate at their convenience" outside the red zone and even to recruit farmers for the white zone.[52] Qualifications to restrictions became increasingly involved. These included collection of deadfalls for fuel in the green and white zones, the cutting of private timber, and extraction of soil and stones for repair of homes and gravesites. Restrictions, however, were not abolished:

> If . . . anyone illicitly cuts down trees belonging to the state,
> opens the mountains to quarry rock, digs deep trenches in the
> earth, sets up kilns to burn charcoal [or fire ceramics], or lights
> fires to set the mountains ablaze for temporary farming in the

zone outside the red posts but within the white posts, this shall be illegal as it would be within the red posts. . . . If such acts are committed outside the line of the green posts but still within the *guanshan* zone [they will also be punished].[53]

Uniform enforcement of any version of these regulations, however, does not seem to have occurred in the records I have been able to examine. One exemplary case occurred in the Xiling (Western Tombs) mausoleum area, located 140 km southwest of Beijing. Xiling had been established in 1729. Little more than seventy-five years later, commoners were found using it for their own interment requirements. A review of the record in 1805 showed that these people had been resident prior to the establishment of the green and white zones and so were not relocated in 1729. The state had little choice but to reaffirm this status quo to avoid the upheaval of barring commoners from the white zone, where their family graves were located. Instead, the red and white zones were contracted and the more permissive green zone extended to encompass all the commoner built space and fields.[54]

Although some unresolved contradictions remain in the record consulted here, it is possible to conclude that the state had taken on a major project of environmental management when it established its royal interment spaces. This Qing project can be summarized as cultural forest protection against the incursions of its own largely provision-seeking subjects, who in the process, also laid out their own robust interment spaces. Of course, this cannot constitute an absolute distinction between Han and Inner Asian woodland services, but it does form the primary contradiction between them within the woodlands under examination. Although commoner graves were unquestionably availing themselves of a cultural service, the main motive for Han commoner incursion into the tomb complexes was clearly provisional, especially evident in game and tree poaching cases, such as those involving fuel thefts in the mid-1800s. Indeed, commoner tombs normally implied descendants living—usually on subsistence agriculture—not far away. Conversely, services mainly sought by Inner Asian elites were cultural, even when they were extractive. Mu-lan wood was not being officially hauled back to Beijing to heat the Forbidden City but instead was used onsite to construct yet more monumental edifices like the Potala Temple.

A series of interrelated cases that broke over a few months in 1822 may convey the challenges that dynastic authorities faced while trying to enforce their own rules under complicated environmental circumstances. A gang of twenty-four had been caught illicitly felling "feng shui mountain trees" (*fengshui shanshu*) in the somewhat ambiguous Dongling green zone, which was nevertheless considered a "great violation of law." Eventually, several gangs were found to have cut well over fifteen thousand logs from the mountain zone into the red zone.[55] Investigators also inadvertently discovered two farming villages of 584 households legally working acreage across the green zone into the adjoining *guanshan* zone. Officials acted to rectify a lack of green zone boundary markers and an absence of penalties, "never clearly enumerated," for *guanshan* tree poaching. As a result, the *guanshan* zone formally became subject to more direct regulation like that of the green zone, although enumerated restrictions were fewer.[56]

The 1822 operations show that 159 years after Dongling was established, its precise boundaries had yet to be set or even to be clearly understood by the personnel specially charged to enforce them. Some of these problems can be attributed to the sheer extent of the complex, largest of the three Qing royal interment sites. The main problem, however, appears to be conflicting visions of woodland services defining the Dongling landscape as a major resource point in equivocal terms that brought ruler and subject into protracted conflict.

Dynastic policy sought to condition people living in proximity to imperial interment complexes to develop a particular "environmentality" that would harmonize agrarian and *fengshu* interests without the need for constant state supervision.[57] The primary spatial means of getting subjects to adopt this dynastic mentality was the regulatory establishment of concentric green, white, and red post zones and the internalization of their spatial restrictions by local residents. Residents' resistance to their formation as what might be called interment site subjects resulted in the addition of another, more lenient space—the *guanshan* zone. It is important to note, however, that prior to 1822, it appears that, in the words of a 1778 report, "there was no restricted land beyond the green zone," at least in fully formal terms.[58]

This process of identity and spatial formation can certainly be understood in terms of purely human cultural interaction like law enforcement, but from the perspective of environmental history, this would substantially miss both the trees and the forest. It is difficult to imagine, for example, how the interpenetrating systems of *fengshu* interment or feng shui landscaping could have ever come about without sustained human interaction and interdependency with woodlands. Woodlands even played a critical role in Wei Wendi's alternative vision of concealed royal interment.

The role trees played in these landscapes was more than just metaphorical. Although trees were culturally imagined as a defining characteristic of royal interment space, the concrete ecological consequences inextricably involved the biology of aesthetically preferred species like pine and cypress, just as that of reeds and willows became linked to the maintenance of dikes or that of fruit and mulberry trees integral to village agriculture.

Regulations on mausoleum tree management show how ecology and culture intertwined. Only in 1748 were procedures established to replace withered trees systematically. Eleven years later, another regulation prohibited the illicit sale of viable trees falsely certified as withered. Bureaucracy expanded with the appointment of "foresters" (*shuhu*) subject to many regulations as they worked replacing worn out trees with viable transplants. By 1760, foresters were advised to shift the spring planting of pine and cypress to winter, when snowfall provided more water for growth. By 1765, foresters were ordered to eliminate competition from any other vegetation surrounding new transplants to enhance their charges' viability.[59]

By the mid-nineteenth century, despite all state measures, royal interment spaces were becoming increasingly degraded. There is certainly evidence in the imperial, and early twentieth-century, record of considerable human adaptation to woodland scarcity.[60] However, this scarcity was rightly considered an environmental crisis—if one with which many inhabitants had learned to cope—ideally remedied by reforestation and conservation.

Under such pressures, woodlands could not remain entombed in restricted areas. In the first year of the Chinese republic, there was an attempt by the new state to evict agrarian intruders in the original Qing mausoleum that had been set up in southern Manchuria before the conquest of China proper in 1644. When these Han farmers were first discovered, officials expressed their obligation to safeguard the tombs as public property confiscated from the recently defunct Qing. In little over a month, however, they determined that cultivators were active within the Zhaoling mausoleum's green zone, and they were not expelled. Instead, Republican authorities decided to plant a perimeter of trees to delineate a white zone, inside which no cultivation could take place.[61] It seems that in this instance, it was easier to dispense with the dynasty than with its regimes for orchestrating complex environmental relations between people and trees that the Qing had fostered in its most vital spaces.

CONCLUSION

The multiethnic Qing state seems to have had considerable trouble protecting its cultural priorities—tied to various aspects of Inner Asian identity formation—from provisioning pressures that were most dramatically exerted by the empire's overwhelming Han majority. However, as the Mu-lan case exemplifies, elite Inner Asian imperial culture experienced internal contradictions that manifested themselves in what appear to have been unsustainable, but authorized, levels of tree extraction for major state building projects. In this case, culture was provisioning, which certainly problematizes the two as distinct analytical categories. The state, moreover, made deliberate, material compromises with its majority Han subjects—primarily to maintain stable cultural relations—when they violated imperial mausoleum complexes for economic reasons.

Despite some unresolved contradictions, both cases clearly show that woodlands should not be considered simply as sites of resource exploitation. Instead, they can be approached more environmentally as habitats—centers of dense and mutually conditioning connections between and within natural ecologies and human cultures. The northern China ecotone's imperial woodland complex habitats were not exactly split down the middle between demands of Inner Asian cultural preservation and Han Chinese subsistence provisioning. They nevertheless did splinter under different environmental pressures that fragmented clean breaks along ethnically determined ecosystem service lines. In many respects, these Qing chips remain to be sustainably pieced together again.

NOTES

1   Miller, *Fir and Empire*; Zhang, *Timber and Forestry in Qing China*.
2   Kinzig, "Ecosystem Services," 573.
3   Chen, "Agriculture Feels the Choke."
4   Kinzig, "Ecosystem Services," 574–75.
5   Gao et al., "Typical Ecotones in China," 298, 299, 301–2; Peters, Gosz, and Collins, "Boundary Dynamics in Landscapes," 458–59. For the existential importance of precipitation gradients for the region's ecotone, see Liu et al., "Vegetation of the Woodland-Steppe Transition," 525–32.
6   Chen and Zhao, *Zhongguo beifang nongmu jiaocuodai shengtai*," 5–6.
7   Chen et al., "Hydroclimatic Changes in China," 98–111; Ge et al., "Temperature Changes over the Past 2000 Yr," 1156, figure 1.
8   Ge et al., "Coherence of Climatic Reconstruction'" 1015, figure 5; Ge et al., "Reconstruction of Historical Climate in China," 676, figure 4.
9   Wang and Hebei beibu, *Nei Menggu dongbu senlin caoyuan jiacuodai*, 63–73; Huang, Liu, and Cui, "Neimenggu gaoyuan dongnanyuan senlin caoyuan guodudai," 262.
10 *Manwen lufu zouzhe* (*MWLF* hereafter), QL 16/9/8 [03-0172-0709-002].
11 *MWLF*, QL 16/9/8 [03-0172-0709-002].

12 *MWLF*, YZ 12/12/11 [03-0172-0902-006]; Quan and Qing, *Da-sheng Wu-la difang xiangtu zhi*, 151–54.

13 For similar trans-frontier interactions in Ningxia between Mongolian herders who sold grass or charcoal to Han farmers in need of scarce fuel, see *MWLF*, YZ 10/4/11 [03-0171-0318-007].

14 Huang, *Fuhui quanshu*, 546–47, 607.

15 Vermeer, "Population and Ecology," 248.

16 Aihara, "Qingchao zhongqi de senlin zhengci," 504–23.

17 Wu, "Pai min zhong liu youjuan wuyi shu," 3:2514b–15a; *Da Qing huidian shili* (*HDSL* hereafter), 10:562b–63a.

18 Cited in Marks, *China*, 233, but see also 240–43. Note that Marks has been updated with a new edition, titled *China: An Environmental History* (2017). References here and throughout are to the 2012 edition. Even today, regional ecological conditions mainly linked to water instability constrain large-scale reforestation; Shixiong Cao et al., "Greening China Naturally," 828, 829; Shixiong Cao et al., "Damage Caused to the Environment," 280.

19 Cao and Wang, "Ming Qing Shaannan yimin kaifa zhuangtai," 50–57; *MWLF* QL 6/10/20 [03-175-559-019] and QL 14/4/9 [03-171-0311-001].

20 Xiao, Fang, and Zhang, "Climatic Impacts," 19–28. For an extreme characterization of serious ecotone degradation arising from Han cultivation, see Huc and Gabet, *Travels in Tartary*, 1:4–6.

21 Lau, *Mencius*, 61. Translation slightly modified.

22 Gugong, *Qing Gaozong yuzhi shi*, 3:168b–69a.

23 Wittfogel and Fêng, "History of Chinese Society," 526.

24 Endicott-West, "The Yüan Government and Society," 136–37.

25 I am not suggesting here that the Mountain Retreat complex as a whole can be instrumentally reduced to any one function. As Stephen H. Whiteman has recently observed in his study of the complex as "a new, fundamentally Qing landscape," the "endogenous and exogenous cultural, artistic, technological and epistemological" elements integrated into the site constitute "a multifaceted mode of ideological expression that, in its simultaneous diversity and coherence, reflects the nature of the Qing"; Whiteman, *Where Dragon Veins Meet*, 4, 10. My primary concern is to emphasize select environmental aspects of the site's imperial Manchu materiality that are likewise integral to the inherent diversity of a Qing landscape.

26 Zhang, "Bishu Shanzhuang shengqi de zhiwu fengjing goutu," 544, 554–55; Han, "Qiantan baohu bishu shanzhuang," 626. Pines also seem to have constituted the majority of residual forest cover in the complex, as observed in the 1930s; Forêt, *Mapping Chengde*, 47–48.

27 He Shen, *Rehe zhi*, 2:831–33. I have modified Sven Hedin's translation of this text; Hedin, *Jehol*, 158–59.

28 Bello, *Across Forest, Steppe, and Mountain*, 48–54.

29 He Shen, *Rehe zhi*, 3:1843–44.

30 Gugong, *Qing Gaozong yuzhi shi* 3:168b–169a.

31 Zhao, *Ziyuan, huanjing yu guojia quanli*, 132–33.

32 Zhongguo diyi lishi dang'an guan and Chengdeshi wenwuju, *Qing gong Rehe dang*, 2:336–37, #132.

33 *Qingshilu* (QSL hereafter), JQ 17/9/6, 31: 534a–35a.

34 *QSL*, JQ 7/8/24, 29:372b.

35 *QSL*, JQ 17/9/23, 29:792b–93a.

36 *QSL*, JQ 17/9/23, 29:792b–93a. For the context of the *Mencius* quote, see Lao, 102.

37 *QSL*, JQ 17/9/23, 29:792b–93a.

38 Zhao Zhen, *Ziyuan, huanjing yu guojia quanli*, 137.

39 *HDSL*, 8:820b–21a.

40 Qian, *Liji zhuyi*, 152–53.

41 Yang, *Zhouli yizhu*, 150–51.

42 *Sanguozhi*, 1:81–82.

43 For the many vicissitudes of royal interment from the Han through the Ming, see Song and Xia, *Qingdai yuanqin*, 1:79–106.

44 Song and Xia, *Qingdai yuanqin*, 1:102.

45 *QSL*, YZ/13/8/27, 9:150b–51a; Wang, "Qingdai lingqin fengshui, 178. Fengshui here can be understood as the systematic attempt to mine qi through landscaping that concentrated it inside encircling waterways preventing its dispersal through exposure to winds. *Fengshu* can be understood as the practice of *fengshui* theory as royal interment, although by the Qing period, feng shui seems to cover both theory and practice.

46 Song and Xia, *Qingdai yuanqin*, 1:126.

47 Wang, *Diguo de xiangzheng*, 74, 199, 220–22.

48 Wang, *Diguo de xiangzheng*, 81.

49 Wang, *Diguo de xiangzheng*, 44–45, 129, 196–97; Wang, "Qingdai lingqin fengshui," 181, 195, 197.

50 In a common official context *guanshan* may be literally rendered as "state mountains" subject to minimal regulation; *QSL*, QL 5/11/25, 10:899b–902a and QL 51/5/4 24:875a–b. This is its most likely meaning in the context of interment sites discussed in the same work; *QSL* DG 2/7/17, 33:684a–b and DG 3/10/9, 33:1047b–48a. In *fengshu* terminology, however, *guanshan* has several more specialized meanings; Xu and Xu, *Dili renzi xu zhi*, 2:543–44. Nevertheless, *guanshan* in both contexts refers primarily to mountains and not forests, although woods are often explicitly included. In contrast, *guanshan* may appear as an administrative reference or "an official term for taxable forests" in an early modern Chinese commercial forestry context; Miller, *Fir and Empire*, 7–8.

51 *HDSL*, 10:826b–27a.

52 *QSL*, QL 6/11/17, 10:1208a–9a.

53 Translated in Elvin, *The Retreat of the Elephants*, 294–95. I have modified Elvin's translation here.

54 *QSL*, JQ 10/11/14, 29:1099b–1100a, JQ 10/12/3, 29:1117b–18b.

55 *QSL*, DG 2/i.c. 3/19, 33:576b–77a, DG 2/i.c. 3/29, 33:584b–85a, DG 2/5/14, 33:631a–32a.

56 *QSL*, DG 2/4/15, 33:602b–3a, DG 2/5/4, 621b–22a, DG 2/5/14 630b–32a.

57 Here, I modify Arun Agrawal's modern concept of environmentality to refer to state employment of various means to ensure its subjects, without supervision, internalize state environmental values; Agrawal, *Environmentality*.

58 *QSL*, QL 13/8/25, 22:245a–b.

59 *HDSL*, 10:850–54.

60 One observer recorded that in 1930, north China villages were somehow producing enough timber for their own use and for export to Japan; Menzies, *Forestry*, 667. However, other contemporary reports are grim. Shandong, for example, was said to have no forests left; Pomerantz, *The Making of a Hinterland*, 137.

61 Yang, Zhao, and Dong, *Shengjing huanggong*, documents dated as "Zhonghua Minguo 1/5/6" and "Zhonghua Minguo 1/6/28," 398–99.

CHAPTER SEVEN

CAMPHOR, CELLULOID, AND COLONIALISM

*The Dutch East Indies and Colonial Taiwan
in Comparative Perspective*

FAIZAH ZAKARIA

F OREST histories often center on exploitation. The felling of the woods
and their constructed afterlives as timber for buildings, monuments,
and ships fed a growing global network that brought up cities from
Venice to Edo. As shown by David Bello (chapter 6) in this volume, however, exploitation coexisted with dependency in multiethnic settings. The
marginalized experiences of peoples who lived in the forest, dependent on
the woods as a sustaining ecosystem, is the focus of this chapter. Developing
identities that were distinct from—and sometimes in opposition to—that of
peoples in polities beyond the forest's edge, interior peoples frequently developed kinship with the more-than-human beings in the forests, reflected
and expressed through ritual, religious beliefs, and myths, all of which
became part of an identity presently termed "indigenous."

These identities are evident in the Dutch East Indies and Japanese-
colonized Taiwan, particularly at an inflection point in the nineteenth
century when imperialism created modern notions of indigeneity. Dutch
imperialistic ambitions in the Southeast Asia region took hold with their
conquest of Malacca and establishment of Batavia in the seventeenth
century, after which they gradually expanded their rule over what is now
the Indonesian archipelago. Their piecemeal conquest of Sumatra over the
course of the nineteenth century is the focus of this chapter. Taiwan was
briefly colonized by the Dutch and Chinese settlers before being occupied
by the Japanese from 1895 to 1945. In these colonial projects, the human
body is entangled with nonhuman natures—material and spiritual—and

colonialism restructures these more-than-human power relations. As in recent work by Donna Haraway and Juno Parreñas on reclaiming a kinship with the nonhuman, the central colonial dynamic highlighted here is an ongoing process of conquest by disempowering indigenous peoples and rearranging kinship connections.[1] In its networked nature, such restructuring of power bears similarity to what political ecologist Pamela McElwee has conceptualized as "environmental rule," where "objects arise and circulate through relational human interactions, but those interactions are shaped by the physical, biological, and social characteristics of the objects themselves."[2] While McElwee's work revealed relatively flat horizontal networks of technocrats and foresters, inequalities are evident in the domination created by imperialism and the tensions generated through evolving anthropocentrism.

This lens allows us to concentrate on the experiences of two interlinked entities that have been sidelined in the historiography: Asia's upland indigenous peoples and trees, specifically, camphor forests. The latter is especially suited to this comparative study as camphor was a resin that was once accessible only through the cooperation of the stateless peoples living in upland forest interiors in East and Southeast Asia. Mutual dependence between stateless peoples and camphor trees in the region disintegrated in the face of accelerated exploitation during the nineteenth century. The synthetic material celluloid, which was made from camphor, was a key driver of these changes. It pushed global demand for camphor to unprecedented levels and also enabled photography that rendered the uplands accessible and legible. The common experiences of indigenous peoples in both colonies were striking despite divergent positionings toward camphor production as an enterprise. Japanese-occupied Taiwan was a major camphor exporter while the Dutch East Indies was a minor player that all but abandoned the enterprise from the mid-1920s. Both powers sought to transform camphor trees into profitable commodities while disentangling these trees from the identities of the indigenous peoples living under their canopies.

The camphor trade in the Dutch East Indies has been sparsely studied, but its history can be reconstructed not only from colonial and missionary records but also from poetry, folklore, and oral traditions that memorialize the camphor tree among the indigenous groups. There is already a fairly robust literature on camphor and indigeneity in Taiwan, which this comparative approach augments to contextualize the history of Taiwan's camphor trees on a global scale.[3] Camphor trees are living, dynamic bodies that shaped kinship connections among upland peoples and coastal peoples prior to the 1860s. Violent military confrontation between colonizer and colonized followed a spike in camphor production to feed the global demand for celluloid from the 1880s to 1920s. These confrontations paved the way for a distant, colonial power to exert closer control of both peoples and forests. Such control was reflected in the policies that the two colonial governments adopted to simultaneously exploit camphor trees and renovate the traditions of upland peoples, leaving visible legacies today.

CAMPHOR TREES: MATERIALITY AND EMBODIMENT

There are two types of trees that produce camphor, each belonging to a different genus. *Dryobalanops aromatica* is a hardwood tree of the dipterocarp family found in the tropical rainforests of Southeast Asia, particularly Sumatra, the Malayan peninsula, and Borneo. *Cinnamomum camphora* is an evergreen of the laurel family native to China, Taiwan, Japan, Korea, and parts of Vietnam. The timber from both trees were valued for their aroma, ability to repel insects, and slow rate of decay.[4] But they became distinguished in human eyes mainly for their valuable resin. Camphor is a waxy, flammable solid, the best versions white in color and exuding a strong aroma. Both trees also secrete an essential oil, utilized widely for pharmaceutical purposes but valued less at the market than the solid resin.

The two trees differed in the production and distribution of their bounty. The sap of the Sumatran *Dryobalanops* accumulated in the cracks and crevices of its inner trunk and flowed inward toward what an early botanist termed as "the pith or heart" of the tree.[5] This sap coagulated into white flakes that clung to the wood and remained solidly hidden under the bark. Only a fraction of the trees contained the valuable resin, and such trees were difficult to identify; the tree might emit a strong scent suggesting camphor but proved empty if felled. The sap in the East Asian *Cinnamomum* trees, on the other hand, flowed outward. Its emergence was announced through a glistening bark or a trickle of camphor oil when shallow incisions were made to the body of the tree. As a laurel, the tree flowered annually. Its yearly profusion of tiny white blooms amid glossy leaves physically manifested its genetic difference from *Dryobalanops aromatica*, which flowered irregularly, depending on the composition of the soil and water on which it grows.[6] European travelers to Sumatra reported that some local informants told them that they had never seen the tree flower in their lifetime.[7]

Almost all *Cinnamomum* trees could be processed into camphor crystals by boiling chopped wood chips in an iron pot. The sap evaporated and stuck to the pot's cover, reforming into crystals.[8] This technique did not work as well on *Dryobalanops* camphor trees; heating the wood yielded only an oily residue. Camphor oil was sold for pharmaceutical purposes but was not expensive or valued, nor could it be used for purposes such as the preservation of a corpse. Solid, white disks of camphor occurred naturally and had to be scraped from under the tree bark. We thus have two kinds of camphor trees; one whose bounty was elusive and slow to reproduce and another that displayed its abundance and fecundity. Folklore emerging from human societies living amid these trees represented these characteristics as living bodies. A legend of the upland peoples who lived under the arboreal shade of *Dryobalanops* narrated how camphor originated from the spirit of a woman named Nan Tar nan Tor Tor (The Dancing One), who tried to escape a malevolent ancestral ghost by seeking refuge in camphor tree after camphor tree. When she inhabited a tree, she stimulated the formation of camphor. Her human husband, whose actions during their marriage had enabled the ghost to plague his wife, was doomed to knock on every camphor tree in search for her without success. Even when he approached the right tree, her soul would flee to a different one and all he would hear was a hollow thumping: *"pagedag pagedog."* Chinese legends involving *Cinnamomum* camphor trees tell of no such frustrations. In ancient times, it was said, a Chinese official ordered a great camphor tree to be felled. As the ax is hewed, blood flowed from the trunk, and when it was finally down, a creature with the face of a man and the body of a dog emerged. The official commands the creature to be cooked, and as he eats it, he comments, "The spirit of the trees is called *p'eng-hou*. It appears much like a black dog with no tail and can be steamed and eaten."[9] The contrast between these two tales illustrates how the materiality of the trees and their respective physical traits are embodied; they personify the rarity of the harvest in *Dryobalanops* and the susceptibility of *Cinnamomum*'s spirits to energetic might.

Fragrant and capable of burning without leaving a residue, camphor was imbricated into religious imaginations across the Indian Ocean. In first millennium South Asia, waving a camphor flame before a sacred image was an extravagant way of supplicating for divine protection. In Sumatra and the Malay peninsula, religious rituals inflected by both Hinduism and animism heavily utilized camphor to perform magic spells either for protection or aggression. Camphor metaphors crept into regional Islamic poetry. Sixteenth-century Sumatran poet Hamzah Fansuri wrote of his soul being "entirely effaced, like wood burnt to ashes, coming from the unruffled ocean to become camphor in Barus."[10] Barus was a port on Sumatra's west coast, famed in the early modern period its high quality camphor and this poem alluded to how love of God incinerated a human's wooden sense of self for a better spiritual existence, represented by camphor.[11] *Dryobalanops* camphor was particularly valued for these spiritual purposes, while the mass market for more pedestrian uses such as pharmaceuticals was captured by the much cheaper *Cinnamomum* camphor.

In both Sumatra and Taiwan, the trees grew mostly at the northern part of upland forests covering a mountain range—Bukit Barisan and Chungyang Range respectively—that divided each island along a north-south axis. This geography impacted the organization of human societies, which became divided by altitude and tree density. Inhabitants of lowland settlements including agriculturalists on coastal plains and traders in ports and towns, considered themselves more civilized than the forest peoples who lived among the trees and loosely congealed as a band of dispersed tribes. In North Sumatra, the upland peoples were collectively known as the Batak.[12] The exact provenance of the name *Batak* is uncertain, but it probably originated as a derogatory label imposed on uplanders by Malay subjects of maritime sultanates on the lowland coasts of the island from the fifteenth century onward.[13] The perception of relative barbarity intensified when many of these sultanates converted to Islam.

In Taiwan, there was a similar divide between upland and lowland, exacerbated by early colonialism. The Dutch East India Company (VOC) was the first imperial power on the island, maintaining several bases at the coast but faltering in the interior. Indigenous peoples, present at least five millennia earlier, were amorphously ill defined.[14] The Dutch referred to them as "blacks" and encouraged migration of Han Chinese, who referred to the latter as *dongfan* (eastern savages).[15] The VOC's colonial project has been characterized as a "Sino-Dutch hybrid colony," driven by Dutch trading ambitions and Chinese settlement.[16] In 1661, however, Ming loyalist Koxinga routed the Dutch from their outposts to set up a government in exile, increasing migration of Han Chinese from the mainland to Taiwan's coasts.[17] After the Qing conquered Koxinga and took control of western Taiwan, sobriquets connoting barbarism continued to define Taiwanese aborigines. Those living near the plains—who conformed to tax obligations and adopted Chinese customs were known as *shoufan* (cooked savages)— and those who remained in the mountains among the trees were referred to as *shengfan* (raw savages).[18] Boundaries between *shoufan* and *shengfan* were rather fluid, as were the divides between Batak and Malay and more broadly, colonizer and colonized; much depended on how kinship was established and with whom.

Kinship consists of connections that provide socioeconomic organizing principles in societies at the forest's edge. Kinship was usually forged in two ways: blood and affect. The making of kin was often expressed in rituals connoting shared experiences, interests, joy, and grief among humans as well as with nonhumans.[19] In both Sumatra and Taiwan, the period from the early eighteenth to the mid-nineteenth centuries was marked by the constant presence of a colonizing power that orbited the upland peoples and the forests but was never able to exert complete authority over either. Such limitations motivated an imperialistic mode of governance that emphasized establishing symbiotic, even familial, relationships to enable extraction of commodities from the forest through commerce.

Batak Dairi oral tradition recounted the story of Si Mbuyuk Mbuyuk, a man born with no bones who was able to talk with camphor trees. This ability yielded him a rich camphor harvest that he ingested to grow a set of bones and marry a princess.[20] The story reflected the more-than-human communications and bodily entanglement that characterized the harvesting of camphor in the Batak uplands.[21] Camphor seekers—a team comprising six to twenty people—were led by a spirit medium called a *bona hajoe* (builder of wood) capable of discerning which trees contain the resin. They built a small hut that served as a base where the *bona hajoe* communed with the spirits and offered sacrifices to receive guidance on which tree to cut. This guidance reportedly took the form of a woman who appeared in the medium's dreams, and her appearance—what she was wearing, the color of her hair— served as indicators for finding the appropriate tree. On identifying the tree, the team then proceeded to cut it down. Unable to transport the tree to a safer place if it contained camphor, the group spent the next few months scraping off the solid camphor, draining the camphor oil, and chopping the remaining wood into chips that they boiled in a pot to distill the final dregs. The yield after three months of work was rarely more than fifteen to twenty pounds of the valuable substance.

Although humans wielded the power of life and death over the tree, that power was not one-sided. The spirit medium who identified the wrong tree was believed to invite retribution by the spirits who could take away the life of some of the members of the camphor-seeking party, a framework for understanding physical dangers encountered in the forest. Such dangers were also vocalized through language taboos, for example, avoiding mentions of elephants and tigers so as not to accidentally invite them to the camp. References to the heart and other organs and mentions of the ax and fire were also avoided so as not to name the act of violence that was to be visited on the tree.[22] These rituals were not necessarily reflections of reverence for the forest per se but short-term bargains for everyday gain. They were an acknowledgment that the tree was not simply a body to be subdued but also a vessel for spirits capable of colonizing human bodies or withholding success from their endeavors. The seekers perceived the frustrating elusiveness of camphor in *Dryobalanops aromatica* as an obstacle that could be navigated with proper conduct and communication. Lowland Malay camphor seekers who joined camphor seeking expeditions adhered to the taboos and the language of the interior to signal affinity with them such that protection and promise of success could be extended to them as well.

Organized into a loose federation of clan-based villages, these Batak territories during this period were essentially autonomous entities with their own chiefs (*raja huta*) running its day to day affairs and priests (*raja baringin*) leading ritual life in the village.[23] It was the chiefs who initiated camphor expeditions and provided supplies. Camphor was further enlisted for the protection and sustenance of the village. When a chief died, his corpse was covered in camphor, tightly packed in a sarcophagus made out of a hollowed-out durian tree, and kept above ground until the rice field was sown and ready for harvest, his ancestral spirit protecting the crop. Only then was the body interred, along with the ears of rice that were sown on the day of his decease.[24] Such rituals made kin of wild trees with cultivated rice and connected the living with the dead.

This camphor trade was initially unperturbed by Dutch colonialism. Dutch colonial presence in Sumatra expanded in a piecemeal fashion over the course of the long nineteenth century. In the 1820s, the Dutch gained entry into the North Sumatran uplands when they intervened in a civil war among the Batak's neighbor, the Minangkabau of West Sumatra, and supported the royal family against a group of militant Islamic revivalists. By 1837, Dutch rule was established over Minangkabau and expanded to include the southern Batak regions of Angkola and Mandailing. Having little money, few men, and not much interest in the upland forests of the northern Batak territories, the Dutch stopped at the door, seeing value in an autonomous, animist Batak zone acting as a buffer against a possible pan-Islamic alliance between Aceh and Minangkabau. There were indications that the Dutch were irked by the restrictions imposed by Batak chiefs in terms of access to mountain passes, but on the whole, until the late 1870s, they acquiesced to an equilibrium long established between lowland Malay and upland Batak where access had to be continuously negotiated through personal ties and required adherence to customary norms (*adat*).

Taiwanese aborigines, on the other hand, were not as invested as the Batak in the camphor trade. Their sustenance was vested in a flourishing forest canopy—including gregarious laurel camphor trees—because it sheltered sika deer, an important source of protein to consume and skins to be traded. Deer was hunted using snares, spears, and bows; the sparse human population and this limited technology kept the deer population at sustainable levels. As with Sumatra, the Dutch were the first to establish a military presence on the island through the VOC, from 1624 to 1662. Their occupation was never absolute and illustrated the difficulties in holding on to the colony through coercive military force. Examples could be seen through the VOC's failed attempts to monopolize the deer trade during its brief tenure.[25] They encouraged migration from the mainland, issuing licenses for Han Chinese migrants to hunt in deer fields previously inaccessible to them and protecting them when conflict inevitably broke out. The Chinese introduced pitfalls as system of still hunting that could bring down hundreds of deer at a time. The population of deer plummeted, forcing Dutch governor Van der Burgh to accept a proposal by an aborigine group to ban pitfalls and restrict Chinese hunters to using only snares.[26]

It was after the Dutch period that the Qing state intensified the production of camphor. The Qing model throughout the eighteenth and early nineteenth centuries encouraged Chinese settlers to be "brokers" in the trade.[27] Camphor merchants (usually Hakka Chinese settlers) advanced capital to camphor headmen, who was in charge of daily operations of camphor stoves set up at the forest's edge.[28] The camphor headman—often a plains aborigine or a Chinese settler who had married an aboriginal woman—negotiated with the forest peoples for the use of their land, paid "mountain fees," and recruited workers to manage these stoves and to bear the risks of attack from hostile aboriginal groups. The camphor produced was then sold back to the camphor merchants, with deductions made for the original capital advanced. Qing provincial officials obtained revenue from the camphor trade mainly through taxes on camphor stoves charged to the owners, not on the product. They largely stayed away from everyday negotiations for forest access, claiming by law that all of Taiwan's forests were theirs, but they were never truly able to enforce these claims despite collecting a "defense fee" from camphor merchants. While the "defense fee" was paid in the form of money, "mountain fees" to the aboriginal tribes were taken in the form of food, arms, and conviviality. A British merchant evaluating the feasibility of participating in the camphor trade described the type of agreements that the Taiwanese aborigines and the camphor headmen might reach thus:

> In consideration of the Chinese providing them at certain
> periods of the year a few necessaries such as rice, salt and a few
> domesticated pigs, a quantity of Chinese gunpowder and perhaps
> a matchlock etc., with a jar or two of samshu [rice wine] thrown
> in, permission is granted to squat within certain limits—to fell
> timber, make charcoal and camphor—and to kill deer and other
> game in the immediate vicinity.[29]

The inclusion of liquor and pig was a ritual to demonstrate belonging and conciliation, with commensalism cementing a trusted bond between headman and tribe. Historian Paul Barclay memorably termed this feasting as "wet diplomacy"—wet being a reference to the copious amounts of alcohol consumed. Shared feasting made kin among potential enemies. The trust gained through these personal encounters that leveraged on emotional affinity was fragile and limited, dependent on honor rather than legalistic enforcement. A different, hostile tribe or a competitive enterprise might have harmed the workers extracting camphor.[30]

Qing officials appeared to view encounters with Taiwanese aborigines as signs of a broad savagery that required little explanation in and of itself, a natural consequence of a culture enamored of headhunting, internecine warfare, and hostile to migrant Chinese. However, they did not seem to recognize that aboriginal hostility might have stemmed from ecological concern. The previous wave of Chinese migration under Dutch protection had depleted the population of deer, restructuring deer trade to the detriment of aboriginal groups.[31] In restricting access to the forest only for those with a claim of symbolic kinship while threatening violence over the uninitiated, Taiwanese upland aborigines retained much of their mountain forest ecology and traditional social structure. As with the Batak in Sumatra, this was accomplished without a unified political structure or common agenda; dispersal and a sense of diffuse danger was precisely what made the forest and its peoples intimidating.

Upland peoples in both places were not isolated; they participated in trade, needing essentials such as salt from the lowlands. There were Batak villages among Malays on Sumatra's coasts, as there were agriculturalist aborigines who adopted Chinese religious practices through contact with migrant Chinese living in the plains.[32] What distinguished them in this period, however, was a sense that access to community and the forests they inhabited was not for sale; it was dependent instead on interpersonal, more-than-human relations. This can be demonstrated by limited circulation of cash in the uplands. In Taiwan, the exchange of cash in these deals was limited to those between state-merchant and merchant-headman and headman-worker. In Sumatra, the limited flow of currency was such that a British East India company official lamented in 1823 that while coins came into the territory, "not a dollar left the country again," a complaint echoed by a few other Europeans who made it to uplands.[33] Any wealth accumulated tended to be channeled back through the patronage obligations that chiefs held toward their villages. Chiefs negotiated the boundaries between upland and lowland, restricting cash flow in a manner that enhanced their social prestige rather than promoted capital accumulation.

A *desire* for wealth among indigenous peoples and camphor workers should not be understated. However, there seemed to be a perception that camphor riches often turned out to be a mirage. It was popularly believed among the Batak that the *bona hajoe*, the chief camphor spirit medium, would die poor.[34] Observers noted the fleeting gains and general poverty of the camphor workers but attributed it to their character. The profits earned after long months in the forests "would dissipate within eight days," a Malay villager reportedly predicted to a Dutch visitor as they witnessed the triumphant return of Batak and Malay camphor seekers to the village, this prediction based on the likelihood that the men would gamble it away or lose it in a cockfight.[35] Similar sentiments surfaced in Taiwan. "A hundred people engage in a hundred toils, but those who make camphor are the most wretched; only coveting mountain-like riches . . . people say camphor-men can really spend money, none have property on their side," expressed an *Ode to the Manufacture of Camphor* published in Taiwan close to the end of the Qing period.[36] The nature of working with camphor—the gender imbalance, long stints in the forest or at its edges—resulted in a trope where these men were perceived as feckless, unpredictable, and unrestrained, much like the forest itself.

These ways of establishing affective, personal connections could enable successful pursuit of camphor up to the mid-nineteenth century. In both cases, the character of the camphor tree partly shaped these relationships. With the unpredictable *Dryobalanops aromatica* in North Sumatra, camphor seekers sought kinship with the spirits that inhabited the trees, and they extended through the camphor gained the protection of ancestral spirits over the living. With the bountiful *Cinnamomum camphora*, Chinese camphor seekers were less concerned about the trees than about the potential hostility of aboriginal tribes. Both systems discouraged accumulation among the aboriginal groups. Material benefits flowed to peoples one step removed from actual interaction with the camphor trees rather than to camphor harvesters. The emphasis on kinship rather than transaction highlighted indigenous interest in a forest ecosystem rather than its parts.

In 1890, Italian anthropologist Elio Modigliani took a picture of a Toba Batak priest, Guru Somalaing Pardede.[37] Accounts of his travels did not include a description of his equipment; we do not know if he used glass plates or if the image of Pardede was frozen into the historical record on celluloid. Early iterations of this light, photosensitive material was invented in the late 1850s, and over the next three decades, coated celluloid gradually displaced heavy glass plates that were used in cameras. Camphor was a key ingredient. A year before Modigliani's encounter with Pardede, scientists in the United States had patented flexible celluloids, a move that would not only revolutionize the film industry by making motion pictures possible but also upend the camphor producing communities in the Asian uplands. "When Charlie Chaplin orders a hundred thousand feet of film to photograph one of his comedies, he little realizes that some Formosan headhunter may meet with a sudden end in order that he may get his film or that some luckless camphor woodchopper may lose his head over the deal," commented an American journalist visiting Taiwan in the early twentieth century.[38]

The disempowerment of autonomous upland peoples in both Sumatra and Taiwan worked through physical dislocation maintained by violence and mental relocation maintained by technology. Guru Somalaing Pardede was one of many Batak priests displaced from his position in society in the wake of Dutch expansion into the highlands. Under the pretext of defending European missionaries threatened by natives in the highlands, Dutch ascendancy was won through two major military campaigns in 1878 and 1883 against a loose coalition of indigenous resistance led by a charismatic and influential priest-king with the title Si Singamangaradja XII. These defeats drove the leaders of this resistance deeper and deeper into the interior, while the Dutch began establishing their governance from the banks of Lake Toba. The process was long and bloody; villages that supported the Singamangaradja resistance were sometimes razed. Conversion to Christianity was indirectly stimulated through this conflict as villagers sought to protect themselves by inviting white missionaries to set up mission stations so that their villages would not be burned.

The new order of political authority imposed by the Dutch reduced the number of village chiefs. In appointing those friendly to their rule, the Dutch cut out local priests (*datu*) from political power. As a *datu* so displaced, Pardede became a key leader in a resistance movement based on a millenarian vision that predicted a Batak victory when they were able to tap both the power of the old spirits and the new gods. This group created a new pantheon that melded reverence of animist leaders like Si Singamangaradja XII with respectful worship of Christian figures like the Virgin Mary and in some cases, charismatic missionaries. Resistance to the Dutch colonial project took both traditional animist and millenarian forms, disrupting the colonizers throughout the 1880s to 1910s. But their impact was limited by swift arrests, surveillance, and aggressive policing that restricted the ability of dispersed Batak traditionalists and millenarians to mobilize at a mass level.[39]

These religious shifts are pertinent to our discussions of the human colonization of the forests in two ways. First, the *datus'* elimination from political life reduced the pregnant power of ritual in their everyday interaction with the nonhumans of the forest, desacralizing and gradually making redundant their old gatekeeping role to the forest. Second, the conversions of the Batak to Christianity did not result in a sharp rejection of old beliefs; many everyday religious practices heterodox to the new faith were still practiced. However, these conversions did limit the Batak's mobility and capacity to navigate their forests and appease its spirits. Surveilled and restricted to what the colonial state defined as their native villages, their free-ranging gathering from forests were severely curtailed. This reduced the quotidian interaction between human and nonhuman that had previously known and respected each other through subsistence work.

Such distancing from local environments was helped by government agronomy programs imposed by the new Dutch authorities. "The more they see demonstration experiments of how seed selection, tillage and the use of organic and artificial fertilizers on their scant fields means an increase in yield, the less they worship their old spirits," reported a Dutch official in the Batak Karo uplands.[40] The church played its part in such encouragement, instituting a number of microcredit schemes so that the Batak could buy seeds and start an agricultural enterprise.[41] Even the unconverted bought into such cash investments. In the early 1900s, another animist anti-Dutch millenarian movement called Na Siak Bagi emerged, led by a goldsmith who, unlike the ascetic Pardede, declared that wealth was his magic staff (*tungkat harajaon*).[42] Capitalistic colonialism precluded indigenous kinship with forests and provoked religious change that estranged the two.

Similarly, colonialism intensified in Taiwan and remade aboriginal identity. From the 1860s, the Qing came under increasing pressure by European global powers to bring autonomous aborigines and lawless forests in line. In 1868, British gunboats sailed to the defense of agents of a British mercantile firm whose camphor had been confiscated for being sourced illicitly from so-called ruffians in the mountains.[43] Meiji Japan sent a punitive expedition in 1874 to southern Taiwan in response to the killings of fifty-four shipwrecked sailors from Ryūkyū islands by a group of Taiwanese aboriginals and the inability of the Qing to bring those responsible to justice.[44] Such incidents exposed Qing weakness with regards to rule of law, facilitating other imperialistic aims over other areas where it held sovereignty. In 1895, following the Japanese defeat of the Qing and the treaty of Shimonoseki, the sovereignty of Taiwan was formally transferred to Japan.

Japan's rule of Taiwan began with familiar feasting and gifting with aboriginal groups, brokering peace necessary to the colony at a minimal budget as well as gaining entry into Taiwan's interior for Japan's camphor merchants. However, like the Dutch in Sumatra, Japanese imperialism eventually reduced the agency of Taiwan's aborigines through intrusive attempts at converting them into modern subjects. Gifting moved away from wet diplomacy toward what Barclay described as a policy of regulated gift giving to "reform indigenous mores or reward and punish."[45] The gifts offered by Hashiguchi Bunzō, director of a newly formed Pacification Office to the Atayal in the late 1890s, demonstrated Japanese modernity: scarlet cotton fabric, red beads, red blankets, flower hairpins, and cigars.[46] In 1898, however, Saitō Otosaku, working at another regional Pacification Office, gave voice to a growing chorus of objections that the gifting of finished goods was inculcating an unconstructive fondness for luxury. He proposed the giving of farm tools, seed, and stock that could move Taiwan's aborigines to embrace agriculture rather than hunting. The discouragement of hunting echoed regulations issued by the Civil Affairs Bureau of the Taiwan Government General that had restricted access to guns and gunpowder to indigenous groups, limited their ability to trade with parties other than government licensed agents, and collectively punished headhunting by withholding gifts from the entire village.[47] Hunting had been a crucial way of building local knowledge about the forest ecosystem. These moves thus reshaped the forest landscape of Taiwan's aboriginal peoples and promoted transactional gifting as well as new mores delinked from the woods. Even without the religious changes underway in Sumatra, the parallel processes occurring were striking—the coming of transactional exchanges and a cash economy, pressure to create a rural indigenous based on agriculture rather than forest dependency, and new ideologies emerging to reinforce both.

As in Sumatra, military force was necessary to implement these changes. Despite their limitations, the Japanese were able to launch punitive campaigns and to aggressively police the frontier between indigenous and nonindigenous more effectively than the Qing; they also had to contend with Han Chinese rebels on top of indigenous headhunters. A key feature of their military power was a guard line manned by up to seven thousand guards, extending to a total length of 226 miles. Large parts of this line were fenced with electric wires and punctuated with guard stations whose perimeters were mined. Foliage was cut down to create a rudimentary surveillance infrastructure in the forest.[48] Military confrontations were sometimes explosive, a key example being the Ri Aguai rebellion in 1902, when an influential indigenous camphor broker organized an indigenous-Hakka/Han campaign of resistance against the Japanese.[49] As a result of Ri's defeat and the brutal elimination of Han Chinese opposition in the same year by head of civilian affairs Gotō Shinpei, the frontier was largely pacified. The continued resources that were used to maintain a military presence well into the 1920s attested to violence that stuttered on for decades. The encircling guard line also, for the first time, marked out a bifurcated territory that created a physical distinction between indigenous and nonindigenous.

UNMAKING AND REMAKING THE INDIGENOUS

Camphor, processed into celluloid film, supported the making of the indigenous in both colonies. Elio Modigliani's photographic gaze of Guru Somalaing Pardede (see figure 7.1) was the first of many in Sumatra that framed the upland indigenous as a parameter for primitiveness. Later photographs told of tutelage: the conversion and baptism of Si Singamangaradja XII's family, Batak students in mission schools posing with a traditional woven cloth draped over their shoulders. From the 1890s, photographs accompanied reports of the missionaries in the Batak territories, helping their external audiences visualize and categorize the Batak peoples. Photography paved the way for Dutch anthropologists who sought to understand human diversity in anthropometric terms, among which was seeking to weld geographical boundaries with racial characteristics.[50] Parallel processes were set in motion in Taiwan. Barclay, studying the anthropometric photography of Taiwan's aborigines, found the years 1895 to 1903 to be "a golden age" for "taxonomic work, photography, collecting and display efforts."[51] The "Face of Savage Taiwan," (see figure 7.2) a woman named Paazeh from Wulai taken in 1902, became globally iconic; she was found in ethnographic picture postcards widely available for sale, in glass-lantern slides of a Canadian travel writer, and in American magazines.[52] Sumatra's and Taiwan's indigenous societies "met" in photographs of the Paris Universal Exposition in 1900, where a Batak house replica was part of a representation of primitive cultural expression of "natural" peoples in the Dutch East Indies. A painting montage of face-tattooed Atayal peoples hung in another part of the

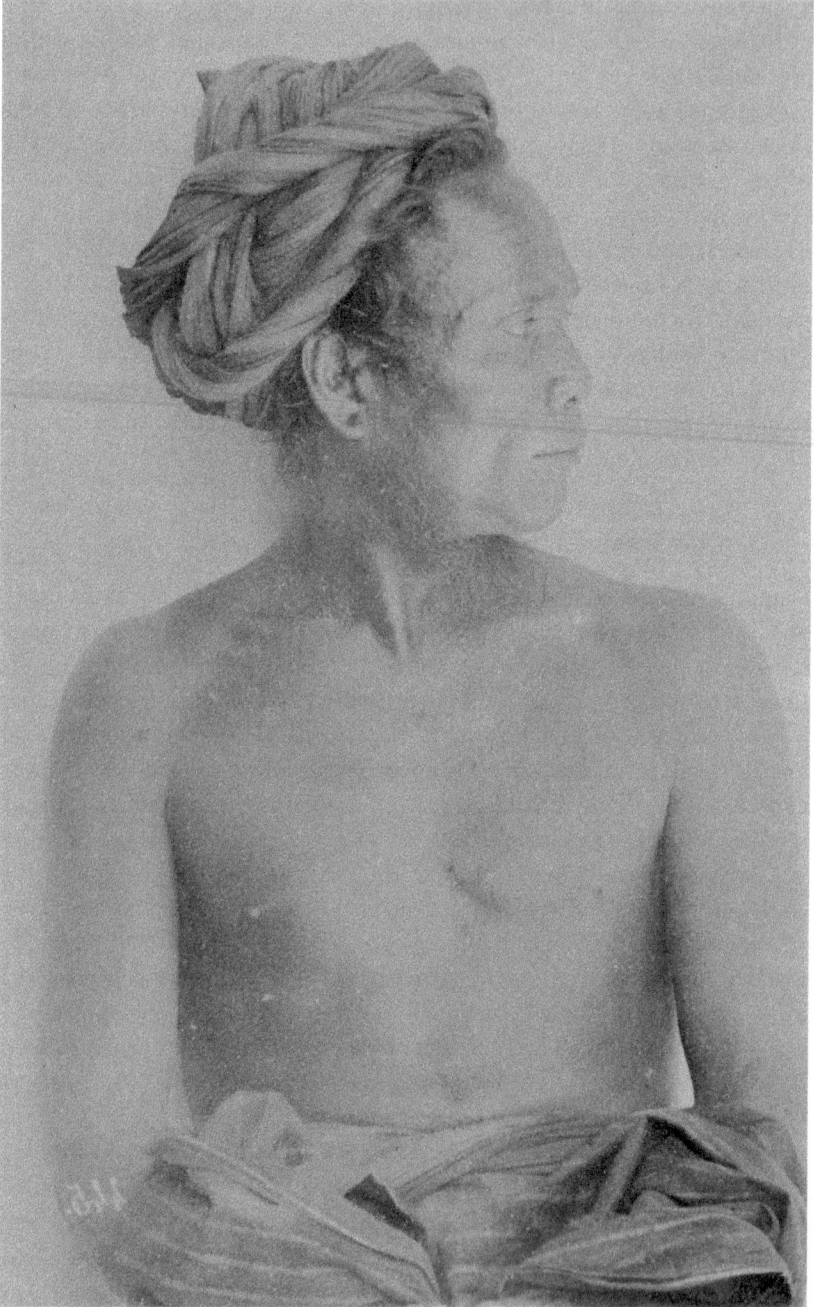

FIGURE 7.1. "Potret van de Toba Batakse goeroe Somalaing." Collection Nationaal Museum van Wereldculturen. Coll.no. RV-A56–18.

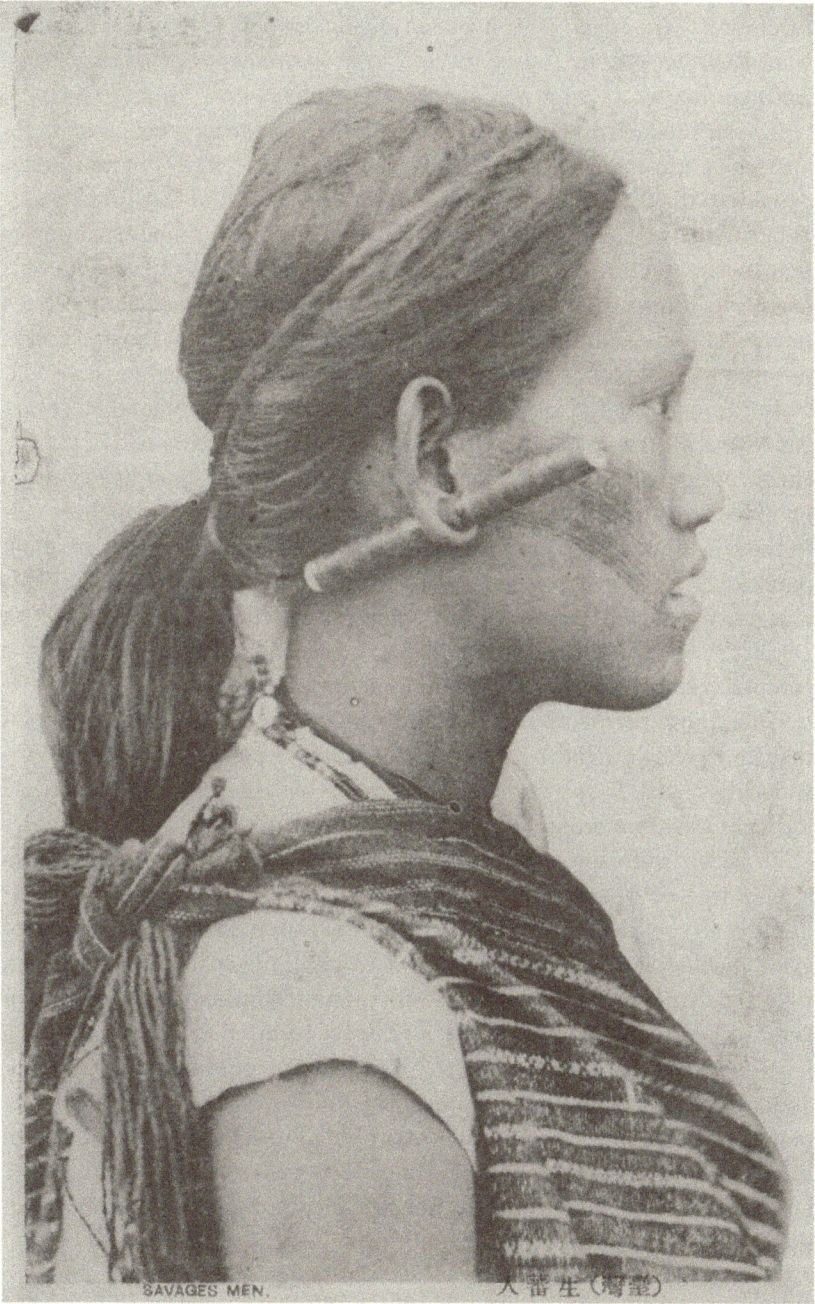

FIGURE 7.2. The "Face of Savage Taiwan." East Asia Image Collection (https://ldr.lafayette.edu/collections/east-asia-image-collection). Special Collections & College Archives, Skillman Library, Lafayette College (http://hdl.handle.net/10385/jd472x50w).

exhibition.[53] The effect was to evoke an identity for peoples that was detached from their ecosystem and connected to accoutrements or objects: wood carvings, houses, face tattoos, and woven textiles.

Conspicuously missing from most of these photographs were the woods. Japanese anthropologist Shinji Ishii's presentation on Taiwan's indigenous peoples to the China Society in London in 1916—the first English language publication by a Japanese person on the subject—was accompanied by more than twenty pictures, including more than ten close-ups of faces but only one of the forest, where a bridge, not the trees, was the focal point.[54] Such images of bodies out of place were symbolic of a deeper transformation occurring in the woods where camphor trees came under tighter state control and global capitalistic interests, removed from the colonies themselves. An American researcher of Taiwan's laurel camphor tree opined in the scientific periodical *Nature* in 1896 that "camphor distilling has been carried on in the most recklessly extravagant manner imaginable. . . . Japanese rule in the island may put a stop to such disastrous waste."[55] Pessimism about Batak forest stewardship were similarly expressed about Sumatra in US pharmaceutical journal *New Remedies*, which predicted a gloomy future for *Dryobalanops aromatica* should the Batak remain empowered to cut down camphor trees "recklessly without a thought for the future."[56] We glimpse through these perspectives a global investment in this new phase of colonialism, driving a division between indigenous peoples and the trees among which they lived. The way forward was a model of management that detached local peoples from profitable wood.

In such a landscape, what happened to the camphor trees which had been a repository of aspirations and ecosystemic ritual life in the two colonies? The greater capacity of the Japanese for military surveillance of forest boundaries enabled them to implement and enforce a licensing system giving rights to camphor trees to Japanese companies, eliminate the former brokers, and put down with force any aggressive reaction from the latter. The Japanese were also able to vertically integrate the production of camphor and celluloid through their technological know-how. Through a monopoly of the raw material and infrastructure to produce celluloid, they were poised to set the terms for the global trade and elbow out competitors who, in the previous era, could have negotiated access to camphor forests directly with the indigenous brokers.

In contrast, the colonial government in Dutch East Indies had a more uphill task profiting from the tricky *Dryobalanops aromatica*. The first few years following Dutch conquest was marked by a spree of cutting camphor trees; exports of camphor from the colony jumped more than fourfold, from

26,000 kg in 1884 to 106,000 kg in 1885.[57] However, from 1890 on, camphor exports plummeted to about 1,000 kg per year.[58] The decline appeared to be a deliberate policy. In 1884, the Dutch Lower House of Parliament (Tweede Kamer) vetoed a proposal to add research on forest resins to the science curriculum in Dutch universities, which educated colonial administrators.[59] No money was allocated for transport or research infrastructure to facilitate camphor extraction in this forest frontier. A tentative plan to build a road from upland Batak forests to a port in Singkil was scrapped despite enthusiastic support by some traders.[60] The tree itself was also frustrating a new generation of camphor seekers, many of whom were cutting down empty tree after empty tree. Indiscriminate cutting, without attention to requisite ritual, drew the scorn of an old Batak *bona hajoe* interviewed by Dutch anthropologist De Ligny in 1917: "In the past, the princes forbade the cutting of trees except in certain tree complexes. Whereas now, no matter how small or young, if men suspect there is camphor, the tree is cut and the beauty of the forest is lost."[61]

In 1907, Dutch resident Louis Welsink issued a moratorium on the cutting of *Dryobalanops aromatica*, citing its vulnerability to extinction.[62] Deterred by *Dryobalanops* but mindful of potential high profits, the Dutch experimented with the possibility of cultivating *Cinnamomum* instead, running experiments at the Cibodas Botanical Gardens on Java to see whether a fast-growing variant of the laurel camphor tree could be cultivated on the island.[63] The project was aborted soon after a pest outbreak ruined the fledgling seedlings.[64] In 1924, at the height of global demand, camphor no longer appeared on the list of exported products in the Dutch Ministry of the Colonies' annual report.[65] This lack of interest should have been good news for *Dryobalanops aromatica*. However, while indigenous access to the tree was restricted, the moratorium on the cutting of *Dryobalanops* was soon lifted to allow a Dutch timber company, Nijverheid Houthandel Singkel, exclusive access to thirty thousand hectares in North Sumatra, half of which were covered in camphor trees.[66] Divorced from supplicatory rituals, the monarch of the forest's final indignity, it seemed, was to be devalued to just another type of timber.

While local forest peoples were disentangled from their traditional associations with camphor trees, they were inveigled into new identities as agriculturalists and woodcraft artisans. An institute for the study of the Batak was established in Leiden, formalizing categorization of Batak subgroups and generating voluminous literature explicating on their cultural variation. Among its research output was the mapping of Batak terrain for the purpose of identifying suitable areas for cash crop agriculture and the expanded cultivation in potatoes, coffee, and frankincense. In Taiwan, a national museum was set up in 1908, with a Japanese expert as curator of aboriginal exhibits. At the center of exhibits were the textiles and wood carvings; the symbol of indigeneity, it seemed, was not to be the *woods* but monocrop cultivable trees and wood products.

Put differently, colonialism entailed both violent displacement from the woods and epistemological relocation of the indigenous to favor wood-related commerce. Its legacy lay in how new generations of indigenous peoples in both zones read back their history. In Sumatra, such historical rereading was intimated as early as 1926, when Angkola Batak journalist Parada Harahap returned to his place of birth and wrote about his experiences in one of the first native travelogues in the colony.[67] He valorized Batak agricultural smallholders over lawless, uncivilized forest foragers of the past *and* the Dutch-educated Batak working for plantations. It was these smallholders, he asserted, who retained the customs of the people while eschewing the stateless wilderness of forest life. This view developed into a merging of smallholder agriculture with indigenous identity that remained potent past the colonial era. One of these cultivated trees, the frankincense tree, was to become to be a symbol of indigenous protest in North Sumatra from the 1980s onward, when pulp and paper companies attempted to change the ecology in these territories by planting fast-growing eucalyptus.[68] The camphor tree, however, faded from historical memory in the uplands.

In Taiwan, the introduction to Sanyi Wood Sculpture Museum's website tells an apocryphal story of how Japanese felling of the woods became an opportunity for indigenous artisans to engage in wood art. "During the Japanese colonial era, the government cut off a significant number of camphor trees for medical and industrial purposes," it narrates. "Some workers found out that the roots of these trees were loaded with profound aesthetic values and professional wood craftsmen could turn these rotted roots into artistic objects."[69] This identification with art and also textiles aptly symbolize what Barclay has termed as Taiwan's "indigenous modernity."[70] Such histories do not detract from indigenous claims for lands rights in both former colonies, which are presently enmeshed with forest conservation efforts. Rather, they underscore that neither forest nor indigeneity is timeless. The conservation targets are not idealized pasts but sustainable, dynamic equilibriums.

CONCLUSION

In 1990, German anthropologist Johann Angerler found that some Christian Batak peasants—not shamans or intellectuals—continued to take part in ritual sacrifices to an ancestral spirit called Raja Uti, whose other aspect was Si Mbuyuk, the man who could talk to camphor trees. These Batak Christians performed these rituals despite the monetary cost and the risk of being temporarily banned from the community's Protestant church. When asked why, one of them replied, "You know, formerly, God was always much closer to us."[71] This affective loss—and the amnesia of conversion—was to these men as real as more concrete measures such as the decline of forest cover and shrinking biodiversity in the evolution of a wood age in their forest frontier. Narrating the colonizing of forested uplands in Asia required an accounting of the complexities of upland people-lowland state relations, the tributary mode of imperialism over multifocal authorities that was prevalent before the nineteenth century and the colonial imperative in Asia to intensify resource extraction rather than promote conquest of territorial settlements. It thereby involved not only material exchange but constant conversions of peoples and natures into ideal imperial subjects.

In the Dutch East Indies and colonial Taiwan, the personality of the trees become enmeshed in local networks of kinship. Both the trees and kinship became increasingly vulnerable in the face of imperialism and the attendant changes to local natures had an atomizing effect on human and nonhuman. With reduced affect for the local forest ecosystem, indigenous identities in both colonies shifted away from the unknowable woods and became reinvested in its more manageable parts, propelled by new innovations such as celluloid. Viewing imperialism from an indigenous perspective in Asia, with an emphasis on the entanglement of human bodies with their changing surroundings, stresses that what Richard White has termed as the middle ground between colonizer and colonized was marked by uprooting *and* rerooting of peoples and trees.[72] The end of the "frontier exception"—to borrow Meng Zhang's phrase in chapter 5—did not eliminate frontier peoples but recast them as actors who navigate, struggle with, and at times resist arboreal changes. Their histories remain relevant as the world seeks an expansion of forests to combat climate change.

NOTES

1   Haraway, *Staying with the Trouble*; Parreñas, *Decolonizing Extinction*.
2   McElwee, *Forests Are Gold*, 24.
3   See Shepherd, *Statecraft and Political Economy*; Barclay, *Outcasts of Empire*; and Tavares, "Crystals from the Savage Forest."
4   Donkin, *Dragon's Brain Perfume*, 27–63.
5   Vriese, *Memoire sur le camphrier de Sumatra et de Borneo*, 31.

6   On flowering of Sumatran *Dryobalanops aromatica*, see Marsden, *The History of Sumatra*, 241–42. Marsden estimates a four-year interval between flowering; de Vriese estimates it to be seven years.

7   Vuuren, "De Handel van Baroes."

8   Davidson, *The Island of Formosa*, 397–421.

9   Ban, *In Search of the Supernatural*, 215–16.

10 Drewes and Brakel, *The Poems of Hamzah Fansuri*, 142.

11 For interpretation of poem, see Naguib al-Attas, "New Light on the Life of Hamzah Fanṣurī."

12 Andaya, *Leaves of the Same Tree*, 151. The Batak were divided into seven subgroups: Dairi, Pakpak, Toba, Angkola, Mandailing, Karo, and Simalungun. Camphor trees grew mainly in the areas occupied by the first three subgroups, but Andaya contends that the premodern trade in camphor catalyzed a broader Batak identity among all seven as it brought them in contact.

13 The description of Batak peoples from accounts of European travelers makes a point of mentioning pigs; the rearing of pigs was an ethnic marker that was linked to lack of civilization and cleanliness in general. This suggests that some of these accounts were drawn from Malay-Muslim perspectives. See by way of comparison Anderson, *A Mission to the East Coast of Sumatra*, 108; Kessel, "Reis in de nog ofhankelijke Batak-landen van Klein-Toba"; and Cabaton, *Java, Sumatra and the Other Islands*, 257063; and Heyne, *Tracts*, 365–400.

14 On early human settlement of Taiwan, see Blust, "Subgrouping, Circularity and Extinction," 31–94.

15 Teng, *Taiwan's Imagined Geography*, 61–65; 104–5. Today, Taiwan's Government Information Office officially recognized sixteen tribes. The Atayal, Sediq, Saisiyat, and Truku, all in the northern part of the island, were the most entangled with the camphor forests discussed in this paper. Scholars agree that these groupings do not correspond to any political entity or social group in premodern Taiwan. Therefore, I will not use these labels until the 1900s, when they emerged in official discourse. For the period before 1900, I follow extant scholarship in referring to them as Taiwan's aborigines.

16 Andrade, "Pirates, Pelts, and Promises," 298–305.

17 Cf. Shepherd, *Statecraft and Political Economy*, 20–41.

18 Tavares, "Crystals from the Savage Forest," 111.

19 For an overview of kinship concepts, see Parkin, *Kinship*. On shared grief and suffering being part of kinship but with animals, see Haraway, *When Species Meet*, 67–90.

20 Brakel-Papenhuyzen, *Dairi Stories and Pakpak Story-Telling*, 51–68.

21 Sources on premodern camphor harvesting are spotty and scant; however, they concur on the same basic process described here. See Marsden, *The History of Sumatra*, 222–40; Heyting, "Beschrijving der Onder-Afdeeling Mandailing"; and Ligny, "Legendarische Herkomst de Kamfer Baroes,"

549–50. The method was also similar to that of the interior peoples of Malaya; cf. Skeat, *Malay Magic*, 373–97.

22 On camphor language of the Batak, see Ligny, "Legendarische Herkomst," 550. And for camphor language of Malaya, see Lake and Kelsall, "The Camphor Tree and Camphor Language of Johor." A list of taboo words provided by Lake and Kelsell on pages 42–58 was particularly interesting; some of these substitute words were not a special language but everyday language of the Jakun or interior peoples of Malaya. What was interpreted as taboo language by European observers could thus also be Malays assimilating by speaking the "ruder" language of the people of the interior when they themselves ventured into the forests.

23 Köhler, *Habinsaran*, 353–54; Kielstra, *Beschrijving van den Atjeh-Oorlog*, 55.

24 Junghuhn, *Die Battalanders auf Sumatra*, 128–29.

25 Cf. Andrade, "Pirates, Pelts and Promises," 301–8; and Koo, "Deer Hunting and Preserving the Common."

26 Koo, "Deer Hunting and Preserving the Common," 201.

27 Tavares, "Crystals from the Savage Forest," 96–125.

28 Davidson, *Island of Formosa*, 400–421; Tavares, "Crystals from the Savage Forest," 124–36.

29 Dodd, *Journal of a Blockaded Resident*, 236.

30 Pickering, *Pioneering in Formosa*, 121, 149, 215, gives some examples of ambush.

31 Andrade, "Pirates, Pelts and Promises," 303.

32 Shepherd, *Statecraft and Political Economy*, 362–94.

33 Anderson, *Acheen*, 188. The cultivators mentioned here refer to pepper cultivators.

34 For this reason, the *bona hajoe* was exempted from labor in a village.

35 Kessel, "Reis in de nog ofhankelijke Bataklanden," 56.

36 Tavares, "Crystals from the Savage Forest," 111.

37 For his account in original Italian, see *Elio Modigliani*. A partial Indonesian language translation is available; see Situmorang, *Guru Somalaing dan Modigliani 'Utusan' Raja Rom*.

38 Priestly, "Formosa," 296.

39 Hirosue, "The Batak Millenarian Response to the Colonial Order."

40 Middendorp, "Het inwerken van Westersche krachten op een Indonesië volk," 461.

41 Tideman, *De Bataklanden*, 17–20.

42 Hirosue, "Prophets and Followers," 217–18.

43 Pickering *Pioneering in Formosa*, 202–39.

44 Barclay, *Outcasts of Empire*, 87–90; Davidson, *The Isle of Formosa*, 123.

45 Barclay, *Outcasts of Empire*, 60. There were eleven such offices, staffed by 105 pacification officers who had to work with about 60 percent of Taiwan's population.

46 Barclay, *Outcasts of Empire*, 176.
47 Barclay, *Outcasts of Empire*, 93.
48 On Japanese violence, see Roy, "The Camphor Question."
49 Tavares, "Crystals from a Savage Forest," 256–67; and Simon, "Making Natives," 65, 82.
50 Sysling, *Racial Science and Human Diversity in Colonial Indonesia*.
51 Barclay, *Outcasts of Empire*, 182.
52 Barclay, "Playing the 'Race Card.'"
53 On Dutch East Indies in the Paris exposition of 1900, see Bloembergen, *Colonial Spectacles*, 190–201; and on Taiwan, Barclay, "Playing the 'Race Card,'" 55.
54 Ishi'i, *The Island of Formosa and Its Primitive Inhabitants*.
55 *Nature*, "Camphor," 116.
56 *New Remedies*, "Camphor," 252.
57 Ministerie van Koloniën, *Koloniaal Verslag*, 1884 and 1885, Bijlage C.
58 Numbers compiled from Ministerie van Koloniën, *Koloniaal Verslag*, from years 1884 to 1900.
59 Ministerie van Koloniën, *Koloniaal Verslag*, (1884), Bijlage D, 5.
60 Vuuren, "De handel van Baroes," 871.
61 De Ligny, "De Legendarische Herkomst," 550.
62 Vuuren, "De handel van Baroes," 872.
63 Ministerie van Koloniën, *Koloniaal Verslag* (1908), 291. It is not quite clear exactly when this experiment started.
64 Ministerie van Koloniën, *Koloniaal Verslag* (1909), 275.
65 The global demand for forest camphor gradually dropped in 1930s when scientists discovered new methods of synthesizing camphor from pinene, a distillation of turpentine that can be obtained from US Southern pine stumps.
66 "Opzet Nijverheid Houthandel Singkel."
67 Harahap, *Dari Pantai ke Pantai*, 113–47.
68 Zakaria, *The Camphor Tree and the Elephant*.
69 "Sanyi Wood Sculpture Museum," www.rtaiwanr.com/miaoli/sanyi-wood-sculpture-museum.
70 Barclay, *Outcasts of Empire*, 161–90.
71 Angerler, "Images of God in Toba Batak Storytelling," 303–4.
72 On the middle ground, see White, *The Middle Ground*.

CHAPTER EIGHT

MODERN TREES FOR BACKWARD CHINA

Arbor Day and the Struggle against Ecological "Backwardness"
in Republican China, 1911–1937

LARISSA PITTS

THE rise of coal and steel did not eliminate the modern state's hunger for timber. During the first half of the twentieth century, forestry and forest cover were subjects of international concern. Western economists and politicians began to warn of a global timber famine as even the New World showed signs of overlogging.[1] For example, in January 1905, President Theodore Roosevelt declared:

> Wood is an indispensable part of the material structure upon which civilization rests, and civilization makes continually greater demands upon the forest. We use not less wood, but more. For example, although we consume relatively less wood and relatively more steel or brick or cement in certain industries than was once the case, yet in every instance which I recall, while the relative proportion is less the actual increase in the amount of wood used is very great.... If the present rate of forest destruction is allowed to continue, a timber famine is obviously inevitable.[2]

In this same speech, Roosevelt announced that the United States should establish bureaucratic structures for the conservation and "efficient" management of the forests in its national parks.[3] The following month, he established the US Forest Service for this purpose.

This fear of a global timber crisis permeated the emerging literature on China's forests in the early twentieth century. British missionary Norman Shaw begins the introduction to his 1914 survey of Chinese timber trees by describing the "world timber famine:"

> Since the closing years of the nineteenth century economists
> have drawn attention to the rapid depletion of the world's timber
> supply through reckless cutting and wasteful methods of
> distribution, and those who have studied the question closely go
> so far as to prophesy a world timber famine in the course of a few
> decades unless steps are taken at once to find a remedy.[4]

Similarly, in their 1928 guide to the timber industry in the Chinese province of Jilin, the Japanese-owned South Manchuria Railway (SMR) begins by describing a 1900 French study that predicted a global timber famine within fifty years. It then claimed that the world was losing 1.7 billion koku of timber each year.[5] Japan, they continued, needed an extra sixty million koku of timber to make up for its own timber deficit.[6] The Japanese nation, the SMR argued, had no choice but to log in timber-rich locations like Jilin Province, no matter what type of resistance they encountered.[7]

As these examples show, modern and modernizing states such as China could not survive in the twentieth century without advanced technologies and infrastructure. Therefore, deforestation represented a serious blow to a nation-state's competitiveness or a colony's value. As the introduction to this volume has shown, the rise of colonial Western governments in the modern world brought with it a global understanding of "forests" as sites for national resource management that accorded with the principles of Western science.[8] Reforestation and afforestation programs sprouted up in many areas considered to be deforested, from eastern Canada to Hawai'i, from colonial Algeria to Imperial Ethiopia.[9] Such programs were designed by foresters, officials, and logging companies to meet economic and/or environmental goals. For instance, during the New Deal, President Roosevelt's tree-planting programs, which were designed to combat the erosion that had created the Dust Bowl, in turn improved local agriculture.[10]

The rise of Western imperialism in China in the nineteenth century led elite Chinese to believe firmly in the importance of national competitiveness as a way of defending the country from the West and Japan. Contrary to what one might expect, elite Chinese came to see forests as an integral part of advancing the Chinese nation economically, militarily, and culturally. During the Republican period (1912–49), Chinese states implemented reforestation programs for similar reasons as those outlined above. For instance, in the first major work on scientific forestry in the Chinese language, Ling Daoyang argues that as of 1918, China was hopelessly dependent on foreign timber from countries such as the United States, Canada, and Japan. State-led scientific forestry held the key to China's economic independence.[11]

Chinese programs distinguished themselves from global trends by also focusing on political and cultural goals, namely the creation of a common political culture that would support the unification of China under a single government. From 1916 to 1927, an ever-shifting set of national governments encouraged Chinese to plant trees on Tomb-Sweeping Festival (Qingmingjie), the day in early April on which Chinese traditionally cleaned the graves of their ancestral dead. Beginning in 1916, the national government renamed this day Arbor Day (Zhishujie) after the American holiday of the same name. In so doing, tree-planting became a way in which national governments reclaimed for the living sentiments that were meant for the dead. During the Nanjing decade (1927–37), the Guomindang (Chinese Nationalist Party) encouraged Chinese to plant trees to commemorate the spirit of Sun Yat-sen, a nationalist figure and the ideological founder of the Nationalist Party. They further promoted this connection between trees and Nationalist unity through the planting of Sun Yat-sen memorial woodlands and the reorientation of Arbor Day to coincide with Sun Yat-sen Memorial Day. In so doing, the Nationalist state relied on previous understandings of woodlands as enchanted through their connection to the spirits of the dead through tomb forests and geomantic theory. In attaching Arbor Day to Tomb-Sweeping Festival and Sun Yat-sen Memorial Day, Republican governments engaged in a process of "political reenchantment" of Chinese trees in order to promote reforestation.

WHY REPUBLICAN REFORESTATION?

Under China's Republican governments (1912–49), reforestation served to unify the country and create a Chinese nation. Both the Beiyang (1916–27) and Nationalist (1927–49) governments sought to accomplish this through the uniting of Arbor Day with practices in which Chinese commemorated the dead. For the Beiyang government, this was Tomb-Sweeping Festival; for the Nationalist government, this was Sun Yat-sen Memorial Day. This association between trees and death was not new to the Republican period. The Dai Temple at the foot of Mt. Tai, the most sacred of Chinese mountains in the imperial cosmology, to this day memorializes the presence of Emperor Han Wudi through the "Han Cypresses." These trees, many of which are more than two thousand years old, were supposedly planted by the emperor himself at the foot of the mountain. Later, they became known more for their connection to Han Wudi than for their natural beauty.

The Confucius Woods (Konglin) are another example of this phenomenon. These woods surround the Kong family seat and temple in Qufu, Shandong. Inside the woods lie the tombs of the Kong family, which is the reason why the character *lin*—literally, "woods"—is sometimes translated as "cemetery." The woodland cemetery reportedly began as trees planted by generations of disciples of Confucius to memorialize their teacher. It has grown to spread across three thousand *mu* (roughly 494 acres). The association between the memory of Confucius and these woods remained so strong that during the Cultural Revolution, when youth across the country attacked sites of "feudal" importance to create a new socialist society, one hundred thousand impassioned Red Guards felled five thousand of the cemetery's ancient pines as they destroyed the graves and defiled the corpses of Confucius and his descendants.[12]

The continued relevance of the memorial trees and woodlands from early in China's history to later periods was no coincidence. Southern Chinese elites during the Song, Yuan, and Ming dynasties (960–1644) used lineage cemeteries to protect their woodlands from state interference. This allowed lineages to maintain exclusive control over the management of their tree farms.[13] This practice appears to have continued in the Han heartland throughout the Qing dynasty (1644–1912), as historical records mention that an artisan had been cutting down trees in his ancestral cemetery before becoming embroiled in the "soul-stealing" scandal of 1768.[14] In addition to cemeteries, trees in the Han heartland were also protected and planted on temple grounds, on sacred mountains such as Mt. Tai, in the Confucius Woods, and in imperial mausoleums throughout the Qing dynasty. David Bello (chapter 6, this volume) discusses the role that imperial mausoleums played in maintaining the spiritual health of the dynasty's qi in imperial cosmology. Conservation of the woodlands in the Mulan Imperial Hunting Grounds along Inner Asian lines also played a fundamental role through which Inner Asian elites asserted their cultural supremacy over the Han majority.[15]

However, the Taiping Rebellion and natural disasters of the nineteenth and early twentieth centuries led to the deforestation of southern China's landscape. As one missionary observer described:

Wherever the rebels encamped, forests, small in extent but the growth of centuries, where they existed, were ruthlessly destroyed to afford fuel and timber to the marauders; and even in those places which escaped such destruction, the deteriorated influence of monks and priests and the lost character of sacred groves, even now allow the sound of the wood-cutter's axe to resound through the otherwise still and somber forests. Thus in 1854 tall fir-trees on the White Cloud Hills near Canton were destroyed, and in the celebrated Lofau mountains many were cut.[16]

By the early Republican period, trees were so scarce that residents of Nanjing stripped branches from trees in a local tree farm to plant them on the tombs of their ancestors on Tomb-Sweeping Festival.[17]

Despite this tradition of protecting memorial trees and woodlands, by the twentieth century, China's land had a far lower rate of forest cover than it had during the times of Confucius and Han Wudi. Chapter 9 in this volume, on Nuosu environmental management, encourages scholars to consider the distinction between ecosystem and social sustainability. The former requires that natural resources retain their biodiversity, while the latter requires that a society be able to persist in maintaining its livelihood.[18] As scholars have pointed out, coastal China's ecosystem has not been sustainable for at least a millennium.[19] However, we know that China was socially sustainable throughout most of that time period thanks in part to both ingenious woodlands management practices and the intervention of a proactive Qing state.[20]

Changes in China's domestic and international circumstances resulted in the fall of China's social sustainability. Foreign observers and Chinese elites alike believed that afforestation was the answer to this problem. The photographs and testimonials of foreign observers made China infamous in the international community for its barren landscape. Ling Daoyang, a Chinese forester who earned a master's degree in forestry from Yale University in 1914, described attending classes and lectures where foresters displayed images of China's landscape as an example of the perils of forestry. "Every time foreigners refer to the damage of China's barren mountains it becomes a warning to the people of that country. This [means] that on the inside [they] receive a careful warning against this loss, but on the outside laughter and denigration remains."[21] Much like Lu Xun, the May Fourth movement author, would later describe in the preface to his first collection of short stories, *Call to Arms*, Ling Daoyang describes this as an edifying experience that motivated him to pursue forestry for the good of the Chinese nation.[22]

During the Republican period, the Beiyang and Nationalist governments began to promote reforestation projects.[23] In 1916, Yuan Shikai's Ministry of Agriculture and Commerce began to mandate the annual celebration of Arbor Day at the national, provincial, and county levels of government.[24] Beginning in 1928, the Nationalist government made Arbor Day part of Reforestation Movement Education Week.[25]

Each government justified Arbor Day reforestation projects in terms of economic, political and health-related benefits, such as improving China's national image, increasing China's timber resources, reducing China's economic dependence on foreign nations, reducing erosion, improving air quality, and even improving the emotional well-being of the Chinese public. However, these were not the only goals behind Republican reforestation projects. Arbor Day ceremonies were also designed to promote national unity. Each year's ceremonies were held on the same day throughout the nation, regardless of regional variations in climate. This meant that some Arbor Day trees froze in the snow while others withered in the heat. Each level of government was also tasked with initiating Arbor Day afforestation projects, regardless of the suitability of the local soil and topography to tree cover. Nevertheless, central governments insisted that Arbor Day projects continue in the hopes of creating a unified, forested China.

Despite regional variations in Chinese tree-planting and conservation practices, Arbor Day activists endeavored to create a unified tree-planting culture that drew on this tradition of memorial trees and forests described earlier. Both the Beiyang and Nationalist governments sought to achieve this goal. Beginning in 1916, Beiyang governments held Arbor Day on the same day as Tomb-Sweeping Festival.

Beginning in 1928, the Guomindang mandated that the celebration of Arbor Day coincide with the anniversary of Sun Yat-sen's death (March 12 on the Western solar calendar). As mentioned previously, the Guomindang also extended Arbor Day activities to include Reforestation Movement Education Week. Images of and references to Sun Yat-sen abounded in these materials. In addition to reforestation projects designed to produce timber or to combat erosion, local governments and elites throughout the Chinese nation were encouraged to plant Sun Yat-sen memorial forests. The spirit of Sun Yat-sen was meant to live in the trees as a testament to the unity of Chinese land under the leadership of the Guomindang. The Nationalist government thus used trees as a means to extend its presence throughout the territory it claimed. During the Nanjing decade, Sun Yat-sen memorial forests thus signaled one's commitment to Nationalist modernization.

For those who believed in the impending deforestation of the Earth, China represented the West's dystopian future: poor, backward, and plagued by natural disasters. Lectures on forestry in the United States showed images of barren Chinese landscapes to their audiences, warning of America's pending doom if it did not reforest.[26] A 1916 editorial in the *New York Times* declared that "China is constantly cited as an example of the vast destruction wrought by floods as a result of deforestation."[27] Joseph Bailie, an Irish-American missionary to China, claims to have singlehandedly founded Chinese Arbor Day upon witnessing the destruction that local residents wrought on his tree farm on Tomb-Sweeping Festival. This tree farm project had been initially created due to Bailie's understanding that forestry was the key to China's economic and ecological salvation. By encouraging the government to set the holiday on Tomb-Sweeping Festival, Bailie hoped to redirect destructive customs into environmentally and economically productive ones.[28]

Chinese elites in both China and the United States took note of this trend in global discourse. Foresters such as Han An used their influence to encourage the Beiyang government to institute reforestation programs, including Arbor Day. In 1916, the Ministry of Agriculture and Commerce sent the following memorial asking for the establishment of a national Arbor Day celebration:

> In a time when axes should be used in moderation, holding a
> ceremony that emphasizes woodlands is truly the method [that
> will have] the broadest effect. For example, strengthening dykes,
> eliminating drought, [and] eliminating [natural] disasters are all
> especially obvious examples of the benefits of forests as they
> relate most to the people's livelihood.[29]

Though the ministry reframes the purpose of Arbor Day in Confucian terms rather than in the language of international forestry, the end goal is the same: to change popular attitudes toward woodlands to those that would be more productive to the state.

That same year, President Yuan Shikai instituted the first national Arbor Day celebration. In his edict, he notes being inspired by a combination of the international notoriety China's landscape had received, China's growing timber imports, and the impact of deforestation on agriculture:

[Whenever] foreigners discuss deforested countries, they all refer to China as an example. Out of all of our products the majority are foreign imports, which has led to the outward flow of our financial power. Fertile soil has become barren. At times [I] worry that our vast land and its many people are in dire straits.[30]

On what had traditionally been known as Tomb-Sweeping Festival, officials throughout the nation, from the president in Beijing to county officials on the Russian border, gave speeches on the importance of forestry to China's future. Local schoolchildren sang songs or read poetry that also glorified reforestation. This was typically followed by tree-planting demonstrations. The ceremony concluded with a photographer capturing a photograph of the most distinguished participants standing beside one or more of the planted trees. Officials then sent copies of these photographs to the Ministry of Agriculture and Commerce as part of their official Arbor Day reports.

Despite the Beiyang government's tenuous control over the territory previously governed by China's last dynasty, many officials, even in remote borderlands, participated in the ceremony. Even in Jilin Province, many (but not all) officials responded to the call to celebrate Arbor Day ceremonies. Jilin's Siberian climate meant that the ground was still frozen solid in early April. Nevertheless, officials still braved the cold to plant trees and take the requisite photographs. For instance, documents related to the celebration of Arbor Day in the counties of Jilin Province in 1917 consistently refer to the ground as not yet thawed.[31]

Many officials and institutions throughout the Chinese "nation" similarly showed enthusiasm for promoting Arbor Day. The governor of Jiangxi Province in warm southern China took the time to write a lengthy vernacular notice directed at the province's rural residents. He urged them to plant trees to improve their financial standings.[32] Students at the prestigious Tsinghua University cited Teddy Roosevelt as they planted trees at all five geomantic directions of their campus.[33] Elementary school students in Dongting County in Henan Province sang about the benefits of reforestation to local industry at an Arbor Day ceremony in 1924: "The fair Tomb-Sweeping Arbor Day promotes forestry. It places the peasant-farmers first as it creates [forests in] all places [so that there is] no wasted earth. It encourages the glory of Dongting's industry. Long live the tree farm! May it live forever!"[34] Arbor Day was thus widely celebrated enough that a Chinese forestry student commented:

Recent years have been marked by continuous internal chaos and we often see conflict. Only [the ritual of] Arbor Day has been continuously and unanimously carried out without regard to [differences between] the North and South . . . gentry, merchants, scholars and commoners, government [officials], students, soldiers and citizens all gather in one place to emphasize planting trees in grand rituals [performed by] distinguished men. Isn't this a bright light for the future of Chinese forestry?[35]

According to these accounts, Arbor Day during the Beiyang period was many things to many Chinese people. It connected people of different social classes and geographical regions, projecting a fleeting image of national unity in a time of discord. It also connected Chinese even in remote regions with a global discourse about the natural environment that privileged forested land.

NATIONALIST ARBOR DAY

The rise of the Guomindang to power in 1927 brought changes to national political ideology. In 1923, advisors from the Soviet Union had helped redesign the party on a Leninist model, despite the party's rejection of Marxism-Leninism. This meant that in addition to establishing its own army, the Guomindang developed its own unified political ideology based on Sun Yat-sen's Three Principles of the People: nationalism, democracy, and livelihood. Party leaders attempted to enforce ideological unity among all its members and to spread the Three Principles of the People throughout the areas under its military control. One of their first tasks upon their tentative unification of China in 1927 was to solidify their control over a vast territory. The Nationalists believed that promoting the philosophy of Sun Yat-sen would be key to accomplishing this task.

They had good reason to put its faith in the ability of Sun Yat-sen's image to garner support for its rule. Throughout the 1910s and until his death in 1925, Sun Yat-sen was a popular nationalist speaker and thinker. In 1912, he nearly became president of the newly founded republic. His ascension to the presidency was quickly thwarted by the military prowess of Yuan Shikai. Despite this setback, Sun remained popular among elite young Chinese in particular, who appreciated his excellent public speaking skills, idealism, and devotion to Chinese national development. On Sun's death in 1925, thousands of Chinese from across the country attended his funeral in Nanjing. Ambassadors and foreign representatives also attended, highlighting Sun's popularity in China and abroad.[36]

Even before their unification of China, the anniversary of Sun Yat-sen's death (March 12) was an important part of the Nationalists' political platform. In 1925, the party used the anniversary to run membership drives throughout the country.[37] Sun Yat-sen was not merely a symbol of a unified China; he was also a symbol of the party's specific vision of a unified China. "Alive, he had been a controversial politician; dead he was to become the Father of the Country," Henrietta Harrison has argued.[38] As Harrison's work has shown, Nationalist events conducted in honor of Sun Yat-sen challenged Beiyang era ideals of citizenship by dividing citizens into social classes, such as women, students, and workers.[39] Harrison also argues that in the 1920s, memorial services served as the means to solidify Sun as a "symbol open to multiple interpretations."[40] Ceremonies ranged from traditional Confucian rituals comprising elite members of the community to populist ceremonies that resembled festivals to commemorate the birth of the Buddha.[41] Sun Yat-sen's presence thus represented the party's goal to change the nature of citizenship and commemoration, just like his presence in Arbor Day would represent the party's goal to change the nature of Tomb-Sweeping Arbor Day.

In 1929, the Division of Woodlands Administration of the Ministry of Agriculture and Mining published a collection of articles on how to reform Arbor Day to accord with the goals of the Nationalist Party. They criticized the Beiyang ceremony for being "superficial and perfunctory."[42] They claimed that officials in the Beiyang period used Arbor Day merely as an excuse to drink tea and socialize. Ceremonies were hidden from the masses and, in supposed contrast to the American ceremony, did little to promote Chinese scientific forestry. This did not accord with Sun Yat-sen's Three Principles of the People, which held a central place in GMD thought at this time. Instead, "the Sun Yat-sen Memorial Arbor Day Ritual should be revolutionary, scientific, and for the masses."[43] It should also support Sun Yat-sen's vision of industrial development as outlined in the Third Principle of the People: the people's livelihood.[44]

Despite this seemingly industrialist approach to reforestation, the idea of trees being more than just timber remained a theme throughout the Ministry of Agriculture and Mining's volume of essays on Arbor Day. In an essay titled "My Humble Plan for Expanding the Reforestation Movement," the Japanese-educated forester Chen Zhi outlined the history of memorial trees in China, noting that the trees planted by Confucius and his descendants still existed. He argued that while stelae must often be repaired, trees can last long beyond the individual's lifetime. Planting memorial trees should thus become a part of national celebrations such as National Day and Martyr's Day. Not only this; tree-planting should also become a part of personal or familial celebrations such as births, graduations, marriages, and funerals.[45]

The rise of modernity across the world has been associated with the rise of scientific rationalism. Historians have argued that the "disenchantment" of Europe in particular began with the Reformation and continued past the Enlightenment. The Reformation separated religion from magic in that it "eliminat[ed] the ideas that religious rituals had any automatic efficacy" and denied the possibility that objects could be endowed with sacred power or that humans could have supernatural effects on the world.[46] Humans could change the natural world, but only through the use of scientific rationalism. With regard to forests, this meant that woodlands were no longer enchanted areas but rather the subject of scientific management practices conducted by trained professional foresters.[47] The Nationalist government implemented scientific forest management in the province of Fujian, a site of China's traditional timber market. Central directives and academic discourse placed Fujian's forests into the realm of scientific management, which in turn meant that they were in service to the nation. This national spirit would undergird Nationalist reforestation efforts of the 1930s.[48]

A similar change occurred in twentieth-century China with the separation of religion from superstition, when the Nationalist Party attempted to create a secular regime based on mass mobilization and popular support. Through the categorization and standardization of religious groups and the concomitant establishment of a religious hierarchy, the Nationalists sought not only to weaken the control of temple associations on Chinese society but also mobilize to them as agents of local power in service of the nation. In this process, some groups were arbitrarily discriminated against in the anti-superstition campaigns for their connections to certain political groups. Other groups, such as those temples sponsored by private citizens rather than public efforts, were merely encouraged to incorporate their activities within the scope of the nation. Campaigns against superstitious practices such as divination intensified under Nationalist rule.[49]

However, not all "superstitious" practices became targets of Nationalist campaigns. Feng shui woods were notable exceptions to this practice. Throughout the late imperial period, communities and individuals created feng shui woods to protect the "geomantic veins" that flowed through the earth, thereby ensuring the region's physical and spiritual well-being.[50] Geomantic veins, just like the veins in a human body, carry spiritual energy, qi, through the earth from nearby mountaintops. According to Chinese feng shui, or geomancy, tree roots could stabilize these veins, preventing flooding and other disasters, such as the failure of the county's men to succeed in the civil service examination. It was particularly important that trees protect the geomantic veins connected with tombs, as these could affect the fate of the entire lineage. Ian M. Miller dates this tradition back to the Song Dynasty (960–1279), when lineages used tombs to protect their woodlands from being utilized by the state.[51] By the Republican period, Chinese of all social classes consistently justified this tradition with fengshui theory.

Republican foresters understood these woodlands' connections to "superstitious" beliefs but were concerned that attacking geomancy would harm the woodlands they sought to protect. In 1936, one forester, named Xu Xiaochun, expressed concern that the "the progress of science [and] the gradual eradication of superstition" had led to the excessive logging of these fengshui woods.[52] "[Though] I am not advocating for superstition," Xu wrote, "I sincerely [believe] in the need for the conservation and use of these forests."[53] Even as he acknowledges the negative effects of anti-superstition campaigns, Xu nevertheless puts his faith in the power of scientific management and government intervention to solve the problem of overlogging in feng shui woodlands.

Proponents of Arbor Day took a different approach to solving the issue of forestry's connection to premodern and "superstitious" belief systems. They intended the traditional use of the dead and the spirit world to conserve woodlands for the good of the nation-state. In 1916, the governor of Jiangxi Province even went so far as to explicitly invoke the spirit world when urging local peasants to protect and plant trees. He warned the farmers that flood dragons might emerge from the mountains if they remained barren, thereby relying on their belief in the importance of covering geomantic mountain veins with trees.[54] Unlike other reforestation movements throughout the world, the Beiyang government did not think of trees as simply an "ecological technology" devoid of connection to the afterlife.[55] Rather, trees were enchanted through their connection to commemorating the dead during Tomb-Sweeping Festival. I refer to this as "political re-enchantment," because the Beiyang state sought to realign the enchantment of trees with the needs of the nation-state.

The Beiyang state was not alone in its political re-enchantment of trees. In 1928, the Nationalist government announced that it would no longer celebrate Tomb-Sweeping Arbor Day. Rather, it would celebrate Arbor Day on the anniversary of Sun Yat-sen's death.[56] This was followed in 1930 by the institution of Reforestation Movement Education Week, during which each level of government would hold other events that promoted reforestation.[57] The act of commemorating Sun Yat-sen would remain a vital part of Reforestation Movement Education Week projects. Chen Yunqian has argued that such ceremonies played a role in promoting the cult of Sun Yat-sen among the Chinese public.[58] Certainly, this was one of the Nationalist Party's goals for its tree-planting projects. As Chen notes, Nanjing's 1929 Arbor Day ceremony took place at the site of the newly completed Sun Yat-sen Mausoleum. More than thirty thousand people participated, planting primarily pine and cypress trees.[59] In 1929, the Beiping municipal government reminded its officials and citizens that the purpose of Arbor Day was to "aid remembrance and emphasize forestry."[60] The following year—in January 1930—Beiping officials laid out a plan to plant the city's first Sun Yat-sen memorial woodland on Jiulongshan. The woodland would spread across one hundred and twenty *mu*, or approximately twenty acres.[61] Beiping's 1931 propaganda leaflet speaks of the forest as the "precursor" to Sun Yat-sen's plan to reinvigorate industry, as it regulates temperature to protect against urban heat spells, regulates rainfall to protect against flood and drought, preserves water sources to protect the cleanliness of drinking water, and prevents erosion to protect agricultural land.[62]

The connection between the memory of Sun Yat-sen and tree planting is revealed in other aspects of Nationalist reforestation programs. Reforestation guides from the Nanjing decade, in direct contrast to those of the Beiyang period, provided model slogans for officials to hang in public places. Some further defined the utility of the forest ("Forests can clean the air, [creating] strong and healthy bodies!"), while others explained the inclusivity of the project ("Protecting forests is the shared duty of the government and the people!").[63] Yet no small number of these slogans, such as "Reforestation is the best way to remember the Premier!" and "Reforestation can realize the Premier's plans for material construction!," ask residents to reforest in the name of Sun Yat-sen's memory.[64] One slogan from a 1930 Arbor Day in Beiping declared that "Reforestation is the most important task in the Premier's industrial plan!" and "Only if [we] can implement the Premier's plan will it count as true remembrance."[65] Such slogans could be found from Gansu to Zhejiang and even in a remote logging county in Manchuria prior to Japanese invasion, well beyond the supposed reach of the Nationalist government in Nanjing.

Local governments and elites were also encouraged to plant Sun Yat-sen memorial woodlands in their jurisdictions. For instance, in 1937, Henan Province claims to have planted 273,726 trees as part of its contribution to the Sun Yat-sen memorial woodlands. These forests covered over 2,220 *mu* (approximately 362 acres) in approximately 101 separate jurisdictions, including rural counties and large cities such as Kaifeng.[66] As such, these spaces extended the idea of the tomb forest to include ostensibly secular sites deprived of access to the physical remains of the Father of the Nation.

Yet Sun Yat-sen was not the only one to receive his own memorial wood-lands. When President Yuan Shikai died in 1916, he was buried in a tomb in his hometown in Henan Province called the Yuan Lin (Yuan Cemetery). Other recently departed members of the Guomindang also earned the right to be memorialized through tree-planting projects. For instance, in 1934, prominent members of the Guomindang, including Chiang Kai-shek, Lin Sen, and the Chen brothers Chen Guofu and Chen Lifu, requested funds to purchase saplings to plant in memorial woodlands for their recently deceased colleague Zhou Bainian.[67] Zhou had been a friend and comrade to Sun Yat-sen and a member of the Guomindang's first Central Committee. To com-memorate him, senior members of the party sought to plant two separate memorial woodlands "to leave eternal thoughts for later generations."[68] Again, this reflects the sentiment expressed above by Chen Zhi: that the leg-acy of trees could last longer than stelae.[69]

The senior members of the Guomindang elected to honor Zhou Baini-an's dedication to China's development by planting fruit-bearing trees that could feed the Chinese people.[70] In the Nanjing decade, utility did not have to be sacrificed for the sake of commemoration; both could be accomplished in the same action. Even though trees planted in Sun Yat-sen's memory were typically not fruit bearing, that did not mean that they were ultimately deprived of utility. Most Sun Yat-sen memorial woodlands were filled with pine trees, which were originally a symbol of imperial longevity.[71] Beyond their symbolic function, they served as an excellent source of timber for tele-phone poles and bridge construction. And according to early twentieth-century forestry, they were just as good as any other tree at functions such as preventing erosion, purifying the air, and conserving sources of water.

Sun Yat-sen memorial woodlands were different from the Yuan Lin, memorial woodlands for the recently departed, and the living trees con-nected to existing officials. While these other examples were individual trees or woodlands planted in an area of importance to the image of the per-son it commemorated, Sun Yat-sen memorial woodlands could be any-where across the Chinese nation, even in sites that were not frequented by Sun during his lifetime. This was a significant change from earlier Chinese models of woodlands as commemoration, in which the trees were tied to the site of the tomb or to the site in which the person had personally visited. Yet Sun Yat-sen was to be commemorated not only by the pine trees on his tomb outside the Nationalist capital of Nanjing but also in the woodlands in rural counties of China's inland provinces. This reflected the Nationalist desire to use Sun Yat-sen Memorial Day and Sun Yat-sen memorial woodlands as a means to extend their ideological control throughout the country.

CONCLUSION

Tree planting played a significant role in the creation of a specific type of Chinese ecological modernity. Chinese in the first half of the twentieth century were very aware of the critical importance of woodlands to modern economies. Many key modern technologies such as the railroad and the telephone relied in great part on access to wood to remain functional, railroads for railroad ties and bridge beams and telegraphs and telephones for utility poles. Chinese were also aware of the ways in which self-professed "civilized" nations equated forest cover with a nation's level of civilization. Government-sponsored reforestation projects through the holiday of Arbor Day represented an attempt to change Chinese landscapes to meet the economic and ideological needs of global ecological modernity.

Chinese states in the Republican period also saw tree planting as a means to exercise and expand their ideological and political control over a fragmented Chinese nation. This was particularly true of the Nationalist regime. The merging of Sun Yat-sen Memorial Day and Arbor Day essentially standardized memorial services. In keeping with Nationalist attempts to standardize religious practices and eliminate unorthodox superstitions, Sun Yat-sen was no longer to be memorialized through superstitious Buddhist festivals or elitist traditional rituals.[72] Rather, his legacy should reflect both Chinese culture and Chinese modernity. Trees, with their associations with traditional Chinese burial culture, global environmentalism, and industrial production, became ideal tools for Nationalist commemoration ceremonies, symbols that Sun Yat-sen's spirit had been properly memorialized that year. The cultivation of Sun Yat-sen memorial woodlands also served as a symbol of allegiance to the principles of Nationalist governance. Trees, as such, did not lose their enchantment with the rise of modernity in China. Rather, they became re-enchanted with new political purpose.

And yet commemoration extended even beyond the spirit of Sun Yat-sen, though only his memory could truly pervade all of Nationalist China. In a period of frequent environmental disasters and warfare, death was a part of the Chinese landscape, both literally and figuratively. In the early 1910s, Joseph Bailie claimed that the presence of one dead body on his doorstop piqued his interest in forestry as a method of poverty relief.[73] During the Nanjing decade, the flood of the Huai River in 1931 brought death, poverty, and despair to the doorsteps of senior Guomindang officials in Nanjing. Linh Vu has shown that in other arenas, the Nationalists were also concerned about reconciling the numerous dead with the lives of the living, to the extent that the dead had "sovereignty" in Republican China.[74] Foresters urged the public to take up memorial tree planting so that the trees could heal their barren landscapes but also heal their souls. Reforestation guides emphasized not only the material and ecological benefits of trees but also their psychological benefits. A 1930 slogan from Jilin Province declared, "Reforestation can adorn the landscape and improve your health!"[75] Another reforestation guide from that same province in the same year reminded readers that forests could "improve your mental/spiritual state."[76]

In short, Republican reforestation projects were shaped by what Chinese elites and forestry professionals considered to be China's economic, political, and even mental/spiritual deficits. All these could be solved by the corrective influence of reforestation, but only if they were done in a way that accorded with the political and even spiritual needs of Republican governments rule. All the Republican governments, including that of the Nationalist Party, thus strove to make reforestation a panacea for China's ills, a symbol of loyalty, a hallmark of modernity, and a way to reconcile the violence and death that pervaded Republican life. To plant trees was to search for healing.

NOTES

1   Olson, *The Depletion Myth*.
2   *New York Times*, "Timber Famine Near, Says Mr. Roosevelt."
3   For more on this link between conservation and efficiency, see Hays. *Conservation and the Gospel of Efficiency*.
4   Shaw, *Chinese Forest Trees and Timber Supply*, 15.
5   Approximately 306 billion liters.
6   Approximately 10.8 billion liters.
7   Nanman tielu diaocha ke, *Jilinsheng zhi linye*, 1–2.
8   See the introduction to this volume.
9   Reforestation refers to the natural or artificial restoration of a forest on land that it had once covered. Afforestation, on the other hand, refers to the establishment of forests on land that has not been forested in the recent past, such as a desert or grasslands. See Sweeney, "Sixty Years on the Margin," 50–51; Lemenih and Kassa, "Re-Greening Ethiopia," 1897; Ford, "Reforestation, Landscape Conservation," 9–10; Woodcock, "To Restore the Watersheds," 624–35.
10   Karle and Karle, *Conserving the Dust Bowl*.
11   Ling, *Senlin yaolan*, 26–30.
12   Ye and Barmé, "Commemorating Confucius in 1966–67."
13   Miller, *Fir and Empire*.
14   Kuhn, *Soulstealers*, 21.

15 See David Bello's chapter in this volume.
16 Haas, "The Feng Tree."
17 Stross, *The Stubborn Earth*, 82.
18 See chapter 9 in this volume.
19 Elvin, *The Retreat of the Elephants*.
20 Miller, *Fir and Empire*; and Will, *Bureaucracy and Famine*.
21 Ling, *Senlin Yaolan*, 2.
22 Lu, "Preface to the First Collection of Short Stories," 2.
23 My 2020 article outlines in greater detail the origins and structure of Beiyang governments' celebration of Arbor Day in the late 1910s and 1920s; Pitts, "Unity in the Trees."
24 Republican Collection, Jilin Provincial Archives, 101-4-413.
25 April 7, 1928, 00100004714A, p. 112, National Government Collection, Academia Historica, Taipei, Taiwan
26 Ling, *Senlin yaolan*, 1.
27 Chittenden, "The Myth of the Forest."
28 Stross, *The Stubborn Earth*, 66–91.
29 A reference to a passage from *Mencius* in which Mencius exhorts King Xuan of Qi to manage the natural world effectively to benefit his people's livelihoods. Republican Collection, Jilin Provincial Archives, 101-4-413.
30 *Nongshang gongbao*.
31 Republican Collection, Jilin Provincial Archive, Changchun, China, 101-6-1378.
32 Jiangxi Xunanshi, "Quan zhishubaihua."
33 "Zhishu jieji," 6–7.
34 "Zhishu dianli," 4.
35 Kang Nongman, "Qingming zhishujie," 1.
36 Harrison, *The Making of the Republican Citizen*, 214.
37 Harrison, *The Making of the Republican Citizen*, 218.
38 Harrison, *The Making of the Republican Citizen*, 144.
39 Harrison, *The Making of the Republican Citizen*, 225–26.
40 Harrison, *The Making of the Republican Citizen*, 144.
41 Harrison, *The Making of the Republican Citizen*, 144–48.
42 Chen Yu, "Zhishushi yu Zhishujie," 2.
43 Chen Yu, "Zhishushi yu Zhishujie," 2.
44 Chen Xuechen, "Zhongshan xiansheng zhi senlin zhengce," 16–23.
45 Chen Zhi, "Kuoda zaolin yundong jihua chuyi," 23–25.
46 Scribner, "The Reformation," 475.
47 Scott, *Seeing like a State*.
48 Songster, "Cultivating the Nation in Fujian's Forests," 461–65.
49 Nedostup, *Superstitious Regimes*.
50 Coggins, *The Tiger and the Pangolin*, 195–213.
51 Miller, *Fir and Empire*.

52 Xu Xiaochun, "Fengshuilin ying baocun," 608.

53 Xu Xiaochun, "Fenshuilin ying baocun," 609.

54 Jiangxi xunanshi, "Quan zhishu baihua."

55 Karle and Karle, *Conserving the Dust Bowl*, 8.

56 Academia Historica 00100004714A.

57 Jilin Provincial Archives, 20-3-101.

58 Chen, "Zhishujie yu Sun Zhongshan chongbai."

59 Chen, "Zhishujie yu Sun Zhongshan chongbai," 79.

60 Economic Archives, Institute of Modern History 17-20-013-02, February 18, 1929.

61 Economic Archives, Institute of Modern History, Academia Sinica, Taipei, Taiwan, 17-20-013-02, January 1930.

62 Economic Archives, Institute of Modern History, 17-20-013-02.

63 *Zaolin yundong xuanchuan dagang*, 15.

64 *Zaolin yundong xuanchuan dagang*, 14.

65 Economic Archives, Institute of Modern History, 17-20-013-02, January 1930.

66 National Government Collection, Academia Historica, 001000006763A, February 21, 1924.

67 National Government Collection, Academia Historica, 001000006798A, February 21, 1934.

68 National Government Collection, Academia Historica, 001000006798A, February 21, 1934.

69 Chen Zhi, "Kuoda zaolin yundong jihua chuyi," 23–25.

70 Academia Historica, 001000006798A, February 21, 1934.

71 Li, *Zhongguo chuantong songbai wenhua*.

72 Nedostup, *Superstitious Regimes*.

73 Stross, *The Stubborn Earth*, 66–68.

74 Vu, "The Sovereignty of the War Dead."

75 Republican Archives, Jilin Provincial Archives, 111-2-1204.

76 Republican Archives, Jilin Provincial Archives, 111-3-1998.

CHAPTER NINE

SUNNY SLOPES ARE GOOD FOR GRAIN, SHADY SLOPES ARE GOOD FOR TREES

Nuosu Yi Agroforestry in Southwestern Sichuan

STEVAN HARRELL, AMANDA H. SCHMIDT, BRIAN D. COLLINS,
R. KEALA HAGMANN, AND THOMAS M. HINCKLEY

F OR the past 1,800 years or so, Nuosu people have inhabited the Liang-shan (Cool Mountain) region, most of which is now in Liangshan Yi Autonomous Prefecture in the southwestern part of Sichuan (figure 9.1).[1] Like most of the upland peoples of what is now Southwest China and neighboring parts of the area that James Scott, following Willem van Schendel, has called Zomia, the Nuosu lived on the margins of empires, subject only indirectly if at all to central, bureaucratic states.[2] Their livelihoods combined crop agriculture, including both swidden and fixed-field cultivation, animal husbandry, and subsistence forestry.[3]

Both imperial and modern Chinese observers and governing authorities saw these and like practices as inefficient and wasteful of land, leading to permanent deforestation and its consequences in erosion, loss of soil fertility, and changes in river depth and course.[4] By engaging in agriculture in forested mountain environments across geography and history, Nuosu exposed the heavily used sunny slopes and ridge tops where they made their swiddens to possible erosion and soil loss. In a 2013 interview, two Nuosu elders living in the Baiwu valley in Yanyuan County described the luxuriant forests they remembered from their youth and explained what happened to them over the past half-century. Although their memories were undoubtedly tinged with nostalgia, they were clear-eyed in recognizing that the swidden agriculture practiced since the time of their ancestors also had

Swiddened after 1750, reverted to forest after 1900, some logging 1980s; now mixed pine-alder, oak, rhodo; thick soils

Clearcut 1970s

Pine forest: heavily cut 1950s - present

Swiddened 1750s-1950s, intensively cultivated 1950s-1980s; heavily grazed by livestock, cut for fuel, construction; thin or no soil

Valley bottom: River braided in lower 3 km; heavily grazed, used for transport. Riverine forest cut 1950s-1980s

▲ Geomorph. soil pits
■ 2002 soil samples
● 2009 forest plots

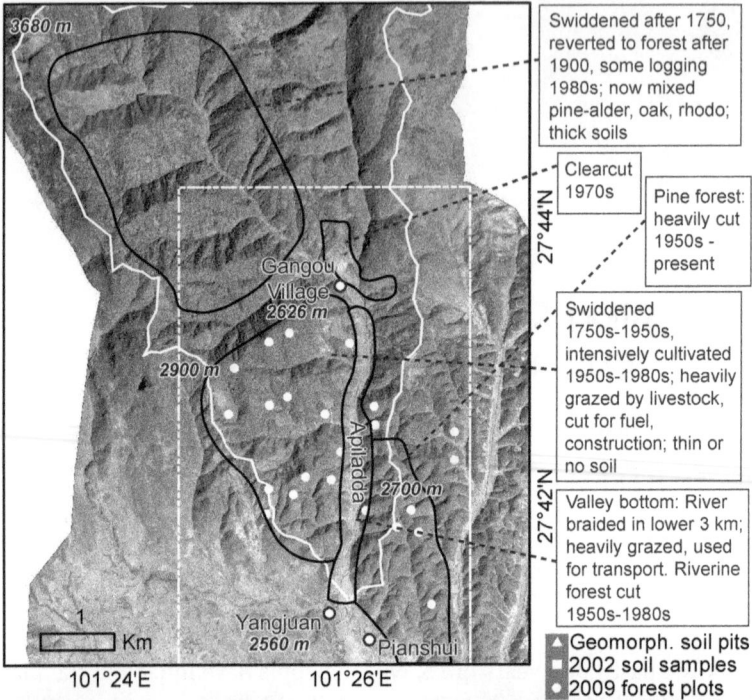

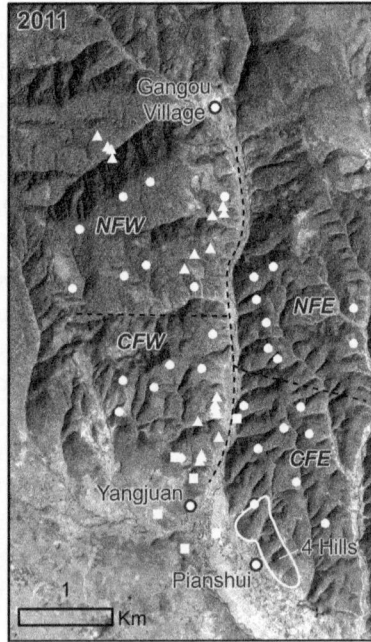

FIGURE 9.1. The Baiwu valley. Top: Watershed boundaries; summary of cultivation and forest history. Bottom Left: 1967 declassified satellite image view showing widespread swiddens west of Apiladda. Bottom Right: 2011 Quickbird view showing extensive regrowth and sites of soil pits and forest plots.

deleterious effects on the local ecology, particularly through erosion of steep slopes and riverbanks:

> Hxiesse Vuga: A long time, a long time ago, there were really big trees here, but now there aren't any big trees . . . thick ones, particularly thick, in places where people can't go [there are, but] . . . in places that are close and you can cut them, big trees, there aren't any.
>
> Hxiesse Vuga: In those times there was still damage. Because in those days we did slash-and-burn. So you cut down the trees, and burned them, and then mixed the ashes into the soil and used them to fertilize the soil. But now almost nobody does slash-and-burn anymore, and the forests are regrowing luxuriantly.
>
> Lurlur Adda: Earlier on, here on the land in the valley, there were alder trees, thorn trees, a lot of them growing, a thick forest . . . with birds everywhere, but then later on, they were cut down for cultivation, and . . . there was erosion.

Despite their knowledge that swiddening can cause erosion, Nuosu in the Baiwu area continued to practice their three-part livelihood for about two hundred years. How did they sustain this livelihood in the face of the environmental changes they brought to the area?

Modern observers have not only criticized Zomian swidden cultivation as degrading to ecosystems; many have also dismissed indigenous knowledge as superstitious, backward, and lacking the insights of objective modern science.[5] They have seen the remedy for this backwardness in scientifically inspired "development."[6] However, many ecological anthropologists have documented systems that persisted for long periods without hampering local people's ability to make a living from the land, and quantitative studies of erosion rates in swidden systems have documented variation of more than three orders of magnitude, from those that erode soil more slowly than it forms to those that would strip topsoil in a few decades.[7]

It is clear that Nuosu traditional livelihood was socially sustainable; their mountain society survived largely independent of imperial or national influence until the mid-twentieth century.[8] Ecological sustainability is more problematic. There is no question that Nuosu habitation altered the environment; they transformed woods into fields, caused erosion, and changed forest composition. At the same time, consciously guided by their environmental philosophy or traditional ecological knowledge (TEK), they continued to gain a livelihood from that environment. Rather than an unchanging system of "ancient wisdom," it appears that Nuosu environmental philosophy has been a guide to continuance in a changing environment.[9]

Since 1956, the Nuosu have no longer lived in Zomia as Scott portrays it; in that year, the Chinese Communist regime assumed effective control over Liangshan and initiated a series of developmental programs that fundamentally altered the relationship of Nuosu people to their forests.[10] No longer able to follow their own environmental philosophy, the people of the Baiwu watershed initiated new practices that diminished the productivity and biodiversity of their forests. Since the 1990s, however, there has been some recovery, shaped by a tacit consensus between modern environmental science and native philosophy, even though it is mostly elders who remember that philosophy in detail.

NUOSU ENVIRONMENTAL PHILOSOPHY

The core of Nuosu natural philosophy is the recognition that the social system and the ecosystem are both parallel and connected. The same ideas guide ethical behavior with other people and ethical behavior with the environment. The patriclan system is central to Nuosu conceptions of the connections and the parallels between the human and the natural worlds. The Nuosu creation epic Hnewo Teyy describes the genealogy of the Snow Clan, which developed after a previous world was destroyed and red snow fell from the sky:

Of the twelve snow tribes
six groups had blood,
six groups had no blood.
Of the six without blood,

one group was grasses.
Black-headed grass
grows in the grassy places,
in three hundred grassy places;
the second group was trees—
white cypress was a snow tribe;
the third group was fir trees—
the fir trees growing in the high mountains;
the fourth group was *bbyp zy* grass—
the long-legged *bbyp zy* grass was a snow tribe;
the fifth group was *put nuo* grass,

black *put nuo* grass was a snow son,
the *put nuo* grass growing in the marshlands.
The sixth group was green vines,
growing at the foot of trees and in caverns.

The six groups with blood were:
One group was frogs,
the frog group had three brothers,
living in the marshy places.

The second group was snakes.
the snake tribe's eldest son
became a *tusi* dragon,
and lived in the high, barren cliffs.
The snake tribe's second son
was the *shy go bbo hlut* snake,
that lived in the top of the fields.
The youngest son of the snake tribe
was the *bbu jjie ke hni* snake,
that lived in the muddy places.
The snake tribe became larger and larger.

The third group were large vultures,
the king of the winged creatures;
the vultures of the vast sky,
living in the white clouds and mountains.

The fourth group was the old bears.
The black bear had one mother and two sons.
They spread out into the fir forests,
and the black bears became plentiful.

The fifth group was monkeys.
The red monkeys had one mother and two sons.
They spread out into the forests,
and the red monkeys became plentiful.

The sixth group was humans.
The humans lived in the human world,
and the humans, in their realm, became plentiful.[11]

Humans and other species thus constitute an ecosystem in the same way that an assemblage of clans constitutes a society. Humans and animals are also related according to a folk taxonomy that divides terrestrial creatures into three "phyla," according to what "hangs" (*ndit*) on their bodies. *Bbipndit* are those who have hooves; they include cattle, pigs, sheep, goats, deer, antelopes, and so on. People are allowed to kill and eat them. *Vopndit*, on the other hand, have claws or fingers, and cannot be eaten; they include horses (because of their dewclaws), dogs, cats, frogs, bears, monkeys, and people. The third category are *ddurndit*, those with wings hanging on them; they include birds and various insects, some of which can be eaten, some of which cannot.

Because the human world and the natural world are both alike and attached, each can serve as an ethical lesson for how to behave with respect to the other. These lessons are expressed in ordinary proverbs and also in parallel couplets (occasionally triplets or quatrains) called *lurby*, many of which refer to natural resources and conservation.

It is not ethical to cut trees unnecessarily: "When a pine is cut, it doesn't grow again." Aside from the obvious dendrological lesson—the Yunnan pine (*Pinus yunnanensis*) does not sprout after coppicing as oaks do, for example— there is a lesson in social ethics here: "Don't burn your bridges." The same sentiment is expressed in another *lurby*: "Do the white, eat the white." White refers to the color of pine wood, and "do" in this case means cut down. If you cut a pine, you have eaten (used) the pine. There is nothing wrong with cutting a pine if you do it at the proper season (see below) and you need it, usually for house construction, since pine posts and beams are the straightest. But you need to consider whether you need it or not.

The relationship to soil is also an ethical one. A *lurby* states, "Land belongs to those who work it; disputes belong to those who initiate them." In other words, do not spoil your relationship with other people any more than you would ruin the land you work. It may be necessary to offend or oppose someone; Nuosu pride themselves on their martial valor. But do not engage in conflict unnecessarily. Conversely, do not ruin the land you work, any more than you should ruin your relationships with other people. The social and the biophysical reflect and reinforce each other—or, "Don't neglect thanks for a gift; don't eat (consume) the fertility of your land."

As with trees and soil, so with trees and water, or with trees, water, and soil. Here it is best to consider two *lurby* together: "Trees are elder kin; water is elder kin," and "Mother's brother gives to father; water flow is maintained." As the structure of society (or put another way, the process of reproduction of people, and thus of the clan) and the process of production (of the natural resources that allow the clan to reproduce and endure) are parallel, so trees standing by water are like the maternal uncle.

Because the clan cannot reproduce itself—marriage within the descent group is incest—the clan needs outside women to marry into it and become mothers, ideally by matrilateral cross-cousin marriage (a man marries his mother's brother's daughter). In a patriarchal society, the males of the mother's clan (the mother's "brothers," who might well be her paternal uncles or agnatic cousins) give the bride to the groom's clan and thus stand beside the father. The trees by the stream are also elder kin like the mother's brother; they prevent bank erosion and keep the water clear for humans and livestock to drink and not get sick. They also prevent the stream bank erosion that might take away valuable pasture or farmland. That is the parallel; the connection is that the trees, ensuring production, feed the mother's clan and allow the mother's brother to give away the bride and thus ensure reproduction.

Structures of time and space are also important in Nuosu ecological ethics. In the Cool Mountains, there is a huge difference in natural forest growth between sunny slopes (*bbuhlit*, or *yangpo* in Chinese) and shady slopes (*bbusi*, *yinpo* in Chinese). In the sections of the Baiwu valley that have not been swiddened for a long time, the forest overstory is mostly pines on sunny slopes and hilltops and mostly alders, oaks, and rhododendron on the shady side. In agricultural terms, a *lurby* sums this up neatly: *bbuhlit zzabbo he, bbusi sybbo he*: "Sunny slopes are good for grain; shady slopes are good for trees."

Another *lurby* emphasizes the parallel between the needs to preserve your relationship with those closest to you and with the landscape you live in: "A rabbit does not eat the grass around its own den; an eagle doesn't poop around its own nest." Sacred groves, where rituals are performed, are also areas that cannot be fouled. This prohibition is observed to this day; people report that those who were forced to cut trees in such groves during the Cultural Revolution have met untimely deaths.

As with space, so with time. Nuosu communities divide the year into two activity seasons, a "growing season" and a "killing season."[12] The growing season starts when the first rhododendrons bloom in spring and lasts until the final crop (usually oats) is harvested in the fall. During this season, crops are in the fields, deciduous trees are in leaf, and all plants are in growth; it is forbidden to cut down trees (though one may cut branches or gather wood lying on the ground), and it is forbidden to hunt wild birds or animals (it is permitted to slaughter livestock). After the last harvest, both crops and wild plants are dormant, and in the fall and winter, one can cut trees (fall is the primary firewood gathering season) and hunt wild animals. Killing trees or wild animals out of season will disrupt the natural order and bring natural calamities, in particular devastating hailstorms.

An orderly arrangement of human activity in space and time should thus, according to Nuosu natural philosophy, lead to sustainability of both the social and the natural order. Neither the natural nor the social is prior to or more important than the other; they are structured in similar ways and depend on each other for their mutual survival.

This is a beautiful philosophy. But beautiful philosophies in many societies have failed to stem the slow progress of resource degradation. The Daoist and Confucian traditions in Han society have also produced admirable philosophies of human harmony with nature. But these elite philosophies did not prevent long-term deforestation and its concomitant environmental degradation starting as early as the Zhou, nor did they prevent the much more devastating degradation of mountain environments that accompanied the Qing population explosion.[13] Did Nuosu natural philosophy do any better? Did it lead to a sustainable relationship between people and the environment? Over the past twenty years, we have conducted ethnohistorical, ecological, and geomorphological research to address this question.[14]

THE UPPER BAIWU VALLEY

The Upper Baiwu valley contains two villages, Yangjuan and Pianshui, inhabited entirely by Nuosu people. The valley floor rises from an elevation of 2,550 meters at Yangjuan to 2,700 at Gangou; surrounding hills rise to over 3,000 meters. Summers are wet and cool, and winters are dry and cold; annual precipitation is about one meter. Current residents' ancestors arrived nine generations before today's young adults, probably in the mid- to late eighteenth century. Until 1956, Nuosu in the Baiwu valley were still living basically independent of technological modernity. Until the early 1900s, local Nuosu lived almost entirely in the hills and benchlands surrounding the alluvial plains of Apiladda and Yiejjoladda downstream and practiced mostly swidden cultivation (figure 9.1).[15]

They lived scattered in clusters of no more than five houses—usually fewer—and cultivated the sunny slopes and ridgetops on a rather fast cycle. In one typical sequence, they would cut trees, burn the residue to fertilize the fields, and plant buckwheat; the second year, they could plant oats, which have a lower yield; and the third year, they planted potatoes, before allowing the field to rest for eight to ten years and repeating the cycle.[16] These slopes did not entirely revert to forest in the eight to ten years they were left fallow, but elders state that they could produce good crops on these plots again after this time. In the twentieth century, after acquiring some valley bottom and benchlands, they could grow corn, but even the alluvial plains and valleys are too cold for rice. They kept oxen (who pulled plows and were also sacrificed on the most important occasions) along with flocks of sheep and goats (kept for both meat and wool). People often pastured these animals on fallow fields in the winter or during the resting phase of the rotation; their manure may have helped fertilize the fields. Pigs went out to pasture with the other ungulates, as did horses, who pulled carts and carried riders, sometimes in holiday races.

As the *lurby* indicates, they left the shady slopes to forests, which provided resources essential to Nuosu livelihood, most importantly fuel, ideally from hot-burning alder, oak, or rhododendron that grow in shady places. The three-needled Yunnan pine (*Pinus yunnanensis*) predominates on the sunny slopes and ridgetops and in some areas on shady slopes as well. Pine is an inferior firewood, but it is strong and straight, ideal for house pillars, beams, doors, agricultural tools, and the minimal furniture that Nuosu kept in their houses.[17] Pine resin also served as a slow-burning lamp or candle in the days before electricity. In all kinds of forests, people gathered foods and medicines from the plants and fungi of the understory, as well as bamboo for making baskets, trays, and the mats spread out on the floor around the hearth in the middle of the house, covered by felt blankets made from the wool of their sheep. They hunted game in the more remote and higher-elevation forests of rhododendrons, oaks, firs, and a species of five-needle pine (*Pinus armandii*) closely related to the white pines of North America.

Everyone who remembers the forests of earlier times recalls their species richness. Some have vanished, and others are now rare, including *Keteleeria davidiana,* which now grows only in a sacred grove in the hills above Yangjuan. Several trees, including willows, alders, and poplars, grew in the alluvial valley of Apiladda but were almost gone by the 1980s. People also remember how big the trees were before so many forests were cut after the 1950s, often stretching their arms out in a not-quite complete circle to indicate the circumference.

Birds abound in distant memories; people woke in the morning to birdsongs, many of which were informative. The magpie darts around and squawks, announcing the arrival of guests; the crow inspects the smoke from a funeral pyre and flies in a certain direction that *bimox* priests can use to divine the fate of descendants; the cuckoo comes in the spring and proclaims that it is time to plant corn. Little boys spent hours setting snares for small forest birds that they could roast over a fire, perhaps with some potatoes or turnips. There were not only several species of cervids—*bbipndit*, and thus edible in the "killing season"—there were also black bears, red pandas, two kinds of wildcats, wolves that stole livestock, and the occasional leopard.

Around 1900, most Nuosu moved out of the mountains north of Gangou Village to the foothills and benchlands to the south, purchasing land on the valley floors, while a few continued to cultivate swiddens in the mountains. In the 1930s, a few households moved to the site of the current Yangjuan Village; others remained on the benchlands until the democratic reforms of 1956. In the early twentieth century, they also began to grow some opium as a cash crop in swiddens, but according to elders, it did not use much land. Their basic patterns of livelihood did not change much.

The relationship between humans and forests changed drastically after 1956, when the Chinese Communists' developmental regime promoted a series of programs designed to boost production and modernize the livelihoods of the "backward" (*luohou*) minority peoples. They concentrated formerly hill-dwelling people in *jumin dian*, or "residents' points," on the sites of the current villages just above the alluvial plains, more than doubling the population of the current site of Yangjuan and settling people in Pianshui where none had lived previously. This relocation put extra pressure on the lower elevation Yunnan pine-dominated forests nearer the new villages in three ways. First, people were required to cut large swaths of trees to build their new houses and to fuel the kilns that roasted the local limestone to make lime for construction.[18] Second, whereas people previously had gathered their firewood in areas near the scattered compounds where they lived, now they all lived in one place, and no one wanted to go too far to cut and carry heavy firewood, so they all began gathering in the same places. Third, development meant agricultural intensification. Farmers were required to eliminate the fallow phase of the swidden cycle in favor of annual cultivation on ridgetops and sunny mountain slopes, and they even had to rake and remove forest litter to provide fertilizer for lowland fields. They also cleared areas in the mountains that had previously been forested and never farmed. In the 1980s, state forestry companies logged some more distant forests for the more valuable species of trees.[19]

As a result, there were further major changes in the environment. Whether these recent changes brought about or accelerated resource degradation provides a partial answer to the question of whether Nuosu traditional livelihoods were sustainable. Did the traditional practices of Nuosu communities result in less degradation of site productivity than the more intensive practices adopted after they became subjects of the developmental state? Did their traditional ecological knowledge allow them to use resources in ways that preserved options for future generations? Do the obviously nostalgic tales of old men reflect several centuries of sustainable resource use, or were landscapes degrading, perhaps imperceptibly, even before the substantial increase in resource use that began in 1956?

More than two decades of ethnographic and historical interviews, guided walks with community elders, community mapping, and collection of quantitative and qualitative data on the forests, pastures, and streams in the watershed help us answer questions about sustainability.[20] Geomorphology provides insight into erosion and deposition of soil over scales ranging from decades to centuries, while forest ecology provides a snapshot of the current state of the forest, from which we can infer processes that have led to its current state.

GEOMORPHOLOGY: OCCUPATION AND EROSION

To understand how Nuosu livelihoods in the Baiwu valley might have affected soils and thus influenced both forest growth and hydrological patterns, we investigated two kinds of sites—the hillside areas where soil might have been lost to erosion and the valley-bottom areas where eroded soil might have been deposited as sediment.

To determine a possible association between soil loss and heavily used areas, we dug soil pits at distances ranging from 0.7–7.1 km from the current villages; we used distance to the Baiwu's headwaters as a proxy for decreased intensity of use. We measured the thickness of soil horizons, or layers, to determine whether there were differences between sites having different use histories. We measured sites on north-facing (shady) and south-facing (sunny) slopes at lower, middle, and upper locations because on a given slope, soil depth varies by both aspect and slope position in addition to climate, vegetation, and other factors and because historic Nuosu land use varied by aspect.[21]

Soil depth in fifteen soil pits on south-facing slopes was highly variable (range 1.5–147.5 cm; median 22 cm) but increased systematically with distance from the villages of Yangjuan and Pianshui.[22] Erosion from land uses likely partially accounts for this gradient because land-use intensity at least since 1900 decreased with distance up-valley; we do not have information on distribution of land use prior to 1900. Soil depth in seven soil pits on north-facing hillslopes, in contrast, was less variable (range 20–72 cm; median 55 cm) and did not vary with distance from the villages.[23] Because elevation also varies with distance from the villages, it is possible that the observed distribution of soil depths on south-facing slopes could reflect a natural increase in soil depth with elevation and associated climatic gradients. However, available data suggest that forest soil depths generally vary with elevation by much less than the amount we document, and we must look to past land use and associated erosion to explain this variation. Indeed, we find that south-facing soils are thinner higher on hillsides and deeper lower down, suggesting that farming and associated land uses on upper slopes were major drivers of erosion. This is confirmed by elders' observation that cleared fields on steep slopes were subject to erosion. The inference that the observed variation in soil depths is largely related to historic land-use intensity is supported by the *absence* of systematic variation in soil thickness on north-facing slopes, where Nuosu did not customarily farm.

To assess *when* soils eroded, we used an increment borer to determine the approximate age of the largest *Pinus yunnanensis* near each soil pit, reasoning that a positive relationship between soil depth and growth rate might suggest that erosion preceded tree establishment, and no relationship might suggest erosion happened during the tree's lifespan. This hypothesis is supported by research elsewhere in Liangshan that shows that *Pinus yunnanensis* is sensitive to soil depth such that deeper soils produce larger trees.[24] The approximate ages of trees in our sample did not vary systematically with distance up-basin, ranging everywhere from twenty-four to sixty years (median 39.5 years), indicating that the trees established in 1950–86.[25] Tree growth rate, however, did increase with distance up-basin, accounting for 77 percent of the variation in growth rate in our sample.[26] Soil depth accounts for part of this variability, weakly but significantly correlating with distance.[27] The influence of climate on tree growth rate could potentially confound the correlation between tree growth and soil depth, but three studies conducted nearby showed that *Pinus yunnanensis* growth rates declined with elevation, making it unlikely that climate confounds the analysis.[28] In addition, we did not observe exposed tree roots or soil pedestals, supporting the hypothesis that A and B horizons eroded prior to tree establishment in 1950–86. The O horizon also thickened with distance from the villages, probably indicating less human use of needle litter in recent decades. O horizon thickness may also be a determinant of tree growth rate, but we find no correlation ($r^2 = 0.001$) in our data between O horizon thickness and growth rate. Moreover, because soil depth explains only part of the variation in our data, other aspects of recent forest use plausibly also influence growth rate; this is explored in the forest ecology section. In sum, our observations of soil thickness, tree growth patterns, and other erosional markers suggest that soil likely eroded prior to 1950.

For another indicator of *when* soils eroded, we described and dated sediments deposited in the valley bottom. Valley bottoms archive, or store, sediments eroded from hillsides in terraces, which are formerly active floodplains that are stranded and preserved when a river incises through the floodplain. Sediments in these terraces, which are exposed in the banks of the river that runs through the valley, are predominantly silt and fine sand in size—deposits that resulted from repeated flooding of the river. Gravelly river-bed deposits are less common. That these deposits are 1–2 m thick tell us that flood deposits accumulated in the valley bottom for a long period in the past. From this we can infer that in the period when these fine sediments were deposited, more sediment was eroded from hillsides than the river could transport, implying rapid rates of erosion; additionally, the abundance of fine-grained sediments is consistent with being sourced from surface erosion. That these sediments are preserved in river terraces in itself tells us that the river has incised after the deposition of these sediments, implying that at some point the amount of sediment contributed to the river diminished. In short, the sedimentary record in the valley is consistent with an earlier period of intense soil erosion in the basin that subsequently stopped.

To quantify when sediment was deposited, we used radiocarbon dating of charcoal and wood samples found in the sediment, along with optically stimulated luminescence (OSL) dates of the sediment itself.[29] We also measured levels of two short-lived radioisotopes, ^{137}Cs (cesium) and ^{210}Pb (lead).[30]

Radiocarbon dates from two stumps at or near the base of the sediments indicate median ages of 1776 CE and 1778 CE and provide a good estimate for the approximate onset of deposition. Detrital charcoal contained at various depths in the sediment returned median ages of 1644–1888 CE; dates for a few samples of detrital wood range from 1580–1844 CE and provide maximum ages because wood, unlike charcoal, can survive for hundreds to thousands of years in fluvial systems. Taken as a whole, the ages indicate that deposition likely began in the late 1700s, which concurs with genealogical accounts of when Nuosu ancestors arrived in the valley.

Multiple dating methods agree on the cessation of sediment deposition. Eight radiocarbon dates from detrital charcoal, in situ stumps, and detrital wood taken from throughout the thickness of alluvial terrace deposits have no dates in the 95 percent confidence interval more recent than 1950 CE, providing a minimum age, confirmed by an OSL date near the top of the deposit indicating that deposition ceased before 1940 CE Additionally, the presence of ^{137}Cs near the top of terrace surfaces indicates that terraces stopped accumulating sediment before 1963 CE, and sediments in the currently active floodplain, which has been created since the river began to incise the silt and sand deposits, stranding them as terraces, contain ^{137}Cs, indicating incision began prior to 1963. Finally, in 2009, local people told us that alders growing on the current floodplain were at least thirty to forty years old. In summary, three independent dating methods and morphological evidence indicate that deposition of the one to two meters of floodplain silt and sand had ceased by around the middle of the 1900s.

Our preliminary analysis of the fine-grained valley-bottom sediments indicates their deposition began around the time when we believe the Nuosu moved to the valley; the intensive use of hillsides, with the associated soil erosion documented by our soil pits, provides a plausible source for the sediment that accumulated in the valley bottom. Such fine-grained deposits in river valley bottoms elsewhere that have been associated with periods of rapid anthropogenic erosion are termed "legacy sediments."[31]

It is less clear why deposition stopped. One possible explanation is that people stopped agricultural or forestry activities after the Communist revolution, but this is implausible, given elders' accounts of converting swidden to yearly cultivation, transporting cut forest materials to villages, and opening up new fields. It also contradicts the evidence from 1960s-era satellite images (figure 9.1, lower left) that show many of the hilltops and sunny slopes on the west side of the valley converted to fields and the hills near Pianshui covered with shrub rather than forest. An alternative explanation, which gains credence from our forest ecology investigations, is that soil on ridgetops and sunny slopes close to the current villages *was already eroded* by the mid-twentieth century, so that there was little further erosion afterward, and hence deposition was minimized.

If soil loss happened entirely in the two-hundred-year period between the time of settlement and the Communist revolution, soil loss rates are as high as ~1 m over two hundred years or 5 mm/year. This is ~5 times the rate of hillslope soil loss from cultivation in both the eastern United States and southwestern China.[32] Such rapid erosion is, however, consistent with documented erosion rates of 1–5 mm/year associated with the early conversion to cropping of native forests and prairies in the eastern and midwestern United States.[33]

Our field observations suggest that lateral fluvial erosion of these legacy sediments stored in Apiladda (the valley of the main river draining the basin), rather than erosion of hillside soils, is currently the dominant source of sediment to the mainstem river. The loss of a riparian forest over the last several decades likely has contributed to the river's destabilization. Satellite imagery from 1967 (figure 9.1, lower left) shows an intact riparian forest; our interpretations of these low-resolution photos are supported by remnant stumps, and by valley residents' statements that the river used to stay in place and run clear. Only a few trees remained by 2008, and the river is now wide and braiding (figure 9.2). Beginning in 2008, villagers planted fast-growing poplars along the river, attempting to retard further erosion and to confine the channel again. The effort appeared partially successful during an unusually large runoff event in August 2015, said by valley residents to have been the biggest in about sixty years. At that time, we observed dramatic rates of lateral retreat of streambanks formed in the alluvial terraces and alluvial fans, but areas planted to poplars appeared to suffer less bank collapse than areas planted with annual crops. While there may be some local hillslope erosion associated with paths and with chutes created to transport cut trees down slope, the bare areas are much smaller than previous swidden patches, and during the 2015 flood, water in the mainstem was highly turbid while water from tributaries remained clear, indicating that erosion was localized and that eroded hillslope material did not make it to streams.

FOREST ECOLOGY: BIODIVERSITY AND FOREST HEALTH

Our geomorphology studies show a period of intense hillside land use and consequent erosion and sediment deposition *before* the Communist revolution. Elders' memories and our own observations indicate intensification of land use in the lower valley, along with deterioration in forest productivity and decrease in diversity of trees in the forest *after* the revolution. Interviews and guided walks with elders indicate that before 1956, the forests included more species of trees: deciduous trees such as *Populus, Salix* (both weeping and straight willows), *Quercus* (oaks), *Acer* (maple), *Betula* (birch), and *Corylus* (hazel); wild fruit trees including *Prunus* (cherries and plums), *Crataegus* (hawthorn), a kind of wild pear called *sy nda lat nuo*, and a kind of wild lychee called *liebbi yienro*; and conifers including *Abies* (fir), *Picea* (spruce), *Juniperus* (juniper), *Cephalotaxus* (plum yew), and the scarce *Keteleeria davidiana*.

Our observations from a number of visits show that forest cover differed both by aspect and by distance from villages. *Pinus yunnanensis* dominated overstories on sunny slopes everywhere. Closer to villages, forests were open (less than 40 percent canopy cover) and pine-dominated regardless of aspect. On more distant plots at higher elevations on shady slopes, alder, oak, rhododendron, and white pine (*Pinus armandii*) dominated the overstory. This suggested that both distance from the villages, as a proxy for intensity of use, as well as environmental variables such as temperature, precipitation,

FIGURE 9.2. Top: *Pinus yunnanensis* forest close to villages, showing eroded soil and heavy cutting of trees. Photo by Keala Hagmann, 2008. Center: Typical shady slope mixed forest more distant from villages. Photo by Lauren S. Urgenson, 2008. Bottom: Apiladda valley, showing braided river course and sparse trees on the floodplain. Photo by Sara Jo Viraldo, 2008.

and soil thickness and quality, might influence forest characteristics and productivity.

Over the entire study area, mixed-conifer and hardwood forests growing on shady slopes appeared to have been less disturbed by felling, branch cutting, or other human activities than pine forests on sunny slopes, which have been heavily impacted by both earlier soil erosion and more recent resource extraction. Elders' reports confirm that large areas on sunny slopes and ridges were cut for intensive agriculture between 1957 and 1968 on both sides of the valley. Consistent with these reports, almost all the large trees we measured were between thirty-five and fifty years old. In addition, hills on the east side of the valley appeared to be covered with a thin shrub layer in a 1979 satellite image, and we found no trees older than forty years on the four hills we studied intensively in 2008 (figure 9.1, lower right). This focused our attention on how differences in management and use affect the sunny, pine-dominated slopes.

To evaluate hypotheses on whether and how governance, use, and site productivity influence forest growth, we turn to the forest conditions we observed in multiple years and measured in two studies in 2008 and 2009. These studies concentrated on sunny ridge tops and south-facing slopes (good for grain), where almost all agriculture in previously forested areas took place. In both studies, we collected quantitative data on basal area, number, species, height, age, and growth rate of trees.[34] We also documented terrain—slope, slope position, aspect, and elevation; soil—compaction and depth; and evidence of human usage—stumps, cut branches, and trails.[35] In the 2008 study, we focused on four hills behind the village of Pianshui (figure 9.1, lower right) with similar environmental parameters and different governance to evaluate the hypothesis that heavier use leads to slower growth rates. In the 2009 study, we expanded the 2008 study by comparing two governance regimes—national and collective forest—and differences in environmental gradients and use patterns between the east and west sides of Apiladda.

Our 2008 research, on the four heavily eroded hills with intensively used pine forests governed differently, demonstrates that differences in governance can affect forest growth. Three of the hills were managed by knowledgeable elders who replanted after earlier clear-cuts and policed random cutting by outsiders, while the fourth was managed as a commons without exclusion rules.[36] Plots on the three privately managed hills differ in individual measurements of forest productivity but generally have higher metrics of productivity than the unregulated commons (table 9.1). The unregulated hill has fewer, younger, smaller trees that grow more slowly than

Management	Unregulated commons	Privately managed		
	Everybody Hill	Jieduo Hill	Lurlur Hill	Vuga Hill
Tree age [years]	**24 ± 8 (7)**	39 ± 4 (6)	33 ± 6 (7)	32 ± 2 (9)
Diameter at breast height [cm]	**13 ± 2.48 (7)**	24.85 ± 4.15 (6)	18 ± 6.41 (7)	21.87 ± 4.76 (9)
Basal area [m²/ha]	4.6 ± 1.7 (3)	6.3 ± 1.1 (3)	10.5 ± 1.7 (3)	9.9 ± 2.3 (3)
Average basal area increment per tree [mm²/yr]	192 ± 78 (7)	641 ± 251 (6)	306 ± 263 (7)	544 ± 293 (9)

Note: Values are means of all measurements plus or minus one standard deviation. The number of trees (or plots in the case of basal area) included is in parentheses. Bolded values are statistically different from all other areas at 90 percent confidence.

the trees on the other three hills. It is unlikely that these differences are due to *differential* erosion in earlier times, since there was essentially no topsoil on any of the four hills.[37] This suggests that even in areas that may have already been heavily eroded before the mid-twentieth century, modifying use can modify site productivity.

To further examine the effect of use intensity on forest conditions, in a 2009 study we examined the collectively managed forests closer to the villages of Yangjuan and Pianshui, where cutting is permitted within limits, and the more distant state-managed (national) forests, where cutting is formally prohibited. In addition, because in the past we observed east-west differences in forest composition and productivity, we compared east and west sides of the valley. This division resulted in the four quadrants of national forest west (NFW), national forest east (NFE), collective forest west (CFW), and collective forest east (CFE) (table 9.2; figure 9.1, lower right), within which we measured plots. To control for variability among different species and slope aspects, we limited our plots to pine forests on sunny slopes.

The national and collective forest plots are statistically indistinguishable in all metrics we considered: distance from the villages, elevation, age and size of largest trees, basal area, tree growth rate, and number of stumps. Qualitative evidence of human use (stumps, trails, branch cutting) was similar, and all four quadrants contained fairly recent swiddens.[38] In addition, we observed almost no trees older than fifty years (i.e., germinated before 1960) anywhere. This presumably reflects the failure to limit use in national forests.

TABLE 9.2. Data from the 2009 study forest health in four quadrants

	Collective Forest East	Collective Forest West	National Forest East	National Forest West
Mean plot elevation [m]	2659 ± 35 (8)	2752 ± 50 (7)	2690 ± 58 (8)	2861 ± 148 (8)
Basal area [m²/ha]	10 ± 6 (8)	12 ± 6 (7)	11 ± 4 (8)	17 ± 3 (8)
Growth rate [m³/ha/y]	25 ± 21 (8)	53 ± 27 (7)	35 ± 12 (8)	73 ± 43 (8)
Mean age largest tree	**34 ± 10 (8)**	45 ± 13 (7)	46 ± 9 (8)	45 ± 10 (8)
DBH largest tree [cm]	**19 ± 12 (8)**	33 ± 9 (7)	25 ± 4 (8)	36 ± 1 8 (8)
Number of stumps	8 ± 10 (8)	3 ± 5 (7)	7 ± 8 (8)	2 ± 2 (8)
Distance from villages [m]	859 ± 343 (8)	1,253 ± 377 (7)	2,088 ± 354 (8)	2,817 ± 441 (8)
Evidence of human use	Light branch cutting, some slashing, moderate trail networks, some animal browsing	Light branch cutting, moderate slashing, moderate to extensive trail networks, light animal browsing	Light slashing, some trails, little animal browsing	Moderate to extensive slashing, some trails, some animals browsing

Note: Values are means of all measurements plus or minus one standard deviation. The number of plots included in the calculation is in parentheses. Bolded numbers are statistically different from all other areas at 90 percent confidence.

In contrast, there was significant variability between the east and west sides of Apiladda. The east-side plots were closer to the villages, at lower elevations, and had more stumps, smaller trees with lower growth rates, and lower basal area. Aside from stumps, qualitative evidence of human use was similar between the east and west. We also found significant correlations between basal area and elevation (larger and higher on the west side) and between basal area and distance from the villages (the west-side forests are more distant).[39] Of the four quadrants, the NFW and the CFE were the most different from one another and the other two quadrants (table 9.2). NFW had significantly greater basal area than the other three quadrants, while CFE had significantly younger and smaller trees compared to the other three quadrants. The only parameter that was statistically identical between the east and west sides of the valley was the age of the largest tree.

These differences between sunny slopes on the west and east sides of the valley may be partly due to site productivity and the way it interacts with geographic boundaries. Productivity appears to be highest on the west side of the valley at higher elevations. This could be in part because soils are deeper at higher elevations on the west side of the study area due to less human use (see geomorphology section), but we lack the soil data to evaluate this. Our geomorphology data and prior studies suggest that greater soil depth leads to faster *Pinus yunnanensis* growth. However, prior work elsewhere in Yanyuan County and in Yunnan Province suggests that wetter summers, due to less sunlight, and higher elevations, due to colder temperatures, both decrease *Pinus yunnanensis* growth rates.[40] If these trends hold true in our study area, they suggest that higher forests are likely to be less productive than lower elevation forests except when decreased soil depth and/or human activity have depleted forest resources.

Our 2009 data lead to the conclusion that the forests on the west side of the valley are significantly healthier than on the east side. As a result of productivity differences between the east and west sides of the valley, Yangjuan villagers, who have legal access to forests on the west of the valley, can cut better-burning hardwoods from shady slopes, easing the pressure on the sunny pine forests we measured. By contrast, the forests on the east side, at lower elevations, are pine dominated regardless of aspect, and villagers of Pianshui have no choice but to cut pine for firewood. Thus, we see more pressure from cutting in the east-side quadrants, which are geographically smaller than the west side quadrants, further exacerbating pressure. This pressure is compounded by the lower heat output of the pine, thus requiring more pine firewood.[41] This is particularly evident in the CFE quadrant closest to Pianshui, where average tree age at breast height (thirty-four years) was lower than in the other three quadrants (forty-seven years), almost certainly reflecting more intensive harvesting. Hence, disturbance affects site productivity. We also observed a negative linear correlation between tree growth rate and number of stumps, suggesting that heavy use of an area may eventually reduce forest productivity, perhaps by promoting erosion, increasing runoff, or depleting soil nutrients.[42] Both this story and that from the four hills support the relationship between excessive use and decreased productivity, as well as the ability to rehabilitate forests with more effective management.

Our forest research thus leads to a set of important, if tentative, conclusions. When developmental policies came to the valley after 1956, much of the forest soil on sunny slopes and in heavily used places was probably already eroded away. After the relocation in 1956, villagers used the forests closer to the relocated village sites much more intensively than more distant sites, simply because cutting and carrying wood, whether for household use or collective projects such as lime kilns, takes immense amounts of energy and time. The forests closest to the villages could not tolerate the intensification of use and thus lost additional productivity, while forests farther away remained more productive.

CONCLUSION

What do our ecological and geological data tell us about the sustainability of Nuosu traditional agroforestry? We know several things for sure:

1. Nuosu practiced agroforestry in the Baiwu valley according to traditional knowledge and practices for about two hundred years. We have evidence that during this time, swidden agriculture and associated practices, such as tree-cutting, firewood gathering, and grazing animals on sloping fields, brought about erosion; sunny ridgetop and south-facing (*bbuhlit*) slopes have thinner soil, and sediment was deposited in the river valley before the revolutionary regime came and altered agricultural practices significantly.

2. Despite considerable soil erosion, Nuosu were able to remain in the area for many generations and to provision themselves with their traditional agroforestry and pastoral practices. In addition, legends and memories testify to the size of the trees in place before the revolution and to the floral and faunal (and perhaps fungal) biodiversity of local forests.

3. Erosion continued after the revolution and village concentration, though probably mostly in different places. On the mountain behind Yangjuan, gullies and visible runoff during storms testify to this, as do muddy waters in the main river during storms that transport legacy sediments previously deposited in the valley bottom. The question of how watershed-wide rates of erosion changed remains unanswered at present.

4. When revolution, development, agricultural intensification, village consolidation, and clear-cutting came to the area starting in the 1950s, the formerly biodiverse forests were cut down for agriculture and fuel, and the forests that have regrown in their place are species-depauperate and provide less habitat for wild birds and mammals.

5. Since decollectivization in the 1980s, some forests have gradually recovered, at least partially. Not only have trees regrown in many places, but carefully managed forests even in nearby locations have grown noticeably since our first visits in the 1990s. In addition, villagers are beginning to report sightings of animals, such as wolves, which were absent earlier.

It is clear, then, that Nuosu people, guided by their traditional knowledge, explicitly attempted to use resources sustainably. However, their attempts had equivocal outcomes. Their guidelines for mountain slope cultivation did not prevent erosion. Slopes where swidden cultivation persisted for centuries have thin soils, while shady slopes (good for trees) continue to have deep O, A, and B horizons. Soils in the far north of the watershed, where people abandoned cultivation after 1900, appear to be undisturbed and are at least a meter deep. It seems implausible on the surface that possibly as much as a meter of soil could erode in about two hundred years, equivalent to as much as 5 mm/yr, but erosion rates from intensive human use are documented to be as high as 100 mm/yr.[43]

We can also say tentatively that revolutionary changes, undertaken in the name of science and without reference to accumulated local knowledge of the environment, did not repair any of the damage from the soil loss that accompanied traditional short-fallow swidden agriculture and herding. In addition, because of the previous soil loss, the revolutionary changes may have brought about more drastic environmental degradation than they would have otherwise. These developmental policies definitely brought about a dramatic decline in biodiversity, although there are now encouraging signs of a partial recovery. Although we will never know precisely what soils were like in the Baiwu valley in 1750 or exactly how many trees of what species grew where, then or two hundred years later, we do know that local people continued to wrest a living from their fields, pastures, and forests, even as they altered them.

NOTES

1   Since the 1950s, the Nuosu have been classified as a "branch" of the Yi "minority nationality," or *minzu*. See Harrell, *Ways of Being Ethnic in Southwest China*.

2   Scott, *The Art of Not Being Governed*, 101.

3   Turner, Bonnin, and Michaud, *Frontier Livelihoods*.

4   Scott, *Seeing Like a State*, 231; Schendel, "Geographies of Knowing, Geographies of Ignorance"; Wu Zhongmin and Zhou Guangyi, "Ecological Consequences of Slash-and-Burn Agriculture."

5   As Piers Blaikie and Harold Brookfield point out in their classic analysis in *Land Degradation and Society*, degradation is in the eye of the beholder. Here we examine topsoil loss, biodiversity loss, and other processes that render the land less suitable for cultivation, other human uses, or ecosystem services. For critique of the prejudicial views dismissive of indigenous knowledge, see Hathaway, *Environmental Winds*, 16–18; Williams, "Representations of Nature," 503–19; and Sturgeon, *Border Landscapes*, 147.

6   Escobar, *Encountering Development*; Escobar, "The Invention of Development."

7   Conklin, *Hanuno'o Agriculture*; Conklin, "An Ethnoecological Approach to Shifting Agriculture"; Altieri, *Agroecology*, 130–32, 156–57; Berkes, *Sacred Ecology*; Hoang, "Forest Thieves?"; González, *Zapotec Science*. Hill and Peart, "Land Use, Runoff, Erosion"; Ziegler et al., "Environmental Consequences"; Montgomery, "Soil Erosion and Agricultural Sustainability." An informative film about swidden agriculture among the Miskito of eastern Nicaragua is "Slash-and-Burn Agriculture," distributed by B & C Films, Sherman Oaks, CA.

8   Harrell, *Ways of Being Ethnic in Southwest China*; Lawson, *A Frontier Made Lawless*.

9   Whyte, "Settler Colonialism."

10 Liangshan was "liberated" in 1950, but the Chinese Communist Party authorities left local social and political systems alone until the "Democratic Reforms" beginning in 1956.

11 From Bender and Aku, *The Nuosu Book of Origins*, 35–37. Note that *tusi* ("a *tusi* dragon") is a Chinese term for a local ruler installed by an imperial regime.

12 Several Nuosu friends have confirmed that these seasonal prohibitions exist, but none has been able to provide names for the seasons when killing is prohibited or permitted.

13 Elvin, "The Great Deforestation."

14 A complete list of publications is available on request.

15 We are indebted to Mgebbu Ashy (b. 1934), Mgebbu Lunzy (Ma Erzi, b. 1957), Hxiesse Vuga (b. 1948), Lurlur Adda (b. 1947), and Mgebbu Vithly (1949–2016), among others.

16 Low-temperature burning makes nitrogen and phosphorus available to plants for a short time, although it results in a net overall loss of nutrients from the environment. See Certini, "Effects of Fire"; and Nguyen et al., "Analysis of the Sustainability within the Composite Swidden Agroecosystem."

17 We dried wood of various species, gathered from local forests, in an oven and compared wet to dry weight, confirming that pine has that highest percentage of water and is thus a less desirable firewood. Chi, "Human Disturbance and Biomass Growth."

18 Much of the forest cut for construction at that time is outside the Apiladda watershed where our geomorphology research was concentrated, so we have no quantitative data on these areas.

19 Trac et al., "Reforestation Programs in Southwest China"; Urgenson et al., "Social-Ecological Resilience."

20 See in particular Urgenson et al., "Social-Ecological Resilience."

21 Jenny, *Factors of Soil Formation*; Phillips, "A Short History of a Flat Place."

22 Soil depth refers to the combined depth of the O horizon, the layer of incompletely decomposed organic matter on top of the ground; the A horizon, the organic-rich topsoil layer; and the B horizon or subsoil, which underlies the A horizon. The correlation for all soil depths as a function of

distance from Yangjuan Village is $r^2 = 0.61$, $p < 0.01$. Considering only soil depth on upper slopes, $r^2 = 0.87$, $p < 0.01$. Soil depths on lower slopes are also significantly correlated with distance from Yangjuan Village ($r^2 = 0.63$, $p = 0.10$).

23 $r^2 = 0.17$, $p = 0.36$.

24 Liu Fuqi, "Relationships."

25 $r^2 = 0.05$, $p = 0.45$.

26 Tree growth rate is the basal area (in cm^2) divided by the approximate tree age. The correlation between tree growth rate and distance from Yangjuan Village is significant ($r^2 = 0.77$, $p < 0.01$).

27 Tree growth rate and soil thickness both vary with distance from Yangjuan Village, and soil thickness explains some of the relationship between tree growth rate and distance from Yangjuan Village. Tree growth rate is significantly correlated with distance from Yangjuan Village ($r^2 = 0.38$, $p < 0.05$).

28 Liu Fuqi, "Relationships"; Bi et al., "Spring Moisture Availability," 446; Yang Rao-Qiong et al., "Radial Growth of *Pinus yunannensis*."

29 See Aitken, *Introduction to Optical Dating.*

30 ^{137}Cs was produced by atmospheric nuclear weapons testing, which stopped in 1963. ^{210}Pb provides information on deposition rates over the last 100–150 years.

31 James, "Legacy Sediment; Walter and Merritts, "Natural Streams."

32 Trimble, "Fallacy of Stream Equilibrium" Reusser, Bierman, and Rood, "Quantifying Human Impacts on Rates of Erosion"; Schmidt et al., "Agricultural Land Use Doubled Sediment Loads."

33 Hupp, "Sedimentation in South Carolina Piedmont Valleys"; Costa, "Effects of Agriculture on Erosion"; Jackson et al., "A Southeastern Piedmont Watershed Sediment Budget."

34 The proportion of ground covered by the bases of trees, usually expressed in m^2/ha.

35 Chi, "Human Disturbance and Biomass Growth."

36 Ostrom, *Governing the Commons*, 90–92.

37 Unfortunately, we do not have evidence on sediment deposition caused by erosion on these hills because creeks there drain downstream from the Apiladda watershed where we collected sediment data.

38 Local interlocutors indicate that swiddening was heaviest between 1957 and the early 1980s and largely ceased after that. We did see a very few swiddens that were probably active within a decade of our visits.

39 $r^2 = 0.47$, 0.42.

40 Liu, "Relationships"; Whitney et al., "Spring Moisture"; Yang et al., "Radial Growth."

41 Chi, "Human Disturbance."

42 $r^2 = 0.13$.

43 Montgomery, "Soil Erosion and Agricultural Sustainability."

GLOSSARIES OF PLANT NAMES
AND NON-ROMAN CHARACTERS

Throughout the glossary, language is indicated as follows:

C: Chinese
J: Japanese
K: Korean
M: Malay
Ma: Manchu
N: Nuosu

For Japanese and Korean, kanji/hanja are not always used and are only given
if different than those used in Chinese. The Korean names generally corre-
late to the Korean word for the tree, not the Sino-Korean gloss.

PLANT NAMES MENTIONED IN THE TEXT

Common name	Scientific name (one word indicates a genus)	Name in Asian Language(s)
alder	*Alnus*	C: 樿 qi; K: 오리나무 orinamu; N: 𖵪 hxobbo
ash	*Fraxinus*	C: 梣 cen; J: toneriko; K: 물푸레나무 mulp'urenamu
beech	*Fagus*	C: 水青 shuiqing; J: 橅 buna
birch	*Betula*	C: 樺 hua; J: kabanoki; K: 자작나무 chajangnamu; N: 𖼝 mgephni
Asian/Siberian/Japanese white birch	*Betula platyphylla*	C: 白樺樹 baihua shu

Common name	Scientific name (one word indicates a genus)	Name in Asian Language(s)
Camphor		
Camphor/camphor laurel	*Cinnamomum camphora*	C: 樟 zhang; J: kusunoki; K: 녹나무 nongnamu
Malay/Sumatran camphor	*Dryobalanops aromatica*	M: pokok kapur barus
Catalpa	*Catalpa*	C: 梓 zi; J: azusa; K : 개오동 kaeodong
Chestnut	*Castanea*	C: 栗 li; J: kuri; K: 밤나무 pamnamu
China fir	*Cunninghamia lanceolata* or *Cunninghamia sinensis*	C: 杉 shan/sha
Chinese juniper	*Juniperus chinensis*	C: 圓柏 yuanbai
Chinquapin	*Castanopsis*	C: 錐栗 zhuili
Cork tree	*Phellodendron*	C: 黃檗 huangbo
Crab apple	*Malus*	C: 蘋果 pingguo, 柰 nai; J: 林檎 ringo; K: 사과나무 sagwanamu
Dawn Redwood	*Metasequoia glyptostroboides*	C: 水杉 shuishan
Dogwood	*Cornus*	C: 茱萸 zhuyu
Elm	*Ulmus*	C: 榆 yu; J: nire; K: 느릅나무 nŭrŭmnamu
Siberian elm	*Ulmus pumila*	C: 白榆 baiyu
Fir (see also China fir)	*Abies*	C: 冷杉 lengshan; K: 젓나무 chŏnnamu; N: [illegible] ssup
Goldenrain tree	*Koelreuteria*	C: 欒 luan
Hackberry	*Celtis*	C: 朴 pu; K: 팽나무 p'aengnamu
Hawthorn	*Crataegus*	C: 山楂 shanzha; N: [illegible] sypbu
Hazel	*Corylus*	C: 榛 zhen; J: hashibami; K: 개암나무 kaeamnamu; N: [illegible] anyut sytu
Hemlock	*Tsuga*	C: 鐵杉 tieshan; J: 栂 tsuga
Hickory	*Carya*	C: 山核桃 shan hetao
Holly	*Ilex*	C: 冬青 dongqing; J: 柊 hiragi; K: 호랑가시나무 horanggasinamu
Honey locust	*Gleditsia*	C: 皂荚 zaojia
Hornbeam	*Carpinus*	C: 鵝耳櫪 e'er li; J: 四手, 椣 shide K: 서어나무 sŏŏnamu
Horse chestnut	*Aesculus*	C: 七葉樹 qiye shu
Japanese cedar	*Cryptomeria japonica*	C: 柳杉 liushan; J: 杉 sugi; K: 삼나무 samnamu
Juniper	*Juniperus*	C: 刺柏 cibai; K: 향나무 hyangnamu; N: [illegible] hasyr;
Katsura	*Cercidiphyllum*	C: 連香 lianxiang
Keteleeria	*Keteleeria davidiana*	N: [illegible] lotcy ssupbbo
Lacquer	*Toxicodendron vernicifluum*	C: 漆 qi; J: urushi; K: 옻나무 onnamu

Common name	Scientific name (one word indicates a genus)	Name in Asian Language(s)
Larch	*Larix*	C: 落葉松 luoye song; J: karamatsu
North China larch	*Larix principis-rupprechtii*	C: 華北落葉松 huabei luoye song
Linden	*Tilia*	C: 椴 duan; J: shinanoki; K: 피나무 p'inamu
Manchurian linden	*Tilia mandshurica*	C: 遼椴 Liao duan
Longan	*Dimocarpus longan*	C: 龍眼 longyan
Lychee	*Litchi sp.s*	C: 荔枝 lizhi; N: 의米#引 liebbi yienro
Maple	*Acer*	C: 槭 qi, 楓 feng; J: kaede; K: 단풍나무 tanp'ungnamu; N: 地尺子 sa'apjjie
Painted maple	*Acer pictum* subsp. *Mono*	C: 色木槭 semuqi
Oak	*Quercus*	C: 櫟 li, 橡 xiang, 青岡 qinggang; K: 참나무 ch'amnamu; N 灬圭 rrubbo;
	Q. acrodonta	C: 岩櫟 yan li
	Q. acutissima	C: 麻櫟 ma li; J: 櫟 kunugi; K: 상수리나무 sangsurinamu
	Q. aliena	C: 槲櫟 hu li; K: 갈참나무 kalch'amnamu
	Q. baronii	C: 墰子櫟 gangzi li
	Q. dentata	C: 柞櫟 zha li; J: 柏 kashiwa; K: 떡갈나무 ttŏkkallamu
	Q. dolicholepis	C: 匙葉櫟 biye li
Mongolian oak	*Q. mongolica*	C: 蒙古櫟 menggu li; K: 신갈나무 sin'gallamu
	Q. serrata	C: 枹櫟 bao li; J: 小楢konara; K: 졸참나무 cholch'amnamu
	Q. variabilis	C: 栓皮櫟 shuanpi li; K: 굴참나무 kulch'amnamu
Paper mulberry	*Broussonetia*	C: 搆 gou; J: 梶の木 kajinoki K: 닥나무 tangnamu
Paulownia	*Paulownia*	C: 泡桐 paotong; J: 桐 kiri; K: 오동 odong
Pear	*Pyrus sp.*	N: 丫艸玤 syrndalatnuo
Persimmon	*Diospyros*	C: 柿 shi; J: kakinoki K: 감나무 kamnamu
Pine	*Pinus*	C: 松 song; J: matsu ; K: 솔 sol, 소나무 sonamu
Black pine	*P. thunbergii*	J: 黑松 kuromatsu ; K: 흑송 hŭksong, 곰솔 komsol
Chinese/Manchurian red pine	*P. tabuliformis*	C: 油松 you song
Horse tail pine	*P. massoniana*	C: 馬尾松 mawei song
Korean/Japanese red pine	*P. densiflora*	J: 赤松 akamatsu; K: 적송 chŏksong, 소나무 sonamu
Yunnan pine	*P. yunnanensis*	C: 雲南松 Yunnan song; N: 灬圭 tepbbo
White pine	*P. armandii*	C: 華山松 Huashan song; N: 业丫 shutsyr
Platycladus	*Platycladus orientalis*	C: 側柏 zebai; K: 측백나무 ch'ükpaengnamu
Plum yew	*Cephalotaxus*	C: 三尖杉 sanjian shan; N: 圹刭 diggu

Common name	Scientific name (one word indicates a genus)	Name in Asian Language(s)
Poplar	*Populus*	C: 楊 yang, N: [illegible] bapla
	P. tomentosa	C: 毛白楊 maobai yang
	P. simonii	C: 小葉楊 xiaoye yang
Redbud	*Cercis*	C: 紫荊 zijing
Rhododendron	*Rhododendron sp.*	C: 杜鵑花 dujuanhua N: [illegible] shuohma; K: 진달래 chindallae
Snowbells	*Styrax*	C: 安息香 anxi xiang; K: 때죽나무 ttaejungnamu
Spruce	*Picea*	C: 雲杉 yun shan, 杄 qian; N: [illegible] shut
Mongolian spruce	*Picea mongolica*	
Sweetgum	*Liquidambar*	C: 楓香 fengxiang
Tallow tree	*Sapium sebiferum* or *Triadica sebifera*	C: 桕 jiu, 烏桕 wujiu
Tree of heaven	*Ailanthus*	C: 臭椿 chou chun
Tung	*Vernicia fordii*	C: 桐 tong, 油桐 youtong
Walnut	*Juglans*	C: 核桃 hetao; J: 胡桃 kurumi; K: 가래나무 karaenamu
Weeping cypress	*Cupressus funebris*	C: 柏木 baimu
Whitebeam/rowan	*Sorbus*	C: 花楸 huaqiu
Willow	*Salix*	C: 柳 liu; J: yanagi; K: 버드나무 pŏdŭnamu; N: [illegible] yyhxox
Wingnut	*Pterocarya*	C: 楓楊 fengyang
Yew	*Taxus*	C: 紅豆杉 hongdou shan; J: 櫟yichī K: 주목 chumok
Zelkova	*Zelkova*	C: 櫸 ju; J: keyaki; K: 느티나무 nŭt'inamu

CHARACTER LIST

bbipndit (N) [illegible]
bbuhlit (N) [illegible]
bbuhlit zzabbo he, bbusi sybbo he (N) [illegible], [illegible]
bbusi (N) [illegible]
bencao (C) 本草
bimox (N) [illegible]
Bishu Shanzhuang (C) 避暑山庄
bugyō (J) 奉行
chammok (K) 雜木
dangjiang (C) 當江
dongfan (C) 東番

dōri (J) 道理
ddurndit (N) ᄂᆞᆷ
fengshu (C) 封樹
fengshui shanshu (C) 風水山樹
fengshui weiqiang (C) 風水圍牆
fushin-yaku (J) 普請役
guanshan (C) 官山
hagye (K) 下契
haishu (C) 海樹
Hanbai (C) 漢柏
Hanjian (C) 漢奸
hibun (J) 非文
houlong (C) 后龍
huang (C) 荒
huangmu (C) 皇木
huo (C) 伙
hyangyak (K) 鄉約
iriai (J) 入会
iriyama (J) 入山
jumin dian (C) 居民點
jungong jiangshou (C) 軍工匠首
Kai Province (J) 甲斐国
kaishan fufan (C) 開山撫番
kamgo (K) 監考
kanyū rinno (J) 官有林野
karishiki (J) 刈敷
Kobayashi (J) 小林
koku (J) 石
Konglin (C) 孔林
kugyong (K) 國用
kŭmp'yo (K) 禁標
kŭmsonggye (K) 禁松契; songgye (K) 松契
Kumssongye Chwamok (K) 禁松契 座目
kye (K) 契
lifen (C) 力分
lin (C) 林
ling (C) 陵
Lingyou (C) 灵囿
linqu (C) 林区
luohou (C) 落後
lurby (N) ᄌᆞᆷ
Miaojiang (C) 苗疆
Miao mu (C) 苗木

minzu (C) 民族

mu (C) 畝

naosu (J) 直す

ndit (N) 𬇙

nei sanjiang (C) 內三江

o'ga chakt'ong (K) 五家作統

Onjŏngdong Kŭmsong Chŏlmok (K) 溫井洞禁松節目

Oyamada (J) 小山田

qi (C) 气, 氣

qianquan (C) 前圈

Qingmingjie (C) 清明節

qiong Miao (C) 窮苗

san dafa (C) 三大伐

sanbang wuxiang (C) 三幫五勷

sanggye (K) 上契

sanjiang (C) 三江

satoyama (J) 里山

sekisho (J) 関所

shan (C) 山

shanke (C) 山客

shanye (C) 山野

shanze (C) 山澤

shengfan (C) 生番

shoufan (C) 熟番

shuhu (C) 樹戶

shuike (C) 水客

shuishan (C) 稅山

sichou yashui (C) 私抽牙稅

Songgye Wanŭi (K) 松契完議

songjŏng (K) 松政

tadashii (J) 正しい

Takeda (J) 武田

tusi (C) 土司

ŭm (K) 陰

ŭmye (K) 陰翳

vopndit (N) ᵇ𬇙

wai sanjiang (C) 外三江

wakashū (J) 若衆

Wangzhi (C) 王制

Wu Shiren (C) 伍仕仁

xi-Hu mu (C) 西湖木

yahang (C) 牙行

yang (K) 陽

yangban (K) 兩班
yangpo (C) 陽坡
yatie (C) 牙帖
yinpo (C) 陰坡
yishu (C) 儀樹
yorioya (J) 寄り親
Yuanlin (C) 袁林
yuqi (C) 余气
Zhang Guangsi (C) 張廣泗
Zhengjiang ji (C) 爭江記
Zhishujie (C) 植樹節
Zhongshan jinian lin (C) 中山紀念林
zhufen (C) 主分

BIBLIOGRAPHY

Agrawal, Arun. *Environmentality: Technologies of Government and the Making of Subjects*. Durham, NC: Duke University Press, 2005.

Aihara Yoshiyuki. "Qingchao zhongqi de senlin zhengci" [Forest policy in the mid-Qing period]. In *Zhongguo lishi shang de huanjing uu shehui* [Environment and society in Chinese history], edited by Wang Lihua. Beijing: Sanlian Shudian, 2007.

Aitken, M. J. *Introduction to Optical Dating: The Dating of Quaternary Sediments by the Use of Photon-Stimulated Luminescence*. Oxford: Clarendon Press, 1998.

Albion, Robert Greenhalgh. *Forests and Sea Power: The Timber Problem of the Royal Navy, 1652–1862*. Cambridge, MA: Harvard University Press, 1926.

Allen, James, L. "Legacy Sediment: Definitions and Processes of Episodically Produced Anthropogenic Sediment." *Anthropocene* 2 (2013): 16–26.

Altieri, Charles. *Agroecology: The Science of Sustainable Agriculture*. 2nd ed. Boulder, CO: Westview Press, 1995.

Amino, Yoshihiko. *Rethinking Japanese History*. Translated by Alan S. Christy. Ann Arbor, MI: University of Michigan Center for Japanese Studies, 2012.

Andaya, Leonard Y. *Leaves of the Same Tree: Trade and Ethnicity in the Straits of Melaka*. Honolulu: University of Hawai'i Press, 2008.

Anderson, James A., and John K. Whitmore. *China's Encounters on the South and Southwest: Reforging the Fiery Frontier over Two Millennia*. Leiden: Brill, 2014.

Anderson, John. *Acheen, and the Ports on the North and East Coasts of Sumatra; with Incidental Notices of the Trade in the Eastern Seas, and the Aggressions of the Dutch*. London: W. H. Allen, 1840.

———. *A Mission to the East Coast of Sumatra*. Oxford: Oxford University Press, 1971. First published 1883.

Andrade, Tonio. "Pirates, Pelts, and Promises: The Sino-Dutch Colony of Seventeenth-Century Taiwan and the Aboriginal Village of Favorolang." *Journal of Asian Studies* 64, no. 2 (May 2005): 295–321.

Angerler, Johann. "Images of God in Toba Batak Storytelling." *Wacana* 17, no. 2 (July 1, 2016): 303–35.

Anmyŏndo minho kŭp wŏnyŏk kŏhaeng chŏlmok [The duties of households and government personnel on Anmyŏn Island]. Kyujanggak Archives (Seoul National University) Kyu 18937. 1895.

Aoki Takeishi. "The Role of Villagers in Domain and State Forestry Management: Japan's Path from Tokugawa Period to the Early Twentieth Century." In *Public Goods Provision in the Early Modern Economy: Comparative Perspectives from Japan, China, and Europe*, edited by Masayuki Tanimoto and R. Bin Wong, 255–75. Berkeley: University of California Press, 2019.

Appuhn, Karl. *A Forest on the Sea: Environmental Expertise in Renaissance Venice.* Baltimore, MD: Johns Hopkins University Press, 2009.

Arioka Toshiyuki. *Satoyama.* Tokyo: Hōsei Daigaku Shuppan, 2004.

Atwill, David G. *The Chinese Sultanate: Islam, Ethnicity, and the Panthay Rebellion in Southwest China, 1856–1873.* Stanford, CA: Stanford University Press, 2005.

Averill, Stephen C. "The Shed People and the Opening of the Yangzi Highlands." *Modern China* 9, no. 1 (1983): 84–126.

Bae, Jae Soo, Rin Won Joo, and Yeon-Su Kim. "Forest Transition in South Korea: Reality, Path and Drivers." *Land Use Policy* 29, no. 1 (January 1, 2012): 198–207.

Ban Gao. *In Search of the Supernatural: The Written Record.* Translated by Kenneth J. Dewoskin and J. I. Crump. Stanford, CA: Stanford University Press, 1996.

Bankoff, Greg. "Almost an Embarrassment of Riches." In *A History of Natural Resources in Asia: The Wealth of Nature*, edited by Greg Bankoff and Peter Boomgaard, 103–22. New York: Palgrave Macmillan, 2007.

———. "Breaking New Ground? Gifford Pinchot and the Birth of 'Empire Forestry' in the Philippines, 1900–1905." *Environment and History* 15, no. 3 (2009): 369–93.

Bao Shichen. *Qimin si shu* [Four arts to nourish the people]. Wikisource digital ed. based on Shanghai: Zhonghua Shuju, 2001.

Barbieri-Low, Anthony J. *Artisans in Early Imperial China.* Seattle: University of Washington Press, 2007.

Barbieri-Low, Anthony J., and Robin D. S. Yates. *Law, State, and Society in Early Imperial China: A Study with Critical Edition and Translation of the Legal Texts from Zhangjiashan Tomb No. 247.* 2 vols. Leiden: Brill, 2015.

Barclay, Paul D. *Outcasts of Empire: Japan's Rule on Taiwan's "Savage Border," 1874–1945.* Berkeley: University of California Press, 2017.

———. "Playing the 'Race Card' in Japanese Governed Taiwan or Anthropometric Photographs as 'Shape Shifting Jokers.'" In *The Affect of Difference: Representations of Race in East Asian Empire*, edited by Christopher Hanscom and Dennis Washburn, 38–80. Honolulu: University of Hawai'i Press, 2016.

Bello, David A. *Across Forest, Steppe, and Mountain: Environment, Identity, and Empire in Qing China's Borderlands.* Cambridge, UK: Cambridge University Press, 2016.

Bender, Mark, and Aku Wuwu, trans. *The Nuosu Book of Origins: A Creation Epic from Southwest China*. Translated from a transcription by Jjivot Zopqu. Seattle: University of Washington Press, 2019.

Berkes, Fikret. *Sacred Ecology: Traditional Ecological Knowledge and Resource Management*. Philadelphia: Taylor & Francis, 1999.

Bi Yingfeng, Corey Whitney, Jianwen Li, Jingchao Yang, and Xuefei Yang. "Spring Moisture Availability Is the Major Limitation on Pine Forest Productivity in Southwest China." *Forests* 11 (2020).

Bian Li. *Ming Qing Huizhou shehui yanjiu* [Research on Ming-Qing Huizhou society]. Anhui Daxue Chubanshe, 2004.

Bielenstein, Hans. "The Census in China during the Period 2–742 AD." *Bulletin of the Museum of Far Eastern Antiquities* 26 (1947): 125–63.

Biot, Édouard. *Le Tcheou-li ou rites des Tcheou*. Paris: Imprimerie Nationale, 1851.

Birdwhistell, Joanne D. "Ecological Questions for Daoist Thought." In *Daoism and Ecology: Ways within a Cosmic Landscape*, edited by N. J. Girardot, James Miller, and Liu Xiaogan, 23–44.Cambridge, MA: Center for the Study of World Religions, 2001.

Birt, Michael P. "Samurai in Passage: The Transformation of the Sixteenth-Century Kantō." *Journal of Japanese Studies* 11–2, (1985): 369–99.

Blaikie, Piers, and Harold Brookfield. *Land Degradation and Society*. London: Methuen, 1987.

Bloembergen, Marieke. *Colonial Spectacles: The Netherlands and the Dutch East Indies at the World Exhibitions, 1880–1931*. Translated by Beverley Jackson. Singapore: Singapore University Press, 2006.

Blust, Robert. "Subgrouping, Circularity and Extinction: Some Issues in Austronesian Comparative Linguistics." In *Selected Papers from the Eighth International Conference on Austronesian Linguistics*, edited by E. Zeitoun and P. J. K. Li, 31–94. Taipei: Academia Sinica, 1999.

Botkin, Daniel B. *Discordant Harmonies: A New Ecology for the Twenty-First Century*. New York: Oxford University Press, 1992.

Brady, Lisa M. "Sowing War, Reaping Peace: United Nations Resource Development Programs in the Republic of Korea, 1950–1953." *Journal of Asian Studies* 77, no. 2 (May 2018): 351–63.

Brain, Stephen. *Song of the Forest: Russian Forestry and Stalinist Environmentalism, 1905–1953*. Pittsburgh, PA: University of Pittsburgh Press, 2011.

Brakel, Clara. *Dairi Stories and Pakpak Storytelling*. Leiden: Brill, 2013.

Braudel, Fernand. *The Mediterranean and the Mediterranean World in the Age of Philip II*. Vol. 1. Berkeley, CA: University of California Press, 1996.

Brown, Philip C. *Central Authority and Local Autonomy in the Formation of Early Modern Japan: The Case of Kaga Domain*. Stanford, CA: Stanford University Press, 1993.

———. *Cultivating Commons: Joint Ownership of Arable Land in Early Modern Japan*. Honolulu: University of Hawai'i Press, 2011.

Cabaton, Antoine. *Java, Sumatra and the Other Islands of the Dutch East Indies*. London: T Fischer Unwin, 1911.

Caffrey, Patrick J. "Transforming the Forests of a Counterfeit Nation: Japan's 'Manchu Nation' in Northeast China." *Environmental History* 18, no. 2 (2013): 309–32.

Campbell, Aurelia. *What the Emperor Built: Architecture and Empire in the Early Ming*. Seattle: University of Washington Press, 2020.

Campbell, Colin D., and Chang Shick Ahn. "Kyes and Mujins: Financial Intermediaries in South Korea." *Economic Development and Cultural Change* 11, no. 1 (October 1962): 55–68.

Cao, Shixiong, Ge Sun, Zhiqiang Zhang, Liding Chen, Qi Feng, Bojie Fu, Steve McNulty, et al. "Greening China Naturally." *AMBIO* 40, no. 7 (November 1, 2011): 828–31.

Cao, Shixiong, Tao Tian, Li Chen, Xiaobin Dong, Xinxiao Yu, and Guosheng Wang. "Damage Caused to the Environment by Reforestation Policies in Arid and Semi-arid Areas of China." *AMBIO* 39, no. 4 (June 1, 2010): 279–83.

Cao Zhihong and Wang Xiaoxia. "Ming Qing Shaannan yimin kaifa zhuangtai xia de ren hu Chongtu." *Shilin* 5 (2008).

Certini, Giacomo. "Effects of Fire on Property of Forest Soils: A Review." *Oecologia* 143 (2005): 1–10.

Chen, Jianhui, Fahu Chen, Song Feng, Wei Huang, Jianbao Liu, and Aifeng Zhou. "Hydroclimatic Changes in China and Surroundings during the Medieval Climate Anomaly and Little Ice Age: Spatial Patterns and Possible Mechanisms." *Quaternary Science Reviews* 107 (January 1, 2015): 98–111.

Ch'en, Kuo-tung. "'Jungong jiangshou' yu Qingling shiqi Taiwan de famu wenti 1683–1875" [Naval lumberjacks and tree-felling activities in Taiwan under the Qing, 1683–1875]. *Renwen ji shehui kexue jikan* 7 no. 1 (March 1995): 123–58.

———. "Non-reclamation Deforestation in Taiwan, c. 1600–1976." In *Sediments of Time: Environment and Society in Chinese History*, edited by Ts'ui-jung Liu and Mark Elvin, 693–727. Cambridge, UK: Cambridge University Press, 1998.

Chen, Stephen. "Agriculture Feels the Choke as China Smog Starts to Foster Disastrous Conditions." *South China Morning Post*, February 25, 2014. www .scmp.com/news/china/article/1434700/china-smog-threatens-agriculture -nuclear-fallout-conditions-warn.

Chen, Wei. *Qin jiandu heji (si): Fangmatan Qin mu jiandu*. Edited by Sun Zhanyu and Yan Changgui. Wuhan: Wuhan Daxue, 2014.

Chen, Wei, Sun Zhanyu, and Yan Changgui. *Qin jiandu heji: Shiwen zhushi xiudingben (si)*. Wuhan: Wuhan Daxue, 2016.

———. *Qin jiandu heji (si)*. Wuhan: Wuhan Daxue, 2014.

Chen Keyun. "Cong 'Lishi shanlin zhichan bu' kan Ming Qing Huizhou shanlin jingying" [A view of Ming Qing Huizhou forest business from the Li lineage forest account book]. *Jiang Huai Luntan* 9 (January 1992): 73–84.

———. "Ming Qing Huizhou shanlin jingying zhong de 'lifen' wenti" [The question of "labor shares" in Ming Qing Huizhou forest business]. *Zhongguo Shi Yanjiu* 1987, vol. 1 (January 1987): 85–87.

Chen Rong. *Zhongguo Senlin Shiliao* [Sources for Chinese forest history]. Beijing: Zhongguo Linye Chuban She, 1983.

Chen Ruizhi. "Hangzhou mucai ye de neimu." In *Zhejiang wenshi ziliao xuanbian (di jiu ji)*, 90–120. Hangzhou: Zhejiang Renmin Chuban She, 1964.

Chen Xuechen. "Zhongshan xiansheng zhi senlin zhengce." In *Zhishu tekan: Zongli shishi jinianri texing*. Nanjing: Nongkuangbu Linzhengsi, 1929: 16–23.

Chen Xuewen. *Ming Qing shiqi shangye shu ji shangren shu zhi yanjiu*. Taibei: Hongye Wenhua, 1997.

Chen Yu. "Zhishushi yu Zhishujie." In *Zhishu tekan: Zongli shishi jinianri texing*. Nanjing: Nongkuangbu Linzhengsi, 1929: 1–4.

Chen Yunqian. "Zhishujie yu Sun Zhongshan chongbai." *Nanjing daxue xuebao: zhexue, renwen kexue, shehui kexue*, no. 5 (2006): 76–90.

Chen Zhi. "Kuoda zaolin yundong jihua chuyi." In *Zhishu tekan: Zongli shishi jinianri texing*. Nanjing: Nongkuangbu Linzhengsi, 1929: 23–35.

Cheng Hai, and Zhao Yunlong. *Zhongguo Beifang nongmu jiaocuodai shengtai—shengchan fanshi quhua ji jianshe yanjiu* [Northern China's agro-pastoral ecotone—A study in regionalization and construction within the ecological production paradigm]. Beijing: Zhongguo Nongye Chubanshe, 2005.

Cheng Zeshi. *Qingshui Jiang wenshu zhi fayi chutan*. Beijing: Zhongguo Zhengfa Daxue Chuban She, 2011.

Chi, Phillip. "Human Disturbance and Biomass Growth in Upper Baiwu Pine Forests." Bachelor of science honors thesis, University of Washington, 2004.

Chi, Xiang. "Chinese Resource Modernity: Environmental Government and the Resource Conflicts in Northeast China's Forests, 1860–1932." PhD diss., University of California Los Angeles, 2019.

Chittenden, H. M. "The Myth of the Forest: If Ever the Last American Walks through Deserted New York, the Cause of Ruin Will Not Have Been National Deforestation." *New York Times*, June 17, 1916.

Choe Wŏnsŏk. "Chosŏn hugi yŏngnam chibang sajok ch'on ŭi p'ungsu tamnon" [The *p'ungsu* discourses of *sajok* villages in the Yŏngnam region in the late Chosŏn era]. *Han'guk chiyŏk chirihakhoe chi* 16, no. 3 (2010): 265–74.

Chŏng Chinyŏng. *Chosŏn sidae hyangch'on sahoesa* [A social history of rural communities in the Chosŏn dynasty]. Seoul: Han'gilsa, 1998.

Clancey, Gregory. "Seeing the Timber for the Forest." In *A History of Natural Resources in Asia: The Wealth of Nature*, edited by Greg Bankoff and Peter Boomgaard, 123–41. New York: Palgrave Macmillan, 2007.

Coedes, George. *The Indianized States of Southeast Asia*. Translated by Sue Brown. Honolulu: University of Hawai'i Press, 1968.

Coggins, Chris. *The Tiger and the Pangolin: Nature, Culture, and Conservation in China*. Honolulu: University of Hawai'i Press, 2002.

———. "When the Land Is Excellent: Village Feng Shui Forests and the Nature of Lineage, Polity and Vitality in Southern China." In *Religion and Ecological Sustainability in China*, edited by James Miller, Dan Smyer Yu, and Peter van der Veer, 97–126. New York: Routledge, 2014.

Conklin, Harold C. "An Ethnoecological Approach to Shifting Agriculture." *Transactions of the New York Academy of Sciences* 17, no. 2 (December 1954): 133–42.

———. *Fine Description: Ethnographic and Linguistic Essays by Hal Conklin.* Edited by Joel C. Kuipers and Raymond McDermott. Monograph 56 ed. New Haven, CT: Yale University Southeast Asia Studies, 2007.

———. *Hanuno'o Agriculture: Report on an Integral System of Shifting Agriculture in the Northern Philippines.* Rome: FAO, 1957.

Cook, Constance A. "Ritual, Politics and the Issue of Feng (封)." In *Shi Quan xiansheng jiushi danchen jinian wenji*, edited by Wuhan Daxue Lishi Dili Yanjiusuo, 215–57. Wuhan: Hubei Renmin, 2007.

Costa, J. E. "Effects of Agriculture on Erosion and Sedimentation in the Piedmont Province, Maryland." *Geological Society of America Bulletin* 86 (1975): 1281–86.

Crosby, Alfred W. *Ecological Imperialism: The Biological Expansion of Europe, 900–1900.* 2nd ed. Cambridge, UK: Cambridge University Press, 2004.

Crossley, Pamela Kyle. *A Translucent Mirror: History and Identity in Qing Imperial Ideology.* 1st ed. Berkeley: University of California Press, 2002.

Crump, James. *Chan-kuo ts'e.* Oxford: Clarendon Press, 1970.

Da Qing huidian shili. Beijing: Zhonghua Shuju, 1991. Reprint of 1899 Guangxu ed.

Dauben, Joseph W. "Suan Shu Shu: A Book on Numbers and Computations; English Translation with Commentary." *Archive for the History of Exact Sciences* 62 (2008): 91–178.

Dauvergne, Peter. *Shadows in the Forest: Japan and the Politics of Timber in Southeast Asia.* Cambridge, MA: MIT Press, 1997.

Davidson, James. *The Island of Formosa, Past and Present.* London: Macmillan, 1903.

Davis, Bradley C. "Black Flag Rumors and the Black River Basin: Powerbrokers and the State in the Tonkin-China Borderlands." *Journal of Vietnamese Studies* 6, no. 2 (2011): 16–41.

———. *Imperial Bandits: Outlaws and Rebels in the China-Vietnam Borderlands.* Seattle: University of Washington Press, 2017.

Dazhi shi tonglüshan gu tongkuang yizhi baohu guanli weiyuanhui. *Tonglüshan gu tongkuang yizhi kaogu faxian yu yanjiu.* Beijing: Kexue, 2013.

Deal, David Michael, and Laura Hostetler, eds. *The Art of Ethnography: A Chinese "Miao Album."* Seattle: University of Washington Press, 2007.

Démurger, Sylvie, Hou Yuanzhao, and Yang Weiyong. "Forest Management Policies and Resource Balance in China: An Assessment of the Current Situation." *Journal of Environment & Development* 18, no. 1 (March 1, 2009): 17–41.

Deuchler, Martina. *Under the Ancestors' Eyes: Kinship, Status, and Locality in Premodern Korea*. Cambridge, MA: Harvard University Asia Center, 2015.

Diamond, Norma. "Defining the Miao: Ming, Qing, and Contemporary Views." In *Cultural Encounters on China's Ethnic Frontiers*, edited by Stevan Harrell, 92–116. Seattle: University of Washington Press, 1995.

Dijk, Wil O. "The VOC's Trade in Indian Textiles with Burma, 1634–80." *Journal of Southeast Asian Studies* 33, no. 3 (2002): 495–515.

Dodd, John. *Journal of a Blockaded Resident in North Formosa during the Franco-Chinese War, 1884–5*. Hong Kong: Daily Press, 1888.

Dongzu shehui lishi diaocha. Bejing: Minzu Chuban She, 2009.

Donkin, R. A. *Dragon's Brain Perfume: An Historical Geography of Camphor*. Leiden: Brill, 1999.

Drewes, G. W. J., and L. F. Brakel. *The Poems of Hamzah Fansuri*. Dordrecht: Koninklijk Instituut voor Taal-, Land-, en Volkenkunde, 1986.

Du Zhengzhen. "Ming Qing yiqian dongnan shanlin de dingjie yu quequan" [The emergence of ownership and boundary demarcation in Chinese southeast mountain land before the Ming and Qing dynasties]. *Zhejiang Shehui Kexue* 2020, no. 6 (June 2020): 117–27.

———. "Wan Qing Minguo shanlin suoyou quan de huode yu zhengming— Zhejiang longquan xian yu jiande xian de bijiao yanjiu" [Late Qing and Republic obtainment and proof of forest ownership rights: Research comparing Zhejiang's Longquan County and Jiande County]. *Jindai Shi Yanjiu* 2017, no. 4 (April 2017): 78–91.

Du Zhengzhen and Wu Zhengqiang. "Longquan Sifa dang'an de zhuyao tedian yu shiliao jiazhi" [The main features and historical values of the judicial archives in Longquan County, Zhejiang Province]. *Minguo Dang'an*, no. 1 (2011): 118–23.

Durrant, Stephen, Wai-yee Li, and David Schaberg. *Zuo Tradition / Zuozhuan: Commentary on the "Spring and Autumn Annals."* Seattle: University of Washington Press, 2016.

Eason, David Anthony. "The Culture of Disputes in Early Modern Japan, 1550–1700." PhD diss., University of California Los Angeles, 2009.

Eastman, Lloyd. *The Abortive Revolution: China under Nationalist Rule, 1927–1937*. Cambridge, MA: Harvard University Press, 1974.

Economic Archives, Institute of Modern History, Academia Sinica, Taipei, Taiwan.

Economy, Elizabeth C. *The River Runs Black: The Environmental Challenge to China's Future*. 2nd ed. Ithaca, NY: Cornell University Press, 2010.

Edmonds, Richard L. "The Willow Palisade." *Annals of the Association of American Geographers* 69, no. 4 (1979): 599–621.

Elio Modigliani: Viaggiatore e naturalista sulla rotta delle meraviglie: Nias, Sumatra, Engano, Mentawei, 1886–1894: Lo sguargo, il racconto, la collezione. Firenze: Pagliai Polistampa, 2002.

Elliott, Mark C. *The Manchu Way: The Eight Banners and Ethnic Identity in Late Imperial China*. 1st ed. Stanford, CA: Stanford University Press, 2001.

Elvin, Mark. "The Great Deforestation: An Overview." In *The Retreat of the Elephants: An Environmental History of China*, 19–39. New Haven, CT: Yale University Press, 2004.

———. *The Pattern of the Chinese Past*. Stanford, CA: Stanford University Press, 1973.

———. *The Retreat of the Elephants: An Environmental History of China*. New Haven, CT: Yale University Press, 2004.

———. "Three Thousand Years of Unsustainable Growth: China's Environment from Archaic Times to the Present." *East Asian History* 6 (December 1993): 7–46.

Endicott-West, Elizabeth. "The Yüan Government and Society." In *The Cambridge History of China*. Vol. 6, *Alien Regimes and Border States, 907–1368*, edited by Denis Twitchett and John K. Fairbank. Cambridge: Cambridge University Press, 1994.

Escobar, Arturo. *Encountering Development*. Princeton, NJ: Princeton University Press, 1995.

———. "The Invention of Development." *Current History* 98, no. 631 (1999): 382–86.

Fang, Jingwu, Zhiheng Wang, and Zhiyao Tang. *Atlas of Woody Plants in China: Distribution and Climate*. Heidelberg: Springer, 2011.

Farris, William Wayne. *Japan's Medieval Population: Famine, Fertility, and Warfare in a Transformative Age*. Honolulu: University of Hawai'i Press, 2006.

Fedman, David. *Seeds of Control: Japan's Empire of Forestry in Colonial Korea*. Seattle: University of Washington Press, 2020.

———. "Wartime Forestry and the 'Low Temperature Lifestyle' in Late Colonial Korea, 1937–1945." *Journal of Asian Studies* 77, no. 2 (May 2018): 333–50.

Fiskesjö, Magnus. "Rising from Blood-Stained Fields: Royal Hunting and State Formation in Shang China." *Bulletin of the Museum of Far Eastern Antiquities* 73 (2001): 48–192.

Ford, Caroline. "Reforestation, Landscape Conservation, and the Anxieties of Empire in French Colonial Algeria." *American Historical Review* 113, no. 2 (April 2008): 1–22.

Foret, Philippe. *Mapping Chengde: The Qing Landscape Enterprise*. Honolulu: University of Hawai'i Press, 2000.

Forsyth, Tim, and Andrew Walker. *Forest Guardians, Forest Destroyers: The Politics of Environmental Knowledge in Northern Thailand*. Seattle: University of Washington Press, 2008.

Frazer, James George. *The Golden Bough: A Study in Magic and Religion*. 12 vols. London: Macmillan, 1919.

———. *The Magic Art and the Evolution of Kings*. Vol. 1 of *The Golden Bough: A Study in Magic and Religion*. London: Macmillan, 1919.

Fujiki Hisashi. *Sengoku no sahō: Mura no funsō kaiketsu*. Tokyo: Heibonsha, 1987.

———. *Toyotomi heiwarei to sengoku shakai*. Tokyo: Tokyo Daigaku Shuppankai, 1985.

Fujiyoshida-shi kyōiku iinkai, ed. *Fujiyoshida-shi shi shiryō sōsho 4, mura meisaichō*. Fujiyoshida-shi: Fujiyoshida-shi Kyōiku Iinkai, 1988.

———, ed. *Fujiyoshida-shi shi shiryō-hen dai nikan (kodai, chūsei)*. Fujiyoshida-shi: Fujiyoshida-shi, 1992.

———, ed. *Fujiyoshida-shi shi shiryō-hen dai sankan (kinsei ichi)*. Fujiyoshida-shi: Fujiyoshida-shi, 1994.

Fujiyoshida-shi shihensan-shitsu, ed. *Myōhōji-ki*. Fujiyoshida-shi shi shiryō sōsho. Fujiyoshida-shi: Fujiyoshida-shi Kyōiku Iinkai, 1991.

Gadgil, Madhav, and Ramachandra Guha. *This Fissured Land: An Ecological History of India*. Berkeley: University of California Press, 1993.

Gale, Esson M. *Discourses on Salt and Iron: A Debate on State Control of Commerce and Industry in Ancient China*. Taipei: Ch'eng-Wen, 1967.

Gao Jixi, Lü Shihai, Zheng Zhirong, and Liu Junhui. "Typical Ecotones in China." *Journal of Resources and Ecology* 3, no. 4 (December 2012): 297–307.

Garrett, Philip. "Bad Neighbors and Monastic Influence: Border Disputes in Medieval Kii." In *Land, Power, and the Sacred: The Estate System in Medieval Japan*, edited by Janet Goodwin and Jane Piggott, 377–402. Honolulu: University of Hawai'i Press, 2018.

Ge, Q., Z. Hao, J. Zheng, and X. Shao. "Temperature Changes over the Past 2000 Yr in China and Comparison with the Northern Hemisphere." *Climate of the Past* 9, no. 3 (May 27, 2013): 1153–60.

Ge, Q.-S., J.-Y. Zheng, Z.-X. Hao, P.-Y. Zhang, and W.-C. Wang. "Reconstruction of Historical Climate in China: High-Resolution Precipitation Data from Qing Dynasty Archives." *Bulletin of the American Meteorological Society* 86, no. 5 (May 1, 2005): 671–80.

Ge, Quansheng, Jingyun Zheng, Yanyu Tian, Wenxiang Wu, Xiuqi Fang, and Wei-Chyung Wang. "Coherence of Climatic Reconstruction from Historical Documents in China by Different Studies." *International Journal of Climatology* 28, no. 8 (2008): 1007–24.

Gernet, Jacques. *Buddhism in Chinese Society: An Economic History from the Fifth to the Tenth Centuries*. Translated by Franciscus Verellen. New York: Columbia University Press, 1995.

Giersch, C. Patterson. *Asian Borderlands: The Transformation of Qing China's Yunnan Frontier*. Cambridge, MA: Harvard University Press, 2006.

Golas, Peter J. *Mining*. Part 13 of *Chemistry and Chemical Technology*. Vol. 5 of *Science and Civilisation in China*. Cambridge, UK: Cambridge University Press, 2000.

González, Roberto. *Zapotec Science: Farming and Food in the Northern Sierra*. Austin: University of Texas Press, 2001.

Grove, Richard. *Ecology, Climate and Empire: Colonialism and Global Environmental History, 1400–1940*. Cambridge, UK: White Horse Press, 1998.

———. *Green Imperialism: Colonial Expansion, Tropical Island Edens, and the Origins of Environmentalism, 1600–1860*. Cambridge, UK: Cambridge University Press, 1995.

Guangxu Liping fu zhi. 18 vols. 1882 ed. Airusheng Zhongguo fangzhi ku.

Gugong Bowuyuan. *Qing Gaozong yuzhi shi* [Imperial compilation of the poems of the Qianlong emperor of the Qing]. Haikou: Hainan Chubanshe, 2000.

Guha, Ramachandra. *The Unquiet Woods: Ecological Change and Peasant Resistance in the Himalaya*. Berkeley: University of California Press, 2000.

Guha, Sumit. *Environment and Ethnicity in India*. Cambridge, UK: Cambridge University Press, 2006.

Gunderson, Lance H., and C. S. Holling, eds. *Panarchy: Understanding Transformations in Human and Natural Systems*. Washington, DC: Island Press, 2001.

Guo Tuotuo [attributed]. *Zhongshu shu* [Book of tree planting]. Wikisource digital ed. based on Siku Quanshu ed. Taibei: Shangwu, 1986.

Haas, Joseph. "The Feng Tree." In *Notes and Queries on China and Japan*. Vol. III, *1869*, edited by N. B. Dennys, 4–7. Frankfurt: Salzwasser Verlag, 2020. First published 1869.

Hall, John Whitney. *Government and Local Power in Japan, 500–1700: A Study Based on Bizen Province*. Princeton, NJ: Princeton University Press, 1966.

Hall, John W., Nagahara Keiji, and Yamamura Kōzō, eds. *Japan before Tokugawa: Political Consolidation and Economic Growth, 1500–1650*. Princeton, NJ: Princeton University Press, 1981.

Han Mira. "Chosŏn hugi kajwa tong kŭmsonggye ŭi unyŏng kwa kinŭng: Kyonggi Yangsŏng hyŏn 'kŭmsonggye chwamok' ŭl chungsim ŭro" [The management and function of the Kajwa pine protection *kye* in the late Chosŏn era: With focus on the 'pine protection *kye* roster' from Yangsŏng prefecture, Kyŏnggi province]. *Yŏksa Minsokhak* 35 (March 2011): 141–73.

Han Zhixing. "Qiantan baohu bishu shanzhuang nei you shengming de wenwu— gusong" [Brief discussion of a living cultural relic—the old pines in the imperial retreat to avoid the heat]. In *Bishu Shanzhuang Luncong*, edited by Bishu Shanzhuang Yanjiuhui. Beijing: Zijincheng Chubanshe, 1986.

Hanks, Jane Richardson, and Lucien Mason Hanks. *Tribes of the North Thailand Frontier*. New Haven, CT: Yale University Southeast Asia Studies, 2001.

Hara Motoko. "Kodai Chūgoku ni okeru jumoku e no ninshiki no hensen: Kan paku shiryō-tō o chūshin." *Tōyō bunka kenkyū kiyō* 163 (2013): 1–45.

———. *Kodai Chūgoku no kaihatsu to kankyō: "Kanshi" jiin hen kenkyū*. Tokyo: Genbun Shuppan, 1994.

Harahap, Parada. *Dari Pantai ke Pantai: Perjalanan ke Sumatra*. Weltevreden: Bintang Hindia, 1926.

Haraway, Donna J. *Staying with the Trouble: Making Kin in the Chthulucene*. Durham, NC: Duke University Press, 2016.

———. *When Species Meet*. Minneapolis: University of Minnesota Press, 2007.

Harper, Donald, and Marc Kalinowski. *Books of Fate and Popular Culture in Early China: The Daybook Manuscripts of the Warring States, Qin, and Han*. Boston: Brill, 2017.

Harrell, Stevan. *Ways of Being Ethnic in Southwest China*. Seattle: University of Washington Press, 2001.

Harrell, Stevan, and Ke Fan, eds. "The Stratification System of the Nuosu (Yi) of Liangshan: A Case Study in Chinese Ethnology." *Chinese Sociology and Anthropology* 36, no. 1 (Fall 2003): 3–10.

Harrison, Henrietta. *The Making of the Republican Citizen: Political Ceremonies and Symbols in China, 1911–1929*. New York: Oxford University Press, 2000.

Hartwell, Robert. "Markets, Technology, and the Structure of Enterprise in the Development of the Eleventh-Century Chinese Iron and Steel Industry." *Journal of Economic History* 26, no. 1 (March 1, 1966): 29–58.

Hathaway, Michael J. *Environmental Winds: Making the Global in Southwest China*. Berkeley: University of California Press, 2013.

Hayes, Peter. "Unbearable Legacies: The Politics of Environmental Degradation in North Korea." *Asia-Pacific Journal—Japan Focus* 7, no. 41 (October 2009): 1–9.

Hays, Samuel P. *Conservation and the Gospel of Efficiency: The Progressive Conservation Movement, 1890–1920*. Pittsburgh, PA: University of Pittsburgh Press, 1959.

He Ning, ed. *Huainanzi jishi*. Beijing: Zhonghua, 1998.

He Shen, ed. *Rehe Zhi* [Gazetteer of Rehe], n.d.

Hedin, Sven. *Jehol: City of Emperors*. 1st ed. London: Kegan Paul, 1932.

Heo, Sunhye, and Inhye Heo. "Discourses on the Natural Environment in North Korea: Changing Regime Dynamics in the 1990s." *Asian Studies Review* 44, no. 3 (July 2, 2020): 533–52.

Herman, John E. *Amid the Clouds and Mist: China's Colonization of Guizhou, 1200–1700*. Cambridge, MA: Harvard University Asia Center, 2007.

Heyne, Benjamin. *Tracts, Historical, Land Statistical on India, Also an Account of Sumatra in a Series of Letters*. London: R. Baldwin and Black, 1814.

Heyting, T. "Beschrijving der Onder-Afdeeling Mandailing en Batang Natal." *Tijdschrift van de Nederlandsch Aardrijkskundig Genootschap* 3, no. 1 (1897): 297–320.

Hill, R. D., and Mervyn R. Peart. "Land Use, Runoff, Erosion, and Their Control: A Review for Southern China." *Hydrological Processes* 12, no. 13–14 (1998): 2029–42.

Hinckley, Thomas M., Philip M. Chi, Keala Hagmann, Stevan Harrell, Amanda Henck Schmidt, and Zong-yong Zeng, "Influence of Human Pressure on Forest Resources and Productivity at Stand and Tree Scales: The Case Study of Yunnan Pine in SW China. *Journal of Mountain Science* 10, no. 5 (2013): 824–32

Hirayama Masaru and Marushima Kazuhiro, eds. *Sengoku daimyō Takeda-shi no kenryoku to shihai*. Tokyo: Iwada Shoin, 2008.

Hirosue, Masashi. "The Batak Millenarian Response to the Colonial Order." *Journal of Southeast Asian Studies* 25, no. 2 (1994): 331–43.

———. "Prophets and Followers in Batak Millenarian Responses to the Colonial Order: Parmalim, Na Siak Bagi and Parhudamdam, 1890–1930." PhD diss., Australian National University, 1988.

Hoang, Cam. "Forest Thieves? The Politics of Forest Resources in a Frontier Valley of Northern Vietnam." PhD diss., University of Washington, 2009.

Hommel, Rudolf P. *China at Work: An Illustrated Record of the Primitive Industries of China's Masses, Whose Life Is Toil, and Thus an Account of Chinese Civilization*. Cambridge, MA: MIT Press, 1969.

Hostetler, Laura. *Qing Colonial Enterprise: Ethnography and Cartography in Early Modern China*. 1st ed. Chicago: University of Chicago Press, 2001.

Hsing, Yi-tien. "Lun Mawangdui Han mu 'zhujun tu' ying zhengming wei 'jiandao fengyu tu.'" *Hunan daxue xuebao*, no. 5 (2007): 12–19.

Hsu, Cho-yun. *Ancient China in Transition: An Analysis of Social Mobility, 722–222 B.C.* Stanford, CA: Stanford University Press, 1965.

Hsu, Mei-Ling. "The Qin Maps: A Clue to Later Chinese Cartographic Development." *Imago Mundi* 45 (1993): 90–100.

Huang Liuhung. *Fuhui quanshu* [A complete book concerning happiness and benevolence]. Translated by Djang Chu. 1894 ed. Tucson: University of Arizona Press, 1894.

Huang Yongmei, Liu Hongyan, and Cui Haiting. "Neimenggu gaoyuan dong-nanyuan senlin caoyuan guodudai jingguang de ruogan tezheng" [Landscape features of the forest-steppe ecotone on the southeastern edge of the Inner Mongolian Plateau]. *Zhiwu Shengtai Xuebao* 25, no. 5 (2001).

Huayang guo zhi. Jinan: Qi Lu, 2000.

Huc, Evariste-Regis, and Joseph Gabet. *Travels in Tartary, Thibet and China, 1844–1846*. New York: Dover, 1987.

Hulsewé, A. F. P. *Remnants of Ch'in Law: An Annotated Translation of the Ch'in Legal and Administrative Rules of the 3rd Century B.C. Discovered in Yün-Meng Prefecture, Hu-Pei Province, in 1975*. Leiden: Brill, 1985.

Hung, Kuang-chi. "When the Green Archipelago Encountered Formosa: The Making of Modern Forestry in Taiwan under Japan's Colonial Rule (1895–1945)." In *Environment and Society in the Japanese Islands: From Prehistory to the Present*, edited by Bruce L. Batten and Philip C. Brown, 174–96. Corvallis: Oregon State University Press, 2015.

———. "Zhanhou chuqi zhi Taiwan guoyoulin jingying wenti: Yi guoyoulin facai zhidu wei ge'an" [Problems of Taiwan's national forest management in the early postwar period: A case study on the institutions regulating lumbering in national forests (1945–1956)]. *Taiwan shi yanjiu* 9, no. 1 (June 2006): 55–105.

Hung, Wu. "The Art and Architecture of the Warring States Period." In *The Cambridge History of Ancient China: From the Origins of Civilization to 221 B.C.*, edited by Michael Loewe and Edward Shaughnessy, 651–744. Cambridge, UK: Cambridge University Press, 1999.

Hupp, Stafford C. "Sedimentation in South Carolina Piedmont Valleys." *American Journal of Science* 243 (1945): 113–26.

Ishi'i, Shiunji. *The Island of Formosa and Its Primitive Inhabitants*. London: China Society, 1916.

Jackson, C. R., J. K. Martin, D. S. Leigh, and L. T. West. "A Southeastern Piedmont Watershed Sediment Budget: Evidence for a Multi-Millennial Agricultural Legacy." *Journal of Soil and Water Conservation* 60 (2005): 298–310.

James, L. Allen. "Legacy Sediment: Definitions and Processes of Episodically Produced Anthropogenic Sediment." *Anthropocene* 2 (2013): 16–26.

Japan Aerospace Exploration Agency. ALOS World 3D (AW3D) 30 meter DEM. V3.2, January 2021. Distributed by OpenTopography. https://doi.org/10.5069/G94M92HB

Jenny, Hans. *Factors of Soil Formation, a System of Quantitative Pedology*. New York: McGraw Hill, 1941.

Jensen, Michael. *Trees Commonly Cultivated in Southeast Asia, An Illustrated Field Guide*. 2nd ed. Bangkok: FAO Regional Office for Asia and the Pacific, 1999.

Jia, Gongyan. *Zhouli zhushu*. Shanghai: Shanghai Guji, 2010.

Jia Sixie. *Qimin yaoshu* [Essential arts to nourish the people]. Wikisource digital ed. based on Siku Quanshu ed. Taibei: Shangwu Yishuguan, 1986.

Jiang Dexue, ed. *Guizhou jindai jingji shi ziliao xuanji*. 1st ed. Chengdu: Sichuan Sheng Shehui Kexue Yuan, 1987.

Jiangxi xunanshi. "Quan zhishu baihua." *Jiangxisheng Nonghuibao* 8 (1916).

Jinping xianzhi, 1991–2009. 2 vols. Beijing: Fangzhi Chuban She, 2011.

Johnston, Ian. *The Mozi: A Complete Translation*. New York: Columbia University Press, 2010.

Jørgensen, Dolly. "The Roots of the English Royal Forest." *Anglo-Norman Studies* 32 (2009).

Junghuhn, Franz Willem. *Die Battalanders auf Sumatra*. Berlin: G. Reimer, 1847.

Kain, Roger J. P., and Elizabeth Baigent. *The Cadastral Map in the Service of the State: A History of Property Mapping*. Chicago: University of Chicago Press, 1993.

Kamala, Tiyavanich. *Forest Recollections: Wandering Monks in Twentieth-Century Thailand*. Honolulu: University of Hawai'i Press, 1997.

Kang Jian. "Ming Qing Huizhou shanlin jingji yanjiu huigu" [Retrospective on research on the Ming-Qing Huizhou forest economy]. *Zhongguo Shi Yanjiu Dongtai*, no. 3 (2013): 43–53.

Kang Nongman. "Qingming zhishujie." *Beijing Daxue Rikan*, no. 1434 (April 1, 1924): 1.

Kang Sŏngbok. *Kŭmsan ŭi songgye* [The pine *kye* of Kŭmsan]. Kŭmsan: Kŭmsan Munhwawŏn, 2001.

———. "Sallim munhwa ŭi chinsu, Kuksabong songgye wa tongje." In *Kyeryong si hyanghal li: Hyangjŏk san charak ŭi sangsŏ roun songgye maŭl*, edited by Kim P'iltong et al., 96–155. Seoul: Minsogwŏn, 2010.

Karle, David, and Sarah Thomas Karle. *Conserving the Dust Bowl: The New Deal's Prairie States Forestry Project*. Baton Rouge: Louisiana State University Press, 2017.

Kelly, William W. *Water Control in Tokugawa Japan: Irrigation Organization in a Japanese River Basin, 1600–1870*. Ithaca, NY: Cornell University Press, 1982.

Kennedy, Gerard F. "The Korean *Kye*: Maintaining Human Scale in a Modernizing Society." *Korean Studies* 1 (1977): 197–222.

Kessel, Oscar von. "Reis in de Nog Ofhankelijke Batak-Landen van Klein-Toba, Op Sumatra in 1844." *Bijdragen Tot de Taal-, Land-, En Volkenkunde van Nederlandsche-Indi* 4, no. 1–2 (1855): 55–97.

Kidder, Tristram R., and Yijie Zhuang. "Anthropocene Archaeology of the Yellow River, China, 5000–2000 BP." *Holocene* 25, no. 10 (2015): 1627–39.

Kielstra, E. B. *Beschrijving van Den Atjeh-Oorlog*. Vol. 1. The Hague: Degroeders van Cleef, 1883.

Kim, Seonmin. *Ginseng and Borderland: Territorial Boundaries and Political Relations between Qing China and Choson Korea, 1636–1912*. Berkeley, CA: University of California Press, 2017.

Kim Kyŏngok. "18–19 segi sŏnamhae tosŏ yŏnan chiyŏk songgye ŭi chojik kwa kinŭng" [The organization and function of pine *kye* in the island and coastal areas of the southwest in the eighteenth and nineteenth centuries] *Yŏksahak Yŏn'gu* 26 (2006): 1–55.

Kim P'iltong. *Han'guk sahoe chojiksa yŏn'gu: Kye chojik ŭi kujojŏk t'ŭksŏng kwa yŏksajŏk pyŏndong* [A history of Korean social organization: Structural characteristics and historical development of *kye*]. Seoul: Ilchogak, 1992.

Kinzig, Ann P. "Ecosystem Services." In *The Princeton Guide to Ecology*, edited by Simon A. Levin, Stephen R. Carpenter, H. Charles J. Godfray, Ann P. Kinzig, Michel Loreau, Jonathan B. Losos, Brian Walker, and David S. Wilcove, 573–678. Princeton, NJ: Princeton University Press, 2012.

Knoblock, John. *Xunzi: A Translation and Study of the Complete Works*. 3 vols. Stanford, CA: Stanford University Press, 1988.

Knoblock, John, and Jeffrey Riegel. *The Annals of Lü Buwei: A Complete Translation and Study*. Stanford, CA: Stanford University Press, 2000.

Knox, J. C. "Historical Valley Floor Sedimentation in the Upper Mississippi Valley." *Annals of the Association of American Geographers* 77 (1987): 224–44.

Köhler, H. J. *Habinsaran (Het Land van Den Zonnestraal)*. Zutphen: W. J Thime & Cie., 1907.

Kolbek, Jirí, M. Srutek, and Elgene E. O. Box, eds. *Forest Vegetation of Northeast Asia*. Dordrecht: Springer, 2003.

Koo, Hui-Wen. "Deer Hunting and Preserving the Commons in Dutch Colonial Taiwan." *Journal of Interdisciplinary History* 42, no. 2 (2011): 185–203.

Ku, Mei-kao. *A Chinese Mirror for Magistrates: The Hsin-Yü of Lu Chia*. Canberra: Australian National University Press, 1988.

Kuhn, Phillip. *Soulstealers: The Chinese Sorcery Scare of 1768*. Cambridge, MA: Harvard University Press, 1990.

Kŭmsonggye chwamok [Pine protection *kye* roster]. Kyujanggak Archives (Seoul National University) Ko 5129–20, 1834.

Kurim taedonggye chi [Records of the Kurim Village *kye*]. Edited by Kurim Taedonggye Sabogwŏn Ch'ujin Wiwŏnhoe. Yŏngam: Kurim Taedonggye Sabogwŏn Ch'ujin Wiwŏnhoe, 2004.

Lake, H. W., and H. J. Kelsall. "The Camphor Tree and Camphor Language of Johor." *Journal of the Straits Branch of the Royal Asiatic Society* 6, no. 3 (1894): 35–58.

Lander, Brian. "Birds and Beasts Were Many: The Ecology and Climate of the Guanzhong Basin in the pre-Imperial Period." *Early China* 43 (2020).

———. *The King's Harvest: A Political Ecology of Early China from First Farmers to First Empire*. New Haven: Yale University Press, 2021.

———. "The Retreat of the Forests—The Advance of the Tree Plantations." *China Review International* 26, no. 4 (2022): 242–51.

Lander, Brian, and Katherine Brunson. "Wild Mammals of Ancient North China." *Journal of Chinese History* 2, no. 2 (2018): 291–312.

Lander, Brian, Mindi Schneider, and Katherine Brunson. "A History of Pigs in China: From Curious Omnivores to Industrial Pork." *Journal of Asian Studies* 79, no. 4 (2020): 865–89.

Lao, D. C., trans. *Mencius*. Harmondsworth: Penguin, 1970.

———. *Mencius: A Bilingual Edition*. Hong Kong: Chinese University Press, 2003.

Lautensach, Hermann. *Korea: A Geography Based on the Author's Travels and Literature*. Translated by Eckart Dege and Katherine Dege. Berlin: Springer, 1988.

Lawson, Joseph. *A Frontier Made Lawless: Violence in Upland Southwest China, 1800–1956*. Vancouver: University of British Columbia Press, 2018.

Lee, John S. "Forests and the State in Pre-industrial Korea, 918–1897." PhD diss., Harvard University, 2017

———. "Postwar Pines: The Military and the Expansion of State Forests in Post-Imjin Korea, 1598–1684." *The Journal of Asian Studies* 77, no. 2 (May 2018): 319–32.

———. "The Rise of the Brokered State: Situating Administrative Expansion in Chosŏn Korea." *Seoul Journal of Korean Studies* 32, no. 1 (June 2019): 81–108.

Legge, James. *The She King, or the Book of Poetry*. Vol. 4 of *The Chinese Classics*. Taipei: SMC Publishing, 1991.

———. *The Works of Mencius*. Vol. 2 of *The Chinese Classics*. Taipei: SMC Publishing, 1991.

Lehner, Bernhard, Kristine Verdin, and Andy Jarvis. "New Global Hydrography Derived from Spaceborne Elevation Data." *Eos, Transactions American Geophysical Union* 89, no. 10 (2008): 93–94.

Lemenih, Mulugeta and Habtemariam Kassa, "Re-greening Ethiopia: History, Challenges, and Lessons." *Forests* 5, no. 8 (July 2014): 1896–1909.

Lévi-Strauss, Claude. *The Raw and the Cooked.* New York: Harper & Row, 1969.

Lewis, Mark Edward. *China's Cosmopolitan Empire: The Tang Dynasty.* Cambridge, MA: Belknap Press, 2009.

Li, Feng. *Bureaucracy and the State in Early China: Governing the Western Zhou.* Cambridge, UK: Cambridge University Press, 2008.

Li Li. *Zhongguo chuantong songbai wenhua.* Beijing: Zhonggguo Linye Cubanshe, 2006.

Liang Cong. *Qingdai Qingshui Jiang xiayou cunzhai shehui de qiyue guifan yu zhixu: Yi Wendou Miao zhai qiyue wenshu wei zhongxin de yanjiu.* Beijing: Renmin Chuban She, 2008.

Lieberman, Victor. *Strange Parallels.* Vol. 1, *Integration on the Mainland: Southeast Asia in Global Context, c. 800–1830.* New York: Cambridge University Press, 2003.

Ligny, J. "Legendarische Herkomst de Kamfer Baroes." *Tijdschrift Voor Taal-, Land-, en Volkenkunde* 23, no. 1 (1923): 549–55.

Ling Daoyang. *Senlin yaolan.* Shanghai: Shangwu Yinshuguan, 1918.

Liu, Hongyan, Haiting Cui, Richard Pott, and Martin Speier. "Vegetation of the Woodland-Steppe Transition at the Southeastern Edge of the Inner Mongolian Plateau." *Journal of Vegetation Science* 11, no. 4 (2000): 525–32.

Liu, Jianguo. "Forest Sustainability in China and Implications for a Telecoupled World." *Asia & the Pacific Policy Studies* 1, no. 1 (2014): 230–50.

Liu Fuqi. "Relationships between the Growth of *Pinus yunnanensis* and the Soil Conditions in the District of Liangshan, Sichuan Province [J]." *Scientia Silvae Sinicae* 4 (1984).

Liu Xiang, ed. *Zhanguo ce.* 3 vols. Shanghai: Shanghai Guji, 1985.

Liu Zongyuan. *Zhongshu Guo tuotuo zhuan* [Biography of tree planter Guo the hunchback]. *Quan Tang Wen* 0592. Wikisource, 1990.

Lowdermilk, W. C., and T. I. Li. "Forestry in Denuded China." *Annals of the American Academy of Political and Social Science* 152 (1930): 127–41.

Lowood, Henry E. "The Calculating Forester: Quantification, Cameral Science, and the Emergence of Scientific Forestry Management in Germany." In *The Quantifying Spirit in the 18th Century*, edited by Tore Frängsmyr, H. L. Heilborn, and Robin E. Rider, 315–43. Berkeley: University of California Press, 1990.

Lu Xun. "Preface to the First Collection of Short Stories, 'Call to Arms.'" In *Selected Stories*, translated by Yang Hsien-yi and Gladys Yang, 1–6. New York: W. W Norton, 2003.

Lu Yin. "Wo ye laitan Longquan ma." *Muye jie* 1, no. 3 (1940): 11.

Major, John S., Sarah A. Queen, Andrew Meyer S., and Harold D. Roth, trans. *The Huainanzi: A Guide to the Theory and Practice of Government in Early Han China*. New York: Columbia University Press, 2010.

Manchester, Steven R., Zhi-Duan Chen, An-Ming Lu, and Kazuhiko Uemura. "Eastern Asian Endemic Seed Plant Genera and Their Paleogeographic History throughout the Northern Hemisphere." *Journal of Systematics and Evolution* 47, no. 1 (2009): 1–42.

Man'gi yoram [Essentials of state affairs]. Kyujanggak Archives (Seoul National University) Kyu 1151. 1808.

Manwen lufu zouzhe [Grand Council Manchu-Language reference collection]. First Historical Archives, Beijing, China.

Marcon, Federico. *The Knowledge of Nature and the Nature of Knowledge in Early Modern Japan*. Chicago: University of Chicago Press, 2017.

Marks, Robert. *China: Its Environment and History*. Lanham, MD: Rowman & Littlefield, 2012.

——. *Tigers, Rice, Silk, and Silt: Environment and Economy in Late Imperial South China*. Cambridge, UK: Cambridge University Press, 1998.

Marsden, William. *The History of Sumatra: Containing an Account of the Government, Laws, Customs, and Manner of the Native Inhabitants*. Cambridge, UK: Cambridge University Press, 2013. First published 1793.

Matteson, Kieko. *Forests in Revolutionary France: Conservation, Community, and Conflict, 1669–1848*. New York: Cambridge University Press, 2015.

McDermott, Joseph P. *The Making of a New Rural Order in South China*. Vol. 1, *Village, Land, and Lineage in Huizhou, 900–1600*. Cambridge, UK: Cambridge University Press, 2013.

McElwee, Pamela D. *Forests Are Gold: Trees, People, and Environmental Rule in Vietnam*. Seattle: University of Washington Press, 2016.

Menzies, Nicholas K. *Forest and Land Management in Imperial China*. Studies on the Chinese Economy. New York: St. Martin's, 1994.

——. *Forestry*. Part 2 of *Agro-Industries and Forestry*, part 3 of *Biology and Biological Technology*, in vol. 6 of *Science and Civilisation in China*. Edited by Joseph Needham. Cambridge, UK: Cambridge University Press, 1996.

——. *Ordering the Myriad Things: From Traditional Knowledge to Scientific Botany in China*. Seattle: University of Washington Press, 2021.

Métaillié, Georges. *Traditional Botany: An Ethnobotanical Approach*. Part 4 of vol. 6, *Biology and Biological Technology*, of *Science and Civilisation in China*. Edited by Joseph Needham. Cambridge, UK: Cambridge University Press, 2015.

Mgebbu Lunzy [Ma Erzi]. "Nuosu and Neighbouring Ethnic Groups: Ethnic Groups and Ethnic Relations in the Eyes and Ears of Three Generations of the Mgebbu Clan." Translated by Stevan Harrell. *Asian Ethnicity* 4, no.1 (2003): 129–45.

Michaud, Jean. "Editorial—Zomia and Beyond." *Journal of Global History* 5, no. 2 (July 2010): 187–214.

Middendorp, W. "Het Inwerken van Westersche Krachten Op Een Indonesië Volk." *Socialistiche Gids* 7 (1922): 329–465.

Ministerie van Koloniën, *Koloniaal Verslag*. Bijlagen bij de Handelingen van de Tweede Kamer der Staten Generaal, 1849–1929. The Hague.

Miller, Ian Jared, Julia Adeney Thomas, and Brett L Walker. *Japan at Nature's Edge: The Environmental Context of a Global Power*. Honolulu: University of Hawai'i Press, 2013.

Miller, Ian M. *Fir and Empire: The Transformation of Forests in Early Modern China*. Seattle: University of Washington Press, 2020.

——. "Forestry and the Politics of Sustainability in Early China." *Environmental History* 22 (2017): 594–617.

Ming Qing Suzhou gongshang ye beike ji. Jiangsu: Jiangsu Renmin Chuban She, 1981.

Miyake Masahisa. *Chōsen hantō no rin'ya no kōhai no gen'in: Shizen kankyō hozen to shinrin no rekishi* [The causes of the devastation of forests on the Korean peninsula: A history of nature conservation and forests]. Tokyo: Nōrin Shuppan, 1976.

Montgomery, David R. "Soil Erosion and Agricultural Sustainability." *Proceedings of the National Academy of Sciences* 104, no. 33 (2007): 13268–72.

Morrison, Kathleen D. "Conceiving Ecology and Stopping the Clock: Narratives of Balance, Loss, and Degradation." In *Shifting Ground: People, Mobility and Animals in India's Environmental Histories*, edited by Mahesh Rangarajan and K. Sivaramakrishnan, 39–64. New Delhi: Oxford University Press, 2014.

——. "Pepper in the Hills." In *Forager-Traders in South and Southeast Asia: Long-Term Histories*, edited by Kathleen D. Morrison and Laura L. Junker, 105–30 Cambridge, UK: Cambridge University Press, 2003.

Morrison, Kathleen D., and Mark T. Lycett. "Constructing Nature: Socio-Natural Histories of an Indian Forest." In *The Social Lives of Forests: Past, Present, and Future of Woodland Resurgence*, edited by Susanna B. Hecht, Kathleen D. Morrison, and Christine Padoch, 148–60. Chicago: University of Chicago Press, 2016.

Morris-Suzuki, Tessa. "The Nature of Empire: Forest Ecology, Colonialism and Survival Politics in Japan's Imperial Order." *Japanese Studies* 33, no. 3 (December 1, 2013): 225–42.

Mostern, Ruth. *The Yellow River: A Natural and Unnatural History*. New Haven, CT: Yale University Press, 2021.

Mueggler, Erik. *The Paper Road: Archive and Experience in the Botanical Exploration of West China and Tibet*. Berkeley: University of California Press, 2011.

Mun Okp'yo et al. *Chosŏn yangban ŭi saenghwal segye—Ŭisong Kim-ssi Ch'ŏnjŏn-pa charyo rŭl chungsim ŭro* [The everyday world of Chosŏn *yangban*:

With focus on the documents of the Ch'ŏnjŏn branch of the Ŭisong Kim lineage]. Seoul: Paeksan Sŏdang, 2004.

Mus, Paul. *India Seen from the East: Indian and Indigenous Cults in Champa.* Translated by I. W. Mabbett. Edited by I. W. Mabbett and D. P. Chandler. rev. ed. Victoria: Monash Asia Institute, 2011. First published 1975.

Na Sŏnha. "16–17 segi Naju sajok ŭi chonjae yangsang kwa hyanggwŏn ŭi ch'ui" [Changes in patterns of persistence and local autonomy of Naju elites in the sixteenth-seventeenth centuries]. *Chibangsa wa Chibang Munhwa* 14, no. 1 (May 2011): 79–114.

Nagahara Keiji. "The Lord-Vassal System and Public Authority (*Kōgi*): The Case of the Sengoku Daimyō." *Acta Asiatica: Bulletin of the Institute of Eastern Culture* 49 (1985): 34–45.

Naguib al-Attas, Syed. "New Light on the Life of Ḥamzah Fanṣurī." *Journal of the Malaysian Branch of the Royal Asiatic Society* 40, no. 1 (1967): 42–51.

Nanman tielu diaocha ke, ed. *Jilinsheng zhi linye.* Tang Erhe yi. Shanghai: Shangwu Yinshuguan, 1930. First published 1928.

National Government Collection, Academia Historica, Taipei, Taiwan.

Nature. "Camphor." June 4, 1896.

Nedostup, Rebecca. *Superstitious Regimes: Religion and the Politics of Chinese Modernity.* Cambridge, MA: Harvard University Press, 2009.

Needham, Joseph, Lu Gwei-Djen, and Huang Hsing-Tsung. *Botany.* Part 1 of vol. 6, *Biology and Biological Technology,* of *Science and Civilisation in China.* Cambridge, UK: Cambridge University Press, 1986.

New Remedies. "Camphor." July 1, 1873.

New York Times. "Timber Famine Near, Says Mr. Roosevelt: Accident and Waste Rapidly Denuding Country. National Forest Service. The President Repeats That One Is Needed—Civilization's Growing Need of Wood." January 5, 1905.

Nguyen, Van Dung, Tran Duc Vien, Nguyen Thanh Lam, Tran Manh Tuong, and Georg Cadisch. "Analysis of the Sustainability within the Composite Swidden Agroecosystem in Northern Vietnam 1. Partial Nutrient Balances and Recovery Times of Upland Fields." *Agriculture, Ecosystems, and Environment* 128 (2007): 37–51.

Nienhauser, William H., ed. *The Grand Scribe's Records,* Vol. 1, *The Basic Annals of Pre-Han China.* 2nd ed. Bloomington and Nanjing: Indiana University Press and Nanjing University Press, 2018.

Nishikawa Kōhei. "Chūsei kai no kuni ni okeru iseki no kaihatsu—Kamijōseki wo taishō ni shite (tokushū chisui to risui no kōkogaku)." *Teikyō Daigaku Yamanashi Bunkazai Kenkyūjo Kenkyū Hōkoku* 14 (2010): 25–33.

———. *Chūsei kōki no kaihatsu—kankyō to chiiki shakai.* Tokyo: Kōshi Shoin, 2012.

———. "Sengoku-ki Kai no kuni ni okeru zaimoku no chōsetsu to yamazukuri." *Takeda-shi kenkyū* 39 (2009): 1–20.

——. "Sengoku-ki ni okeru kawayoke fushin to chiiki shakai: Kai no kuni wo jirei toshite." *Rekishigaku Kenkyū*, no. 889 (February 2012): 1–17.

Nijverheid Houthandel Singkel. *Opzet Nijverheid Houthandel Singkel*, 1916.

Nongsang jiyao [Essentials of agriculture and sericulture]. China Text Project digital ed. based on Siku Quanshu ed. Taibei: Shangwu Yishuguan, 1986.

Nongshang gongbao. "Zunyi xingban senlin bing chen benbu tichang zaolin qingxing you." Vol. 2, no. 1 (August 1915), 4.

Nye, Peter Hague, and D. J. Greenland. *The Soil under Shifting Cultivation*. Farnhammap Royal, Commonwealth Bureau of Soil Science, 1951.

Olson, Sherry H. *The Depletion Myth: A History of Railroad Use of Timber*. Cambridge, MA: Harvard University Press, 1971.

Osano Asako. "Takeda ryōgoku no dogōsō to chiiki shakai." In *Sengoku daimyō Takeda-shi no kenryoku to shihai*, edited by Hirayama Masaru and Marushima Kazuhiro, 325-354. Tokyo: Iwada Shoin, 2008.

——. "Takeda ryōgoku-ka ni okeru kokujin Oyamada-shi to Gunnai no zaichi seiryoku." *Takeda-Shi Kenkyū* 30 (2004).

Osborne, Anne. "Highlands and Lowlands: Economic and Ecological Interactions in the Lower Yangzi Region under the Qing." In *Sediments of Time: Environment and Society in Chinese History*, edited by Ts'ui-jung Liu and Mark Elvin, 203–34. Cambridge, UK: Cambridge University Press, 1998.

——. "The Local Politics of Land Reclamation in the Lower Yangzi Highlands." *Late Imperial China* 15 (January 1, 2011): 1–46.

Ostrom, Elinor. *Governing the Commons: Evolution of Institutions for Collective Action*. Cambridge, UK: Cambridge University Press, 1990.

Pae Suho and Yi Myŏngsuk. *Sallim kongyu chawŏn kwalli rosŏ kŭmsonggye yŏn'gu: kongyu wa sayu rŭl nŏmŏsŏ kongyu ŭi chihye ro* [A study of the pine protection *kye* as forest commons resource management: Toward an understanding of commons beyond public and private]. Seoul: Jipmoondang Publishing, 2018.

Pak Chongch'ae. "Chosŏn hugi kŭmsonggye ŭi yuhyŏng" [Types of pine protection *kye* in the late Chosŏn era]. *Yŏksa Sok e Sup Kwa Imŏp* (2000): 192–204.

——. "Chosŏn hugi tonggye ŭi unyŏng kwa hyangch'on chojik: Naju Kŭman tonggye ŭi sarye rŭl chungsim ŭro" [Village organization and the administration of late Chosŏn ward compacts: A case study of the Naju Kŭman ward compact]. In *Han'guk ŭi hyangyak tonggye* [Community and ward compacts in Korea], edited by Hyangch'on sahoesa yŏn'guhoe, 165–98. Seoul: Sinyong Hyŏptong Chohap Chunganghoe, 1996.

Pak Wŏn'gyu, and I Kwanghŭi. "Uri nara kŏnch'uk e sayong toen mokchae sujong ŭi pyŏnch'ŏn" [Changes in tree species used in Korean architecture]. *Kŏnch'uk Yŏksa Yŏn'gu* 16, no. 1 (February 2007): 9–27.

Palais, James. *Confucian Statecraft and Korean Institutions: Yu Hyŏngwŏn and the Late Chosŏn Dynasty*. Seattle: University of Washington Press, 2002.

Parkin, David. *Kinship: An Introduction to the Basic Concepts*. Oxford: Wiley-Blackwell, 1997.

Parpia, Shaha. "The Imperial Mughal Hunt: A Pursuit of Knowledge." In *Ilm: Science, Religion and Art in Islam*, edited by Akkach Samer, 39–58. South Australia: University of Adelaide Press, 2019.

Parreñas, Juno Salazar. *Decolonizing Extinction: The Work of Care in Orangutan Rehabilitation*. Durham, NC: Duke University Press, 2018.

Peluso, Nancy Lee. *Rich Forests, Poor People*. Berkeley: University of California Press, 1992.

Peluso, Nancy Lee, and Peter Vandergeest. "Genealogies of the Political Forest and Customary Rights in Indonesia, Malaysia, and Thailand." *Journal of Asian Studies* 60, no. 3 (2001): 761–812.

———. "Political Ecologies of War and Forests: Counterinsurgencies and the Making of National Natures." *Annals of the Association of American Geographers* 101, no. 3 (April 25, 2011): 587–608.

Peters, Debra P. C., James R. Gosz, and Scott L. Collins. "Boundary Dynamics in Landscapes." In *The Princeton Guide to Ecology*, edited by Simon A. Levin, Stephen R. Carpenter, H. Charles J. Godfray, Ann P. Kinzig, Michel Loreau, Jonathan B. Losos, Brian Walker, and David S. Wilcove, 458–63. Princeton, NJ: Princeton University Press, 2012.

Phillips, Jonathan D. "A Short History of a Flat Place: Three Centuries of Geomorphic Change in the Croatan National Forest." *Annals of the Association of American Geographers* 87, no. 2 (1997): 192–216.

Pibyŏnsa tŭngrok [Records of the border defense command]. 16 vols. Seoul: Kuksa P'yŏnch'an Wiwŏnhoe, 1949.

Pickering, W. A. *Pioneering in Formosa*. London: Hurst and Blackett, 1898.

Pitts, Larissa, "Unity in the Trees: Arbor Day and Republican China, 1917–1927." *Journal of Modern Chinese History* 13, no. 2 (January 2020): 296–318.

Pomeranz, Kenneth. *The Making of a Hinterland: State, Society, and Economy in Inland North China, 1853–1937*. 1st ed. Berkeley: University of California Press, 1993.

Prange, Sebastian R. "'Measuring by the Bushel': Reweighing the Indian Ocean Pepper Trade." *Historical Research* 84, no. 224 (2011): 212–35.

Priestly, W. E. "Formosa, Isle of Camphor." *Asia* 33, no. 5 (1933): 297–301.

Qian, Sima. *Records of the Grand Historian: Han Dynasty*. Vol. 2. Translated by Burton Watson. Hong Kong: New York: Columbia University Press, 1993.

———. *Shi ji*. Beijing: Zhonghua, 1959.

Qian Miaojin, trans. *Liji Zhuyi* [Annotated translation of the *Record of Rites*]. Hangzhou: Zhejiang Guji Chubanshe, 2007.

Qianlong Qingjiang zhi. 8 vols. Manuscript copy. Airusheng Zhongguo fangzhi ku.

Qiannan shilue. 32 vols. 1847 ed. Airusheng Zhongguo fangzhi ku.

Qing Shilu [Veritable records of the Qing Dynasty]. Reprint. Taibei: Huawen Shuju, 1963.

Qingdai Gongzhong dang zouzhe ji Junji Chu dang zhejian ziliao ku. National Palace Museum, Taipei. https://rbk-doc.npm.edu.tw/.

Quan Ming, and En Qing, eds. *Da-sheng wu-la difang Xiangtu Zhi* [Local gazetteer of the Butha Ula region]. 1891 ed. Changchun: Jilin Wenshi Chubanshe, 1898.

Rackham, Oliver. *The History of the Countryside: The Classic History of Britain's Landscape, Flora and Fauna.* London: Phoenix, 2001.

Radkau, Joachim. *Nature and Power.* Translated by Thomas Dunlop. Cambridge, MA: Cambridge University Press, 2008.

———. *Wood: A History.* Cambridge, MA: Polity Press, 2011.

Rawski, Evelyn S. *The Last Emperors: A Social History of Qing Imperial Institutions.* Berkeley: University of California Press, 1998.

Republican Collection, Jilin Provincial Archives, Changchun, Jilin Province, People's Republic of China.

Reusser, L. J., Bierman, P. R., Rood, D. H. "Quantifying Human Impacts on Rates of Erosion and Sediment Transport at a Landscape Scale. *Geology* 43 (2014): 171–74.

Richards, John F. *The Unending Frontier: An Environmental History of the Early Modern World.* Berkeley: University of California Press, 2003.

———. *World Deforestation in the Twentieth Century.* Edited by Richard P. Tucker. Durham, NC: Duke University Press, 1988.

Richardson, S. D. *Forests and Forestry in China.* Washington, DC: Island Press, 1990.

Rickett, W. Allyn. *Guanzi: Political, Economic and Philosophical Essays from Early China: A Study and Translation.* Vol. 2. Princeton, NJ: Princeton University Press, 1998.

Rikugun Sanbōkyoku. *Chōsen zenzu* [complete map of Korea]. Tokyo: Rikugun Sanbōkyoku, 1875. Library of Congress.

Roberts, Luke S. *Mercantilism in a Japanese Domain: The Merchant Origins of Economic Nationalism in 18th-Century Tosa.* Cambridge, UK: Cambridge University Press, 1998.

———. *Performing the Great Peace: Political Space and Open Secrets in Tokugawa Japan.* Honolulu: University of Hawai'i Press, 2012.

Roosevelt, Theodore, "To the Schoolchildren of the United States." Reproduced in *Report on Farmers' Institutes Held under the Auspices of the West Virginia State Board of Agriculture.* Issue no. 5. Tribune Printing Company, 1907: 9.

Rosen, Arlene. "The Impact of Environmental Change and Human Land Use on Alluvial Valleys in the Loess Plateau of China during the Middle Holocene." *Geomorphology* 101 (2008): 298–307.

Rosen, Arlene M., Jinok Lee, Min Li, Joshua Wright, Henry T. Wright, and Hui Fang. "The Anthropocene and the Landscape of Confucius: A Historical Ecology of Landscape Changes in Northern and Eastern China during the Middle to Late-Holocene." *Holocene* 25, no. 10 (2015): 1640–50.

Roy, Toulouse Antonin. "'The Camphor Question Is in Reality the Savage Question': Indigenous Pacification and the Transition to Capitalism in the Taiwan Borderlands (1895–1915)." *Critical Historical Studies* 6, no. 1 (March 1, 2019): 125–58.

Sanft, Charles. "Environment and Law in Early Imperial China (Third Century BCE–First Century CE): Qin and Han Statutes Concerning Natural Resources." *Environmental History* 15, no. 4 (2010): 701–21.

Sanguozhi [Annals of the three kingdoms]. Beijing: Zhonghua Shuju, n.d.

Sano Shizuyo. *Chū-kinsei no sonraku to suihen no kankyōshi: keikan seigyō shigen kanri*. Tokyo: Yoshikawa Kōbunkan, 2008.

——. "Traditional Use of Resources and Management of Littoral Environments at Lake Biwa." In *Environment and Society in the Japanese Islands: From Prehistory to the Present*, edited by Bruce L. Batten, and Philip C. Brown, 75–95. Corvallis: Oregon State University Press, 2015.

Sasamoto Shōji. *Sengoku daimyō Takeda-shi no kenkyū*. Kyoto: Shibunkaku Shuppan, 1993.

Schafer, Edward H. "The Conservation of Nature under the T'ang Dynasty." *Journal of the Economic and Social History of the Orient* 5, no. 3 (December 1, 1962): 279–308.

——. "Hunting Parks and Animal Enclosures in Ancient China." *Journal of the Economic and Social History of the Orient* 11, no. 1 (January 1, 1968): 318–43.

Schendel, Willem van. "Geographies of Knowing, Geographies of Ignorance: Jumping Scale in Southeast Asia." *Environment and Planning D: Society and Space* 20, no. 6 (December 1, 2002): 647–68.

Schlesinger, Jonathan. *A World Trimmed with Fur: Wild Things, Pristine Places, and the Natural Fringes of Qing Rule*. Stanford, CA: Stanford University Press, 2019.

Schmidt, A. H., V. S. Gonzalez, P. R. Bierman, T. B. Neilson, D. H. Rood. "Agricultural Land Use Doubled Sediment Loads in Western China's Rivers. *Anthropocene* 21 (2018): 95–106.

Scott, James C. *The Art of Not Being Governed: An Anarchist History of Upland Southeast Asia*. New Haven, CT: Yale University Press, 2009.

——. *Seeing like a State: How Certain Schemes to Improve the Human Condition Have Failed*. New Haven, CT: Yale University Press, 1999.

Scribner, Robert W. "The Reformation, Popular Magic, and the 'Disenchantment of the World.'" *Journal of Interdisciplinary History* 23, no. 3 (1993): 475–94.

Shapiro, Judith. *Mao's War against Nature: Politics and the Environment in Revolutionary China*. Cambridge, UK: Cambridge University Press, 2001.

Shaw, Norman. *Chinese Forest Trees and Timber Supply*. New South Wales: T. F. Unwin, 1914.

Shepherd, John Robert. *Statecraft and Political Economy on the Taiwan Frontier, 1600–1800*. Stanford, CA: Stanford University Press, 1993.

Shi Nianhai. *Huangtu Gaoyuan lishi dili yanjiu*. Zhengzhou: Huanghe Shuili, 2001.

Shibatsuji Shunroku. *Sengoku daimyō-ryō no kenkyū: Kai Takeda-shi ryō no tenkai.* Tokyo: Meicho Shuppan, 1981.

———. "Sengoku-ki no suiri kangai to kaihatsu." *Minshū-Shi Kenkyū* 11 (1973): 79–98.

Shibatsuji Shunroku, Hirayama Masaru, Kuroda Motoki, and Marushima Kazuhiro, eds. *Takeda-shi kashindan jinmei jiten.* Tokyo: Tokyodo Shuppan, 2015.

Shidei Tsunahide. *Shirin wa mori ya hayashi dewan nai: watakushi no shirinron.* Kyoto: Nakanishiya Shuppan, 2006.

Shih, Sheng-han. *A Preliminary Study of the Book Ch'i Min Yao Shu: An Agricultural Encyclopaedia of the 6th Century.* 2nd ed. Beijing: Science Press, 1982.

Shin, Leo Kwok-yueh. *The Making of the Chinese State: Ethnicity and Expansion on the Ming Borderlands.* Cambridge, UK: Cambridge University Press, 2006.

Shuihudi Qin mu zhu jian zheng li xiao zu. *Shuihudi Qin mu zhujian.* Beijing: Wenwu, 1990.

Skinner, G. William. "Regional Urbanization in Nineteenth-Century China." In *The City in Late Imperial China*, edited by G. William Skinner, 211–49. Stanford, CA: Stanford University Press, 1977.

Skeat, Walter. *Malay Magic.* London: W. W. Norton, 1900.

Simon, Scott. "Making Natives: Japan and the Creation of Indigenous Formosa." In *Japanese Taiwan: Colonial Rule and Its Contested Legacy*, edited by Andrew D. Morris, 75–92. London: Bloomsbury, 2015.

Singh, Chetan. "Forests, Pastoralists and Agrarian Society in Mughal India." In *Nature, Culture, Imperialism: Essays on the Environmental History of South Asia*, edited by David Arnold and Ramachandra Guha, 21–48. Oxford: Oxford University Press, 1997.

Sivaramakrishnan, K. "Forests and the Environmental History of Modern India." *Journal of Peasant Studies* 36, no. 2 (April 1, 2009): 299–324.

———. *Modern Forests: Statemaking and Environmental Change in Colonial Eastern India.* Stanford, CA: Stanford University Press, 1999.

Situmorang, Sitor. *Guru Somalaing dan Modigliani 'utusan' raja rom.* Jakarta: Penerbit Grafindo Mukti, 1993.

Sivasundaram, Sujit. "Trading Knowledge: The East Indai Company's Elephants in India and Britain." *Historical Journal* 48, no. 1 (March 2005): 27–63.

Smil, Vaclav. *The Bad Earth: Environmental Degradation in China.* New York: M. E. Sharpe, 1984.

Song Dachuan and Xia Lianbao. *Qingdai yuanqin zhidu yanjiu* [A study of the Qing mausoleum system]. Beijing: Wenwu Chubanshe, 2007.

Songster, E. Elena. "Cultivating the Nation in Fujian's Forests: Forest Policies and Afforestation Efforts in China, 1911–1937." *Environmental History* 8, no. 3 (July 1, 2003): 452–73.

———. *Panda Nation: The Construction and Conservation of China's Modern Icon.* New York: Oxford University Press, 2018.

Songgye chŏlmok [Pine *kye* regulations]. Kyujanggak archives, Seoul National University, Kyu 12329, 1800.

Songgye wanŭi [Pine kye resolution]. Kyujanggak archives, Seoul National University, Ko 5129-30, n.d.

Spafford, David. *A Sense of Place: The Political Landscape in Late Medieval Japan.* Cambridge, MA: Harvard University Press, 2013.

———. "War and Territorial Imagination in Late Medieval Japan." PhD diss., University of California Berkeley, 2006.

Spengler, Robert N. *Fruit from the Sands: The Silk Road Origins of the Foods We Eat.* Berkeley: University of California Press, 2019.

Stephens, Holly. "Agriculture and Development in an Age of Empire: Institutions, Associations, and Market Networks, 1876–1945." PhD diss., University of Pennsylvania, 2017.

Stromgaard, Peter. "The Immediate Effect of Burning and Ash-Fertilization." *Plant and Soil* 80, no. 3 (1984): 307–20.

Stross, Randall E. *The Stubborn Earth: American Agriculturalists on Chinese Soil, 1898–1937.* Berkeley: University of California Press, 1986.

Sturgeon, Janet C. *Border Landscapes: The Politics of Akha Land Use in China and Thailand.* Seattle: University of Washington Press, 2005.

Sun, Xiangjun, Changqing Song, Fengyu Wang, and Mengrong Sun. "Vegetation History of the Loess Plateau of China during the Last 100,000 Years Based on Pollen Data." *Quaternary International* 37 (1997): 25–36.

Sun, Yirang. *Zhouli zhengyi.* Beijing: Zhonghua, 1987.

Sutton, Donald S. "Ethnicity and the Miao Frontier in the Eighteenth Century." In *Empire at the Margins: Culture, Ethnicity, and Frontier in Early Modern China,* edited by Pamela Kyle Crossley, Helen F. Siu, and Donald S. Sutton, 190–228. Berkeley: University of California Press, 2006.

Swann, Nancy Lee. *Food and Money in Ancient China: The Earliest Economic History of China to A.D. 25.* New York: Octagon Books, 1974.

Sweeney, Brendan. "Sixty Years on the Margin: The Evolution of Ontario's Tree Planting Industry and Labour Force: 1945–2007." *Labour* 63 (Spring 2009): 47–48.

Sysling, Fenneke. *Racial Science and Human Diversity in Colonial Indonesia.* Singapore: National University of Singapore Press, 2016.

Takagi Shōsaku. "Hideyoshi's Peace and the Transformation of the Bushi Class: The Dissolution of the Autonomy of the Medieval Bushi." *Acta Asiatica: Bulletin of the Institute of Eastern Culture* 49 (1985): 46–77.

Tambiah, Stanley J. "The Galactic Polity: The Structure of Traditional Kingdoms in Southeast Asia." *Annals of the New York Academy of Sciences* 293, no. 1 (1977): 69–97.

Tan Qixiang, ed. *Zhongguo lishi dituji*. 8 vols. Shanghai: Zhonghua Dituxue She, 1975.

Tang Bingnan. "Hankou ce mucai zhi fa." *Hubei sheng nonghui nongbao* 2, no. 9 (1921).

Tavares, Antonio C. "Crystals from the Savage Forest: Imperialism and Capitalism in Taiwan's Camphor Industry, 1800–1945." PhD diss., Princeton University, 2004.

Taylor, Rodney L. "Companionship with the World." In *Confucianism and Ecology: The Interaction of Heaven, Earth, and Humans*, edited by Mary Evelyn Tucker and John Berthong, 37–58. Cambridge, MA: Center for the Study of World Religions, 1998.

Teng, Emma Jinhua. *Taiwan's Imagined Geography: Chinese Colonial Travel Writing and Pictures, 1683–1895*. Cambridge, MA: Harvard University Asia Center, 2006.

Thomas, Julia Adeney. *Reconfiguring Modernity; Concepts of Nature in Japanese Political Ideology*. Berkeley, CA: University of California Press, 2001.

Tideman, J. *De Bataklanden, 1917–1931*. Leiden: Bataksch Instituut, 1932.

Tonomura, Hitomi. *Community and Commerce in Late Medieval Japan: The Corporate Villages of Tokuchin-Ho*. Stanford, CA: Stanford University Press, 1992.

Totman, Conrad D. *The Green Archipelago: Forestry in Preindustrial Japan*. Berkeley: University of California Press, 1989.

———. *The Lumber Industry in Early Modern Japan*. Honolulu: University of Hawai'i Press, 1995.

Trac, Christine Jane, Stevan Harrell, Thomas M. Hinckley, and Amanda C. Henck. "Reforestation Programs in Southwest China: Reported Success, Observed Failure, and the Reasons Why." *Journal of Mountain Science* 4, no. 4 (2007): 275–92.

Trac, Christine Jane, Amanda H. Schmidt, Stevan Harrell, and Thomas M. Hinckley. "Is the Returning Farmland to Forest Program a Success? Three Case Studies from Sichuan." *Environmental Practice* 15, no 3 (2013): 350–66.

Trautmann, Thomas R. *Elephants and Kings: An Environmental History*. Chicago: University of Chicago Press, 2015.

Trimble, Stanley W. "Fallacy of Stream Equilibrium in Contemporary Denudation Studies." *American Journal of Science* 277 (1977): 876–87.

Troost, Kristina Kade. "Common Property and Community Formation: Self-Governing Villages in Late Medieval Japan, 1300–1600." PhD diss., Harvard University, 1990.

Turner, Sarah, Christine Bonnin, and Jean Michaud, *Frontier Livelihoods: Hmong in the Sino-Vietnamese Borderlands*. Seattle: University of Washington Press, 2015.

Urgenson, Lauren S., R. Keala Hagmann, Amanda C. Henck, Stevan Harrell, Thomas M. Hinckley, Sara Jo Shepler, Barbara L. Grub, and Philip M. Chi.

"Social-Ecological Resilience of a Nuosu Community-Linked Watershed, Southwest Sichuan, China." *Ecology and Society* 15, no. 4 (2010). www .ecologyandsociety.org/vol15/iss4/art2.

Vandergeest, Peter, and Nancy Lee Peluso. "Empires of Forestry: Professional Forestry and State Power in Southeast Asia, Part 1." *Environment and History* 12, no. 1 (2006): 31–64.

Vermeer, Eduard B. "The Mountain Frontier in Late Imperial China: Economic and Social Developments in the Bashan." *T'oung Pao* 77, no. 4 (January 1, 1991): 300–329.

———. "Population and Ecology along the Frontier in Qing China." In *Sediments of Time: Environment and Society in Chinese History*, edited by Ts'ui-jung Liu and Mark Elvin, 235–82. Cambridge, UK: Cambridge University Press, 1998.

Vesey, Alexander. "Temples, Timber, and Negotiations: Buddhist-Lay Relations in Early Modern Japan through the Prism of Conflicts over Mountain Resources." *Japan Review* 28 (2015): 67–101.

Von Glahn, Richard. *The Economic History of China: From Antiquity to the Nineteenth Century.* Cambridge, UK: Cambridge University Press, 2016.

Vriese, Willem Hendrik de. *Mémoire sur le camphrier de Sumatra et de Bornéo, Par W. H. de Vriese.* Leiden: Brill, 1856.

Vu, Linh, "The Sovereignty of the War Dead: Martyrs, Memorials, and the Makings of Modern China, 1912–1949." PhD diss., University of California Berkeley, 2017.

Vuuren, Louis van. "De Handel van Baroes, Als Oudste Haven Op Sumatra's Westkust, Verklaard; En Voor the Toekomst Beschouwd." *Tijdschrift van Aardrijksche Genootschap* 2, no. 25 (1908): 1–25.

Wagner, Donald B. "The Administration of the Iron Industry in Eleventh-Century China." *Journal of the Economic and Social History of the Orient* 44, no. 2 (January 1, 2001): 175–97.

———. *Iron and Steel in Ancient China.* Leiden: Brill, 1993.

Waley, Arthur, and Joseph R. Allen. *The Book of Songs: The Ancient Chinese Classic of Poetry.* New York: Grove Press, 1996.

Walker, Brett L. *The Conquest of Ainu Lands: Ecology and Culture in Japanese Expansion, 1590–1800.* Berkeley: University of California Press, 2006.

———. *The Lost Wolves of Japan.* Seattle: University of Washington Press, 2008.

Walsh, Michael. *Sacred Economies: Buddhist Monasticism and Territoriality in Medieval China.* New York: Columbia University Press, 2010.

Walter, Robert C., and Dorothy J. Merritts. "Natural Streams and the Legacy of Water-Powered Mills." *Science* 319 (2008): 299–304.

Wang, Chi-Wu. *The Forests of China.* Cambridge, MA: Harvard University, 1961.

Wang Liqi. *Xin yu jiaozhu.* Beijing: Zhonghua, 1986.

———. *Yantie lun jiaozhu.* Beijing: Zhonghua, 1992.

Wang, Xianqian. *Han shu buzhu.* 12 vols. Shanghai: Shanghai Guji, 2012.

Wang, Zijin, and Li Si. "Fangmatan Qin ditu linye jiaotong shiliao yanjiu."
Zhongguo lishi dili luncong 28, no. 2 (2013): 5–10.

Wang Haiyan. *Diguo de xiangzheng: Qing dongling de zhengzhi—shehui shi yanjiu*
[Symbol of empire: A study of the political and social history of the Qing
eastern tombs]. Jinan: Jinan Daxue Chubanshe, 2012.

Wang Qingsuo and Hebei beibu. *Nei menggu dongbu senlin caoyuan jiacuodai
Zhibei he shengwu duoyuanxing yanjiu* [A Study of vegetation and biodiversity
in the forest-steppe ecotone of northern Hebei and eastern Inner Mongolia].
Beijing: Qishang Chubanshe, 2004.

Wang Qixiang. "Qingdai lingqin fengshui: lingqin jianzhu sheji yuanli ji yishu
chengjiu gouzhen" [Qing mausoleum feng shui: An in-depth inquiry into
mausoleum construction design principles and aesthetic achievements]. In
Fengshui lilun yanjiu [Studies on feng shui theory] no. 2, edited by Wang
Qixiang. Tianjin: Tianjin Daxue Chubanshe, 1992.

Warde, Paul. *Ecology, Economy, and State Formation in Early Modern Germany.*
Cambridge, MA: Cambridge University Press, 2006.

———. *The Invention of Sustainability: Nature and Destiny, c. 1500–1870.* New
York: Cambridge University Press, 2018.

Weinstein, Jodi L. *Empire and Identity in Guizhou: Local Resistance to Qing
Expansion.* Seattle: University of Washington Press, 2013.

Weld, Susan. "Chu Law in Action: Legal Documents from Tomb 2 at Baoshan."
In *Defining Chu: Image and Reality in Ancient China*, edited by John S.
Major and Constance A. Cook, 76–97. Honolulu: University of Hawai'i Press,
1999.

Whiteman, Stephen H. *Where Dragon Veins Meet: The Kangxi Emperor and His
Estate at Rehe.* Seattle: University of Washington Press, 2020.

White, Richard. *The Middle Ground: Indians, Empires and Republics in the Great
Lakes Region, 1650–1815.* Cambridge, UK: Cambridge University Press, 1991.

Whyte, Kyle. "Settler Colonialism, Ecology, and Environmental Injustice."
Environment and Society 9 (2018): 125–44.

Will, Pierre-Etienne. *Bureaucracy and Famine in Eighteenth-Century China.*
Paolo Alto, CA: Stanford University Press, 1990.

Williams, Dee Mack. "Representations of Nature on the Mongolian Steppe: An
Investigation of Scientific Knowledge Construction." *American Anthropologist*
101, no. 3 (2002): 503–19.

Williams, Michael. *Deforesting the Earth: From Prehistory to Global Crisis, An
Abridgment.* Chicago: University of Chicago Press, 2006.

Williams, Raymond. "Ideas of Nature." In *Culture and Materialism*, 67–85.
London: Verso, 2005.

Willis, Katherine J., and Jennifer McElwain. *The Evolution of Plants.* 2nd ed.
Oxford: Oxford University Press, 2014.

Wing, John T. *Roots of Empire: Forests and State Power in Early Modern Spain,
c.1500–1750.* Leiden: Brill, 2015.

Winichakul, Thongchai. *Siam Mapped: A History of the Geo-body of a Nation*. Honolulu: University of Hawai'i Press, 1997.

Wittfogel, Karl August, and Chia-sheng Fêng. "History of Chinese Society Liao (907–1125)." *Transactions of the American Philosophical Society* 36 (1946).

Wolters, O. W. *History, Culture, and Region in Southeast Asian Perspectives*. rev. ed. Ithaca, NY: Southeast Asia Program Publication, 1999.

Woodcock, Deborah. "To Restore the Watersheds: Early Twentieth-Century Tree Planting in Hawai'i." *Annals of the Association of American Geographers* 93, no. 3 (September 2003): 624–35.

Worster, Donald. *Nature's Economy: A History of Ecological Ideas*. 2nd ed. Cambridge, UK: Cambridge University Press, 1994.

———. *The Wealth of Nature: Environmental History and the Ecological Imagination*. New York: Oxford University Press, 1993.

Wu, Shellen Xiao. *Empires of Coal: Fueling China's Entry into the Modern World Order, 1860–1920*. Stanford, CA: Stanford University Press, 2019.

Wu Dashan et al., ed., *Hunan shengli*. Digital ed. based on ed. held at Peking University Library, ca. 1800.

Wu Jing. "Pai min zhong liu youjuan wuyi shu" [Dispatching commoners to plant willows will incur expense to no benefit]. In *Qing jingshi wenbian* [Collected writings on statecraft from the Qing dynasty], edited by He Changling, 1826. Reprint. Beijing: Zhonghua Shuju, 1992.

Wu Zhenyu. *Qian yu*. 1887 ed. Airusheng Zhongguo fangzhi ku.

Wu Zhongmin and Zhou Guangyi. "Ecological Consequences of Slash-and-Burn Agriculture in Tropical Areas of China." *Ambio* 25, no 3 (1996): 210–11.

Xiao, Ling Bo, Xiuqi Fang, and Yujie Zhang. "Climatic Impacts on the Rise and Decline of 'Mulan Qiuxian' and 'Chengde Bishu' in North China, 1683–1820." *Journal of Historical Geography* 39 (January 1, 2013): 19–28.

Xu, Jiongxin. "Naturally and Anthropogenically Accelerated Sedimentation in the Lower Yellow River, China, over the Past 13,000 Years." *Geografiska Annaler. Series A, Physical Geography* 80, no. 1 (1998): 67–78.

Xu Guangqi, ed. *Nongzheng quanshu* [Complete book of agricultural administration]. Wikisource digital ed. based on Siku Quanshu ed. Taibei: Shangwu Yishuguan, 1986.

Xu Xiaochun. "Fenshuilin ying baocun yu liyong zhi biyao." *Nongbao* 3, no. 10 (April 1936): 608–9.

Yamamoto Takeshi, and Owada Tetsuo, eds. *Sengoku Daimyō kashindan jiten: Tōgoku-hen*. Tokyo: Shin Jinbutsu Ōraisha, 1981.

Yamanashi-ken shihensan iinkai, ed. *Yamanashi kenshi shiryō sōsho mura meisaichō: Yatsushiro-gun hen*. Kōfu-shi: Yamanashi Nichinichi Shinbunsha, 1996.

———, ed. *Yamanashi kenshi shiryō-hen 4: Chūsei 1, kennai monjo*. Kōfu-shi: Yamanashi Nichinichi Shinbunsha, 1999.

———, ed. *Yamanashi kenshi tsūshi-hen 2: Chūsei*. Kōfu-shi: Yamanashi Nichinichi Shinbunsha, 2006.

Yan, Changgui. "Tianshui Fangmatan muban ditu xintan." *Kaogu xuebao* 3 (2016): 365–84.

Yang, Rao-Qiong, Ze-Xin Fan, Zongshan Li, and Qingzhong Wen. "Radial Growth of *Pinus yunannensis* at Different Elevations and Their Responses to Climatic Factors in the Yulong Snow Mountain, Northwest Yunnan, China." *Acta Ecologica Sinica* 38, no. 24 (2018): 8983–91.

Yang Bojun. *Chun qiu Zuo zhuan zhu*. Beijing: Zhonghua, 1990.

Yang Fengbai, Zhao Huanlin, and Dong Yue, eds. *Shengjing huanggong he guanwai sanling dang'an* [Archives from the imperial palace at Mukden and the three tombs beyond the passes]. Shenyang: Liaoning Minzu Chubanshe, 2003.

Yang Tianyu, trans. *Zhouli zhuyi* [Annotated translation of the classic of rites]. Shanghai: Shanghai Guji Chubanshe, 2007.

Yates, Robin D. S. "Some Notes on Ch'in Law: A Review Article of Remnants of Ch'in Law by A. F. P. Hulsewé." *Early China* 11–12 (87 1985): 243–75.

Ye, Sang, and Geremie R. Barmé, "Commemorating Confucius in 1966–67: The Fate of the Confucius Temple, the Kong Mansion, and Kong Cemetery." *China Heritage Quarterly*, no. 20 (December 2009).

Ye Mengde. *Bizhao lühua* [Notes while avoiding the summer heat]. Wikisource digital ed. based on Siku Quanshu ed. Taibei: Shangwu Yishuguan, 1986.

Yeh, Emily T. "The Politics of Conservation in Contemporary Rural China." *Journal of Peasant Studies* 40, no. 6 (November 1, 2013): 1165–88.

Yuan Cai. *Yuanshi shifan* [House instructions of Mr. Yuan]. Wikisource digital ed. based on Siku Quanshu ed. Taibei: Shangwu Yishuguan, 1986.

Zakaria, Faizah. *The Camphor Tree and the Elephant: Religion and Ecological Change in Maritime Southeast Asia*. Seattle: University of Washington Press, 2023.

Zaolin xuzhi: Zongli shishi shizhounian ji senlinfa shixing. [Nanjing?]: Shoudu Zaolin Yundong Weiyuanhui Yinzeng, 1935.

Zaolin yundong xuanchuan dagang. [Nanjing?]: Zhongguo Guomindang Zhong-yang Zhixing Weiyuanhui Xuanchuanbu, 1931.

Zhang, Meng. "Financing Market-Oriented Reforestation: Securitization of Timberlands and Shareholding Practices in Southwest China, 1750–1900." *Late Imperial China* 38, no. 2 (2017): 109–51.

———. *Timber and Forestry in Qing China: Sustaining the Market*. Seattle: University of Washington Press, 2021.

———. "Timber Trade along the Yangzi River: Market, Institutions, and Environ-ment, 1750–1911." PhD diss., University of California Los Angeles, 2017.

Zhang Ji'an. *Jiaqing Yuhang Xianzhi* [Jiaqing era Yuhang County gazetteer]. Minguo Banian Chongkan Ben. Zhongguo Fangzhi Ku Yi Ji, 1919.

Zhang Yingqiang. "Cong Guazhi 'Yishi Yongzun' shike kan Qingdai zhonghou qi de Qingshui Jiang mucai maoyi." *Zhongguo shehui jingji shi yanjiu*, no. 3 (2002).

———. *Mucai zhi liudong: Qingdai Qingshui Jiang xiayou diqu de shichang, quanli, yu shehui* [The movement of timber: Market, power, and society in the lower Qingshui River region during the Qing dynasty]. Beijing: Sanlian Shudian, 2006.

———. "The Qingshuijiang Documents: Valuable Sources for Regional History and Cultural Studies of the Miao Frontier in Guizhou." *Journal of Modern Chinese History* 11, no. 1 (January 2, 2017): 145–60.

Zhang Yuxin. "Bishu shanzhuang shengqi de zhiwu fengjing goutu ji qi dui tigao yuanlin pingjia de zuoyong" [The botanical landscape composition of the imperial retreat to escape the heat and its role in enhancing the appraisal of its gardens and parklands]. In *Bishu Shanzhuang Luncong*, edited by Bishu shanzhuang yanjiuhui, 542–58. Beijing: Zijincheng Chubanshe, 1986.

Zhang Zhenglang. "Buci poutian ji qi xiangguan zhu wenti." *Kaogu xuebao* 1 (1973): 93–120.

Zhang Zhuangxi. *Zhongguo lidai qiyue huibian kaoyi* [Annotated collection of Chinese deeds from duccessive eras]. Vol. 1. Beijing: Beijing Daxue Chuban She, 1995.

Zhao Yanfeng. "Yuandai Huanjing Shi Zhuanti Yanjiu." Xi'an: Shaanxi Normal University, 2016.

Zhao Zhen. *Ziyuan, huanjing yu guojia quanli: Qingdai weichang yanjiu* [Resources, environment and state power: a study of the Qing hunting preserves]. Beijing: Zhonghua shuju, 2012.

Zheng Chinlong. "Ershi shiji Taiwan de shequ linye zuzhi" [Twentieth-century Taiwan's community forestry organizations]. *Linye yanjiu zhuanxun* 17, no. 1 (2010): 1–5.

Zheng Zhenman. "Ming Qing shiqi de linye jingji yu shanqu shehui—Fujian yongtai qiyue wenshu yanjiu" [Forestry economy and local society of mountain areas in Ming and Qing periods—Investigating contracts from Yongtai County]. *Xueshu Yuekan* 52, no. 2 (February 2020): 148–58.

"Zhishu dianli." *Xuesheng Wenyi Congkan* 1, no. 7 (1924): 4.

"Zhishu jieji." *Qinghua Zhoukan* 105 (1917): 6–7.

Zhishu tekan: Zongli shishi jinian ri kanxing. Nanjing: Nongkuangbu Linzhengsi, 1929.

Zhongguo diyi lishi dang'an guan and Chengdeshi wenwuju, eds. *Qing Gong rehe dang* [Rehe archives from the Qing palace]. Beijing: Zhongguo Dang'an Chubanshe, 2003.

Zhu Xi. *Hui'an xiansheng Zhu Wen gong wenji* [Collected works of Zhu Xi]. Edited by Rao Pingsu. Wikisource digital ed. based on 1532 Jingshang haiyuanfenlou ed.

Zhuang, Yijie, and Tristram R. Kidder. "Archaeology of the Anthropocene in the Yellow River Region, China, 8000–2000 Cal. BP." *Holocene* 24, no. 11 (2014): 1602–23.

Ziegler, Alan D., Thilde B. Bruun, Maite Guardiola-Claramonte, Thomas W. Giambelluca, Deborah Lawrence, and Nguyen Thanh Lam, "Environmental Consequences of the Demise in Swidden Cultivation in Montane Mainland Southeast Asia: Hydrology and Geomorphology." *Human Ecology* 37 (2009): 361–73.

Zou, Songbing, Guodong Cheng, Honglang Xiao, Baorong Xu, and Zhaodong Feng. "Holocene Natural Rhythms of Vegetation and Present Potential Ecology in the Western Chinese Loess Plateau." *Quaternary International* 194, no. 1–2 (2009): 55–67.

CONTRIBUTORS

David A. Bello is E. L. Otey Professor of East Asian Studies at Washington and Lee University. He is the author of *Across Forest, Steppe and Mountain: Environment, Identity and Empire in Qing China's Borderlands* (2016) and *Opium and the Limits of Empire, Drug Prohibition in the Chinese Interior, 1729–1850* (2005).

John Elijah Bender is assistant professor of history and environmental studies at Concordia College in Moorhead, Minnesota.

Brian Collins is associate teaching professor of earth science at the University of Washington. He is author of more than thirty peer reviewed articles on how physical processes shape the landscape and interact with ecosystems and human societies.

Bradley Camp Davis is associate professor of history at Eastern Connecticut State University. He is the author of *Imperial Bandits: Outlaws and Rebels in the China-Vietnam Borderlands* (2017) and is currently writing a multispecies environmental history of Vietnam.

Keala Hagmann is a research ecologist and affiliate assistant professor at the University of Washington School of Environmental and Forest Sciences. Her most recent publications address climate change and western wildfires.

Stevan Harrell is professor emeritus in the School of Environmental and Forest Sciences and the Anthropology Department at the University of Washington. He is coauthor of *Fieldwork Connections* (2007) and author of *Ways of Being Ethnic in Southwest China* (2001).

Tom Hinckley is professor emeritus in the School of Environmental and Forest Sciences at the University of Washington.

Brian Lander is assistant professor of history at Brown University and a fellow at the Institute at Brown for Environment and Society. He is the author of *The King's Harvest: A Political Ecology of China from the First Farmers to the First Empire* (2021).

John S. Lee is assistant professor in East Asian history at Durham University. He is preparing a monograph on state forestry and the making of early modern Korea.

Ian M. Miller is associate professor of history at St. John's University. He is the author of *Fir and Empire: The Transformation of Forests in Early Modern China* (2020).

Larissa Pitts is assistant professor of history at Quinnipiac University.

Amanda Schmidt is associate professor of geology at Oberlin College. She is the author or coauthor of more than twenty peer reviewed papers on human-land use interactions and related topics.

Faizah Zakaria is assistant professor of history at Nanyang Technological University. She is the author of *The Camphor Tree and the Elephant: Religion and Ecological Change in Maritime Southeast Asia* (2023).

Meng Zhang is assistant professor of history at Vanderbilt University. She is the author of *Timber and Forestry in Qing China: Sustaining the Market* (2021).

INDEX

afforestation, xxi, 144, 147, 158n9.
  See also reforestation
Agrawal, Arun, "environmentality,"
  114, 119n57
Ainu, xviii
Akimoto Yasutomo, 50, 58n44
alder trees, 16n4, 17n10, 163, 167, 169,
  174, 175
Amino Yoshihiko, 42, 56n5
Andong (Korea), 68
Angerler, Johann, 138
Angkor (Cambodia), xxiv
Anmyŏn island, 64
Annals of Master Lü (Lüshi
  chunqiu), 11
anthropocentrism, 95, 121
anthropologists, 133, 136, 137, 138, 163
anti-superstition campaigns, 153–54, 157
Apiladda river valley, 168, 169, 177, 179;
  sediment data, 174–75, 183n18,
  184n37; sparse trees on the floodplain, 176*fig*.
apricots, 3, 14, 23
Arbor Day, xxi, 148, 159n23; and
  reforestation, 155, 157; and Sun
  Yat-sen Memorial Day, 145, 148, 152,
  157; and Tomb-Sweeping Festival,
  145, 148, 149–51, 152, 154–55
ash trees, xv, 17n10
Atayal peoples, 132, 133, 140n15

Bagán (Burma), xxiv
Bailie, Joseph, 149, 157
Baiwu valley, 161–63, 162*fig*.; under
  Chinese Communist control from
  1956, 164, 180, 181, 182; forest health,
  175–77, 180; forest management,
  177–79; forest recovery after
  decollectivization, 164, 181;
  geomorphology, 171–75, 180; soil
  erosion, 171, 177, 181; sunny slopes
  and shady slopes in, 167; Upper,
  168–69. *See also* Apiladda river
  valley; Nuosu peoples; Pianshui
  Village; Yangjuan Village
bamboo, xiii, xx, 8, 9, 16n1, 20, 169;
  cultivation of, 23, 24, 25, 26
Bao Shichen, *Four Arts to Nourish the
  People* (Qimin sishu), 25
Barclay, Paul, 128, 132, 133, 138
Batak peoples, 124, 140n13; as agriculturalists, 137–38; Batak Dairi oral
  tradition, 125; camphor harvesting by,
  125–26, 141n22; camphor language of,
  141n22; conversions to Christianity,
  130–31, 138–39; death rituals of, 126;
  and Dutch colonialism, 130–31, 137;
  photographs of, 133; priests, 130–31;
  subgroups, 137, 140n12; upland-
  lowland relations, 121, 126, 127–29,
  139; village organization, 126, 129

and Western colonialism, 144.
See also forest ownership rights;
state forestry
"forest monks" (*thudong*), xxiv
forest ownership rights, 20–21, 28–33,
34–35, 73. *See also* land deeds
forest peoples, xx–xxi, xxvi, xxvii, 97.
See also indigenous peoples
forest products. *See* camphor; timber
extraction
forest-steppe ecotone, 97, 103, 104–5
forest surveys, x, xxv, 26–28, 39; maps,
12–14, 13*fig.*
frankincense tree, 138
"frontier exception," 91, 139
fruit and nut trees, xx, 1, 2, 3, 14, 23, 115,
156, 175
fuel scarcity, xx, 1, 99, 113–14. *See also*
firewood
Fuji, Mt., 41–42
Fujiki Hisashi, 53, 59n55
Fuling, 110
Funatsu checkpoint, 43, 47, 51, 58n44

Gadgil, Madhav, xxiii
Gangou Village, 162*fig.*, 168
gazetteers, 79, 85
geomancy, x, xx, 69; geomantic veins,
153–54
geomorphology, 171–75, 180
ginger, xxiii
gingko, xiv
ginseng, xx
global timber crisis, 143–44
Gotō Shinpei, 133
gravesite groves, 62, 66, 68, 70–71, 73
Great Leap Forward, xxii
Great Peace, 56n1
Grove, Richard H., xxiii
guanshan (state mountains), 112, 113,
114, 118n50
Guanzhong basin, 7
Guanzi, "Categories of Land" text, 15

Guha, Ramachandra, xxiii
Guo the hunchback, 23
Guomindang (Nationalist Party), 151;
reforestation programs, 145, 148,
153–55, 157, 158

habitat contraction, 101
Hadong district (Korea), 65
Han An, 149
"Han Cypresses," 146
Han shu, 18n49
Hansŏng (Seoul), 63
Harahap, Parada, 138
Haraway, Donna, 121
Harrison, Henrietta, 152
Hashiguchi Bunzō, 132
hazel, 175
historiography, xvii–xxvi
Hmong peoples, xxv
Hnewo Teyy, 164–65
Hoeryong (Chŏlla Province), *kye*,
71–72
hornbeam, xv
horsetail pine, xx
Hu Yuanqing, 29
Huai River flood of 1931, 157
Huainanzi, 4–5, 9, 10
Huang Liuhong, 100
Huizhou land contracts, 21, 32
Hunan Provincial Precedents (Hunan
shengli), 25
hunting: of deer on Taiwan, 127, 132;
imperial hunting grounds, 97, 101–4;
and loss of forest, 106; Manchu and
Mongol, xx, 103; as military
preparedness, 104–5, 106, 108.
See also Mu-lan hunting ground
Hxiesse Vuga, 163

illegal logging, 65, 66, 67, 69, 71, 72.
See also timber extraction
Imagawa daimyo house, 57n21
Imjin War, 63

Liangshan Yi Autonomous Prefecture, 161, 164, 172, 184n10. *See also* Baiwu valley; Nuosu peoples
Liao Taizong, 103
licensed brokerage (*yahang*) system, 78, 83. *See also* timber brokerages
Lijin taxes, 89
Lin Sen, 156
linden trees, 17n10, 97
lineage cemeteries, 146
Ling Daoyang, 145, 147–48
Little Ice Age, 96–97, 101
Liu Zongyuan, 23
local elites, 55, 62, 68, 69. See also *yangban*
local militias, 44–45, 47, 49, 55, 57n12, 57n27
logging. *See* illegal logging; timber extraction
Longjiang Customs Station (Nanjing), 93n33
Longquan County (Zhejiang), 32–33
Lu, Duke of, 11
Lu Xun, *Call to Arms*, 147–48
lumberjack head (*jungong jiangshou*) system, xxii
lurby, 166, 167, 169
Lurlur Adda, 163

Manchukuo, xxi
Manchurian forest peoples, xx–xxi, 97. *See also* Qing dynasty
"mandala state" (Wolters), xxiv
maple trees, xv, 16n4, 97, 106, 175
McElwee, Pamela, 121
Medieval Warm Period, 97
memorial trees, 146, 148–49, 152, 155–56, 157–58
Mencius: on access to forest resources, 11, 102; on ecosystem management, 6–7, 16, 69, 106–7, 159n29
Menzies, Nicholas K., xxixn34

merchants: camphor, 127, 132; native-place organization, 78, 84, 91n3; "three large groups," 84–85, 86, 90; timber traders, 80, 81–82, 84–85, 86, 93n29
metal production, ix, 5–6, 8
Miao frontier, 77, 79; ethnic conflicts in, 83, 87–88; Ming-Qing administration of, 79, 80; Qing ethnic policies in, 82, 89, 90–91; timber disputes in, 84, 85–88; timber markets and trade routes in, 77–78, 78*fig.*, 80. *See also* Jinping timber market; Miao peoples; timber brokerages
Miao peoples, xxi, 77, 79; acculturation, 79, 89; "Black Miao," 81, 83; categorization, 79, 92n7; revolts, 79, 87, 89. *See also* Jinping timber market; Miao frontier; timber brokerages
militias. *See* local militias
Miller, Ian, 154
Minangkabau, 126
Miyabayashi forest (Yoshida), 47, 48–49, 49, 50–51; as Mt. Otare, 50–52, 54, 58n43
Miyake Masahisa, xxviii–xxixn14
Modigliani, Elio, 130, 133
Mongolian herders, 99, 108, 117n13
monsoon forests, xv
montane Asia, xxiv–xxv
monumental architecture, 6, 113
Mountain Retreat to Escape the Heat (Bishu Shanzhuang), 103–4, 117n25
"mountains and marshes" (*shanze*), 26
Mozi, 7
muang, xxiv, xxxin73
Mu-lan hunting ground, 97–98; cultural ecosystem services, 103–5; decline in wildlife, 101, 106–8; and Inner Asian culture, 105, 146; tree extractions, 102, 105–6, 107–8, 113, 116; woodland habitat, 101–3, 105

state forestry, 64–66, 68, 73, 74; upper and lower branches, 66–67, 69, 70–71; upper Naktong basin, 68; use by local elites, 62, 66–67, 73

"Pine Protection *Kye* Roster" (Kajwa), 70

pine trees: in China, xv, 3, 12, 16n6, 97, 100; as construction timber, 156; cultivation of, 23–24, 25, 81; cutting of, 9, 106, 166; five-needle, 169; horsetail, xx; and imperial mausoleums, 115, 156; as inferior firewood, 169, 180, 183n17; in Korea, xv, xvi, xix, xxixn28, 60, 63; at Mu-lan, 103, 117n26; white pine, 21, 169, 175. *See also* conifers; pine protection *kye*; Yunnan pine (*Pinus yunnanensis*)

poaching, 99, 100, 101, 105–7, 108, 111, 113, 114

"political re-enchantment" of trees, 154, 157

poplars, xx, 3, 12, 14, 15, 16n4, 16n6, 23, 169, 175

population records, Han dynasty, 7–8, 8*fig.*

post horses (*tenma*), 56n6

precipitation, xiv–xv, 3, 96–97, 168, 175

provisioning services, 96, 97, 115–16

Qi, Duke of, 11

Qianlong emperor, 102, 103–4, 107, 110; "Passing through the Ongni'ud [Mongol] Tribes," 105

Qin dynasty forestry, 11–14, 13*fig.*

Qing Dongling, 97, 108

Qing dynasty: dynastic tombs, 97–98, 108; ethnic policies, 79, 82, 89, 90–91; frontier administration, xx–xxi, 79, 80; Taiwan under, 127, 128, 131–32. *See also* imperial tombs; Mu-lan hunting ground; Qianlong emperor

Qing Xiling, 97, 108

Qingshui River, dredging of, 80

Qinling Mountains, 3, 12

Radkau, Joachim, 4

rainforests, xiv, xv, 122

Raja Uti, 139

Record of Rites (Liji), discourse on "The Royal Order," 109

Records of the States South of Mt. Hua (Huayang guo zhi), 9

reeds, 100, 115

reforestation, 158n9; and erosion, 148, 155, 156, 175; in Korea, xix; in PRC, xxii, xxxin53; in Qing China, 100; in Republican China, 145, 148, 153–55, 157, 158; by United Nations, xix. *See also* afforestation; conservation

Reforestation Movement Education Week (China), 148, 154

Reform and Opening, xxii

Reformation, 153

"retreat of the elephants," xvii

rhododendrons, xiv, xvi, 167, 169, 175

Ri Aguai rebellion (1902), 133

river valleys, xvi, 2, 8, 9, 18n49, 20. *See also* Apiladda river valley; Yellow River valley

Roosevelt, Franklin, 144

Roosevelt, Theodore, 143, 150

royal interment, 97–98, 109–10. *See also* imperial tombs

rubber, xxv

Ryūkyū islands, 132

sacred tree groves, 2, 147, 167

Saitō Otosaku, 132

salt production, 5

Sanyi Wood Sculpture Museum, 138

satoyama, 40, 56n4, 58n53

Schendel, Willem van, xxv, 161

scientific rationalism, 153

Scott, James C., xxxin68; Zomia, xxv, 161, 163, 164

"Tale of the Struggle for the River" (Zhengjiang ji), 85
Tan Jing, 29
Tan Yongxian, 29, 30
Tang Code with Commentaries (Tanglü shuyi), 27
taxation: construction duty, 51, 58n49; timber taxes, 89; and village *kye*, 63–64; of Yoshida, 51, 52
tea, xvi, 25, 27, 34
teak, xv, xxv
temple forests, 26
Temporary Regulations for National and Public Forests (Guanyoulin gongyoulin zanxing guize), 27–28
"three great cuttings" (*san da fa*), xxii
"three-town market." *See* Jinping timber market
Tibetan uplift, xiii–xiv, xvi
tigers, 101, 125
timber brokerages, 77–78, 83–88, 89–90, 93–94n38, 94n51; licensing, 78, 83, 86–87, 90, 91n3
timber cultivation, xx, xxi, 3, 14–15, 20, 24–26, 28, 81, 100. *See also* tree planting
timber extraction: colonial, xxvii; commercial, 8–9; coppicing, 23, 27, 166; ethics, 166; and floating wood downstream, 9–10; illegal logging and, 65, 66, 67, 69, 71, 72; and imperial tombs and hunting grounds, 98, 105–6, 113–14, 116; state regulation of, 10–12; in Yellow River valley, 6–7
timber famine, 143–44
timber imports, xviii, xx, 149
timber trade: with foreign capital and foreign timber, 90, 91; measurement and pricing in, 77; Miao frontier and, 77, 78*map*, 79, 80; along the Yangzi River, xx, 1, 77, 80, 86, 91; in

Yuan River basin, 80–82, 90. *See also* Jinping timber market
timber tribute, 80, 84, 86
T'oegye Yi Hwang, 68
Tokugawa Japan, xvii, xviii, 50, 53, 56n1, 58n47, 59n62
tolls, 43
tombs, commoner, 113. *See also* imperial tombs
Tomb-Sweeping Festival (Qingmingjie), 145, 147, 148, 149–51, 152, 154
Tonglüshan, 17n17
Totman, Conrad, xvii, xviii; *The Green Archipelago*, 43
traditional ecological knowledge, 163–64, 171; Nuosu environmental philosophy, 164–68. *See also* forest knowledge
tree growth rates, 172, 184n27
tree planting: New Deal, 144; Republican China, 145, 152, 155–57. *See also* timber cultivation
tropical Asia, xv
Tsinghua University, 150
tung oil trees, 81
tusi, 165, 183n11
tutelary shrine associations, 59n64

Ŭisong Kim lineage, 68
United Nations reforestation projects, xix
upland-lowland divide, 121, 124, 126, 128–29, 139. *See also* Batak peoples; Taiwan
Upper Baiwu valley, 168–69
US Forest Service, establishment of, 143–44

"venery" (Bello), 104
village militias (*wakashū*), 44–45, 47, 49, 55, 57n12, 57n27

www.ingramcontent.com/pod-product-compliance
Lightning Source LLC
Chambersburg PA
CBHW031416270326
41929CB00010BA/1472